DISCARD

THE EUROPEAN RITUAL

Football constitutes a vivid public ritual in contemporary European culture through which emergent social solidarities and new economic networks have come into being. This fascinating and unique volume traces the transformation of European football from the 1950s to the present, focusing in particular on the dramatic changes that have occurred in the last decade and linking them to the wider process of European integration.

The examination of football illuminates how the growing dominance of the free market has changed European society from an international order in which the nation-state was dominant to a more complex transnational regime in which cities and regions are becoming more prominent than in the past. The study is supported by detailed ethnographic accounts emerging from the author's fieldwork at Manchester United and interview data with some of the most important figures in European football at clubs including Juventus, Milan, Bayern Munich, Schalke and Barcelona. It also includes a highly topical examination of racism in European football.

The European Ritual

Football in the New Europe

ANTHONY KING

ASHGATE

© Anthony King 2003

All rights reserved. No part of this publication may be reproduced, stored in a retrieval system, or transmitted in any form or by any means, electronic, mechanical, photocopying, recording or otherwise without the prior permission of the publisher.

Anthony King has asserted his right under the Copyright, Designs and Patents Act, 1988, to be identified as the author of this work.

Published by
Ashgate Publishing Limited
Gower House
Croft Road
Aldershot
Hants GU11 3HR
England

Ashgate Publishing Company
Suite 420
101 Cherry Street
Burlington, VT 05401-4405
USA

Ashgate website: http://www.ashgate.com

British Library Cataloguing in Publication Data
King, Anthony, 1967-
 The European ritual : football in the new Europe
 1. Soccer - Europe 2. Soccer - Europe - History 3. Soccer - Social aspects - Europe
 I. Title
 796.3'34'094'09049

Library of Congress Cataloging-in-Publication Data
King, Anthony, 1967-
  The European ritual : football in the new Europe / Anthony King.
    p. cm.
  Includes bibliographical references and index.
  ISBN 0-7546-3652-6 (alk. paper)
   1. Soccer--Europe--History. 2. Soccer--Europe--Social aspects. I. Title.

GV944.E85K56 2003
796.334'094--dc21

2003045350

ISBN 0 7546 3652 6

Printed and bound in Great Britain by
Antony Rowe Ltd, Chippenham, Wilts

Contents

Acknowledgements	*vii*
Preface	*ix*

PART I: THE TRANSFORMATION OF A RITUAL

1	From 1968 to 1999	3
2	The New Europe: Cities, States or Superstate?	19

PART II: FOOTBALL IN THE OLD EUROPE

3	The Early Years of the European Cup: 1955–70	37
4	Eurosclerosis	49

PART III: FOOTBALL IN THE NEW EUROPE

5	Bosman	69
6	The Television	97
7	The New Business of Football	119
8	The League of Champions	137

PART IV: FOOTBALL FANS IN THE NEW EUROPE

9	The Politics of Football	169
10	Localism	191
11	Racism	223
12	The Contours of a New Europe	245

Bibliography	*261*
Index	*281*

Acknowledgements

This book could not have been written without the assistance of numerous individuals. Thanks are due to the following fans who consented to be interviewed by me (and helped me in many other ways): Mike Adams, Carlo Balestri, Michael Barth, Peter Boyle, Monica Brady, Andi Bröck, Graham Byrne, Gian-Carlo Capelli, Armand Caraben, Richard Chorley, Wayne Connolly, Duncan Drasdo, Stuart Dykes, John Early, James Edwards, Ray Ekersley, Massimo Finizio, David Gildea, Alfons Godall, Lutz Hepperle, Richard Kurt, Serafino Leporati, Domenico Lo Forte, Mark Longden, David Mitchell, Andy Mitten, Dominic Müller, Tizio Rapello, Mark Southee, Anthony Southgate, Matt Starenton, Andy Walsh and Luke Zentar. The names of fans who do not hold formal public roles have been changed in the text.

I am also grateful for the following professionals who consented to be interviewed: Jaime Andreu, Marcel Benz, Roberto Bettega, Nicolas Casaus, Tony Cascarino, Adam Crozier, Jeff Farmer, Alex Flynn, Edward Freedman, Umberto Gandini, Brian Glanville, Peter Kenyon, Rudolfo Hecht Lucari, Brian McClair, Etienne Moati, Juan Onieva, Rick Parry, Rod Petrie, Nissat Satarr, Juame Sobriques, Gordon Taylor and Richard Worth.

I am grateful to Tony O'Neill for his assistance on trips to Europe, and to Dirk and Vera Martensen for their hospitality. I would also like to thank Malcolm Wilson and Jane Morwood. Francisco Cordero, Francesca Daldella, Francesco Guala, Roger Michaelson and Simona Pezzano acted as translators without whom the interviews in Italy and Spain could not have happened.

Ian Hawkey provided valuable guidance.

For academic support I am grateful to Barry Barnes, Adam Brown, Grace Davie, Roz Davies, Eric Dunning, James Eastham, Tia de Nora, Patrick Overy, Nigel Pleasants, John Vincent, Bob Witkin and to the ESRC who funded the project (R000222891). I am particularly indebted here to Keith Hart for his comments throughout the project. I would also like to thank Jeanne Brady and Caroline Wintersgill, my editor at Ashgate.

Finally, I am indebted to Cathy King, my wife. This book is dedicated to her.

Preface

What is Europe? Since the early 1990s, this question has become an increasingly central concern for the social sciences as sociologists, political scientists, economists and historians attempt to comprehend the nature of European integration. This question is difficult because it is becoming clear that the European Union is a reality without obvious historical precedents although various commentators have used historical examples to predict the future form of the European Union. Larry Siedentop (2000) has recently tried to draw parallels between Europe in the 1990s and the creation of the United States. Siedentop looks to the Federalists and to De Tocqueville to provide a framework for understanding the European Union. Indeed, he believes that the formation of the United States in the late eighteenth and early nineteenth centuries can usefully suggest an appropriate political structure for Europe today; the principles of political organisation on which that Union was founded may be applicable to the European Union in the twenty-first century. Yet, although Siedentop is correct when he claims that De Tocqueville illuminates the historical reality of the time in which he wrote, we should be careful about applying the political principles which De Tocqueville identified to an era entirely different to that which he examined. The best use we can make of De Tocqueville is to imitate his close attention to the details of everyday existence in America in the early nineteenth century. His works endure as they do precisely because of their compelling empirical orientation. The best lesson which De Tocqueville teaches is that we should focus on the reality which actually confronts us rather than speculating what that reality should be. Following De Tocqueville, we should recognise that Europe cannot be understood by applying the principles of the past to the present but by confronting the present in all its confusing reality. We cannot answer the question 'What is Europe?' except by focusing directly on the reality of Europe as it is currently lived by millions of individuals in differing circumstances across this north-western peninsula of the Eurasian continent.

This book employs the example of European football to provide one possible answer to this question. By engaging closely with one form of social practice in Europe today, it is hoped that a more sustainable account of contemporary reality is proffered than by Siedentop and others like him who are disappointed by the nature of the European Union because it does not match their idealisations of what it should be. In order to come to terms with the reality of the European Union, it is necessary not to abstract from everyday life but to become immersed fully in it. Yet, this immersion brings with it certain problems which have to be recognised. Avoiding unrealistic idealisation risks the danger of falling into an empirical provincialism which, while rich in detail, throws no light on general processes. This is the unavoidable dilemma of every researcher. In the belief that the interest lies in the detail, this book takes the empirical and ethnographic route. It tries to illuminate the reality of Europe by analysing the process in one specific form of life. It is hoped that focusing on the specific will illuminate the general and that this study will outline the broader architecture of Europe today. I accept the risks entailed by that decision.

While empirical research faces certain limitations, theoretical work confronts some equally serious difficulties. Although theories of European integration try to illuminate general processes, it is misleading to claim that there is an overarching 'European' position from which abstract theorising speaks. Abstract theorising does not enjoy a panoramic view denied to empirical research. The view from nowhere does not exist; there are only views of Europe from Germany, Spain, Italy or France, from Scotland, Catalonia, Lombardy or from Marseilles, Milan or Amsterdam. Most often abstract theorising, in fact, adopts a particularistic perspective which it disguises rhetorically. To understand the complete reality of Europe, it would be necessary to immerse oneself ethnographically in all these diverse and countervailing positions. Only the synthesis of all these particular positions could produce a genuinely general theory of European integration. A total synthesis of this sort is impossible. However, if the analysis at one point is compelling enough it may be able to shed light on similar, though differentiated processes occurring elsewhere. It is hoped that in some small way the analysis proffered here might contribute in this way to a more general understanding of Europe. It is hoped that other social scientists find that there are parallels between the processes described here and their own areas of study. Whether this book is able to perform that function is uncertain. However, whatever the merits or demerits of this book, it is hoped that it will convince on one point: football is a central social practice in Europe today and its analysis can illuminate the contemporary reality with unusual lucidity. If anything can help us to answer the critical question of 'What is Europe?', it is this extraordinary public ritual which dominates the lives of so many Europeans.

Anthony King
University of Exeter

PART I
THE TRANSFORMATION OF A RITUAL

Chapter 1

From 1968 to 1999

It was, perhaps, one of the most dramatic moments in the history of European football. Since scoring in the sixth minute, it seemed certain that Bayern Munich would win the 1999 European Cup Final. They had dominated most of the game, scoring early and hitting Manchester United's post and crossbar in the second half, while United had made few significant attacks. Halfway through the second half, Teddy Sheringham was brought on to replace United's left-winger, Jesper Blomquist, bringing Ryan Giggs back into his favoured position on the left. With Giggs on the left and Beckham out wide on the right, Manchester United looked a more balanced side but the changes appeared to have been made too late. Later, in the eightieth minute, Ole Gunnar Solskjaer replaced Andy Cole but, despite Solskjaer's record of late scoring, this substitution also seemed futile. In the ninetieth minute when the game seemed already lost, United won a corner and while David Beckham prepared to launch the team's final effort, Peter Schmeichel, as he had done in other games, left his own net and joined the rest of his team in Bayern's penalty area. As the ball swung over, Schmeichel, whose presence had drawn Bayern defenders out of position, jumped for the ball. It passed clear over the head of this mêlée, falling to Dwight Yorke on the far side of the goal. He headed the ball back and it eventually fell to Ryan Giggs who struck the ball weakly towards the Bayern goal. As the ball passed Teddy Sheringham he hooked it into Bayern's net. Three minutes later, now deep into stoppage time, United won another corner. Again Beckham swung the ball in. Sheringham rose and deflected a header down towards the left-hand post where Ole Gunnar Solskjaer threw out his boot, driving the ball high into the net. Now familiar scenes of mayhem followed, while Sammy Kuffour, on all fours, pummelled the ground in despair.

1968: An International Match

Thirty-one years earlier, on 29 May 1968, Manchester United had beaten Benfica of Portugal 4–1 in the 13th European Cup Final at Wembley Stadium. Although the United players in 1999 lifted the same trophy as their forebears in 1968, any formal similarity between these two events is deceptive. In fact, historical transformations separate these dates decisively from one another though it is often difficult to recognise these wider changes. In the famous opening pages of *Discipline and Punish*, Foucault juxtaposes the brutal execution of the attempted regicide Damiens in 1757 with the penal regimen instituted in the following century in order to highlight the distinctiveness of European society (Foucault 1977). While the pitiful Damiens was ripped limb from limb, his various body parts displayed or burnt in a ferocious act of regal revenge, the criminal of the nineteenth century was subjected to a measured and private regime of mental and physical discipline. For Foucault, the two penal systems reflect the political regimes of the time; Damiens' torture symbolised the personal revenge of the king, whose very self had been insulted by insurrection, while the new penal system denoted the imposition of abstract laws on deviant individuals. For Foucault, the peculiar cruelty of the familiar penal system can be recognised fully only when set against a sharply differing system of retribution. As Foucault demonstrated, that juxtaposition allows the familiar to be illuminated in dramatically new ways, providing dulled perceptions with new insights (see Baert 1998). Similarly, in order to recognise the current transformation of football, it is useful to juxtapose contemporary practices against those of the past. To this end, the comparison of 1999 with 1968 serves a useful heuristic purpose of illuminating the direction and extent of present changes, just as the execution of Damiens in 1757 and the prison regulations of 1828 economically highlight an important historical transformation in the penal system.

A brief examination of the main newspaper coverage in the respective years of Manchester United's European victories is instructive. Throughout the 1968 season, the English newspapers had covered each of United's games with previews and reports and there was an understandable expansion of reports for the final. Not only was this the first final that an English team had ever reached but it was also particularly significant because of the death of the Manchester United team, the so-called 'Busby Babes', in an aircrash ten years earlier in Munich.[1] The English newspapers interpreted Manchester United's matches in a historically distinctive fashion; they were international games and the club itself was the unproblematic representative of England and Britain. The line adopted by *The Times*' correspondent, Geoffrey Green, was typical.[2] For instance, after Manchester United had eliminated Real Madrid in the 1968 semi-final, Green commented: 'Manchester United now stand as the heroes of England' (Geoffrey Green 1968a: 16). He highlighted the qualities which brought these English heroes victory: 'In the end it was English temperament, fibre and morale that won through' (ibid.). Contrasting with the English national character, Green invoked a stereotypical account of Latin temperament of which he saw evidence both in the Real Madrid team and the crowd itself. 'This was siesta time for the hot-blooded crowd whose wrath flamed out as Stiles stabbed at fleeting Amancio ... All day the sun had beaten down like a hammer and the night, exquisitely still, was humid. It should have favoured the Spaniards ... ' (ibid.). Contrasting with the phlegmatic English, Green implies that the Spanish players were 'hot-blooded', reflecting the climate in which they lived. This nationalistic paradigm was evident elsewhere in Green's writing. Discussing the prospect of the 1968 final on the day of the game itself, Green similarly drew upon the concept of an English character. 'There will be no question where the hopes of the 100,000 crowd and of the nation as a whole will lie ... if there is any valid explanation it probably rests in their moral fibre, temperament and unquenchable spirit that lifted them off the floor recently' (Geoffrey Green 1968b). Once again, Green emphasised the 'English' virtues of the Manchester United team.

Although Green assumed that Manchester United represented England, the team, in fact, included players from the other home nations of Britain. Indeed, the team even fielded two Republic of Irish internationals (Tony Dunne and Shay Brennan).[3] For Green, England and Britain were synonymous; Scottish, Welsh, Northern Irish and even Republic of Ireland players were viewed by him as English when playing for English clubs. It was significant that during this period the term 'Europe' or 'Europeans' was rarely used in English newspapers. Rather, the preferred term for Europeans in these early years was 'Continental' or the 'Continentals' (for example, *The Times* 1962a; *The Times* 1963b), emphasising Britain's distinctive maritime isolation. British teams were seen as the embodiment of the common national virtues of manliness, perseverance and strength against the effete (though skilful) showiness of 'Continental' teams. Thus, in describing Tottenham's 4–2 defeat by the Polish team Gornik Zabrze, *The Times* drew on stereotypical accounts of English temperament (which saved Tottenham from an even heavier defeat) but were surprised that the Polish team did not demonstrate these typically 'Continental' characteristics: 'In the end it was fitness, temperament and luck (or ill luck) of that injury to the Polish left-half that saved them from disaster. Most Continental sides in a similar position would have faded like a smoke ring' (*The Times* 1961b). This reading was repeated when Tottenham played Benfica later in the same season; 'In terms of pure football technique these Portuguese were the greater artists. But technique is not everything at times, and last night they found themselves in a man's game where spirit and fibre and courage and the last drop of breath counted' (*The Times* 1962e). While the newspapers recognised the skill of the 'Continentals', they were invariably portrayed as temperamentally suspect. After their controversial defeat by Internazionale in 1965,[4] Liverpool 'walked off the pitch at a hot, hysterical San Siro stadium' (Horridge 1965) while in 1967, a Naples player, Sivori, 'showing his quick South American temperament, jabbed his opponent, lashed out at Morgan, then kicked O'Neil' (Green 1967b). Similarly, in his description of Manchester United's game against Sarajevo in 1967, David Meek drew on this same motif which figured heavily in Green's work of the disciplined English and the hot-blooded foreigner. He noted that the 'Yugoslavs are a tough, passionate people' (Meek 1967), concluding that the outcome of the game 'was a matter of temperament'. While Manchester United 'though often flattened [by fouls] got straight up again to play football', the Yugoslavs 'lost their heads' (ibid.). This contrast between the English and British and the 'Continentals' culminated with assertions about the inherent disposition of different races towards certain kinds of behaviour. For instance, Benfica's defeat by Sunderland in 1963 was explained in significant fashion: 'Certainly last night was not the sort of weather to excite their Latin and Negroid blood' (*The Times* 1963a).

It followed from his assumption that Manchester United represented England and its national virtues that Green interpreted the final as an international match between two nations. Club and nation were interchangeable for Green: 'For this is a national occasion make no mistake. It is seen as revenge for Portugal's World Cup defeat and Benfica's humiliating 5–1 defeat by Manchester United ... two years ago' (Green 1968b). This assumption that clubs represented their nations was long-standing. After Manchester United's drubbing of Anderlecht in 1956, *The Times* reported that, 'They stayed to roar their heads off and to dream dreams of English football showing its true stamp once more' (*The Times* 1956). Similar language was employed to describe Manchester United's game against Real Madrid later in that year's competition: 'But now [having gone 2–0 down] United, remembering what they stand for in Britain, seemed suddenly inspired by the danger' (Green 1957). This close connection between Manchester United and the nation was emphasised by other journalists. In his coverage of the 1968 Cup Final, David Meek, the *Manchester Evening News* football correspondent, similarly drew a connection between Manchester United and Britain when describing fans gathered in London before the game. 'A group of youngsters in Trafalgar Square decided to back Britain as well as United. Over their sober suits, they had draped large Union Jacks' (Meek 1968b).

Reflecting this nationalistic interpretation of European competition, club games were often conceived of in military terms; an analogy was drawn between the games and war. Thus, the opposition was regularly described as the 'enemy' (*The Times* 1962b) and metaphors of 'arrows' (*The Times* 1962d; *The Times* 1961a), 'shafts', 'grape-shot' (*The Times* 1963b), 'spearheads', 'ripostes' (*The Times* 1962f) or 'barrages' (Green 1967a) were often used to describe attacks or shots at goal. Milan made 'a sneak raid' against Ipswich in 1962 (*The Times* 1962c) while in a game against Internazionale, Everton were criticised for their unsubtle tactics; 'It was physical exertion and the old frontal attack with no ideas of subtle infiltration' (*The Times* 1963c). Similarly, to describe defensive play, martial metaphors were liberally employed. Thus, while Real Madrid were excellent in attack, 'their shield could be dented' (McGhee 1957) and against Ipswich, Milan's sneak raid was mounted from a 'chainmail defence' (*The Times* 1962c). These military metaphors could reach the lyrical heights as a description of the semi-final between Real Madrid and Manchester United at Old Trafford in 1957 reveals: 'The field had all the appearance of a battlefield. Smoke from the stone-fingers of surrounding chimneys drifted over the lividly-lit pitch' (McGhee 1957). Similarly, Meek also drew on florid military references to frame his reports: 'Having seen their mountains and watched their football, I can fully understand how the Germans found it impossible to beat Marshal Tito and the partisans into submission' (Meek 1967). The most elaborate use of military metaphor was saved for matches against German opposition such as Manchester United's match against Borussia Dortmund in 1956:

> The Borussian forwards in their eagerness fell repeatedly into United's off-side trap, much to the satisfaction of the British Tommies who were present in large numbers ... Two superbly judged sorties by Wood held the ravening Germans at bay ... Here was history repeating itself: the Thin Red Line against the German hosts. [*The Guardian* 21 November 1956, cited in Meek 1988, p. 21][5]

In the 1950s, the Second World War was still a vivid memory. Consequently, the military metaphor was apt, denoting the status of European football as an international competition between the representatives of different nations.

The reports of the 1968 Final itself traversed the same nationalist line which was typical of the era. Thus, *The Times* carried a front-page piece which emphasised the national satisfaction that could be taken from this game: 'How fitting too, that this memorable triumph should go now to a club which has done so much for the game England first gave to the world' (Ecclestone 1968). On the sports pages, Geoffrey Green continued this theme.

> At last Manchester United have climbed their Everest and after 11 years of trial and effort their dreams have come true. So the crown sits on the first English club to enter this competition ... They have helped to beat back the Latin domination that for so long had taken Continental football by the throat ... they [United] fell back on their morale and unconquerable spirit. Again it made giants of men who seemed to have given their last ounce of strength as they searched for the final yard to the summit. [Green 1968c]

Significantly, not only were United's virtues of morale and spirit emphasised but the dubious character of foreigners was also highlighted. *The Mirror*'s reporter was critical of the game: 'It was not a great match. Indeed at times it was an ugly one ... In defeat Benfica do not retain the label of sportsmanship that the Portuguese acquired during the World Cup. They showed their true colours last night. It was difficult to admire anything they attempted' (Jones 1968). In fact, Eusebio was fouled many more times than Best. United were much more petulant than Benfica, and there were a couple of examples of outstanding sportsmanship from Eusebio. Yet, once Benfica had been interpreted as foreigners, unfounded attributions concerning their temperament followed.

The 1968 Final was seen as an international match between the representatives of two discrete nations. This interpretation was all but universal in papers such as *The Times*, *The Manchester Evening News* and *The Mirror*. However, although the nationalist paradigm was dominant in this period, it is worth noting that the final could occasionally be interpreted in a different way. In his report on the 1968 Final, Green noted with relish that in the following season both Manchester City, which had just won the league title, and Manchester United would be 'treading the paths of Europe'. He added: 'What rivalry that will engender in the years to come' (Green 1968c). Here Green begins to recognise that European competition could be understood not in nationalistic but in localistic terms. European competition could stimulate local rivalry between the fans of different clubs. However, given the brevity of this comment especially in relation to the volume of Green's reporting on European football and the positive tone of the sentence, it cannot be invested with too much significance. For Green, European competition was still understood in internationalist terms. On the same theme, the *Manchester Evening News* published a single letter which called for a 'Truce time' between United and City fans, noting that 'there has always been the keenest rivalry between Manchester City and United fans', but insisting 'that on this night of nights ... a United fan living in London calls for a truce and a linking of Reds and Blues in the name of Manchester, "home of champions" ' (Frame 1968). Frame's letter is interesting in that it calls for unity between the fans on a local rather than a national basis. These brief comments by Frame and Green suggest that a localistic interpretation of European football was theoretically possible even in the 1960s. Yet, examples of a localistic interpretation were so rare that they were all but irrelevant in comparison with the hegemonic nationalist account of European football.

The nationalist account of the Final was not a mere construction, any other interpretation of these games providing an equally accurate account of the game. One of the reasons for the dominance of this interpretation is that it did accord broadly with the realities of European football at the time. At this time, national federations were sovereign, with the clubs subordinate to them. The federations administered both domestic and European competition with the aid of their international representative, UEFA (The Union of European Football Associations). These federations defended the sovereignty of their leagues carefully. In particular, in the 1960s, and indeed in the 1950s in all countries except Spain and Italy, foreign player restrictions were enforced. These restrictions ensured that European club teams were drawn from the nation in which the club was situated and were intended to protect the development of native talent for the national team.[6] Thus, Benfica fielded only Portuguese nationals including former colonies so that Eusebio and Coluna, both from Mozambique, were qualified to play. Similarly, in England, although there was no restriction on home nation players from Scotland,

Wales, Northern Ireland and Eire, no foreigners were allowed to play in English club teams. Consequently, the connection between the club and nation which journalists like Green and Meek drew, and the metaphor of war which hyperbolically suggested an international struggle, were valid accounts of European football at the time. A reading which emphasised the priority of the city or region was certainly not *a priori* impossible in 1968, but given the structure of European football, a nationalistic reading reflected contemporary realities most accurately. The Final in which Manchester United played some 31 years later was a very different occasion and was interpreted in significantly different ways.

1999: A Transnational Event

In 1968, the nationalist interpretation of European football was supported by the national composition of the teams. The players were natives of the countries in which the clubs were located and consequently, in European competition, the matches could be straightforwardly interpreted as international games. By the late 1990s, by contrast, the composition of the teams was far more cosmopolitan. For instance, in the 1999 European Cup Final, although both Manchester United and Bayern Munich had unusually few foreign players in comparison with their European peers, their squads were much more diverse. Manchester United's 1999 team included seven foreign players (Blomqvist, Johnsen, Schmeichel, Yorke, Van der Gouw, Solskjaer, Stam) while Bayern's team included two (Kuffour and Salihamidzic). The increasingly transnational composition of the teams in 1999 was reflected in public discussions of the event.

The nationalist interpretation remained very important in 1999. As in 1968, most of the reportage framed the Final as a match between England and Germany where Manchester United represented England and Bayern Munich, Germany. A typical example of this nationalistic reading was provided by ex-Liverpool player and European Cup winner, Tommy Smith: 'I wore England's three lions over my heart with pride and I would back any English side in Europe – we all should. It's all about regaining ground in Europe' (Smith 1999). The leader in *The Mirror* affirmed Smith's stance insisting that 'it is the night our football nation sets aside lifelong rivalries and stands United. The red of Old Trafford, Manchester, will be everyone's colour' (*The Mirror* 1999). It was notable that the other major tabloid, *The Sun*, also adopted an unproblematically nationalist line in its coverage to the point of xenophobia. The paper delighted in the fact that Manchester United had in the course of the season 'brought the Italians down in Milan and Turin and on Wednesday they put the Germans on their knees' (Greaves 1999). *The Times* sometimes traversed a similar line. On the day before the game, in a humorous article which listed ten reasons to support United (*The Times* 1999b), it was argued that a Manchester United victory would assist English football by providing more places for clubs in European competitions in the next season. In a piece of crude nationalism, the article asked: 'A football match between an English and a German team? What other reason do you want?' (ibid.). Similarly, although *The Manchester Evening News* recognised that many in the city did not support United (Everett 1999) and appeals to urban pride also featured in their coverage (for example, Everett 1999; Hince 1999), the regional paper generally adopted a simplistic nationalistic line delighting in the defeat of the 'Germans': 'Manchester United made you proud to be English' (Hince 1999). The same interpretation was demonstrated in the coverage of the game itself on ITV. The commentator Clive Tyldesley persistently drew on common satirical stereotypes of the Germans. Thus, for Tyldesley, United unproblematically represented England and the defeat of Bayern Munich automatically also meant the defeat of Germany by England. He introduced the match by citing the fact that England had not beaten Germany since 1966 in a major tournament. However, Tyldesley noted that while England's national record against Germany was poor, at club level, English sides had a record of six victories and two defeats in their last encounters. It should be noted that the idea of the nation mobilised in 1999 was somewhat different from 1968: while Manchester United sometimes represented England in 1999 (even with its many foreign players), England was no longer conflated with the rest of Britain, reflecting what Nairn has called the incipient 'break-up of Britain' (1981). Consequently, while some commentators appealed to a nationalistic interpretation which seemed to echo Green's own understanding of European football in the 1950s and 1960s, in fact, this nationalist interpretation had undergone significant renegotiation. In addition different accounts of the event were given prominent public airings in 1999 which contrasted strongly with 1968.

Thus, directly opposing Tommy Smith's reading, in a piece entitled 'Why I back Bayern' on the same page, Brian Reade proclaimed; 'I will be singing Deutschland, Deutschland Uber Alles' (Reade 1999). Reade justified his support for Bayern because of Manchester United's domestic dominance and the unjustifiable level of media coverage the club received. Reade concluded the article in significant terms: 'Football will always be first and foremost about tribalism. One-upmanship. Love and jealousy' (ibid.). For him, the urban and regional rivalry between fans at a club level was more important than artificial unification behind putatively national representatives. Interestingly, even in his nationalistic interpretation of the Final, Tommy Smith emphasised the local rivalry between Manchester United and Liverpool, pointing to Liverpool's greater honours list and the putative superiority of Liverpool's 1977 European Cup-winning team in which he played: 'Players like Beckham are great but we could have whacked them' (Smith 1999). Smith was not alone in recognising a tension within the nationalist reading of the 1999 Final. Significantly, many of the pieces in *The Times* which drew on this nationalistic interpretation simultaneously recognised its problematic nature:

> In practice, it is the Bundesliga's finest who will have to lie awake and torment themselves with the thoughts of what might have been. English glee must be forgiven. The wait for the role reversal has been a long one and the only trick still beyond Manchester United may be the gift uniting the entire country. Their power and wealth will continue to irk some and cause envy to others, but, at Old Trafford, England's 30 years of hurt has been avenged. [McCarra 1999]

Here, the nationalist interpretation of the event which revels in the defeat of a national rival is cross-cut by a recognition of Manchester United's ambiguous relationship to England and its fans. In line with this, *The Times* carried a number of articles which promoted a new interpretation of European football. For instance, the list of ten reasons for supporting United was matched by ten others for not supporting them (*The Times* 1999a). Typically, Manchester United's domestic domination, its financial power and its pervasive position in the national media were cited. Furthermore, in an article which discussed an opinion poll saying that 86 per cent of people wanted Manchester United to beat Bayern Munich, the author rejected this support for United as false and highlighted the increasing antipathy of many English football fans towards the club:

> So what accounts for United's new-found national status? Whatever has changed, it is not the hearts of die-hard football fans, many of whom remain enthusiastic supporters of the ABU (Anybody but United) Club. The sad Liverpool fans waving Bayern flags on the Kop were not the only ones to sing 'Stand up if you hate Man U' on the day United won the Premiership this month. The pollsters also found 27 per cent of people insisting that they would never support United 'under any circumstance'. [Hume 1999]

A notable transformation had taken place between 1968 and 1999. Manchester United was no longer necessarily seen as England's representative when playing foreign opposition. European competition is no longer unproblematically viewed as a form of international competition. The major European football clubs are becoming differentiated from the nation and different forms of solidarity are emerging around and against them when they play other European competition. This is a decisive shift in public understandings. This is not to say that some fans in 1968 did not want Manchester United to lose; there is evidence that many Manchester City fans were not pleased by United's European victory. Rather, the two Finals differ because in 1968, the public understanding of the event was nationalistic; the competition was understood in international terms. It may be possible to claim tentatively that, by 1999, a transformation of the once dominant international interpretation is evident.

The nationalistic interpretation has not been effaced but it has undergone significant renegotiation as allegiances to the local club and city have been prioritised. Just as the international reading corresponded to the political economic organisation of European football at the time, so does this new localistic reading of the competition reflect current political economic developments. The nationalistic interpretation corresponds to an international regime, the localistic reading to a transnational one.

The Ritual of Football

The two Finals of 1968 and 1999 demonstrate that European football is undergoing profound change. Like Foucault's disciplinary examples, these dates stand on opposite sides of a decisive historical transformation. Yet, the significance of these changes is often overlooked because it is difficult to adopt an analytical stance towards the sport. For many, football is entertainment and therefore unworthy of serious consideration. Yet, the difficulties of analysis are not automatically obviated for those who are interested in the game. For enthusiasts, football is compelling because the outcome is uncertain. The game thrives upon the random and the accidental, which inspire ecstasy and despair among players and fans alike. Yet, the very excitement which the game engenders obstructs a proper appreciation of the social significance of the game. Although the exciting contingencies of football are not irrelevant to the analysis of it, contingencies need to be situated within a wider historical context which render them meaningful in a deeper but less emotive sense. In order to comprehend European football and its position in European society, a different relationship to the game must be adopted. It is necessary to become detached from the game and to become defamiliarised with it while at the same time recognising its profound social importance. That is not easy but there is a method by which an appropriate analytic position can be attained.

Durkheim's *The Elementary Forms of the Religious Life* provides a profound sociological account of ritual which, nearly a century after its publication, is still one of the most fruitful resources for comprehending these social events. In that work, Durkheim argued that the ritual constituted a key mechanism by which the social solidarity of aboriginal clans in Australia was sustained. For most of the year, aboriginal clans were engaged in the profane activity of hunting and gathering during which time they would fissure into smaller groups. Periodically, the clan would gather together and engage in ecstatic rituals in which they would worship their totemic god. Durkheim appositely noted that since the totem which the clanspeople worshipped represented their clan, aborigines, in fact, worshipped their own society in their rituals (Durkheim 1976, p. 225). The physical sensations which the aborigines experienced in the ritual and which they attributed to their god was, in fact, the power of their social group which was amassed ecstatically around them. Indeed, they did more than simply worship this social god. Through their participation in these heightened moments of collective effervescence, the clanspeople recreated this god, their society, for themselves. Only insofar as the clan gathered together periodically, reaffirming its existence which was represented by the totem, did this social group exist at all. Against the interpretations of Victorian anthropology, which dismissed rituals as the product of irrational primitive mentality, Durkheim highlighted the comprehensible and necessary role which ritual played in the social life of aboriginal groups, with the heavy hint that such ritualistic performances are universal. Without these periodic congregations in which group members mutually recognise each other, social groups cannot continue to exist: 'A society can neither create itself nor re-create itself without at the same time creating an ideal. This creation is not a sort of work of supererogation for it, by which it would complete itself, being already formed; it is the act by which it is periodically made and remade' (Durkheim 1976: 422).

For Durkheim, the ritual inculcates a certain idea of society into the minds of its members, which idea is essential to that social group. Group members have to recognise their social relations to each other if the group is to cohere. The group has a reality only if members understand what kinds of social practices their shared idea of society enjoins. However, this ideal does not impose itself upon individuals automatically or inevitably, as Durkheim seemed to suggest in much of his early work where society was given autonomous existence. Rather, this ideal has to be recreated by the group, for which re-creation the ritual constituted a key site. As Durkheim emphasises, this ritualistic recreation is not otiose. It is essential that individuals gather together and celebrate their membership of a unified social group if that group is to exist. The implication is clear. Without periodic ritual interaction, a social group fragments into profane and separate existence. Without ritual, the social group ceases to exist.

It is important to recognise that ritual has no less significance in modern society, although our familiarity with frequently informal and secular modern ritual forms often obscures the continuing centrality of ritual to our lives. Certainly, in modern society, rituals do not always involve the collective effervescence which Durkheim described in relation to aboriginal clans. Yet, even in contemporary European society, if any social grouping is to sustain itself, the members of that group must periodically meet in order to affirm the existence of the group and their commitment to it. These periodic congregations are not supererogatory to a group's existence. Durkheim himself was well aware of the continuing importance of ritual in contemporary life. At the end of *The Elementary Forms*, Durkheim wistfully remarks: 'A day will come when our society will know again those hours of creative effervescence' (Durkheim 1976: 427–8). Durkheim believed that these vital moments of creative effervescence would appear among the professional groups which he promotes as the only possible solution to social anomie. In a secularised, industrial society in which paid employment is a central experience, Durkheim argued that the professional group could become an important source of social solidarity. Strangely, though, Durkheim completely ignored a key public ritual which could also produce 'hours of creative effervescence': sport. It is possible that he ignored the significance of sport as a modern ritual because of the relative under-urbanisation of France. The mass urban spectator sports such as football developed slowly and weakly in France in comparison with other European countries. Its relative insignificance in France may have led Durkheim to ignore it. Yet, despite Durkheim's failure to recognise sport, some of the most important social groups in Europe are reconstituted through their ecstatic participation in sporting rituals. Consequently, the sporting ritual provides an illuminating focus for sociological research because it is an arena in which social relations and shared understandings are viscerally recreated. These recreations are not supererogatory to the social order which would exist without them. Because social relations have meaningful dimension, they have to be recognised by those who are party to them and the ritual constitutes the critical site at which this communal recognition takes place. Certainly, sport is not the only European ritual but it has been a very important one and is likely to be increasingly significant in the future.

Although Durkheim himself may have failed to acknowledge the importance of sport as a European ritual, it is possible to adopt an appropriate analytical relation to football in the light of his work. Rather than seeing this event as a mundane form of entertainment, football is defamiliarised when it is looked at as a ritual. As a ritual, football is not analysed alongside other equally familiar leisure activities but juxtaposed against the most exotic rituals uncovered by history and anthropology. Viewed as a ritual, football can become as strange and powerful as the spectacles of classical Rome, which illuminate Roman culture in all its stark brutality. Like the Greek games, the gladiatorial combats of classical Rome originated as an element in a wider religious rite; they were initially associated with funerals where the combats were intended to honour the deceased. The first recorded gladiatorial combat took place in 264 BC in honour of an aristocrat's dead father and involved only three pairs of gladiators (Hopkins 1983: 4). Over the next two centuries, the scale and frequency of gladiatorial shows steadily increased so that in 65 BC Julius Caesar organised a combat of 320 pairs of gladiators in an elaborate funeral rite for his father (Hopkins 1983: 4). Developing from this funerary origin, the spectacles which occurred in the amphitheatres of most towns and cities throughout the empire eventually consisted of three defined events: the execution of criminals, wild animal hunts and, finally, the combats themselves. Gradually, as the spectacles became more elaborate, they became the prerogative of the emperor himself. For instance, in 80 AD, the emperor Titus organised a spectacle in which nearly 9,000 wild and exotic animals were killed in a single day (Hopkins 1983: 9). The monopolisation of the Roman spectacle by the emperor demonstrated the transformation of an oligarchical republic into an absolutist state. Through huge spectacles, emperors demonstrated their absolute authority. At the beginning of the spectacle, criminals were often executed by being thrown to exotic wild animals (Hopkins 1983: 11) which would themselves be killed in subsequent hunting displays within the arena. This process ritualistically equated criminals with the status of mere beasts and was a powerful statement of the social hierarchy. The Roman spectacle was a graphic demonstration of the social abjection of slaves and criminals (Auguet 1994: 184; Hopkins 1983: 12). Significantly, although the crowd might plead for the life of a gladiator who had fought well, the decision of life and death – as in the rest of Roman life – rested with the emperor alone. Although gratuitous to modern sensibilities, the Roman spectacle was not supererogatory to Roman society. Roman society was recreated periodically in the fervid atmosphere of the arena. The spectacle was a central ritual in later Roman civilisation whereby the social hierarchy from emperor, to citizens and down to slaves, criminals and finally animals was reaffirmed in the arena. Although the strangeness of Roman culture often makes the parallel difficult, in the spectacle of European football, social hierarchies are similarly demonstrated through graphic performances on the field of play. These events are bloodless in comparison with the gruesome Roman spectacle but their effervescent power is no weaker. European football illuminates the realities of the New Europe just as the Roman spectacle displayed the brutal power of the *Pax Romana*. The different ritual form reflects the different social orders of which these events are part.

The Sociology of Europe

If European club football is analysed as a ritual, it can become as strange and unfamiliar as the Roman spectacle. Then, this apparently mundane social practice can begin to shed as much light on contemporary European society as Foucault cast upon nineteenth-century European society through the contrast of two differing penal systems. Once football is recognised as a social ritual rather than an escape from social reality, important new horizons are opened up. European football provides a prominent arena in which important social relations in European society are periodically remade. The game offers a particularly clear view of the wider society for in it, many of the key values and relations of contemporary society are intensely visible. In these ecstatic moments, such as the 1968 and 1999 European Cup Finals, a lucid vision of society comes into view in a way that is rare in any other aspect of social life. In the effervescent moments of this ritual – Best turning away from the goal in

1968 acknowledging victory with a raised arm, or Kuffour pummelling the earth in despair – the social relations and social groups which are central to European society emerge with a clarity and force which is often absent elsewhere. In explaining the transformation between the 1968 and 1999 Finals, it is essential that the development of this sporting ritual and its changing position in European society at the beginning of the twenty-first century is connected to wider changes across western Europe. It is essential that the significance of the historical transformation of European society from the 1970s onwards is recognised. These European Cup Finals are a powerful expression of wider social realities in contemporary European society and they can be understood only in the light of this wider social context of which they are an inseparable part. In order to achieve this contextualisation, we need to distance ourselves from the aspects of the game with which we are most familiar and to transform that which is most obvious and taken-for-granted into the something which is as strange as the Roman spectacle.

If football can be successfully analysed as a ritual, then the sociology of football may begin to make a serious intellectual contribution by analysing in rich empirical details the actualities of contemporary social transformation. In this way, the analysis of football will begin to transcend its current marginal position to make a serious interjection into current debates about Europe. Theoretical accounts of contemporary social transformation do not provide a better insight into the actualities of current historic changes. On the contrary, those who have ignored the intense reality of this ritual remaining cocooned in their own self-spun worlds should recognise the inadequacies of their idealisations. In his famous work on cricket, published in 1963, C.L.R. James demonstrated the social significance of this sport by altering Kipling's famous comment about England. At the beginning of that work, James demands: 'What do they know of cricket, who only of cricket know?' James' challenge can be usefully applied to current concerns to ask: what do they know of Europe, who nothing of football know? Without intimate knowledge of the activities which inspire Europeans today, discussions of the reality of Europe are merely academic. We do not live in theoretical abstractions but in actual social relations. These relations, the passions which they inspire, must always be the focus of genuine social analysis. This book attempts to make a small contribution to our understanding of Europe today by analysing one of its most important contemporary rituals.

Notes

1 Glasgow Celtic had defeated Internazionale in the 1967 Final to become the first British team to lift the European Cup.

2 Geoffrey Green was recognised as one of the most prominent sports journalists writing in Britain at the time (see Glanville 1999: 187–9).
3 Since the Irish league was not fully professional, Irish players were always considered as British nationals by the football authorities and so Green's conflation of Irishness and Britishness was understandable.
4 See Chapter 4. The match referee was almost certainly bribed.
5 The reference here is to British soldiers stationed in West Germany who were watching the game but the use of the highly charged term 'Tommies' (by which British infantrymen were colloquially known during the two World Wars) is significant.
6 As we shall see in Chapter 4, in the 1950s, the Italian and, especially, Spanish federations had few or no restrictions on foreign players. Only in the early 1960s were rules limiting foreign players introduced to protect the development of indigenous talent for the national team.

Chapter 2

The New Europe: Cities, States or Superstate?

The Origins of the Europe Union

The European catastrophe of the Second World War provided the immediate impetus for integration between the nation-states of Europe. In particular, the Resistance movement against fascism promoted the notion of a united Europe in which future European wars might be avoided. The idea of unifying the nation-states of Europe and particularly of binding Germany to France was first formally proposed in July 1944 when the Resistance movements from several countries signed a declaration that new federal structures were required for the whole of Europe after the war (Urwin 1991: 9). Even Winston Churchill, a committed nationalist, regarded the integration of Germany into the rest of Europe as essential to prevent further conflict. However, although the Resistance movement promoted the idea of European integration any serious political reformation was difficult during the 1940s. The primary role for nation-states after the war was reconstruction. Many of Europe's industries and infrastructures had been badly damaged and it was necessary to stabilise national economies in order to provide employment for the millions of demobilised servicemen. Aid from the United States, especially the Marshall Plan, was essential in this reconstruction but, although highly successful, it was not until the 1950s that nation-states were in any position to implement plans of European integration (Urwin 1991: 25–42; Williams 1992: 16–17). By that time, the Resistance movement had itself lost credibility, partly as a result of its involvement in the summary justice meted out to collaborators after the end of the war in 1945. However, while the Resistance movement was not politically significant in implementing its vision of a unified Europe in which future war was impossible, it did play an important role in conditioning people to a new way of thinking about Europe (Urwin 1991: 24). This new way of thinking was significant in the initial stages of integration.

Although there were preliminary agreements in the 1940s such as the treaties of Dunkirk and Brussels in 1947 and 1948 and the establishment of the European Assembly in 1948 (ibid.: 48), the first serious moves towards European integration were initiated on 9 May 1950 when Robert Schumann launched the union of German and French steel and coal production, the so-called Schumann Plan. The creation of this economic community had been regarded as essential since, as Schumann noted in his declaration, 'the solidarity in production thus established will make it plain that any war between France and Germany ... becomes not merely unthinkable, but materially impossible' (Nelsen and Stubb 1994: 12). In April 1952, France, Germany, Belgium, Holland, Luxembourg and Italy joined the European Coal and Steel Community to establish the first supranational institution in post-war Europe and the model of all future European institutions. Efforts were also made to create a European Defence Community which unified the military defences of European countries but this attempt failed rapidly. However, the six signatories of the Steel and Coal Community were successful in establishing EURATOM, a supranational atomic energy community (Urwin 1991: 118).

The successful establishment of these two communities encouraged the development of the European Economic Community (EEC) which would reduce tariffs and international obstructions to intra-European trade and economic development. This third community, which has subsequently become by far the most important, was ratified, along with the previously existing communities at the Treaty of Rome in 1957. This Treaty was concerned with advancing the interests of liberal capitalism and was formally, at least, committed to deregulation and unfettered private capitalist accumulation as a major engine of economic integration (Williams 1992: 26). Many of the key articles (for example, Articles 48, 85, 86) of the Treaty of Rome, for instance, were explicitly neoliberal before neoliberalism had become the dominant paradigm for western European capitalism. These articles were concerned with improving the standard of living in Europe and increasing Europe's economic competitiveness, especially in relation to the United States, through liberalisation. In addition, according to functionalist theorists of European integration in the 1950s and 1960s such as Haas (1964) and Lindberg and Scheingold (1970), this liberal economic integration would promote further political integration through a series of 'functional' spillovers. The Treaty of Rome and the creation of the European Economic Community involved the rapid and relatively uncontentious creation of a customs union and the elimination of many internal trade barriers (Middlemas 1995: 59).

However, while the abolition of tariffs involved the surrender of a degree of national autonomy, the nation-states retained control over the new Community. Notably, the Council of Europe and the Council of Ministers, which were intergovernmental bodies, determined policy, rather than the more radically supranational Parliament or Commission (Williams 1992: 28). The inalienable sovereignty of the nation-states in the European project was also formally recognised in 1966, when member states, ultimately at the behest of France and Charles de Gaulle, instituted the so-called Luxembourg Compromise (Wallace 1990: 78; Wallace 1997: 26–7; Middlemas 1995: 52; Williams 1992: 31; *The*

Economist 1997: 11). This compromise allowed any state the option to refuse to implement those aspects of European legislation which it found offensive, outlawing majority rule and therefore genuine supranational government. Consequently, although the language of the Treaty of Rome was often liberal, prioritising the free market as the key driver of European integration, the first 15 years of European integration should not be seen primarily as a period of economic liberalism in which the free market dominated as states surrendered sovereignty. As the Luxembourg Compromise showed, national sovereignty persisted. Moreover, although the liberalisation of tariffs did increase transnational European trade considerably, they were only a minor and relatively uncontentious part of the political agreements which were made in those early years of the European community. By contrast, the most significant political agreement which constituted the greatest bulk of the Community's work in the 1950s and 1960s was the Common Agricultural Policy (CAP), the development of which was in direct opposition to the liberal language of the Treaty (Williams 1992: 41, 73; Anderson 1997: 67). CAP was not concerned with the application of the free market to European farming but with the establishment of a corporatist international agreement which aimed at sustaining the agricultural sector in the face of economic competition by redistribution and subsidy. CAP was concerned with alleviating the effects of market competition for the agricultural sector rather than promoting a transnational market. Moreover, throughout the early years of European integration and indeed up to the present day, the Commission has had no independent tax-raising powers but is dependent upon national governments (Anderson 1997: 67).

Andrew Milward (1992) has famously demonstrated that, in the early years of the European Union (EU), at least, the sovereignty of the nation-states was not significantly challenged (Wallace 1997: 28). Those commentators who regard European integration as the surrender of national sovereignty to supranational authority have paid no attention to the details of European integration. They have imposed false theoretical teleologies onto European development. For Milward, European integration was the means by which European nation-states preserved their sovereignty and political authority (Milward 1992: x, 2), a point which becomes clear when the actual historic interactions between the nation-states at the heart of the union are considered in detail (ibid.: 12). Milward claims that the Second World War constituted a disaster for the nation-states of Europe where they almost collapsed as a result of external aggression or internal extremism which drove them, in the case of Italy and Germany, to self-destruction (ibid.: 3–4). Against teleological accounts of European integration which point to the surrender of sovereignty by states to supranational bodies, Milward insists that the European project was a key method by which these states reinvigorated themselves in the 1950s ensuring their popular legitimacy by creating economic growth and stability for their citizens (ibid.: 27). He traces the rise of the three communities of Europe as well as subsequent policy developments such as CAP after the Treaty of Rome, to show that in each case, nation-states always retained control over developments and lost none of their sovereignty. For instance, the European Coal and Steel Community, while putatively supranational, could never have imposed anything on the Belgian government (ibid.: 117) while the French government accepted only what it wanted from Europe (ibid.: 220).

Milward undermines the myths which have grown up around the founding fathers of Europe, such as Schumann, Monnet, Adenauer, Spaak and de Gasperi. He demonstrates that the interpretation of these individuals as committed federalists is the convenient fabrication of those who themselves espouse a federal image of Europe. For Milward, by contrast, these individuals were always faithful nationalists who saw European integration as the best way to create peace and prosperity in each European member state. He appositely cites Robert Schumann: 'Our European States are a historical reality; it would be psychologically impossible to make them disappear. Their diversity is in fact very fortunate and we do not want either to level them or to equalize them' (ibid.: 329). He also notes that Monnet was one of the most important figures in the reconstruction of the French state after the war and, therefore, it was unlikely that this same individual would wish to dismantle his work and surrender the sovereignty of the state he had helped resurrect to a supranational body (ibid.: 334).[1] Milward provides compelling evidence that while the language of some parts of the Treaty of Rome may well have been neoliberal, the nation-state remained dominant in the first 15 years of integration and that any economic liberalisation was initiated by nation-states for their own benefit. However, although Milward's argument for the early years of European integration seems broadly accurate, it does require some minor qualification. As Woever argues, if nation-states had to choose European integration to survive, it means that the nation-state cannot be what it once was. The state could survive only in a transformed form as a bargaining state which contradicts Milward's programmatic statement (Woever 1995: 427; Anderson 1997: 58). Certainly Milward is correct to emphasise the centrality of nation-states to the European project – the power of the Council of Europe and the importance of the Luxembourg Compromise demonstrate this – but it is unsustainable to argue that states now have to take other states into account even in domestic policy and then claim that there has been no erosion of state authority or sovereignty. However, although Milward's thesis might require qualification to claim that from the 1950s European states gave up small parts of their sovereignty in order to guarantee national economic prosperity on which their legitimacy was founded, it is also clear that within the historical period with which Milward is particularly concerned, the early years of integration up to the 1970s, his argument is sustainable. European integration was driven by nation-states for their mutual benefit.

The liberalisation of trade as a result of the Treaty of Rome did not undermine European nation-states. Rather, integration enhanced nationally-based Fordist regimes of production by extending the market for mass manufactured commodities. Significantly, the reduction of tariffs applied only to industrial goods and to neither services nor workers themselves (Williams 1992: 32). This arrangement was in the interests of Fordist industries and the interventionist states, committed to guaranteeing economic stability and prosperity, because it expanded the markets for these goods without threatening the internal political settlement between labour unions, capital and the state. The liberalisation of labour markets would have undermined the Fordist regime by threatening the position of workers in the post-war period with imported foreign competition. It would therefore undermine the corporatist settlement between trade unions, capital and state which was central to the Keynesian post-war consensus. Consequently, there was no attempt to reduce non-tariff barriers since these would interfere too seriously with the macroeconomic policy of each nation-state. The success of the early years of the EEC from 1957 until 1972 took place under a Fordist regime. As the Luxembourg Compromise of 1966 demonstrated, the nation-states of the Union only consented to international liberalisation insofar as it was in the interests of their national economic development.

Eurosclerosis

The early progress of the EEC under the Treaty of Rome was substantially the result of the post-war boom but, towards the end of the 1960s, contradictions within the Keynesian international order appeared. As the political economic regime which had given rise to the EEC tottered, the project of European integration stagnated and governments sought to address domestic crises. There were four central reasons for the collapse of the Fordist post-war regime of regulation. First, the Bretton Woods international monetary system became increasingly unstable from the early 1970s as the position of the dollar, which underpinned the system, eroded. The obvious response to this decline of the dollar's position in relation to other currencies would have been to devalue the dollar but since a devaluation would have had serious domestic repercussions for the United States government, it was delayed (Dunford and Kafkalas 1992: 50). Eventually though, the dollar's fixed value had to be abandoned producing currency speculation and economic destabilisation (Williams 1992: 52–3). This destabilisation was serious for Fordist companies with large overheads and long production runs. Second, alongside the collapse of the stable Bretton Woods monetary system, relations between labour and capital were becoming more strained from the late 1960s onwards. Full employment had reduced profitability by encouraging wage inflation, but as the Bretton Woods system came under pressure, that inflexibility in the labour market became increasingly intolerable for capital, resulting in growing confrontations between the two sides which became increasingly impossible for the state to mediate (Williams 1992: 53). Third, from the late 1960s, increasing global competition, especially from Japanese transnational corporations, reduced profit rates and rendered labour inflexibility and monetary instability even more problematic to capital accumulation. Of course, the US's inability to act as an anchoring currency in the world markets was itself a partial result of its relative economic uncompetitiveness in comparison with new Japanese modes of manufacture. Fourth, the oil crisis of 1973 (and later 1978–79) constituted the final blow for post-war Fordist stability and growth. As a result of the 1973 Yom Kippur war, OPEC quadrupled oil prices with obvious consequences for retail prices and profitability in Europe and North America.

For the following ten to fifteen years, Europe and North America experienced crisis until a new post-Fordist political settlement emerged. Given the level of economic uncertainty between the early 1970s and the mid-1980s, the nation-states of Europe were in no position to implement further steps towards European integration at this time. There were other far more pressing issues and after the initial achievements of European integration in the 1950s and 1960s, the European project stagnated in the 1970s as 'Eurosclerosis' set in (Nelson and Stubbs 1994: 179; Wallace 1997: 34; Bulmer and Scott 1995). However, although there was little progress in the field of economic integration, there was an expansion of the Union to include three further countries in 1973. Denmark, Great Britain and Ireland joined the EEC just before the economic crisis occurred.

The New Europe: Deregulation

As a result of the collapse of Fordism, the EEC remained a minor aspect of state policy until the mid-1980s when the nine nation-states of the European Community began to see the need for economic integration once again. In the light of rapid globalization which increased economic competition and reduced any single government's control of their domestic economy, political integration and cooperation at an intergovernmental level was becoming ever more urgent by the mid-1980s. Indeed, the calls for the development of a genuinely federal Europe became increasingly loud from this time. Although Germany and France still operated with far more interventionist states than Britain, the new post-Fordist settlement which was emerging from the late 1970s was more economically liberal (Wallace 1997: 36–9; Van Creveld 2000: 365, 370). As multinational corporations became increasingly important actors on the global stage and as financial markets became more international and less stable, European nation-states have been forced to adopt an increasingly more *laissez-faire* approach to the economy. Clearly, under Prime Minister Thatcher and with its traditional bias towards the financial institutions of the City of London, Britain exemplified the most radically liberalised post-Fordist settlement but throughout Europe the emergent regime of regulation was decidedly more market-oriented; states increasingly resorted to deregulation to promote economic development. Even the putatively socialist government in France under Mitterand passed a series of deregulatory legislation.

After the Eurosclerosis of the 1970s, the Single European Act of 1986 constituted the first serious attempts to reinvigorate the project of European integration. Although the Single European Act was only a restatement of the principles already enshrined within that Treaty, in the transformed economic conditions of the late 1980s, this restatement amounted in practice to a quite profound transformation of the European project. In particular, the reinvigoration of the European project applied the free market principles of the Treaty of Rome in a way that was incompatible with the previous Fordist regime in order to create the conditions for full economic union. Consequently, although the Single European Act, Project 1992 and, later, the Maastricht Treaty seemed to be a mere restatement of the 1957 Treaty and therefore simply a return to a project which was untowardly interrupted by the crises of the 1970s, European integration of the 1980s and 1990s was, in fact, a quite different phenomenon to that of the 1950s and 1960s. The importance of the Treaty of Rome in both periods disguises the significant difference between them; while one was carried out under the paradigm of Keynesian and Fordist common sense in which the state was dominant, the other has been prosecuted under the free market orientation of post-Fordism (Klein and Welfens 1992). For instance the Single European Act proposed a programme for eventual monetary union which became known as Project 1992. The Single European Act insisted not only on a free market in goods (as had been the case in the 1960s) but also, highly significantly, on a free market in persons, services and capital as well (Williams 1992: 94) thus creating a genuinely transnational market across Europe which reduced the sovereignty of the nation-state. Under this liberalised regime, certain regulatory policies whereby nation-states attempted to protect their workforce became unworkable as well as illegal. The Single European Act and Project 1992 sought to create a genuine single market in which fiscal, physical and technical barriers were removed and, in this, it has been highly successful. For instance, although progress with Project 1992 was difficult, decisions had been taken on 60 per cent of the required measures by March 1990 and the success of the project prepared the way for a single European currency. In the light of globalization, European integration is now primarily informed by free market principles and in line with this, large sectors of the European economy have been privatised over the last 15 years.

Corporatist social policy provisions which echo the spirit of the Keynesian era have been subordinate to these deregulatory reforms (see Boornschier and Ziltener 1999).

The Nation-State in the New Europe

While Andrew Milward's claim that the state reached its zenith in the early years of European integration (1992) is broadly sustainable, his claim of the inviolable sovereignty of the nation-state even into the 1990s seems less convincing. The problem for Milward, of course, is that since the reinvigoration of the European project, the situation has changed dramatically and the kinds of erosion of state sovereignty and authority which the functionalists of the 1950s, like Haas and Lindberg, advocated seem much more in evidence. Nevertheless, while the post-Fordist regime is marked by the retreat of the state from direct economic intervention, this does not mean that the state is becoming irrelevant or will do so in the near future. Even though weakened, the state of the late twentieth and early twenty-first centuries, is one of the key institutions in the contemporary world (Mann 1993; Cable 1995; Strange 1995; Muller and Wright 1994). States now compete for market shares in the world economy rather than territory, but they are still a prime source of authority in the world system (Strange 1995: 55, 57; Held 1991: 149). Despite the growing economic importance of multinationals, the nation-state still retains the monopoly of violence at the turn of the millenium; only the state can prosecute war and institute legitimate criminal punishment within its borders.[2] Moreover, the nation-state retains its legitimacy in the eyes of its citizens and imagined national communities uniting a people behind a state remains one of the most significant forms of identification. The nation-state is changing and in certain spheres, primarily the economic, its authority is declining. As certain commentators have noted, the nation-state is being 'hollowed out' (Strange 1995: 57); it administers the same or similar geographical areas but it has devolved many of its former functions and responsibilities. The state is finding new roles in the contemporary Europe to offset the loss of old ones as intergovernmental bargaining becomes an increasingly important element of state policy (Mann 1993: 118). It is notable that the success of the single European currency is dependent upon the active intervention of the nation-states of Europe. Crucially, the Council of Europe – the intergovernmental element of the Union where nation-states meet and negotiate – is becoming increasingly important in developing legislature and policy which is then effectively endorsed by the Commission and Parliament even though the Commission is the formal legislative chamber. Europe is a complex new political phenomenon which defies definition because it transcends conventional political categories. The emergent order differs from the national liberal democracies which have been prominent in the last two centuries of European history (Anderson 1997: 68). Against the polemics of individuals like Siedentop who call for a federal politics which merely transposes the past into the future, emergent European politics is a bewildering reality. It involves states, intergovernmental relations, supranational institutions and subnational, urban and regional bodies. Announcements of the state's death are certainly premature. Political sovereignty has not shifted conveniently to the supranational level with the emergence of a European superstate. Rather, transformed nation-states now operate in an increasingly marketised environment within a complex intergovernmental regime.

New Medievalism and the Rise of the City

In his polemics on globalisation, Kenichi Ohmae has announced the imminent demise of the state, insisting that 'the nation-state has become an unnatural even dysfunctional, unit for human activity and managing economic endeavour in a borderless world' (Ohmae 1993: 78).[3] The claim that the nation-state is unnatural is plainly incorrect since for many individuals it is the most immediate and obvious form of identity and allegiance. Similarly, Ohmae's belief in the dysfunctionalism of the nation-state is overstated. The nation-state's intervention into the operation of the market can be counterproductive in the post-Fordist era and it might therefore be possible to say that in this sphere the nation-state can act in dysfunctional ways, if its purpose is to maximise economic output. Yet many of the traditional and key areas of nation-state policy, namely the provision of healthcare and pensions, the protection of property and the maintenance of civil order, are not dysfunctional roles. On the contrary, without states to guarantee social and economic order, multinationals could not sustain profits. The problems which a corrupt or weak state in the Third World, for instance, present to investing multinationals demonstrates the continuing importance of the state even in a globalised world. Ohmae exaggerates the existence of a 'borderless' world in which only markets matter but he does illuminate the rise of a new subnational entity which is becoming increasingly important: the region or city. In opposition to the 'obsolete' nation-state, Ohmae promotes the 'region-state' as the optimum political economic unit in the post-Fordist world (ibid.: 78): 'The region-state make such effective points of entry into the global economy because the very characteristics that define them are shaped by the demands of the economy' (ibid.: 80). The region-state ideally consists of between five and twenty million people which is sufficiently small for its citizens to share certain economic and consumer interests but of adequate size to provide an attractive market and to justify infrastructural development such as an international airport and a good harbour with international freight-handling capacity. These are essential for competitiveness. Most interestingly, Ohmae highlights the fact that corporate managers themselves are increasingly looking upon the world as a network of region-states rather than in terms of national units. Thus, when Nestlé and Proctor and Gamble expanded into Japan, they did not treat Japan as a single market but focused specifically on the Kansai region of the country (ibid.: 81–2). Ohmae's insight into the way that senior corporate management prepare market strategy is highly significant for, while his claims that the nation-state is in decline are unreliable, his description of corporate decision making highlights the empirical processes by which the nation-state is being undermined and fragmented by regionally specific foreign direct investment.

Above all, Ohmae's recognition – albeit exaggerated – of the growing significance of the 'region-state' is profoundly important because it highlights a new development which is central to the New Europe: the rise of cities and regions and their growing transnational connection with each other. The increasing influence of multinational corporations on the internal economic affairs of nation-states and the growing importance of foreign direct investment has produced new levels of uneven development (Keating 1998: 162). Certainly in the Fordist era, there were poorer and richer regions in every nation-state. However, the nation was unified under a single regime of regulation imposed by the state irrespective of particular interests; the state attempted to sustain a national basic standard of living through programmes of aid and assistance (Rhodes 1995). In the light of new forms of fluid investment, this centralised regime has been fragmented. The state is no longer in a position to assist backward regions and the autonomy of various regions and cities has grown. Thus, while the nation-state remains critical, the city and region or the 'region-state', as Ohmae calls it, are becoming increasingly significant actors, attracting international capital to themselves through individual strategies. Cities and regions are becoming more important in Europe and especially in those dynamic areas which have been constrained by backward or exploiting nation-states such as north-western Italy (see Mingione 1993), Catalonia or Scotland. The moves towards regional autonomy are predicated on the belief that the system of regulation provided by the nation-state has hamstrung a region's participation in the global economy (Sheridan 1995; Sznajder 1995). Significantly, from the 1980s, cities in Europe have prioritised the attraction of international capital above the provision of social and welfare services which was the dominant concern in the Keynesian era. Related to this growing 'entrepreneurialism', the major cities of Europe have increasingly developed networks of cooperation and competition with other cities which has enabled them to exploit their potential (Jensen-Butler 1997: 3); a reorientation which has been described as 'New Urban Politics' (Peck and Tickell 1995; Boyle et al. 1996; Harding 1997; Peck 1995; Cox 1993; Cochrane et al. 1996; Shaw 1993; Corner and Harvey 1991). Major European cities are increasingly disembedded from the national context and reintegrated into a transnational matrix with other cities (Castells 1998: 380–81) so that 'the major cities throughout Europe constitute the nervous system of both the economic and political system of the continent' (ibid.: 23). With declining mediation from the nation-state, these new informational cities, as Castells calls them, are acting independently to attract global capital for their own economic and cultural benefit (Wilson and Smith 1993). It is important not to overexaggerate the new autonomy of cities and regions. Various commentators, for instance, have emphasised the continuing dependence of regions and cities on their nation-states, noting, for instance that in approaching the European Union they require the support of their nation-state (Keating and Jones 1985; Sharpe 1993; Keating 1998; Storper 1995).

Sassen's (1991) and Castell's (1996) now-classic works on the post-Fordist city highlight the new position of the city in the global order. Both Sassen and Castell analyse the way in which cities have played a key role in the development of a post-Fordist global economy by providing milieus of innovation in which new technologies, cultures and networks are able to develop. Although for the most part, innovative centres in the 'informational' era are located in the old metropolises of the industrial eras (and thus, for Sassen, New York, London and Tokyo are the key 'global cities'), new urban hierarchies are emerging in which formerly peripheral cities have become very significant actors in the new economy. Cities and regions are increasingly seen as the drivers of innovation. Moreover, the growing independence of cities from their national context has led to a more complex situation: in place of the old cores and peripheries, there is now a complex hierarchy of cities (Dunford and Kafkalas 1992: 25; Featherstone 1997: 12). In addition, given the shift in emphasis within New Urban Politics away from social welfare to entrepreneurialism, the cities themselves are increasingly internally divided into what Sassen calls the 'dual city' (Sassen 1991: 266) where the wealth and affluence in those sectors of the city which are integrated into the global economy are juxtaposed against the marginal elements of urban population excluded from the market and no longer protected by the social services (also Dunford and Kafkalas 1992: 258; Davis 1990: 232; Parkinson and Harding 1995). The rise of cities and regions in the deregulated post-Fordist era is likely to produce distinctive forms of identification, solidarities and political cultures in the future.

New European Identities

The growing autonomy of cities and the new transnational networks which are developing between them cast current debates about European identity and democracy in an interesting light. There has been a wide-ranging debate in Europe about the threat of a 'democratic deficit' which refers to the potentially autocratic dangers of the European Union when a new supranational level of government is matched neither by the affective ties nor formal democratic procedures which characterised the era of the nation-state. Various theorists (for example, Chryssochoou 1996; see Schmidt 1995) and institutional bodies such as the German Federal Constitutional Court have insisted that the only way to bridge this deficit is to create a European demos so that individuals across the European Union feel the same bond with the institutions of the Union and its mythical traditions as they do to their own nation-states (Weiler 1997). Thus, particular European nationalisms need to be replaced by a pan-European nationalism which operates in exactly the same way as former nationalisms, taking the same exclusive form, but merely incorporating wider European traditions. Affectively committed to the Union, individuals will then feel a close attachment to the institutional core of the European Union, demoting their relation to their nation-state below that to the European Commission and the Parliament. By contrast, the spectre of a pan-European nationalism has worried many recent commentators (for example, Touraine 1994; Balibar 1991; Habermas 1993; Derrida 1992; Delanty 1995, 1996; Pietersee 1991; Morley and Robins 1990; Bance 1992; Weiler 1997). For these commentators, European supranationalism does not promise democracy but rather, for those who cannot be incorporated into white European culture, it threatens exclusion and, at its most extreme, the gas chambers. This is exemplified in some of Gerard Delanty's recent writings: 'There is a direct continuity in the idea of Europe from the crusading genocides of medieval Christendom to the systematic extermination of other civilizations of Europe to the gas chambers of the Nazis and the pogroms of ethnic cleansing of the new nationalisms in the post-Cold War period' (Delanty 1995: 157). Although the somewhat teleological implications of this statement may require qualification, it neatly summarises the concerns of a large number of critical and leftist intellectuals in Europe. Against the idea of a homogenous European demos, these intellectuals argue for a post-national citizenship which does not seek to exclude on cultural or racial grounds but which defines citizenship on purely political grounds. Thus, a European post-national citizenship does not look for cultural homogeneity but rather seeks to maximise democracy by allowing everyone regardless of ethnic status, including newly arrived migrants, to have a formal say in the political process (for example, Balibar 1991: 19; Habermas 1993: 66, Delanty 1996: 104).

Despite the theoretical importance and ethical rectitude of these commentaries, there is a serious problem with them in the light of more empirical accounts of the nation-state and cities; they are simply barking up the wrong tree. They assume that the Europe of the future is seriously threatened by a pan-European nationalism and by the imposition of cultural homogeneity. Yet, while concerns over immigration and political or economic marginalisation are entirely legitimate, it is unlikely that any such cultural homogenisation will take place. In the end, these critics make the same error as those theorists who argue for a European demos as a solution to the democratic deficit; they anachronistically impose rapidly superseded understandings from the past onto the future (Schlesinger 1994; Weiler et al. 1995; Smith 1992). Particular groups such as marginalised white men may well appeal to specious and racist European traditions but these grand traditions are usually drawn upon to refer to quite specific local struggles brought about by globalisation. Although neofascist politics is a credible force in parts of the new Europe, the threat of an exclusivist Euronationalism engulfing the entire Union seems unlikely. In relation to a pan-European supranationalism, there is little evidence for any such identity among the peoples of Europe, outside the Commission itself. Although the legislative influence of certain supranational bodies such as the Commission or the European Court of Justice cannot be denied, pan-Europeanism is not so much a cultural reality as a legitimating claim by bureaucrats who putatively operate (and are paid) in the name of Europe (Shore and Black 1994: 288–9).

It is highly unlikely that we are entering a period of exclusive supranationalism as the democratic deficit theorists and the cultural critics suggest but instead a historical moment which is usefully captured by the term 'new medievalism' (Woever 1995; Mann 1993: 129; Strange 1995: 56). Europe is likely to be contoured by a set of overlapping sovereignties and allegiances between transformed nation-states, emergent supranational institutions (the Commission and multinational corporations, for instance), and cities or regions, just as medieval Europe was constituted by the simultaneous and often contradictory claims of monarchy, papacy and local nobility. In line with these overlapping political and economic networks, social solidarities and cultural identifications in the new Europe are likely to be similarly complex. In place of identification with the nation-state which was the primary, though not exclusive, basis of political affiliation for most of the twentieth century, it is more probable that there will be shifting, overlapping social relations and cultural identities between region, nation and supranation where individuals are simultaneously embedded in different and competing networks of relations.

It is therefore important to recognise three key planes of identification and activity which are becoming increasingly significant in the new Europe: region, nation and supranation, although at the level of identification, the supranational is all but irrelevant (see for example, Smith 1992; Weiler et al. 1995; Weiler 1997; Tassin 1992; Schlesinger 1994; Touraine 1994). Thus, although undergoing quite radical transformation especially in regard to their public spending, nation-states are still extremely powerful forces economically, politically and militarily and their legitimacy has, at most, been renegotiated rather than undermined. By contrast, the dialectical result of globalization is the increasing importance of local, urban and regional affiliations and structures as the multinational forces of globalisation undermine and bypass the territorial sovereignty of the nation-state. Nationalism is far from dead but in the face of increasingly independent cities (and regions) it is being renegotiated in important ways. The key transformation in identification in the new Europe is not at a higher supranational level but rather at a subnational level where identification with cities and regions is becoming ever more significant as these entities have a greater say in their destiny.

Football in the New Europe

In Chapter 1, it was argued that rituals serve the crucial social purpose of providing an arena in which social relations are realised and social groups come into being. Through the ritual, key social relations are reaffirmed and renewed. If the ritual is the key site by which social relations are re-created, and football is a primary public ritual in the new Europe, then the game must be situated in the social context outlined in this chapter. The mutation of football between the two Finals of 1968 and 1999 is best understood when situated within this historical context of European integration from its initial successes, through its stagnation in the 1970s until its neoliberal reinvigoration in the 1990s. The transformation of the European ritual must be connected with the increasing interpenetration of national markets by multinational corporations, the 'decline' of nation-states, the rise of new networks of cities (and regions) and the increasing prominence of new urban or regional affiliations, just as Foucault connected the emergence of new penal regimes of the nineteenth century with the rise of the modern state. The social relations which have been actualised through European football between the fans, the players, the owners of the clubs and the television stations since its inception in 1955 to the present are inseparably bound up with these wider historic transformations and can only be understood in relation to them. In particular, the emergence of these new political and economic networks is transforming the kind of social solidarity which is possible at the local level and, while nationalism remains an important source of identification, new local regional or urban solidarities are becoming ever more salient. The rise of these new local solidarities, which finds expression in the new opposition between a club like Manchester United and England, reflects the shift from an international order that characterised the early years of European integration in which the sovereignty of the nation-state was all but untouched, to a transnational future in which that sovereignty is likely to be seriously contested and compromised.

It is the purpose of this book to analyse the emergence of new economic networks between football clubs and new solidarities among the fans. In this way, the analysis of the transformation of European football is intended to cast light on the nature of contemporary Europe more widely. European football does not reveal the emergence of any saccharine supranational accord which the Commission and certain commentators have promoted. We are not all becoming good Europeans now; a European demos is no nearer. On the contrary, European integration today is characterised by increasingly ferocious transnational competition between cities and regions in which there are winners and losers. The growing dominance of the market as the key reference point for economic, political and social organisation in Europe has led certain commentators to disparage the notion of the European Union which is seen as a purely economic community. Political sovereignty and identity have been surrendered to the market. The historian, John Pocock is a prominent critical commentator:

> The institutions jointly operated and or obeyed by member states would then not be political institutions bringing about a redistribution of sovereignty but administrative or entrepreneurial institutions designed to ensure that no sovereign authority can interfere with the omnipotence of the market exercising 'sovereignty' in the metaphorical because non-political sense. There would be an empire of the market. [Pocock 1991: 9]

Although the market is the driving force behind European integration in the 1990s, Pocock's objections are overstated. The free market has stimulated transnational competition between cities in Europe and, consequently, it has given rise to new local solidarities and identities. New groups as well as new forms of politics are emerging within the new transnational flows of capital. Against the notion of a placeless world to which various commentators have subscribed (for example, Henderson and Castells 1997), these new transnational flows have, in fact, encouraged an ever greater sense of place among those affected by them. Increasingly, nascent social groups are mobilising an idea of the city or region which operates alongside or, sometimes, against more traditional ideas of nationhood. We are entering a new period of transformation which is as dramatic as the 'birth-time' of which Hegel wrote at the beginning of the nineteenth century (1977: 6) but, although this millennial 'birth-time' will certainly involve the destruction of many old ways of life, new forms of existence, solidarity and resistance will emerge from the ashes of the old. Where critics like Pocock can only see decline and decay, we must train ourselves to stare unblinkingly into the future to see also resurrection and transformation. For Hegel, the owl of Minerva flew only at dusk and he insisted that the 'birth-time' of the late eighteenth century could be comprehended only in retrospect (1967: 13). Perhaps that is also true of contemporary Europe and we will only know it when looking back on it in the middle of the twenty-first century. Yet, it might just be possible that the ritual of football can provide us with a glimpse of the new dawn before day has even broken, like a bird flying so high that it sees first light before those on the ground. In this still pale light, the outlines of the new landscape may be seen.

Notes

1 This claim is open to argument. Anderson believes that Monnet was working for a supranational Europe (1997: 70).
2 The development of private security companies in Britain suggests a demise of state authority in the protection of property (see Van Creveld 1999: 405).
3 It seems that Ohmae's position as a chairman of a major corporation (McKinsey and Company) has led him to exaggerate contemporary developments so that his commentary envisages the kind of world in which his company would most like to exist.

PART II
FOOTBALL IN THE OLD EUROPE

Chapter 3

The Early Years of the European Cup: 1955–70

The Origins of the European Cup

In December 1954, the prestigious French sports magazine, *L'Equipe*, published an article by the journalist Gabriel Hanot proposing the development of a European club competition between the champions of each domestic league in Europe. He suggested that each country should nominate a side to play in a mid-week European league (Rippon 1980: 2; Motson and Rowlinson 1980: 14; Macwilliam 2000: 6; Radnedge 1997c: 74). The idea of the competition appealed to most of the clubs in Europe, although many favoured a cup competition which would require less fixtures than a league (Motson and Rowlinson 1980: 15). Real Madrid was particularly enthusiastic about the competition and the Spanish Liga replied to *L'Equipe* unequivocally on behalf of the club: 'This project appeals to me enormously and to my friend, Santiago Bernabeu. We are ready to receive, in this stadium which has room for over 100,000 spectators, all the top teams in Europe and those from behind the Iron Curtain' (Juan Touzon, cited in ibid.: 15).

The enthusiasm of Real Madrid was understandable. The club had been closely linked to the Spanish monarchy before the civil war (it was awarded the 'Royal' title by King Alfonso XIII) and after 1936 was associated with General Franco, as a symbol for Spanish nationalism (Burns 1999: 156–7). Significantly, Santiago Bernabeu, who became club chairman, had well-known Fascist sympathies and had fought with Franco's troops on the Catalan front during the Spanish Civil War.[1] The prospect of Franco's club beating the most famous teams in Europe was attractive to a regime shunned by the European Community on political grounds. Moreover, there were obvious economic incentives behind Real's enthusiams. Bernabeu had redeveloped Real's Charmartin ground into a huge new stadium which would establish Real Madrid as a major European force, but the financial risks of this reconstruction, which was funded through membership payments (Glanville 1991: 13), required the development of European competition. The stadium had to attract capacity crowds if the club was to remain solvent. It would not be the last time when an overly ambitious Real Madrid would look to new

European competitions as a way of rescuing them from local economic difficulties.

Given the enthusiastic response to their proposal, in January 1955, *L'Equipe* sent out an invitation to 18 clubs which Gabriel Hanot, Jacques Ferran, the editor-in-chief of the paper, and Jacques Goddet, had selected. Not all the invited clubs were national champions. Some were selected for their potential attractiveness to fans, though *L'Equipe* suggested that from the second year of the competition, places should be reserved for domestic champions and this became established as the norm (Moston and Rowlinson 1980: 15; Rippon 1980: 3).[2] The 18 clubs were invited to a meeting in the Ambassador Hotel in Paris on 2 April 1955 when the exact format of the new competition was decided. The meeting ratified the development of the European Cup and established a steering executive committee. However, the viability of the competition relied on the support of the football authorities, as Jacques Ferran recognised:

> The Paris meeting was the turning point in getting the European Cup off the ground. It was, in effect, a bluff by a committee who had neither the means nor the experience to apply themselves to such a difficult task as running this type of competition. It would have been inconceivable for directors and secretaries of clubs to organise a cup of this kind, because there would be new teams involved each year. [Ferran cited in Moston and Rowlinson 1980: 18]

Although *L'Equipe* had successfully initiated the competition and the clubs were enthusiastic about such an event, neither could administer the competition themselves. Like all sporting competitions, a higher authority was required which mediated between the interests of competing clubs. Fortuitously, UEFA, the Union of European Football Associations, had been established the year before but, as yet, had no clear role. The development of European competition offered this new institution the ideal opportunity to establish itself and UEFA agreed to administer the new competition, under whose auspices the European Cup quickly established itself as the premier club competition in European and, indeed, world football.

The International Organisation of European Football

The first 15 years of the European Cup between 1955 and 1970 were dominated by four teams: Real Madrid, Benfica, Internazionale and AC Milan. Between them, these clubs won the competition twelve times and featured in a further seven finals. Thus, until 1970, one of these four teams featured in every single final. The dominance of the biggest European clubs seemed to extend beyond the pitch. For instance, in 1956, Manchester United ignored the Football

League's ruling that it should not play in the European Cup and entered the competition anyway. The dominance of the biggest clubs on the pitch and their ability to get their own way off it in the 1950s and 1960s seems to suggest that the clubs were dominant even in the earliest years of European competition. In fact, while the dominance of the biggest clubs on the pitch cannot be denied during this period, the clubs were not as politically dominant as Manchester United's defiance implies. The creation of the European Cup demonstrates this point.

The *Federation International des Associations de Football*, FIFA, were aware of *L'Equipe*'s plan for a European Cup and sanctioned its development on three conditions: participating clubs had to receive permission from their national associations, the tournament had to be organised by UEFA, and the title 'European Cup' had to be reserved for a proposed competition between national sides (Motson and Rowlinson 1980: 18).[3] The sovereignty of the national federations was guaranteed and UEFA was appointed as international mediator between these national institutions. UEFA had no direct communication with the clubs but spoke only with the federations. The sovereignty of the national federations was demonstrated most explicitly in 1958 when UEFA invited Manchester United to participate in the European Cup as compensation for the Munich disaster even though the club were not English Champions. The Football League overruled UEFA, insisting that UEFA's own rules stipulated that only national champions or European Cup-holders could enter the competition (Macdonald 1968: 69; Glanville 1991: 51). As Glanville noted: 'Quite apart from the fact that UEFA were presumably entitled to waive their own rules, they had, in fact allowed teams which came into neither category to compete' (Glanville 1991: 51; also Cameron 1995: 210). Glanville's statement highlights an important historical point. Although formally in charge of European competitions, UEFA was in the final instance dependent upon the national federations in the administration of the competitions and the application of competition rules. Since national federations alone had the authority to impose UEFA's rules on the clubs, the final tribunal in European football in its earliest years was not UEFA, the international institution, but rather the national federations. UEFA was ultimately a forum for these national organisations (much as the European Communities were actually intergovernmental forums for the national governments). European football was organised on an international basis, in which the relations between sovereign national federations mediated by UEFA were the most important factor. In England, the centrality of the sovereignty of the national federation in this era was exemplified most extremely by Alan Hardaker, secretary of the Foreign League between 1956 and 1979, when he commented to Brian Glanville. 'Hardaker ... once, in an unguarded aside, confided to me with a grin that he didn't much enjoy dealing with football on the Continent: "Too many wogs and dagoes!"' (Glanville 1991: 6). Hardaker's xenophobia was extreme and idiosyncratic but it suggests that the sovereignty of the national federations was supported by strong cultural ideas about national distinctiveness, if not superiority.

The transfer system at the time was also organised on an international basis, prioritising the autonomy of nations. In the 1950s, Spain and Italy allowed foreign players to play for club sides. Real Madrid had an unusually large number of foreign players, including Puskas (Hungarian), Di Stefano and Dominguez (Argentinian), Santamaria (Uruguayan), Canario and Didi (Brazilian) and Kopa (French) (Macdonald 1968: 69). However, in the early 1960s, foreign players were restricted from playing in the formerly open Italian and Spanish leagues (Cresswell and Evans 1999: 342; Green 1978: 95, Rippon 1980: 25) and, in 1966, Bernabeu fulfilled his ambition when Real won the European Cup with a Spanish side. In the rest of Europe, there were long-standing limitations or outright bans on foreign players. These rules were significant because they reflected a concern about the effects which foreign players had on the development of indigenous players. The influx of foreigners was regarded as detrimental to the production of native talent and therefore the prospects of the national team in international tournaments.[3] The national federations, which imposed these rules, also conveniently earned a substantial portion of their revenue from international matches. The foreigner restrictions institutionalised the autonomy of the national league and the priority of the national team. From the 1960s, European Champions typically fielded four or five players capped for the national team in which the club was situated and six other good native players (Glanville 1977c). Both Manchester United's and Benfica's 1968 teams accorded exactly with this model. As noted in Chapter 1, the national basis of the team facilitated an international interpretation of European competition, where matches were seen as games between national representatives.

Significantly, the international structure of the European Cup reflected the wider reality of European integration at the time. As Milward has argued, integration (at least up until the late 1980s) did not primarily involve the loss of national sovereignty. European integration was an intergovernmental process from which states could withdraw at any time. Similarly, the European Cup was organised as a competition between different national leagues; it was an international competition between the representatives of national federations. Moreover, as an expansion of cross-border trade in football matches, the European Cup reflected the European Economic Community. The European Cup increased the international trade in football matches but eschewed radical liberalisation of the market for labour which would have undermined the international regime of organisation. The emergence of the European Cup in the mid-1950s and its format were consistent with wider social realities. UEFA and the competition itself were created at the same time as the European Communities in the mid-1950s and took a similar international form.[4]

The Economics of the European Cup: The Unity of Sporting and Financial Principles

The European Cup was initially organised on an international basis. Given the current romanticisation of the early years of the European Cup, where it is commonly seen as a competition determined solely by sporting considerations, it is vital to recognise the economic principles which underpinned European club competition from the 1950s onwards. European football was a professional sport, involving significant and sometimes large wage bills. Consequently, European football was never determined by sporting considerations alone where only exciting play and the honour of winning were relevant. This is not to say that sporting integrity was not a significant factor in the European Cup from the 1950s, however. For instance, the purely sporting reason of gaining honour on the playing field did encourage clubs to take part in this competition. Matt Busby, the successful manager of Manchester United between 1947 and 1969 expressed these sporting reasons articulately: 'I had the feeling at this time that football was no longer an English game or a British game but a world game. I said this to the Board [of Manchester United] and they were happy about it' (Motson and Rowlinson 1980: 3; Rippon 1980: 40). Busby explicitly prioritised the sporting benefits of the development of European competition at other times: 'The experience gained in competition against the finest clubs in Europe would be invaluable to my young players. After England's two failures in the World Cup, prestige alone demands that the Continental challenge should be met, not avoided' (Macdonald 1968: 35). For Busby, honour and recognition gained from success on the pitch were among the key motivations for European football. David Meek, the former *Manchester Evening News* correspondent, who knew Matt Busby personally, confirmed these sporting motivations for entering this competition:

> Why bother? Why go into Europe? Why put ourselves to all that trouble and expense. But that philosophy came across to me from Matt Busby. He felt that once you'd proved yourself the best in England, football is a global game and the next logical step was to prove yourself, to test yourself against the best of Europe. That is what took him into Europe and he fired me personally with that sort of spirit. There was one particular game when United played, as European Champions, in Argentina against Estudiantes. They had a torrid time. It represented the not so nice face of football and I remember saying to Matt Busby after the game. 'Well, I don't expect you'd accept an invitation to go through all that again?' And he said, 'Oh yes I would.' And this was right in the heat of it, when he was watching his players being kicked and he was counting the cost. But even then he was far-sighted enough to say, 'Oh yes, we would because unless we play these people, the game globally won't progress. They'll live in their world – they think that is how football is played. We have to try and influence them and steer the game to a better standard.' And he said, 'Maybe we have to change our approach a little as well. You won't make progress by

running away. It has to be faced and met and so I would accept an invitation to play again.' It took me by surprise but it also made me realise that here was someone who had his face up from the trough. It wasn't just the pursuit of more money but the pursuit of his vision of football being played on a global level – and played the right way on a global level. [David Meek, personal interview; 19 April 2000; see also Green 1978: 147]

For Busby, sporting success was crucial but his sporting principles also emphasised the development of the game itself, whereby technical standards would be improved. It is highly likely that *L'Equipe*'s main motivation for devising this new competition was also sporting. For instance, Gabriel Hanot's idea for such a competition was a response to the English press's crowning of Wolverhampton Wanderers as 'Champions of the World' after they had defeated the famous Hungarian club, Honved, in December 1954 (Rippon 1980: 2; Macwilliam 2000: 6; Radnedge 1997c: 74; Motson and Rowlinson 1980: 14). Hanot thought such a claim premature: 'We must wait for Wolves to visit Moscow or Budapest before we proclaim their invincibility. There are other clubs of international prowess notably Milan and Real Madrid' (Rippon 1980: 2). For Hanot, the European Cup was a way of determining the sporting merit of the best European teams. Santiago Bernabeu was similarly motivated since he wanted to establish Real Madrid as a club of international stature.

Although sporting considerations were central to the European Cup, the financial aspect of this competition should not be denied. This competition offered the clubs involved in it a supplementary source of revenue. Given the financial risks which Bernabeu had taken to create Real Madrid's new stadium, it is difficult to believe that the financial advantages of competing in the European Cup were lost on him. Real's acquisition of Alfredo Di Stefano, for instance, undermines the idealised interpretation of these early years of the European Cup. In the 1950s, Di Stefano was regarded as the best player in the world, remaining to this day one of the greatest footballers who has ever existed. He was instrumental in bringing five European Cups to Real Madrid, establishing them as one of the most important clubs in world football. However, although his play was certainly sublime, his recruitment to Real Madrid contrasted with the idealised memories which have condensed around this player. Pepe Samitier, FC Barcelona's informal chief scout, had spotted Di Stefano in Argentina in 1952 when he played for Millonorios against Real Madrid but Bernabeu, who had also been present at the game, had been similarly impressed (Burns 1999: 155). Barcelona rushed to sign the player and, with Di Stefano arriving in Barcelona with his family on 17 May 1953 it seemed that they had successfully captured the player (Burns 1999: 157). At this point, however, Real Madrid became involved, pressurising the Spanish Football Federation to oppose the transfer. Although it is impossible to corroborate, there have been many accusations that Franco's government itself opposed the transfer, concerned about the political implications of the Catalonian club signing the greatest player in the world (ibid.: 158–9). In the end, the Spanish Football Federation ruled that Di Stefano should be shared by Barcelona and Real Madrid, with the player going to Real in the first instance for the 1953–54 season. In the event, Barcelona relinquished their right to him partly in outrage at this compromise (ibid.: 159), but it also seems likely that with Kubala in such form, Di Stefano was seen as potentially superfluous to requirements, especially given the expense of the transfer (King, J. 2000a: 66–7). Clearly, Barcelona were responsible for giving Real Madrid a player who would be instrumental in their European Cup victories but Real Madrid's political tactics must be recognised. Moreover, the federation's decision that Di Stefano should play for Real Madrid in the first instance seems to indicate clear bias toward the Castilian club on behalf of the national authority. Real's acquisition of Di Stefano demonstrates that Bernabeu and European clubs more widely recognised the importance of signing professional talent and would use all their financial and political resources to do so. Star players would bring success, large crowds and therefore revenue into the club. Financial imperatives were not absent from European Cup in its early years and, as the Di Stefano case highlights, certain European clubs were ruthless when it came to signing top players.

The financial benefits of European competition must also have been clear to the clubs since they kept their home gate revenue from these games, giving only 4 per cent to UEFA (Rippon 1980: 7). In the first season of the competition, Hibernian of Scotland made £25,000 by reaching the semi-final. Although Matt Busby has always been employed as a symbol of an unsullied past in which financial affairs were irrelevant, he certainly recognised the financial benefits which accrued from competing in the European Cup:[5] 'Certainly, I was eager to be part of this new European challenge and the reasons were many. *There was money to be made for the club*, there was a new kind of adrenalin inducing excitement for the players and there was an opportunity for spectators to enjoy the skills of Continental players' (Meek 1988: 11, emphasis added).

Busby's awareness of the financial realities of profession in the 1950s and '60s is demonstrated elsewhere. For instance, when his team lay at the bottom of the table in the autumn of 1952, having won the title that spring, Busby commented, 'There is no deep cause for worry although we have slumped at the moment. We have £200,000 worth of skill in our youth and reserve sides' (Green 1978: 58). He emphasised the point: 'Don't let anyone run away with the idea that our method of team building is cheap or easy' (Macdonald 1968: 90).[6] In addition, his purchase of Albert Quixall from Sheffield Wednesday in June 1958 for £45,000 was considered a 'staggering sum' at the time (Green 1978: 119). Indeed, Busby employed methods of recruitment which while doubtless commonplace were not strictly ethical. As Glanville noted: 'United made it their business to track down and acquire the best young talent. Other clubs were not always happy about their methods' (Glanville 1991: 42). It was significant, for instance, that Bobby Charlton, who was raised in Newcastle, might reasonably have been expected to sign for Newcastle United while Duncan Edwards, raised in Dudley, Birmingham, might similarly have been expected to play for West Bromwich Albion or Wolverhampton Wanderers. Busby was able to attract both to Manchester United. Busby's success was not due to his ignorance of financial matters but to his acumen at purchasing the correct players and then bringing out their full potential. Similarly, Jock Stein, the first British manager to win the European Cup with Celtic in 1967, confirmed this pragmatic attitude. When Celtic were invited to be the opposition for Di Stefano's testimonial, Stein dismissed the suggestion of the Celtic chairman, Bob Kelly, that playing in such a game was an honour and financial considerations were irrelevant: 'Real's first offer of a guarantee was a joke. Bob Kelly, the chairman, was saying never mind the fee, it's an honour to be asked to play. But I said we had arrived in Europe now, and this was a matter of business' (Stein, cited in Motson and Rowlinson 1980: 104). Similarly, Real Madrid was well aware of the financial potential of European competition. In the 1956–57 season, Real and Rapid Vienna drew over the two legs. The play-off should have been played on a neutral ground but Real offered to pay Rapid £25,000, a large sum of money at the time, if the game took place at Charmartin, Real's home ground. With home advantage, Real won the play-off 2–0, more than justifying their £25,000 investment (Glanville 1991: 20).

Football in this era was not a sporting idyll in which financial considerations were irrelevant. Even Geoffrey Green who was prone to extravagance stated the point bluntly:

> A football club by definition is a business, a company which has to try to balance profit and loss. And football after the war was to become a vast entertainment industry. Having been in the red so long it was clearly uplifting to the directors to find their stock on the rise. Attractive football and success on the field was reflected in the balance sheets of 1946, 1947 and 1948 when the profits of the club rose dramatically from £10,215 15s. 1d. to £13,393 2s. 1d. and then £22,329 13s. 0d. as the weight of debt was off-loaded. [Green 1978: 43]

Interestingly, although a degree of nationalistic xenophobia cannot be discounted, one of the primary reasons why the English Football League denied Chelsea entry to the European Cup in 1955 was similarly financial. Arthur Drewry, the president of the League, emphasised the financial dangers of entering European competition by noting the effect which mid-week friendly fixtures had had on Saturday attendances in the Football League:

These figures are inclined to make one think that the league's Saturday fixtures are suffering as a result of all the extra matches which are being played, outside the league programme. The time has come to give serious consideration to a curtailment of the number of friendly and other matches which clubs are arranging. [Motson and Rowlinson 1980: 18]

Although they have always been vilified for their insularity, the economic reasoning behind the League's stance was not absurd, for the clubs involved benefited financially from their participation in Europe. Although European football did not have a decisive impact, the benefits of European competition for the bigger clubs was a contributory factor in undermining the solidarity of the national leagues; successful clubs received additional income which they did not have to redistribute to the lesser clubs in their own league. The Football League's opposition to the European Cup was an attempt to defend a particular national economic regime, over which the federation presided. This regime was different to the one which emerged in the 1990s but it is wrong to think that professional European football at this time was only or even primarily informed by ideas of sporting prestige.

The format of European competition similarly reflected the economic reality of this regime. As we have noted, Hanot originally intended to create a genuinely European league which would take place alongside the national leagues throughout the season. The constraints of the fixture list, infrastructure and spectator demand reduced that plan to a knock-out cup competition but not of the traditional knock-out form. Each round of the competiton was competed over two legs, home and away. Until 1967, if there was no outright winner from the two legs, a third deciding leg was played at a neutral location and if this game was drawn as well, a large blue and red disc tossed by the referee and called by the captains decided the tie (Rippon 1980: 4). After 1967, aggregate goals decided the tie.[7] Consequently, the European Cup was never structured on the same lines as the FA Cup or as other cup competitions in Germany or Italy, where there was only one game in each round and where, therefore, the defeat of big clubs by smaller ones (so-called 'giant-killing') was likely (ibid.: 8). The two-legged rounds weighted 'the scales in favour of Goliath against David, when the whole magic allure of the FA Cup had been its opportunity for giant killing' (Glanville 1991: 7). The organisation of the cup into two-legged competitions was partially justified on the grounds of fairness. If clubs were to compete in Europe and go to the expense of travelling to away games, then they should compete on parity so that both teams suffered the disadvantage of playing away from home. Doubtless, the sporting rationale for two-legged rounds was significant, but one of the primary reasons for competing rounds over two legs was financial. The two legs gave each club the chance to collect the revenue from an enlarged home gate, attracted by the presence of exotic and often very entertaining European teams.

Coverage of the new competition in the British press demonstrates this consonance between financial and sporting considerations precisely. The press saw football as a business and therefore regarded the financial opportunities which the European Cup offered as entirely consistent with sporting integrity. This consonance between the financial and sporting aspects of the game is demonstrated most vividly in the reporting of the Munich aircrash of 1958. The *Manchester Evening News*' coverage of that disaster is instructive. Beneath the headline on the front page, the report stated: 'One of the greatest disasters to befall British football struck Manchester United this afternoon when a plane carrying the £350,000 wonder team crashed at Munich' (1958: 1). The piece continued in similar vein (although it contradicted its own valuation of the team): 'It was a team which carried a transfer market value of more than £250,000 according to present-day value.' To the contemporary ear, so used to the intense conflict between market imperatives and sporting values, this emphasis on the monetary value of the team seems improper, demeaning the deaths at Munich. However, given the *Manchester Evening News*' close relationship to the club and their Mancunian readership, it is likely that they had a very good understanding that these sentences would be interpreted not as a denigration of the team who were reduced to the status of mercenaries with a debased market value (which would become a common motif in the 1990s) but rather as a vindication of their sporting superiority. It was a matter of celebration that these young men could be worth so much on the transfer market, a testament to their skill. To cite their financial worth was, therefore, a suitable mark of the magnitude of their loss. Significantly, there were no letters complaining about their coverage of the disaster.

Similarly, journalists often mentioned the size of crowds and gate receipts in their reports with candid approval. For instance, West Ham's victory against 1860 Munich in the European Cup-Winner's Cup was played 'before a wildly excited crowd of 100,000 who paid £76,000 for their pleasure' and, according to the reporter, 'never was money better spent' (*The Times* 1965b). In the same month, the financial rewards of Liverpool's game against Milan were similarly approved: 'The big bowl of the San Siro stadium will be filled to its capacity of 90,000. The takings will reach nearly £100,000' (*The Times* 1965a). As they were in the match between Everton and Internazionale in 1963: 'At the end of the first leg a crowd of some 63,000 had paid a record figure of £31,450 for a club match in England' (*The Times* 1963c). Commentators in the 1990s who have argued, as we shall see, that the transformation of the European Cup in the last decade has been a betrayal of the competition's history, misrepresent the reality of the Cup in its early years. The European Cup was always regarded as a very effective method of raising money for the clubs who had to pay professional players their wages. Financial factors were always important to the European Cup. Crucially, however, and marking a profound difference from the 1990s, in the early years of the European Cup, sporting values which prioritised the honour of winning were regarded as entirely compatible with economic realities. In order to hire and retain the services of attractive players, clubs required financial resources. Since European competition provided these financial resources, it was regarded as legitimate.

In the early years of the European Cup, the competition may have been dominated by the biggest clubs on the pitch but they were not the dominant force. The competition was organised on an international basis in which European football was divided into discrete national economies. The national leagues were governed by sovereign national federations to whom even the biggest clubs were subordinate. The biggest clubs came into contact with each other only in European competition through the mediation of these national federations and their international representative, UEFA. Under this international regime, no contradiction was recognised between financial and sporting values. Moreover, organised on this international basis, European football paralleled the wider process of European integration which similarly preserved the sovereignty of nation-states. Football was certainly a business at this time, therefore, but it took this distinctive international form. This international order was extremely successful in promoting European football for just over 15 years and various commentators were enthusiastic about its financial and sporting benefits. However, from the early 1970s, echoing the wider difficulties faced by the European Communities, this international basis of organisation became increasingly problematic. Football experienced its own 'Eurosclerosis'.

Notes

1 When the Spanish Civil War broke out, Bernabeu was denounced as a fascist by the other members of the Real Madrid board and had to take refuge in the French Embassy (Burns 1999: 156).
2 The 18 teams were: Rot-Weiss Essen, Chelsea, Rapid Vienna, Anderlecht, BK Copenhagen, Hibernian, Real Madrid, Stade de Reims, Holland Sport, Voros Lobogo, AC Milan, Sporting Lisbon, FC Saarbrucken, Malmo, Servette Geneva, Partizan Belgrade, Moscow Dynamo and Sparta Prague.
3 In line with FIFA's proviso, UEFA named *L'Equipe*'s new competition, the 'European Champion Clubs' Cup', but in fact, it was from the first always simply known as the European Cup and when a national championship between European teams did develop in the late 1960s it was known as the European Championships.
4 European competitions had been proposed before the development of the European Cup. In 1927, Henri Delaunay, secretary of the French Football Association, put the idea of a European club competition to FIFA; in 1934, Hanot himself had proposed that two clubs from different leagues should play in other national leagues from their native ones in order to promote international relations. These schemes were never implemented but, in 1927, Hugo Meisl, an Austrian, created the Mitropa Cup which brought teams together regularly from central Europe (Czechoslovakia, Hungary,

Yugoslavia and Austria). Reasonable geographic proximity allowed for regular fixtures between teams from these countries. Despite the failure of Hanot and Delaunay's plans, the increasing number of friendly matches between European teams which took place from the 1920s were very important in creating the demand for European football. For instance, Dynamo Moscow were famously watched by 100,000 in a game against Chelsea at Stamford Bridge in November 1954 (Downing 2000).

5   See for instance Dunphy (1991) or Crick and Smith (1989) for historical accounts of Manchester United which interpret Busby as untainted by financial consideration and indeed the antithesis of the corrupting influence of money on the game.

6   The journalist Mihir Bose also highlights Busby's skill in exploiting the economic situation in which he found himself, describing him as a 'street smart operator'. Mihir Bose notes that 'backhanders' were paid to parents to encourage boys to sign for United (Bose 1999: 130). Busby's financial acumen and hard-nosed managerial capacities were also described by Meek who experienced them at first hand in his interview. Although less overtly confrontational than the present Manchester United manager Alex Ferguson, Meek insisted that Busby was certainly able to command fear as well as respect among players and journalists. Meek confirmed Roger Macdonald's description of Busby as 'an iron fist in the velvet glove' (personal interview, 19 April 2000; Macdonald 1968: 19).

7   Wismut KMS were the first to go through in this manner against Guardia Warsaw in 1957–58. If this aggregate away goal rule had been in force from the beginning of the competition, Real Madrid would have been eliminated in the 1956–57 season when they beat Rapid Vienna 4–2 in Madrid but lost 3–1 away.

Chapter 4
Eurosclerosis

Foul Play and Corruption

Real Madrid, with its all-white strip representing the purest principles of sporting integrity, has become an important symbol for the early years of the European Cup. While currently powerful, this image of Real Madrid is not an accurate reflection of that club's sportsmanship. At the time, various questions were asked about the manner of some of the team's play. In the semi-final in 1957 against Manchester United in the Bernabeu, for instance, Real Madrid were guilty of rough play. Although provoked, Di Stefano openly kicked Jackie Blanchflower in the course of the game but was not sent off (Ledbrooke 1957; *Manchester Evening News* 1957):

> he [Di Stefano] executed some exquisite dummies and tricks it is true ... but he lost his head and made, on Blanchflower of all people, the most squalid foul one remembers to have seen in either representative or cup-tie football. The pretence of a reproof conveyed to Di Stefano at the referee's insistence by his captain almost made one vomit at its cynicism. It seemed incredible that such an artist could trail his wings in the gutter in this way. [*The Guardian*, 11 April 1957, cited in Meek 1988: 28]

John Charles, who played for Juventus in the 1950s, confirmed that there was a physical side to Real's play: 'Yes, Real were a truly great team, make no mistake about that. But they could dish out the hard stuff too, especially Santamaria. People gloat about them and say they never kicked anybody. Well, they certainly kicked me' (Motson and Rowlinson 1980: 65). The physical side of Real Madrid has been conveniently forgotten as the team has become established in common European football folklore as the sanctified representatives of the European Cup.

By contrast, in the 1970s there was a decisive shift in the perception of the game. The European Cup was seen to have been corrupted by foul play. It was curious that these criticisms of the competition coincided with the ascendancy of the great Ajax team of the early 1970s. Ajax, inspired by Johan Cruyff, applied the concept of 'total football' to win three successive European Cups between 1971 and 1973.[1] Doubts about the worth of this competition may have been more legitimate in the early to mid-1960s as Italian defences dominated but these concerns surfaced only in the 1970s. As Hans Bangerter, UEFA secretary, put it: 'The ideals of fair play and sport ethics are more and more trampled down by what can only be called criminal elements' (Green 1978: 91). In September 1974, Bangerter warned the clubs: 'Any and all undisciplined action must be punished. In order to stop further escalation of such lamentable events, the disciplinary committee has no alternative but to apply in full the increased sanctions' (Green 1978: 91; Green 1974b). Geoffrey Green's book *Soccer in the Fifties*, which was published in 1974, was a prominent example of this pessimism among journalists.

> And, most importantly in my opinion, what has gone from the game – I suspect irretrievably – is fun ... I don't think it could have been better put than by a remark of Mr Joe Mercer, once an outstanding captain of England. A compassionate, fair-minded person, a born leader of men, he once said to me: 'Compared with our day, when I see the boys running out of the tunnel nowadays they all look as if they are on their way to Vietnam.' [Green 1974d: 7–8]

The journalist Norman Fox concurred. In his review of Green's book in *The Times* significantly titled 'When football was fun and a sweeper was someone who pushed a broom', he nostalgically contrasted the overly technical, defensive and serious nature of football in the 1970s with the 1950s (Fox 1974). Interestingly, Gabriel Hanot himself became disillusioned by the European Cup in the early 1960s but Hanot's comments in the 1960s were ignored. However, a decade later, as journalists themselves became pessimistic about the competition, they resurrected Hanot's criticism: 'Even Hanot himself on occasion regretted letting loose what he felt was rapidly growing into a Frankenstein monster. The desire to win and the rivalry engendered as the prizes and incentives increased, tended to spill over the bounds of fair play' (Green 1978: 90; Green 1974b). It was not simply the players motivated by financial incentives who fell some way below the sporting ideal. The clubs themselves were heavily implicated in this corruption. For instance, in October 1971 the Internazionale striker, Roberto Boninsegna, collapsed after being hit by a soft drink can in a game against Borussia Dortmund. Inter were losing 2–1 at the time but they went on to be routed 7–1 (Macwilliam 2000: 49; Motson and Rowlinson 1980: 144). Inter, whose team had ultimately thrown the game when Boninsegna went off, demanded that they be awarded the match. Eventually, having applied various forms of nefarious pressure on UEFA, the result was declared void and a replay was arranged on a neutral ground (Motson and Rowlinson 1980: 144). Inter eventually went through, winning in Milan and drawing the rescheduled game in Berlin.

While it was certainly true that the financial rewards on offer for players in the 1970s had increased, it was inaccurate to imply that footballers in the 1950s and 1960s played merely for 'fun'. Players were intensely competitive, foul play was common and professional players received lucrative bonuses in that period. Real Madrid players earned a £650 bonus for beating Eintracht Frankfurt in 1960 (Cameron 1995: 18) while the players of FK Sarajevo lost their £300 win bonus when they went out to Manchester United in the European Cup in November 1967 (Bellamy 1967). Moreover, although there are indications that foul play may have increased in the 1970s, this assumption needs to be treated with care. For instance, Bobby Charlton, who experienced European football from the 1950s, complained not that play had become too rough in the 1970s but that legitimately physical play had been driven out of the game by overprotective referees (Redhead 1986: 82). In the light of this, it may be more accurate to say that there was no dramatic transformation in the way the game was played but rather in the way in which the game was viewed by players, managers, journalists and spectators. From the 1970s, a growth in foul and unethical play is probable but by far the most decisive divide from previous decades was that European competition was viewed with increasing pessimism. This pessimism, and not any intrinsic corruption of the European Cup, was the genuinely new social phenomenon. There had been foul and violent play in the early era but it was not looked upon so seriously until the 1970s.

Significantly, the new pessimism of commentators focused on putatively national dispositions which impelled certain players to cheat. Perhaps the most notorious example of this debasement of European football was the European Cup match between Celtic and Atletico Madrid in 1974 in which there were nine bookings and three members of the Atletico team sent off:

> It was not football. It was Armageddon, a sick nightmare which will become an infamous scar on the game in these islands ... There was nothing in the black book that they did not turn to – ankle tapping, scything tackles, body checking and blatant obstruction. It was destruction pure and simple, obvious, brutal and subtle. The effigy of football was burned ... This was a bull ring. All we lacked was the sun and hot sand. The rest was there. The intimidation and the blade. [Green 1974a]

Significantly, Green was explicit about the reasons for this corruption of football: 'The craze for power and money shown by the Latins every now and then goes beyond the bounds of reason and decency' (ibid.) Although it is generally agreed that in this match the Spanish team were guilty of foul play, Green's discussion demonstrates a nationalistic interpretation of their foul play.[2] There is a strong implication that 'Latins' are more predisposed to this kind of play than Anglo-Saxon footballers. Clearly, this is an echo of the kind of essentialist nationalist interpretations which featured in his writings in the 1950s and 1960s but here the tone and purpose is different. Green does not merely distinguish the temperamental Continentals from the virtuous Englishmen, but implies that this temperament was a threat to the integrity of the competition. The tournament was being degraded as a result of the defects in Latin national character and, of course, Green employs the metaphor of the bull-ring to emphasis this brutality.

The validity of European football was further dented by the exposure of bribery scandals in European Cup matches in the 1970s by Brian Glanville; the so-called 'Years of the Golden Fix' (Glanville 1991: 82). These bribery scandals were first exposed in 1973. During the semi-final of the European Cup between Juventus and Derby County, Derby County players noted Helmut Haller, one of the Juventus substitutes, entering the referee's changing rooms before the game and again at half-time. This was an irregular practice which was rightly looked upon with suspicion (Glanville 1991: 82–112; Glanville 1999: 213, 219–28; Cameron 1995: 48). Fuelling suspicions of bribery and corruption, the referee booked two key Derby players, Macfarland and Gemmill, conveniently ensuring that they would miss the return leg at Derby since they had been booked earlier in the competition. As Brian Clough, then manager of Derby County, stated: 'In any other industry, there would have been a full scale inquiry into the behaviour of Juventus. But UEFA just looked the other way' (Motson and Rowlinson 1980: 151). The scandal was exposed after the return leg when the referee, Francisco Lobo, informed UEFA that he had been approached by one Dezco Solti, who offered Lobo rewards if he favoured Juventus. After an ineffectual inquiry, UEFA weakly banned Solti from European competition but believed Juventus's incredible defence that the club had no relation with Solti. The club unfeasibly claimed Solti was acting on his own volition. When given the opportunity to explain the actions of the club to Brian Glanville later, Giampiero Boniperti, the Juventus president, memorably denied responsibility with the exasperated words 'Brian, if there are these madmen going about!' and proceeded to inquire about the state of English football. As Glanville has recently forcefully stated.

> Look at the Lobo-Solti case, Keith [Botsford] and I had them bang to rights. Absolutely bang to rights. But what can we do? Nothing happened because, who was behind the whole thing? Juventus. And who was behind Juventus, Agnelli, one of the most powerful men in Europe. What chance have you got, even with *The Sunday Times*, which was a very powerful paper? [Brian Glanville, personal interview, 2 October 2000]

In 1977, Brian Glanville produced incontrovertible proof that Juventus were guilty of bribing the referee. Glanville published a letter from Deszo Solti to Juventus which categorically tied the club to their agent: 'Deszo Solti, proscribed corrupter of referees, did have official connections with Juventus which the club has always denied' (Glanville 1977a; see also Glanville 1999: 213, 219–28). Not only did this letter demonstrate that Juventus were connected to Solti but that they had also lied to UEFA about this connection.

In his article in 1977 which brought the Solti letter to light, Glanville cast much wider aspersions about the extent of corruption in the European game, based on the initial report in 1975: 'On March 16 1975, *The Sunday Times* published a chart to show how astonishingly often certain referees had been in charge of European club cup games played by the big three Italian clubs, Milan, Inter and Juventus; and how well those clubs had done when they refereed between 1962 and 1969' (Glanville 1977a).

Glanville listed a series of curious connections. For instance, when the Swiss referee, Dienst, was in charge of games involving these clubs, the Italians won six and drew three out of nine game. Ortiz de Mendibil of Spain, who gave two highly suspect goals against Liverpool in the 1965 European Cup semi-final against Inter, presided over five wins out of five for the Italian teams. Then there was the Yugoslavian referee, Tesamic, who in the summer of 1964 was found at an Italian holiday resort at Inter's expense having failed to send an Inter player off during the notorious semi-final against Borussia Dortmund. In the light of this manifest corruption, other results in European football began to look increasingly unsound, such as AC Milan defeat of Leeds in the Cup-Winner's Cup Final in 1973, Bayern Munich's defeat of Leeds in the European Cup Final of 1975 (when both a clear penalty and good goal against Bayern were not given[3]), and Real Madrid's 1976 match against Borussia-Moenchengladbach.

The timing of Glanville's report was significant for, while it was clear that most of the dubious practices had mainly taken place in the 1960s, especially by Inter, these revelations were made in the 1970s just at a time when there was widespread disillusionment with European football. These revelations of bribery affirmed the suspicions that the game had become too serious and that the pursuit of money was now debasing this once prestigious competition. Nothing demonstrated that debasement more categorically than the corruption of those very officials who were supposed to be the guardians and enforcers of sporting rectitude. The revelation that some of Inter's victories in the 1960s were almost certainly invalid did not, in fact, undermine the memory of the early period of the competition or necessitate a renegotiation of the meaning of that era. Those early years signified by the sporting probity and excellence of the all-white Real Madrid's were beyond de-canonisation, whatever evidence might be produced to sully them. Rather the web of corruption that Glanville uncovered in the middle of the 1970s played a crucial role in casting a pall of pessimism over the competition then.

Significantly, although Glanville himself was in no way xenophobic, living and working in Italy for a number of years and constantly emphasising the need to introduce Europe training techniques into Britain (for example, Glanville 1955), the corruption he uncovered was an Italian affair, with Inter at its heart (Glanville 1999: 225). Thus, Glanville coruscated Angelo Moratti, the chairman of the club during this period, whom, he claimed 'was behind the whole crooked business' (personal interview, 2 October 2000). He was equally scathing about Italo Allodi, Juventus' fixer: 'Allodi died recently and the encomia were just beyond belief. There was this man who had been completely exposed. He was the quintessence, the incarnation of corruption. And you should have seen the tributes ... This man was the controlling influence' (ibid.). Glanville's criticisms were certainly severe but they were neither nationalistic nor xenophobic. They were plainly motivated out of a genuine desire to protect the integrity of European competition. However, they were interpreted exactly as rantings of a xenophobe inspired by national self-interest. Glanville's report was interpreted not as the exposure of a few well-placed individuals but rather as impugning the national integrity of Italy. 'The Years of the Golden Fix' become an affront to national honour in Italy. Nationalist sensitivities were, in fact, evident from the beginning of this affair. It was notable that Brian Clough's memorable phrase to the waiting Italian journalists in 1973 – 'No cheating bastards will I talk to. I will not talk to any cheating bastards' – was translated by Glanville, who was attending the match, for those journalists. The phrase became the headline in Italian newspapers the next day: 'Bastardi Truffatori [cheating bastards]!' (Glanville 1991: 82). Given his other comments about foreigners, Clough may very well have thought that Italians as a nation were 'cheating bastards' but the Italian headline demonstrated that to Italians this is what he meant. During the 1970s, the European Cup was undergoing its own process of Eurosclerosis. The international basis of organisation had been very successful up to 1970 but from then on national conflicts threatened the competition. The competition was not promoting international amity and mutual respect but intensifying national rivalries and hostility which were diminishing the status of the competition.

Hooliganism

Tensions within European football in the 1970s were not confined to the pitch: certain aspects of fan culture became problematic at the same time. Hooliganism was recognised as a serious social problem in Britain from the early 1960s. The problem had, in fact, begun to appear in the late 1950s but regular terrace violence and public discussion about it became widespread only in the early 1960s, when the vandalism of trains carrying supporters to away games became a focus of concern. Throughout the 1960s, the levels and frequency of violence increased at English and Scottish league grounds where a ritualistic form of combat, called 'the taking of the ends', developed; opposition fans would forcibly infiltrate the terrace behind the goal occupied by home supporters. During the 1960s, hooliganism began to be a serious problem at football grounds in Britain and there developed something of a 'moral panic' about it which misrepresented the phenomenon (in ways which are likely to have exacerbated fan violence) (King 1997b) and promoted inappropriate remedial measures for it (see Ingham 1978). However, the moral panic rightly recognised the very serious implications of fan violence for the economic and social viability of football which was wholly borne out by events over the next twenty years.[4] While football hooliganism was a serious problem in Britain in the 1960s, it was not generally a feature of European Cup games at the time. There had been serious crowd disturbance at the semi-final between Rapid Vienna and Benfica in 1961. When the referee failed to give Rapid a penalty, Rapid fans had joined their players on the pitch in protest (Motson and Rowlinson 1980: 60).[5] While serious, this incident was not really a case of hooliganism, according with the crowd disturbances which Dunning et al. (1988) noted as typical before the First World War in England when the crowd spontaneously threatened or attacked the referee. This spontaneous reaction to decisions on the field directed at officials is a quite different phenomenon to the ritualistic gang-fighting between opposition fans which emerged in the 1960s in England and Scotland. This changed in the 1970s when hooliganism became a key feature of European football.

Some fans had travelled to European away games in the 1950s and 1960s. A small group of Manchester United fans were mentioned in the reports of the semi-final with Real at the Bernabeu in 1957 and in Lisbon at the Cup Final in 1967 very large numbers of Celtic fans were present, many of whom hindered their club's lap of honour by invading the pitch (in generally good-natured though not entirely sober delirium). Travel to European away matches in the 1960s was difficult and expensive but, as air travel developed, it became increasingly easy for fans to travel to European away games.[6] Hooliganism began to be a major issue in European football when violently inclined British fans, who were always among any club's most committed support, began to take advantage of cheaper air-travel. A very large number of minor incidents of fan violence took place at European games during the 1970s and up to 1985 but five dates are widely cited as being the most significant events in the litany of European football violence: the European Cup-Winner's Cup Final between Rangers and Dynamo Moscow in 1972, the UEFA Cup Final between Tottenham Hotspur and Feyenoord in 1974, the European Cup Final between Bayern Munich and Leeds in 1975, the European Cup-Winner's Cup tie between Manchester United and St Etienne in September 1977 and, finally, the European Cup Final between Liverpool and Juventus in 1985 (the Heysel disaster). There are obvious parallels between these matches. All, except the incident involving Manchester United at St Etienne, were European finals and, consequently, far more fans travelled to these games than to normal European ties. The increased number of fans at these games created a critical mass which raised the usual (though not of course inevitable) occurrence of minor confrontation to a different level; the sheer number of fans increased the likelihood of a confrontation with locals. The presence of Manchester United in this group proves this rule about the significance of numbers, for this club has been unusual for its very large away following. Consequently, Manchester United were likely to be involved in more trouble abroad since even relatively minor ties would attract large numbers of supporters.

However, the mere number of British fans who travelled abroad does not in itself explain the resulting violence. British football fans were frequently involved in violence not only because there were simply more of them but because violent confrontation was an organic element of British football culture at the time, though this violence cannot be understood simply by demonising the individuals involved. Hooliganism was not the product of a few 'deviant' individuals but was instead the result of a complex interaction between fan groups or between fans and the police (see King 1995, 1999a; Stott and Reicher 1998). It is extremely rare for English fans to engage in entirely unprovoked violence. Male fans in England and, indeed, in the rest of Europe, have prioritised a notion of masculine honour which emphasises the violent assertion of superiority. English fans, in particular, have often been drawn into conflict because they are so sensitive to their masculine honour (Dunning 1999: 142; Armstrong 1998; King 1995). (For more on the nature of the masculine fan, see Chapter 9.) Their definition of what constitutes provocation is very broad. Since they are concerned with their status, these men are extremely quick to resort to violence to reassert their honour in the face of insult and provocation. Often, the violence of these fans is not premeditated but, as unforeseen situations arise which threaten their status, they are pulled into relations of escalating conflict which eventually lead to violence itself. Indeed, even in premeditated violence, provocations and insults are exchanged before fighting occurs.

Crucially, this sense of honour which sensitised English fans to insult when abroad was heavily informed by ideas of nationhood. As Williams et al. demonstrate, when travelling abroad in the early 1980s – either with the club or country – English fans drew consistently on the Falklands War as evidence of English superiority and as a means to denigrate especially Hispanic opposition (Williams et al. 1990: 132). Williams et al.'s work, as well as the writings of fans (for example, Ward 1989) and other commentators (for example, Buford 1992) demonstrate the unignorable role which the nationalism of these men played in the subsequent violence in which they were involved. As Ward noted: 'Most of the England fans travelling saw themselves as a sort of reincarnation of Winston Churchill. "We'll show the Krauts why they lost the last war" was heard on the cross-channel ferry' (Ward 1989: 184). When they travelled abroad, English football fans have gathered in certain bars or public places to drink and socialise. In the course of this socialising, fans have often displayed flags and sung nationalistic chants such as 'No surrender to the IRA' or simply 'England' to unify the group. The use of nationalistic songs and symbols to unify these social groups has been significant, for these men effectively created an imagined nation for themselves in various corners of European cities. Their social group came to represent England to them and consequently had to be protected from insult or attack. Moreover, to allow the reputation of the English nation to be impugned was not only an affront to England but it also questioned the masculinity of these fans who had created this little imagined community for themselves. If these fans did not defend the honour of the nation by repelling all insult to their social group, they were simultaneously dishonoured themselves. Since their extreme national pride often encouraged a negative view of the countries to which these individuals were travelling, promoting unruly, uncivil if not outrightly provocative behaviour, the violence which occurred between English and other European fans or local police was unsurprising.[7] Informed by ideas of national superiority, English fans behaved in a way which made offence and confrontation likely and usually necessitated some restraint. Yet, any action on behalf of locals or police was always seen as an affront to these men's status and their national pride. Significantly, it was not simply English hooligans who were influenced by nationalist ideas in their activities. Ultra fan cultures which emerged across Europe in the 1970s self-consciously imitated British hooligan culture, including its emphasis on nationalism. For instance, the Black and White Fighters of Juventus not only consciously imitated English hooligan crews but also tried to organise national alliances of Italian ultra groups for international tournaments or when they were travelling to difficult destinations such as Germany or England (Seve and Claudio 1999). Echoing events on the field of play, European hooliganism emphasised the negative aspects of international competition, vilifying other nations and thriving on international hostility.

Although often not premeditatively violent, the possibility of confrontation was always an organic part of English travelling supporting in the 1970s and 1980s. Given the organic possibility of violence, it is essential that the Heysel stadium disaster of 1985, when European hooliganism reached its nadir, is not seen as a random accident. While the scale of the Heysel disaster was extraordinary, that British football hooliganism would eventually result in a major incident in Europe involving fatalities was inevitable. It required simply the unfortunate coincidence of poor stadium facilities, bad policing and a sufficiently antagonistic opposition. All these factors happened to be present at Heysel. Significantly, however, British fans had been involved in various incidents which anticipated Heysel, none more so than at the game between Manchester United and St Etienne in 1977. At that game, there was no segregation between the fans and fighting had broken out between Manchester United and St Etienne fans in what should have been the reserved home end of the ground. Manchester United were by far the more aggressive group in this confrontation and French supporters fled towards the fence at the bottom of the stand, where a serious crush developed: 'An hour before kick-off about a hundred Britons started a fight behind one of the goals. Armed with bottles, sticks and knives, they went for the supporters of the French team. Panic-stricken spectators rushed down towards the wire-netting around the pitch where they piled up' (Fox 1977a). Unlike the Juventus fans in 1985, the St Etienne fans were fortunate that no wall or barrier gave way and that there was also an effective though initially slow intervention by French riot police which prevented this crush becoming any more dangerous: 'The rest of the crowd shouted "Les flics, les flics" because the riot police on hand were slow to intervene. It took three charges by truncheon-swinging police to clear the battlefield expelling most of the Manchester United supporters' (ibid.).

At the Heysel stadium on 29 May 1985, Liverpool and Juventus fans stood together at one end of the ground, separated only by a flimsy fence with police ineffectually stationed on the perimeter of the pitch rather than on the terraces. Mutual antagonism arose between the fans before the start of the match which led to scuffles and finally a full 'charge' by Liverpool fans from which the Juventus fans, most of whom were unused to hooligan confrontations, fled, causing a crush at the far side of the terrace. At this point, a wall collapsed, causing most of the 39 deaths.

The Heysel stadium disaster was substantially caused by the nationalist masculinity of English travelling fans. It also highlighted the inadequacy of the administration of European football at this time which could allow a major final to take place in such inadequate surroundings. As such, the Heysel disaster constituted a crisis of the international regime. The measures which were taken to remedy this crisis further weakened the international order. UEFA had imposed punishments and banned certain English clubs from competing in Europe for short periods throughout the 1970s and early 1980s. Leeds was banned for a year after the 1975 Final and Manchester United was lucky to escape a similar ban after the incident at St Etienne. After Heysel, UEFA were forced to take more extreme measures and they ruled that all English clubs should be banned from European competition for five years. The ban was imposed by UEFA in consultation with the English Football League, the Football Association and other national federations and was applied to the national league as a single and discrete administrative entity. It was a national solution to a problem substantially precipitated by nationalist ideas and sentiments and it was a further serious blow to the viability of this international competition. English clubs brought added interest and revenue to European matches, even if they lacked the skill of other European teams. It is significant that while this solution was acceptable in the 1980s when the sovereign national federations agreed to implement it, it would be impossible for UEFA to impose such a sanction in the 1990s. No European club would now tolerate a ban on its activities as a result of the behaviour of the fans of other clubs simply because they happened to play in the same league. It is inconceivable that a publicly listed company like Manchester United and its shareholders could accept a restriction on a key part of its core activities as they did in the 1980s. In fact, Martin Edwards, the chairman of Manchester United publicly opposed the ban as an unreasonable restriction of the club's legitimate trade but his view was dismissed. In the 1990s, the clubs would never have been overruled by the national federations and UEFA and it is also certain that no national sanction would have stood up in a European court. The Heysel ban was, perhaps, the last significant legislative act undertaking by UEFA as the ultimate authority of the international order of European football.

The Decline of Playing Standards

In the early part of the 1970s, Ajax had raised the standard of European club football, possibly to heights that even Real had rarely reached, and the Bayern Munich team which dominated the competition in the middle part of the decade winning the trophy between 1974 and 1976 was certainly an excellent though less spectacular team. However, after Bayern's run ended, concerns about playing standards began to be raised. On the face of it, this was peculiar because from 1976 until 1984 Liverpool dominated the competition with clearly outstanding teams which eventually won four European Cups. Alan Hansen, the Scottish international and Liverpool captain in the early 1980s, has argued that the Liverpool team of 1978–80 was among the best English club sides which had ever existed (Cameron 1995: 156).[8] Brian Glanville has similarly praised Liverpool in these years but with significant qualification:

> Of Liverpool's astounding resilience as a club, there can be no doubt ... Meanwhile, the fact that Liverpool is there at all is a solid tribute to the solidarity of British football. Ill-led, ill-chosen, ill-instructed, the England team have been neither an advert for, nor a true reflection of our game. We know its faults which are largely of technique, conservatism and lack of imagination. Some of these Liverpool themselves share. But they also manifest its many virtues; not least of which is an endless capacity for self-regeneration. [Glanville 1977b]

Even while recognising the qualities of Liverpool and their deserved victories in the European Cup in this period, Glanville has repeatedly emphasised both Liverpool's own weaknesses and the decline in standards at this time: 'The era of English supremacy was not, let it be said, a brilliant one. I wrote at the time, and displeased Liverpool's Bob Paisley in the process, that it coincided with a decline in the standard of European football' (Glanville 1991: 10), and that 'English clubs had surely prevailed through organisation, stamina, pace and morale in a way they never could when Real Madrid, Ajax and Bayern Munich were at their peak' (ibid.: 151).

Other journalists concurred with Glanville;

> After two finals in which Borussia Moechengladbach and Bruges have failed to offer the intense competition one would expect in this last stage of a senior European club competition it will still be Liverpool's lot to endure reservations of those who claim that standards are lower than in the days when Bayern Munich won the title for the first time in 1974 and Ajax before them. [Fox 1978]

More than any other, the 1979 European Cup Final between Nottingham Forest and Malmo demonstrated the decline in playing standards in the European Cup. Although Nottingham Forest's victory was a vindication of Brian Clough's extraordinary management, the final was forgettable. The European press found Malmo's offside tactics monotonous and boring, while one journalist argued that the European Cup was finished as a spectacle (Motson and Rowlinson 1980: 214). Nottingham Forest's victory against Hamburg in the following year only confirmed these unfortunate views. The Spanish press in particular were extremely pessimistic about the game, describing Forest's football as 'compact and strong, but without a soul' (ibid.: 240).

> So many finals then were such drab, dull affairs. Oh, the longueurs and the mediocrity of such dire games as Liverpool against Bruges at Wembley, against Real Madrid in Paris; of Nottingham Forest against Malmo and Hamburg. These were Finals won without flair, without panache ... But after the grand epoch of Total Football, this was anticlimax. [Glanville 1991: 10–11]

The problem with the playing standards was that while Liverpool themselves were a very good team, there were few other outstanding teams. During this period between 1976 and the late 1980s, the big city teams which had dominated the early years of the competition were notable by their absence; Real Madrid, Milan, Inter, Benfica, Manchester United and Celtic possessed only mediocre teams and Milan and United had even been relegated during the 1970s. Reflecting the decline of the European giants in this period, in the 1977–78 and 1978–79 runs, Liverpool meet only one major European club, Benfica, who were in serious decline by then. In the 1950s and 1960s, the champion would normally meet two big European clubs; Manchester United played Real Madrid in the semi-final in 1968 and then, of course, met Benfica in the final. By contrast, only in 1981 when they played Real Madrid and in 1985 when they lost to Juventus in ignominious circumstances did Liverpool compete against a club of similar stature. The other three finals were played against Borussia Moechengladbach, Bruges and Roma. Bill Shankly, the renowned Liverpool manager, summarised the 1977 final appositely: 'Winning the European Cup is supposed to be better than a domestic title, but most English clubs would have given us a better game than Borussia did tonight' (Fox 1977b). Perhaps demonstrating Shankly's point, an entertaining but certainly average

Manchester United team had beaten Liverpool somewhat fortuitously in the FA Cup Final on the Saturday before the 1977 European Cup Final.

Although a degree of nostalgia about the standards of play in the 1950s and 1960s seems likely, a drop in playing standards does seem apparent in the late 1970s until at least the late 1980s when the great Milan team emerged. The reasons were certainly partly related to the particular management structures in place at each club at the time. The decline of Manchester United after the 1968 Final and the rise of Liverpool in the same period highlight the contingent factors which could determine a club's success or failure. After the 1968 Final, Matt Busby had achieved his goal and ultimately had lost his ambition to continue. The 1968 team was ageing and required complete rebuilding around the young Brian Kidd and George Best, who was just reaching maturity. No such rebuilding took place and the team declined the following year, after which Busby announced his retirement. However, his continuing presence at the club was detrimental to those managers who succeeded him, especially since they were manifestly not competent enough for a job of that magnitude. Above all, they were unable to control the now alcoholic George Best who was destabilising the team. Manchester United declined rapidly and were relegated at the end of the 1973–74 season. Under Tommy Docherty they returned to the First Division but, although playing in a manner consistent with the attacking traditions established by Matt Busby, they were not an especially good team. Docherty's successors, until Alex Ferguson's arrival in 1986, were similarly incapable of producing a team of sufficient quality to challenge for the Championship.

By contrast, Liverpool went from strength to strength. Bill Shankly who had managed Liverpool from 1959 had developed an institution known as the 'boot-room' where the manager and coaches developed strategies and decided upon player transfers in close collusion. This system sustained Liverpool at the summit of English and European football by obviating the problem of succession. Bill Shankly retired on grounds of ill-health in 1974 to be effortlessly replaced by Bob Paisley who quickly won two European Cups and who, in turn, was replaced by Joe Fagan (Radnedge 1997c: 117; Macdonald 2000: 78). The contrasting fortunes of Liverpool and Manchester United demonstrate that a degree of contingency is important in the successes of particular clubs.

Yet, mere contingency cannot explain why in the late 1970s and early 1980s, only Liverpool of all the big European clubs had an outstanding team. The general lack of quality suggests that there were underlying reasons which affected all the big city clubs alike. It seemed likely that the economic structure of the football industry at the time prevented the big city clubs from accumulating talent in the way they had done in the 1950s and 1960s. The restriction on foreign players seems to have been critical here. In Germany, Italy and France, the biggest clubs were not allowed any foreigners at all until the 1980s, while in Spain, although the complete restriction on foreigners was lifted in 1973 (allowing Cruyff to go to Barcelona), there were limitations on the numbers of foreigners that any single club could field. Up to the 1990s, the market for European footballers was divided into a series of autonomous national markets in which cross-border transfers were the exception. In a sense this was an admirably democratic situation since it allowed smaller clubs such as Nottingham Forest with an extraordinary manager but generally very average players to win the European Cup. Illustrating the significance of this access to an international market for players, Liverpool were in a very advantageous position compared with the rest of Europe because they had access to two large national pools of players (Scotland and England) and three smaller ones (Wales, Northern Ireland and the Republic of Ireland) and their management structure exploited this situation to the full. However, although Liverpool itself should not be denigrated, this dispersal of talent caused by the economic regime of the industry at the time seems to have been one of the prime reasons for the reduced standard of European football in the late 1970s.

However, while the restriction on foreign players was likely to have been a necessary factor in the decline in playing standards in the late 1970s, it cannot have been a sufficient cause: by contrast, in the 1960s and 1970s, Milan, Inter, Benfica, Manchester United, Ajax and Bayern all developed outstanding teams within this international structure. Other identifiable economic factors played a crucial role in limiting the biggest clubs' ability to accumulate the best available talent in the late 1970s and 1980s beside the foreign player restrictions. The big clubs were not simply constrained by legal restrictions in their hiring of foreign talent but, from the late 1970s to late 1980s, the big clubs were severely limited by certain economic restrictions. In this period, the biggest clubs earned little television revenue. In all of the five major television markets, France, Germany, Britain, Italy and Spain, the broadcasting rights for football were sold to a public service monopoly (or, in the case of Britain, to a cartel of public and private sector broadcasters) which suppressed the value of football. Moreover, the sovereign national federations not only redistributed television revenue to the whole league but they also eschewed live coverage which significantly reduced the market values of television rights. For instance, in Germany in 1986, closely echoing the English situation, the two main public channels ARD and ZDF offered the Bundesliga only £6 million a year and the Bundesliga could not attract the new private companies, SAT 1 or RTL Plus. There were problems over dates and the fear that live broadcasts would cause a serious slump in attendance (Rotmil 1986a). Bayern Munich's general manager, Uli Hoeness, described this television fee as 'derisory', claiming that it should have been £10 or even £16 million. He insisted that 'we should not be selling our product so cheaply.' The biggest clubs were unable to exploit the potential value of their television rights, preventing the accumulation of playing talent. The problem for the big clubs was that while wages had increased dramatically, they were no longer earning sufficient revenue to accumulate this talent, despite their obvious potential for increasing their earnings. From the mid- to late 1970s, as a result of the economic regulations governing football, the biggest clubs were being forced into a position of relative equality with the more moderate-sized teams around Europe like Malmo, Nottingham Forest and Steaua Bucharest. Arthur Rotmil, the veteran German football correspondent, noted, for instance, that the lull in the transfer market at this time was substantially due to the fact that most clubs were in debt (Rotmil 1985: 28–9). Certainly, the big clubs still remained the dominant forces in their domestic league; they attracted the highest attendances and the most media attention. However, their position in relation to the other large clubs in the top divisions at the time had declined. The economic restrictions imposed by limited television revenue and increasing player wages prevented the big clubs from accumulating talent in the way that Inter, Milan, Real and Benfica had been able to in the 1950s and 1960s.

The big clubs were fully aware of the disadvantageous of this economic situation as their ferocious criticisms of the national leagues and their regulations demonstrate. Uli Hoeness, Bayern Munich's general manager, pointed to a new economic regime in which the biggest clubs would be able to exploit their real value:

> In ten years, there will be a European league composed of the richest clubs. They will play each other and make the biggest profit from private cable television. The fans will be able to see the matches only on pay-as-you-view television sets. Add to this the television fee, perimeter advertising, sponsorship, plus gate receipts and the total income from just one match would be in excess of 9DM million (£3 million). Home clubs would keep all the receipts and meet only the costs of travelling to away matches. [Hoeness, quoted by Rotmil 1986a]

By the mid-1980s, the international organisation of European football disadvantaged the biggest clubs, preventing them from exploiting their true market value. The big clubs became increasingly militant in their criticisms of this order but, in fact, the decline of the biggest clubs under this regime was detrimental to the competition itself. By the late 1970s, the most famous European clubs were less successful in the European Cup and so the competition lost much of its attraction for spectators and commentators. Significantly, the loss of spectacular finals between the biggest teams was openly regretted; 'the dream of a Barcelona–Juventus European Cup Final was shattered when the quarter-final draw for the European competition produced the star-studded pairing' (*World Soccer* March 1986: 3). Sporadic giant-killing added to the attraction of the European Cup but the consistent absence of those teams which *L'Equipe* had originally recognised as having box-office attraction diminished the competition. During the 1970s and early 1980s, the organisation of European football with its limited market for players, declining attendance and derisory television revenue undermined the hegemony of the biggest clubs. This allowed smaller but far less attractive teams such as Nottingham Forest, Hamburg or Steaua Bucherest to win the competition. The decline in playing standards in the late 1970s and early 1980s was product of the international regime of European competition at the time in which the national federations were sovereign. These federations, assisted by UEFA, protected the national market for players and reduced the value of television. In this structure, it was increasingly difficult for the top clubs to develop strong playing squads to produce football of the highest quality. In this middle era of the European Cup, therefore, the international basis of organisation was becoming a threat to the integrity of European competition itself, especially since the competition was already tarnished by foul play, corruption and hooliganism.

Towards a Transnational Order

The Heysel stadium disaster denotes a quite specific historic moment in European football, when the international regime which had initially proved very successful in the 1950s and 1960s was becoming increasingly untenable. Significantly, at this time, the big clubs began to oppose the restrictions imposed by the international regime more actively. From the late 1970s, they had pressurised UEFA and their national federations into increasing the number of foreigners they were allowed to play and, from 1979, following an intervention by the European Commission, European clubs were allowed to play two foreigners in European competition, liberalising the transfer market somewhat (Radnedge 1985a: 26). Ernesto Pellegrini, president of Internazionale, for instance, had two foreign nationals, Liam Brady and Karl-Heinz Rummenige, on his books in 1985 following this ruling (ibid.). Keir Radnedge noted the growing desire of the biggest European clubs for an even more open player market: 'The likes of Barcelona and Real may even now be dreaming of a return to the good old days of the 1950s when they often had more foreign players in their first team than Spaniards' (ibid.). The biggest clubs were becoming increasingly aware of the restrictiveness of the international regime and, while the clubs did not initially demand formal liberalisation of the market, they did develop strategies to subvert these rules. In 1985, Inter, Juventus and Roma evaded the import bans by buying foreigners internally from Serie B clubs which process legally naturalised these players (*World Soccer* 1985).

Although Juventus, Inter and Roma developed ways around the player restrictions, AC Milan eventually played the decisive role in eliminating the increasingly untenable restrictions of this order. Highlighting the financial problems which the biggest clubs faced under this regime, AC Milan recorded a £12 million debt in 1986. However, recognising the potential of the club and requiring 'content' for his emergent private television networks, the media mogul Silvio Berlusconi offered to buy Giuseppe Farina's majority shareholding for £6 million and to recapitalise the club with a further investment of £3 million. In fact, Berlusconi quickly provided more capital for the club to fund the transfers of Frank Rijkaard and Ruud Gullit from PSV Eindhoven in 1987. Shrewdly, he signed Marco Van Basten for a nominal fee from Ajax, describing his policy aptly: 'We have bought the best, we will give our fans entertaining football and intend to bring the league championship to Milan' (Nottage 1986: 30–31). Berlusconi exploited the mild liberalisation of the rulings on player restrictions in order to produce a new kind of team. With these international stars, Milan exceeded even Berlusconi's expectations for the team quickly established itself as the outstanding team of the late 1980s and the early 1990s, winning its first European Cup in 1989, with a 4–0 thrashing of Steaua Bucherest. Its domination continued into the 1990s, with a further European Cup against Benfica in 1990 and an extraordinary 4–0 victory over Cruyff's Barcelona in 1994. Berlusconi exploited the potential of an increasingly liberalised market for players and it is significant, that after the emergence of AC Milan in the late 1980s on the back of this liberalisation, the European Cup has been dominated by big city clubs. Out of the Eurosclerosis of international club competition, the outlines of a new regime began to emerge in the course of the 1990s which was to produce a new ritual for a New Europe.

Notes

1 For a very interesting analysis of Dutch football, which argues that the clever use of space on the football field by the Dutch reflects the scarcity of space in the Netherlands, see Winner 2000.
2 The team contained one of the players from the Argentinian team which Alf Ramsey had described as 'animals' after England's game against them in the 1966 World Cup.
3 It seems more likely that this game involved poor rather than corrupt refereeing.
4 Football hooliganism was minimally an indirect factor in the Hillsborough Disaster on 15 April 1989 (see Russell 1997: 188).
5 Williams et al. (1990) note that the first recorded incidence of fan violence occurred in 1965 when Manchester United played SV Hamburg.
6 Buford's description of Manchester United fans' trip to Turin in 1982 highlights both the anti-social behaviour in which fans could become involved and also the creative ways in which they travelled cheaply to these games. Buford's account includes an amusing description of United fans 'jibbing' the flight back home; that is, gaining access to the plane without a ticket.
7 I use the term English rather than British here because English fans were more persistently involved in trouble in Europe during the 1970s and 1980s. Moreover, after Heysel, the behaviour of travelling Scottish fans was markedly different from

English fans. Increasingly wishing to highlight their difference from the English and therefore to emphasise the reality of Scotland as a nation, they often adopted boisterous but non-violent and non-confrontational forms of celebration when they followed their teams abroad.

8   Unlike many other commentators, Hansen argued that the standards were as good in the 1970s and 1980s as in the 1990s (Cameron 1995: 156). He is contradicted by Bruges manager, Ernst Happel who described the 1978 Final as 'weak' and went on to say that Liverpool 'were a shadow of that team' which Bruges had played two years before (Fox 1978).

PART III
FOOTBALL IN THE NEW EUROPE

Chapter 5
Bosman

The employment conditions of professional players are among the most important factors in a sport. Players' wages and the restrictions on which players a club can employ determine the distribution of the players between the clubs. Consequently, employment conditions substantially determine the level of inequality between clubs in any league. The abolition of the maximum wage in England in 1961 demonstrates the importance of employment conditions for professional players to the structure of the sport, for that deregulation of wages led to a steady accumulation of talent among the biggest clubs in England and a concomitant decline of the small town clubs (which had been very significant forces in English football) (King 1998c). In the United States, the professional sports leagues recognise the structural implications of the players' labour conditions. They and have created draft systems so that the worst teams have first choice of upcoming college players to offset the inequalities which arise from the favourable market position of the big city teams (see Rosentraub 1999). Apparently small alterations in the legislation concerning labour conditions can transform the balance of power between the clubs over the long term. In European football, the so-called Bosman ruling of 1995 constituted a critical moment of legislative change which echoes the abolition of the maximum wage in England in 1961.

Towards Bosman

From the 1970s, the clubs gradually undermined the international regime through their demand for star players. Once discrete national player markets were penetrated as foreigners were hired by the big clubs. The Spanish league readmitted foreign players in 1973 but by the early 1980s, the other major European football leagues, Britain, Italy and Germany had also allowed a restricted number of foreign players to be fielded by league sides, although British and German clubs never exploited the possibility of foreign signings due to financial limitations. Barcelona was the first Spanish club to take advantage of the liberalisation of foreigner restrictions, signing Johan Cruyff from Ajax for £922,000 in 1973 (Radnedge 1997c: 172) and, later in 1982, Diego Maradona from Boca Juniors in Argentina (Burns 1999: 65–6). In 1984, Maradona was transferred to Napoli, the southern Italian club, for £5 million and was instrumental in winning two Italian Championships, the UEFA Cup and the Italian Cup, thereby breaking the dominance of the northern clubs (Radnedge 1997c: 120). The clubs recognised the financial significance of foreign stars for their immediate operations. For instance, not only did Maradona bring unprecedented success to Napoli in the mid-1980s but the club recouped most of the £5 million transfer fee in season ticket sales within a fortnight of the transfer; Maradona consistently played to sell-out crowds of 85,000. However although clubs lobbied UEFA for the liberalisation of the player market, they showed little interest in challenging the foreigner rulings legally. The clubs were not ideologically committed to a free market for European players; they were motivated by pragmatic and short-term self-interest which recognised the practical advantages of signing foreign stars. Foreign players brought success to the club, increased the gate and, therefore, contributed doubly to the club's finances. However, their increasing use of the transnational player market created a situation in which the legal basis for these restrictions on foreign players could begin to be questioned.

In the 1970s, the Commission had ruled on two significant sports cases, *Dona* vs *Mantero* and *Walrave*. Both cases addressed the question of discrimination against professional sportsmen on the grounds of their nationality but while these cases set important legal precedents for the European Community, they were specialist rulings with little immediate economic effect. However, the Commission also became interested in football at the same time expressing concern about the foreign player restrictions. As a result, UEFA eased the ban on foreign players and allowed two European Union players to play for club sides from 1979. Following further discussions with the Commission, the national football federations in Europe promised to lift this two-player limit but, in the event, the Commission did not enforce this ruling. The Commission was easily deterred by the football authorities at the time. Brian Glanville, for instance, recorded the successful diplomacy of the president of UEFA at the time, Artemio Franchi: 'Franchi held them off with extreme diplomatic skills for a long time ... Franchi was absolutely brilliant because, as I said before, he was like a man who confronts an armed burglar with no weapons and somehow gets the better of him or at least staves him off' (Brian Glanville, personal interview, 2 October 2000). Franchi's diplomatic skills were well known but it is likely that he was able to deter the Commission only because that institution was itself less than determined to enforce European legislation on football in the late 1970s. The Commission was a weaker institution then and had other concerns.

By the mid-1980s, the Commission could no longer be assuaged by individual diplomatic skills. For instance, at the 1985 Milan conference when the Single European Act was initiated, the Addonino report recognised sport as a serious concern to the European Union for the first time; sport provided 'a unique opportunity for promoting a sense of belonging to the single Community' (The Commission 1992: 5). Recognising the cultural significance of sport, the Commission now began to focus on foreign player restrictions more seriously. The Commission attempted to set a deadline for the abolition of all restrictions on European Union players for the start of the 1986–87 season. However, even with the reinvigoration of the European project and the growing power of Brussels, the lifting of restrictions was extremely difficult in practice and in June 1985, UEFA proposed a compromise. Instead of an open European transfer market, restrictions should be eased so that any player who had played in a league for more than five seasons was 'naturalised', that is, he was counted as a native player (Radnedge 1985b: 26). But even this measure was not implemented immediately and there was extensive debate in the course of the late 1980s between the Commission and UEFA about this liberalisation. UEFA finally agreed to expand the foreigner restrictions so that from 1992, three foreigners and two naturalised players were eligible to play for any European club.

Although the Commission accepted this agreement in 1992, it was clear that the Commission fundamentally opposed the transfer system and the foreigner rulings since they were were incompatible with the Treaty of Rome (Glanville 1989). That opposition became stronger during the early 1990s as the financial position of European football improved dramatically as a result of the influx of new television money. The growing economic and cultural significance of European football impelled the Commission to consider it more seriously. As Rick Parry, the chief executive of Liverpool Football Club, commented, 'There is an element of European Commissioners jumping on the football bandwagon because it's high profile and immediately grabs headlines, it is far more sexy than the chemical industry' (personal interview, 9 February 2000). Consequently, during the early 1990s, the Commission urgently wanted to impose European legislation on football and the most effective way of achieving this end was by means of a court ruling. The foreigner restrictions could be most decisively challenged at the European Court of Justice. In contrast with lengthy political bargaining with UEFA, a court ruling was attractively non-negotiable. Yet, in order to challenge the restrictions legally the Commission required an appropriate test-case and for that, they had to wait until a legal challenge appeared. In the event, the disputed transfer of Jean-Marc Bosman from Standard Liege to Dunkerque in 1990 provided the ideal opportunity for the Commission to achieve its objectives of applying Union laws to European football.

The Bosman Ruling

In 1990, Jean-Marc Bosman was suspended at a third of his pay by his club, Standard Liege. Standard Liege had originally agreed to transfer Bosman to the French club Dunkerque but fearing the French club would be unable to finance the transfer fee – even though they had no evidence from Dunkerque or their bank that this was the case – Liege abandoned the transfer. Nevertheless, the club retained Bosman's contract in line with the restrictive Belgian transfer system. Bosman was effectively deprived of his livelihood, since Liege had reduced his pay to a third while preventing him earning a living at another club. Significantly, because the Bosman dispute involved a cross-border transfer, this case provided an excellent opportunity for the Commission to challenge both the transfer system and the foreigner rulings. In 1993, the Liege Court of Appeal upheld the first judgment against Standard Liege and referred the matter to the European Court of Justice for a preliminary ruling on whether the transfer system and nationality clauses were compatible with Articles 48 (free movement of workers), 85 and 86 (free competition) of the Treaty of Rome (Blanpain and Inston 1996: ix).

The manifest injustice of the Belgian transfer system and the obduracy of the football authorities assisted the Commission's case. F. Messleman, the vice-president of the Belgian Football Association declared, for instance: 'We have no lessons to learn from somebody who, in a manner of speaking, doesn't even know that a football is round' (ibid.: 1). Rick Parry confirmed the inappropriateness of UEFA's stance:

> I got involved with some debates with the Commission on behalf of the Premier League. There was no doubt that UEFA handled the whole thing appallingly – just supreme arrogance – and there is no doubt that a deal could have been done with the Commission. There is no doubt, for instance, that the transfer system could have been preserved if UEFA had agreed a relaxation on the three foreigner rule. No question about that, in my view. The debate we had with the Commissioners and with politicians showed that the Commission do do deals. That is how the Commission works. [Personal interview, Rick Parry, chief executive, Liverpool Football Club, 10 February 2000][1]

Richard Worth, a senior executive at UEFA's marketing wing, Television and Event Marketing (TEAM) confirmed Parry's point: 'It was because they had a distant and rather arrogant attitude to what they felt that the EU was capable of doing' (Richard Worth, TEAM, 2 March 2000).[2] The attitudes of the football authorities only confirmed the arbitrariness of their law.[3] Profiting from UEFA's mismanagement of the case, Advocate General Lenz gave his final statement on 20 September 1995 which was finally endorsed as a ruling on 15 December 1995 by the European Court of Justice. Out-of-contract transfer fees and all foreign restrictions for European Union players were outlawed. It was a historic moment in European football.

Lenz's Ruling on Transfers

The plaintiffs, the Belgian Football Association and Standard Liege, supported by UEFA, defended the system of transfer fees on the grounds that it redistributed revenue between the bigger and smaller clubs and, therefore, went some way to protecting sporting equilibrium. Football relies on a degree of competitive equilibrium between the teams to assure uncertainty of outcome (Blainpain and Instow 1996: 17–19). This maintains the attractiveness of the competition. The Court's decision finally rested on the question of whether the public good of competitive equality outweighed the restrictiveness of the transfer system. Transfer fees 'would be lawful only if they were justified by imperative reasons in the general interest and did not go beyond what was necessary for attaining those objectives' (ibid.: 243–4). Lenz himself accepted that sporting equilibrium was important in professional leagues and that smaller clubs were an important reservoir of talent for the big clubs (ibid.: 246). He therefore recognised that there were general interests which European legislation should recognise. However, he rejected the claim that transfer fees could be accepted as a method of sustaining this equality. In particular, it was uncertain whether transfer fees really were as significant for the redistribution of wealth as clubs and federations maintained:

> Empirical studies have likewise consistently failed to show any connection between the existence of the transfer market and the sporting equilibrium of the competition ... If we carry out analysis that takes the dynamics of the market mechanisms into account, it shows that the abolition of the transfer market has no harmful effect on the financial position of smaller clubs. [ibid.: 20]

Appositely, Lenz noted that when clubs bought players from other national leagues they were not contributing to the competitive equality of their own but this practice was regarded as entirely acceptable. Lenz also disputed the claim that transfer fees represented compensation for the training costs (ibid.: 252, para. 239) mainly because 'the amount of the transfer fee quite evidently is not in relation to the costs of training' (ibid.: 252, para. 237). Consequently, Advocate General Lenz ruled against the transfer system: 'it thus follows in my opinion that transfer fees ... are not justified by a reason in the general interest' (ibid.: 255, para. 247). However, he did not ban transfer fees completely, ruling only that the payment of transfer fees after the expiration of a player's contract was illegal. That was certainly a significant legislative amendment but not quite the cataclysm for which it has often been taken. Although Lenz dismissed the transfer fee as an appropriate means of redistributing wealth within football leagues, he did advocate various other means by which competitive equality might be achieved. He suggested that clubs could share television revenues or gate receipts (ibid.: 248, para. 226): 'In the German cup, for example, the two clubs involved each to my knowledge receive half of the receipts remaining after the deduction of their share due to the Deutsche Fussball Band' and Lenz noted a redistribution of income by UEFA to clubs involved in the Champions League. Lenz concluded his argument for other forms of redistribution to be introduced which neither infringed the legal rights of players nor impinged upon the laws of the European Union: 'It must be observed that a redistribution of a part of their income appears substantially more suitable for attaining the desired purpose than the current system of transfer fees. It permits a club concerned to budget on a considerably more reliable basis' (ibid.: 251, para. 233).

It was logical for Lenz to advocate new forms of redistribution given his recognition of the importance of competitive balance. However, in arguing for voluntary schemes of redistribution to be introduced, Lenz flew blissfully in the face of the economic realities of European football. Moreover, Lenz's German cup example was tendentious for a number of reasons. Germany is, along with France, still one of the most corporatist leagues structures in Europe. Moreover, cup competitions are not accurate indicators of redistributory policy since they are usually played over one leg and therefore, it is regarded as only reasonable that the teams share the gates. Even in England, one of the most marketised leagues, clubs still share gate receipts for the FA Cup. In Germany gate receipts are not shared for League matches, though television revenue is still pooled more equally than in Spain, Italy and England. Lenz's example of the Champions League is also problematic since it is not true that clubs share receipts there. Each club keeps its home gate receipts in the competition, while UEFA, which markets the tournament centrally, then distributes the television money to competing clubs according to their performance. The reason that the clubs involved accept this situation is that this central marketing method has increased the value of the competition and therefore the revenue which clubs earn. Moreover, the entire structure of that competition is elitist, favouring the biggest clubs in each nation. Lenz's untenable assumption that clubs would voluntarily give up portions of their revenue has not been lost on those within football:

> Of course, you could dream up all sorts of theoretical bases for clubs redistributing wealth but get real. Do you imagine that somehow the big clubs are voluntarily going to give money away to their smaller brethren? Nonsense. It isn't going to happen. What the transfer system did was to provide a market mechanism that redistributed wealth. There is no way you are going to do it voluntarily. [Personal interview, Rick Parry 9 February 2000]

Operating in a competitive economic environment, football clubs will give up revenue only if they receive something in return. The transfer system was a way of exploiting this economic reality for the good of disadvantaged clubs. The transfer system operated in line with economic realities rather than in the face of them.

Lenz's Ruling on Foreign Players

In the first instance, the Bosman case was concerned with the legality of the Belgium transfer system alone. However, Bosman was sponsored by FIFPro, the European union of professional players, which appended to this grievance the question of foreign player restrictions. FIFPro opposed the three-plus-two rule on the grounds that this rule was still a major restriction of trade for professional players. Clubs were still predominantly bound to national markets in hiring players. Consequently, although Bosman himself was only affected by the Belgian transfer system, the legality of foreigner restrictions were considered as part of Bosman's case from the first. UEFA argued that the consideration of the foreigner restrictions were artificially attached to the Bosman case since these restrictions had nothing to do with his contractual difficulties. UEFA were surely correct here but since foreigner restrictions breached EU law so obviously and since the Bosman case presented such a good opportunity to consider them legally, the Commission was unlikely to allow these restrictions to remain unchallenged. Predictably, Advocate General Lenz opposed restrictions on foreign players; 'No deep cogitation is required to reach the conclusion that the rules on foreign players are of a discriminatory nature'. They represent an absolutely classic case of discrimination on the gounds of nationality. Those rules limit the number of players from other Member States whom a club in a particular Member State can play in a match' (Blanpain and Instow 1996: 210, para. 135). Given that free labour movement had been accepted as one of the pillars of European integration since the 1980s, it was self-evident that the foreigner ruling was unsustainable. Nevertheless, Lenz went to some lengths to demonstrate that its loss would not have the effects which the football authorities had predicted and that their position on this matter was illogical, if not hypocritical. The foreigner restrictions were defended on the grounds that national sovereignty was an important part of football since fans identified more closely with players from their own member states. Lenz rebutted this argument decisively:

> The vast majority of clubs in the top divisions in Member States play foreign players. The greater majority of supporters are much more interested in success of their club than in composition of the team. If nationals who come from other parts of the relevant State are accepted without question, one cannot see why that should not also be the case for nationals of other Member States. [ibid.: 214–15]

Indeed, confirming Lenz's point, not only were players from other parts of a Member State regarded as legitimate, but fans rarely objected to foreign players. Cruyff established himself as something of an honorary Catalan at FC Barcelona while Maradona became a symbol of the depressed south during his time at Napoli. More recently, Eric Cantona was a key symbol for fans at Manchester United in the 1990s. Although there are important exceptions to this point, especially when it comes to players from ethnic minorities, Lenz was generally correct to emphasise that in many cases the origin of players is irrelevant to the fans.

Throughout the Bosman case, Lenz recognised the importance of competitive balance. As already stated, he went to considerable lengths to advocate theoretical methods of redistribution. He affirmed the solidarity of the national leagues in which the strong helped the weak. Overtly, he supported corporatist principles. However, market logic assumed a position of priority. While he might have nodded to certain corporatist principles, Lenz's statement finally rested on the sovereignty of the market:

> Now it is certainly undeniable that sports associations have the right and duty to draw up rules for the practice and organisation of sport and that that activity falls within the associations' autonomy which is protected as a fundamental right. That does not mean, however, that for resolving conflict between the rights of freedom of movement and the right of association, a simple 'balancing of rights' would suffice. The fundamental importance of Article 48 for the internal market which the Court has expressly emphasised on several occasions, would not be given sufficient account thereby. [ibid.: 245, para. 216]

Lenz's statement is clear. Article 48 is paramount in a European Court of Law, denoting the absolute priority of the free market above all other legal principles and his statement formally asserted this priority. The free market overruled redistributive corporatism in every instance. Significantly, Lenz recognised the likely effects of market logic but – against his weak espousal of corporatist redistribution – he vindicated those effects fully. Discussing the financial problems which faced many football clubs in the increasingly marketised environment which his own statement promised to introduce, Lenz simply declared: 'Many club managers have not yet learned to cut their coat according to their cloth. The fact that sound management will result in fewer professional footballers and fewer professional clubs in a small country like Belgium is no more than straightforward economic logic' (ibid.: 20). In dismissing the problems confronted by smaller clubs as examples of individual malpractice, Lenz promoted deregulation extremely strongly for, on this interpretation, liberalisation was opposed only by the inefficient and expendable.

In prioritising the free market, Lenz's statement and the subsequent ruling by the European Court of Justice reflected the spirit of the SEA and Project

1992 which was eventually enshrined in the Maastricht Treaty of 1994. 'Maastricht leads to an obliteration of what is left of the Keynesian legacy' (Anderson 1997: 131) and Lenz's ruling constituted the end of Keynesian arrangements in football. In line with the central premise of Maastricht legislation, Lenz promoted the radical deregulation of European football. Consequently, the Bosman ruling denotes a critical moment in European football when free market logic was established as the fundamental principle of European football, determining labour contracts for professional players. In a single legislative stroke, the principles of national sovereignty and the separation of national markets which were a prime feature of the international regime were replaced. Bosman swept away the principle of national sovereignty and discrete player markets, creating, in a single stroke, a new economic regime. In place of an international structure, Bosman instituted a new transnational order in which there was an open European market for players where national boundaries were irrelevant. The abolition of the maximum wage in England in 1961 had profound long-term effects on the game since it inflated wages and increased the gap between the big city clubs and the smaller town clubs. Over a thirty-year period, the abolition of the maximum wage eventually necessitated the reformation of the English league in line with the new dominance of the big city clubs (see King 1998c). In the long term, the effects of the Bosman ruling are likely to be similar but these effects have begun to be realised almost immediately.

The Effects of the Bosman Ruling: Wage Increases

Most obviously, the Bosman ruling has increased the financial pressure on the clubs by inflating wages. Following the ruling, player wages have increased because in order to protect themselves from losing the transfer fee of players after the expiry of their contracts, clubs had to sign players on longer contracts. Players have accepted these longer contracts only if they were a substantial improvement on what they had previously received (Szymanski and Kuypers 1999: 108–10). There are some notable recent examples of this process. At the beginning of the 1999 season, the contract of Roy Keane, Manchester United's captain, was due for renewal since it expired at the end of the season. As a result of Bosman, Manchester United were in an awkward financial situation which was exploited by Roy Keane and his agent to the full. It was no secret that Roy Keane was content to stay at the club. He had won all that he could have reasonably expected (except the European Cup itself, having been suspended for the Final) and the club had given him a genuinely global stage on which to perform. Moreover, he and his family were settled in Manchester. Until 1999, Manchester United as a public limited company (Plc) had imposed very successful wage caps on the players so that, relative to some of the top players in Italy or Spain, Roy Keane was underpaid. Roy Keane's demand for a new contract took account of this imbalance and demanded a very substantial increase in wages from about £25,000 a week to over £40,000 a week. Despite Keane's importance to the club, it was highly likely that the Plc would have rejected this demand before Bosman and would have transferred Keane for many millions of pounds to Italy or Spain. It was notable that Christian Vieri was transferred from Lazio to Inter in 1999 for £31 million, while Real Madrid paid Arsenal £23 million for Nicholas Anelka. Given this market, Roy Keane's fee was likely to have been between £25 and £30 million. The abolition of post-contract transfer fees presented the Plc with a dilemma. If he left after his contract expired, the club would receive no compensation; they had either to break their wage structure or lose a multi-million pound transfer fee. Since they would have to replace Keane anyway, they chose to break their wage cap and award Keane his contract. Amateurishly, the club tried to blame the rise in season ticket prices in the following season on Keane's contract, but it was certainly true that Keane's contract – and the wider inflation of wages at United among the whole playing staff that has followed – has had a significant effect on the club's financial figures. Profit dropped by a third in the accounts returned in the year following Keane's renegotiated contracted. Not all of this decline in profit can be put down to the Keane contract, but the inflation of wages was certainly not irrelevant as Peter Kenyon, the chief executive of Manchester United Plc, and Rick Parry, his counterpart at Liverpool, have affirmed:

> There is this continual pressure upwards on salaries – on everybody. I think we controlled it better than anybody but you don't escape the pressure. You don't see an end to that. So it is hard to understand what the economic business model is when costs are going up 35 per cent a year and none of the other stuff is. So however sustainable those other clubs are, there has to be some fall-out. [Peter Kenyon, personal interview, 3 March 2000]

'You have to accept the reality of it now. It is posing different pressures. The spiral of players' wages is going ever upwards. There is no end to that in sight' (Rick Parry, chief executive Liverpool Football Club, personal interview, 9 February 2000).

Post-Bosman inflation has affected all the clubs. In the Premier League as a whole there was a 35 per cent rise in average player earnings in 1997 (Demsey and Reilly 1998: 26) while, in Germany, the average expenditure per year has risen by more than 500 per cent since 1990 (Kipker 2000a: 4). In Italy and Spain, although the data is less reliable than in England, there are signs of similar increases in player wages (Demsey and Reilly 1998: 26). The renewal of Keane's contract is an excellent example of how the Bosman ruling has increased wage costs in professional football even for those clubs who had instituted long-term wage structures to suppress costs. In this deregulated and transnational economic environment, it is simply impossible to suppress wage costs if a club has any pretensions of advancing, or even maintaining, its status.

Although this inflation of the players' wages is not ideal, either financially or ethically (since it is not clear why the players should earn very large sums of money while the fans struggle to pay for season tickets), professional football is a long way from the chaos which some predicted would follow Bosman. The importance of transfer fees to smaller clubs has always been exaggerated. Some small clubs have sometimes employed transfer fees as a means to buttress their core income but so uncertain is this source of income that it would not be sensible to rely on it as a core form of financing (Szymanski and Kuypers 1999: 111).

> The truth is that the current transfer system does provide a number of smaller clubs a decent income but it is a payment that is completely arbitrary and irregular. In England for example recent trends show that rather than support smaller clubs in the UK, the transfer system has allowed Premier League clubs to support foreign clubs. Only 40 per cent of the £200m spent by Premier League clubs in the summer of 2000 went back to English clubs and more than half of that share went to other Premiership clubs. [*Soccer Analyst* 2000d: 1]

Moreover, after Bosman, these smaller clubs have not had to pay transfer fees to others in turn. However, while the abolition of transfer fees does not intrinsically threaten smaller clubs more than the bigger one, the inflation in wages following Bosman has had a disproportionate effect on the smaller clubs. In particular, in the 1990s, the big clubs funded by deregulated television contracts have been in a much stronger position to cope with the increase in wage costs. Indeed, with this increased television revenue, the big clubs have effectively inflated wage costs in every division of the national leagues while the small clubs have had no new revenue streams on which to draw. Relatively, wage inflation has had a worse effect on the smaller clubs than the bigger ones. Thus, in the English Football League, while wage bills in the Second and Third Division constituted 84 and 97 per cent of the clubs' total income, wages costs for the top division accounted for only about 50 per cent of total expenditure (Szymanski and Kuypers 1999: 81), even though the average wage bill in the Premier League was eight times the average turnover in the Third Division (Deloitte and Touche 1999: 7). The wage bills are much higher in the Premier League but the Premier League clubs are much better able to sustain these costs. Peter Kenyon is correct to highlight the inflationary pressure which has been introduced since Bosman, but while the biggest clubs may have been seriously affected by this inflation, the smaller clubs have become almost unviable as fully professional operations as a result of it. The 'fall-out' which Kenyon predicted is likely to be borne by the smaller clubs in the lower divisions. After Bosman, there has been a general inflation of wages which has, in the end, concentrated power at the biggest clubs.

The Effects of Bosman: transnational competition and the rise of the big clubs[4]

Not only have the inflationary effects of the Bosman ruling been differential but the ruling has allowed the biggest clubs to build up international squads unrestricted by the foreigner restrictions. In 1992, Berlusconi purchased an extra striker, Jean Pierre Papin, for AC Milan. Papin could not be played all the time because of the three foreign (plus two assimilated) player ruling. Berlusconi seems to have bought the player in case one of the other strikers was injured and, possibly, to prevent competitors from playing Papin against AC Milan. Papin spent much of the season on the bench and Berlusconi was vilified at the time for introducing a strategy which prevented one of the stars of European football from performing regularly. Yet, in the post-Bosman era, this strategy is now regarded as standard practice. With the ending of nationality restrictions, the big clubs have been able to create large playing squads which have become essential if the clubs are to remain successful in domestic and European competition. For the big clubs, this transnational context is certainly more costly than the international regime, but funded by new television monies, they are now much freer to exploit the transfer market and to develop diverse playing squads.[5] The liberalisation of the international market for players has allowed these clubs to recruit talent. The Bosman ruling has effectively redressed the decline in playing standards in the late 1970s and early 1980s where the biggest clubs could not accumulate talent while smaller teams, like Nottingham Forest or Malmo, could thrive. The biggest clubs are conscious that this deregulation has benefited them:

> In the Spanish league, any poor player from the second division can cost us £5–£10 million. The stupidest of presidents of club boards sees that a player is being widely recognised and he raises the players' wages by 10 per cent, while adding a club fee of £5 to £10 million. As the latter occurs throughout Europe it helps to close the market down. [Jaume Sobriques, FC Barcelona, personal interview, 22 May 2000]

For Sobriques, the restriction on foreign players put a false market value on national talent and effectively allowed smaller teams to exploit their oligopolistic position within national markets. They put a false market value on their players when selling them to the big clubs. For Barcelona, the Bosman ruling has opened access to a Europe-wide transfer market.

Although the biggest clubs have benefited most from this deregulation, it has also created new difficulties and pressures for them. When football was divided into discrete national player markets under the international regime, the smaller clubs in each league were protected from unfettered competition but the biggest clubs were also shielded from market forces as well. After Bosman, the biggest clubs confront those forces directly. In particular, the transnationalisation of the European player market following Bosman has introduced direct competition between all the clubs in Europe:

> I think one of the consequences of the Bosman ruling was the creation of a European market more than a national transfer market. It is natural that when there is a talent that can play in any given country in the European Union, it is quite normal now that it is not only his own country's team that are trying to buy him but that all the top countries are trying to lure him away because we all need superstars. For many reasons ... Competition between the big clubs is bigger now for talent. It could be the talent from Ukraine or from France. [Umberto Gandini, organisation director, AC Milan, personal interview, 15 March 2000]

> Ultimately, one of your core entities as a club are players and players, by their very nature, are certainly pan-European now. [Peter Kenyon, chief executive, Manchester United, personal interview, 3 March 2000]

> What do the people want in any country and all the supporters of any club want? They want good players and results and in the professional world that means you have to spend money. You have to get the best players. And then you have competition and the competition is the other big clubs. Of course. You have to look to the other important clubs in Europe, instead of looking at the other clubs in your country, because the normal competitor is the big clubs. [Juan Onieva, personal interview, 19 April 2000]

By necessity, the number of highly talented players in Europe is limited and, as a result of the Bosman ruling, the top European clubs are now in direct competition for these valuable assets.

The significance of this direct transnational competition should not be underestimated. It constitutes a quite profound change in the economics of European football which denotes a new period in the history of the game. Of course, as we shall see later on, there are important social and cultural dimensions to this open transnational competition which are beginning to appear and are expressed by the fans of European football clubs. However, there are immediate economic effects which the directors of clubs recognise. Clubs now must consider the financial advantages of their transnational competitors in a way which was irrelevant when the international regime limited transnational market forces:

> It is not just the case now that we have to keep an eye on the Premier League TV deal. We have to keep an eye on the Spanish deal, the Italian deal, the German deal because that is the marketplace which we are competing in. [Rick Parry, personal interview, 9 February 2000]

We knew about the contract they had signed in Italy. It makes us very, very worried. Because Italian clubs in the next two years are going to receive a large amount of money. Much bigger than we will receive. We are professional clubs. The players are professionals. That means that if other clubs have more money, they are going to have the best players. This is normal. But we have to accept this, we can do nothing. The contract is signed. We have the contract until 2003. We know that. This process is going to happen in the next two or three years; we are going to suffer. [Juan Onieva, personal interview, 19 April 2000]

The ability of business deals, or structures, or TV deals in Italy or Spain do make you less competitive in the European market. [Peter Kenyon, personal interview, 3 March 2000]

The liberalisation of the market has put the major clubs in direct competition for players but, since players must be paid, the transformation of this labour market has automatically introduced ferocious transnational competition across Europe. Every aspect of a club's operations are now relevant to European competitiveness in a way which was simply not the case in the international era. For European clubs situated in small markets, such as Scotland or Holland, the transnational market is a very serious threat: 'After Bosman you have a free European market for players which means that, for example, Anderlecht is competing with Juventus for all players because Anderlecht no longer has a privilege on any national kind of players' (Jean Dupont, *Soccer Analyst* 2000a: 10).

The predicament of teams in small markets is nowhere better highlighted than in the case of Ajax Football Club in Amsterdam. Since the late 1960s, Ajax has always been famous for producing highly skilled players. This production of young talent was part of a wider strategy at the club: young players initially played for the club but would later be transferred for large fees which would sustain the club's finances. Cruyff and Neeskens were the earliest and most famous examples, but Ajax has employed this strategy consistently throughout the 1980s and early 1990s. From 1990 to 1995, for instance, Ajax had sold more than twenty players for a transfer value of £33 million (Kelly and Radnedge 1996: 18). For a major club like Ajax operating in a small market, the foreigner ruling and the transfer fee were key factors in their business strategy. The Bosman case transformed the business environment in which Ajax operated and rendered this strategy unworkable since 'the kids can go just as soon as they like' (Radnedge 1997a). No longer limited in the number of foreigners they can field, financially stronger clubs are now able to asset strip Ajax's youth system without restriction and often without even compensating Ajax for the loss. After their victory in the European Cup Final in 1995, Ajax lost most of its talented squad and in the cases of Clarence Seedorf, Patrick Kluivert, Edgar Davids, Marc Overmars – and later Winston Bogarde – no transfer fees were received (Banks 1998). PSV Eindhoven has confronted similar problems which their president describes succinctly: 'In recent years PSV have lost most of their best players. The players we buy or train only stay a couple of years. Every year we have to start again whereas the big countries can construct a team on a long-term basis' (Harry van Raaij, club president, *Soccer Investor* 2000a). The unification of the player market has facilitated a concentration of playing power in the core football markets of the New Europe – in England, Germany, Spain and Italy – because the clubs in these countries are financially better equipped than those in smaller leagues (now unprotected by national trade limitations) to buy players. The emergent network of large clubs, especially located in these key leagues, comprises the core of the new transnational order fostered by the post-Bosman deregulation. It should be noted that while a new economic regime is emerging around the biggest clubs, the old international order is not completely irrelevant. The biggest European clubs are located in the main national markets with, above all, the biggest television markets. Consequently, although the regulatory regime and the market for players is transnational, the nation as a cultural and organisational unit remains significant. Nations are still significant but their importance has been altered in the light of this transnational order. Clubs have become relatively more important. It is notable that in some cases these national television boundaries have begun to break down. The Premier League has been broadcast very successfully across Europe especially in Norway, while Channel 4 in Britain has televised live Serie A games on Sunday afternoons. In the 2002–03 season, the BBC has broadcast Old Firm games between Celtic and Rangers live on English television. The national television markets are still very important but these boundaries are themselves breaking down and in each case the biggest clubs benefit from the new transnational market.

Unsurprisingly, the new transnational competition has led to new disputes between clubs of different countries which were extremely rare in the past. The growing antagonism between clubs as they squabble over transfers is an inevitable feature of post-Bosman football, especially given the often divisive interventions of the players' agents. The Nicholas Anelka case provides an excellent example of this new transnational antagonism. In 1997, Arsene Wenger, the recently appointed French manager of Arsenal Football Club, arranged the transfer of 17-year-old Nicholas Anelka from Paris Saint-Germain, where Anelka was on a youth contract, to a fully professional contract at the London club. Having coached in France for many years, Wenger was aware of Anelka's potential. However, Paris Saint-Germain were incensed by Wenger's actions, arguing that Wenger had approached Anelka illegally and poached one of their prime assets – without even paying a transfer fee. In fact, Wenger had acted legally though perhaps unethically, and relations between the clubs cooled distinctly as a result of the transfer (Duclos 1997). In 1999, the tables were reversed for in the close season, Anelka was approached by Real Madrid. The transfer reached almost comical proportions when David Dein, the Arsenal chief executive, and Lorenzo Sanz, the president of Real Madrid at the time, became locked in a mutually demeaning dispute over the affair. Transnational transfers have, of course, occurred before and some of them had required UEFA tribunals to set appropriate fees. However, the international acrimony between clubs is a post-Bosman phenomenon when clubs find themselves in direct transnational competition with each other for assets (players) which are critical to their operations.

However, the transnational relations between clubs which are developing in the post-Bosman era are not only competitive and antagonistic. New forms of cooperation have also emerged in this era which are partly due to the Bosman ruling:

> It's probably not for the first time but it has been going on more than a few years. And it's not just a matter of buying and selling players but wider questions: 'What is my problem?' 'What is your problem?' 'What are you doing with this?' It is changing. It is new. Why do we have to stay in different worlds? We are playing in the same world and so talking together is just a way of improving, of learning from somebody else, or teaching somebody else something. Or to make our clubs bigger and better than in the past. It is not just a question of more sales and more buys following the Bosman case. [Roberta Bettega, Juventus FC, personal interview, 14 March 2000]

> We had good connections and good relations with major European clubs even before the Bosman, probably because, as we said before, we are all working in a broader market. It is natural probably, that you develop many more relations than you did before. You have to be more present in more countries and on more occasions. You are conscious now of the fact that you are important, that you are fundamental. A lot of people are looking at the way you work, the way you do things. They are trying to understand you. Tomorrow, we have Bordeaux coming here to talk to us. They are trying to model themselves on us. In the G14 we have big clubs, which have decided to come and scout and look at our organisation, trying to understand why Milan is there. [Umberto Gandini, organisational director, AC Milan, personal interview, 15 March 2000. The G14, established in November 1998, is a grouping of the largest European clubs – see Chapter 8.]

The liberalisation of the transfer fee and the abolition of foreign player restrictions has transformed the political economic structure of European football, ushering in a new transnational order. This order is more financially competitive than the internationalist regime and the changes which are being made to the game as its implications are worked out are both radical and bewildering, but the anarchy predicted by those who have interests in or who preferred the international order has not occurred. Rather, definite strategies have been adopted by the clubs whose identification provides an outline of European football in the new era. The liberalisation of the market has promoted the biggest clubs, throwing them into ever closer relationships with each other involving both competition (and antagonism) and cooperation. Like the major European cities which Castells described, the big European football clubs are becoming 'the nervous system of both the economic and political system of the continent' (Castells 1994: 23). A new geography of European football is emerging.

The New Geography of European Football

In the light of the new transnational order, clubs have developed new strategies to improve their competitiveness. Ajax, for instance, which was very successful under the old regime, is likely to be sufficiently innovative to succeed even against the market odds in this new era. In order to counteract its financial disadvantages, the club supports the development of a regular European Superleague which would increase their market base:

> If you take the position of an Ajax, for example, in a weakish domestic league with modest revenues, they are in a hugely difficult position. Again traditionally they developed their own players very successfully. If they lost the players, they would command transfer fees. Post-Bosman they are getting nothing back. To remain a major power is enormously difficult for them. I can see that a European Super League would suit them down to the ground. [Rick Parry, chief executive, Liverpool Football Club, personal interview, 9 February 2000]

Similarly PSV Eindhoven have suggested that they too would support moves to form such a league: 'To survive economically and evolve on a sporting level, PSV will in the future have to play on a higher level' (Harry van Raaij, club president, in *Soccer Investor* 2000a). While a European super league looks a long way off, Ajax have also been at the forefront of other radical proposals which would increase their market size, allowing them to compete more effectively in the post-Bosman era. Ajax, with the other big Dutch clubs, PSV Eindhoven and Feyenoord, held discussions with the major clubs in Scotland, Belgium, Denmark and Portugal in February 2000 about the possibility of a so-called 'Atlantic League' (ibid.). This league would involve regular competition between the major clubs in each league with the intention that by combining all three leagues, these clubs will create a television market which can compete with Italy, France, Germany, Spain and England. The exact format of this league remains very unclear but it is deliberately intended as a business strategy which would offset the disadvantages which major clubs like Ajax face by being situated in a small market in the post-Bosman, transnational era. The proposal that Rangers and Celtic might join the English Premier League in August 2001 was part of the same strategy. It denotes a decisive breakdown of the international order because these plans ignore the historic national boundaries between countries and the sovereignty of national federations. They are examples of economic logic which ignore formerly binding national solidarities in favour of transnational integration. Although new kinds of leagues like the Atlantic League are rational solutions to the transnational market and they may eventually emerge, they are fraught with difficulties. Although the Commission itself would support such cross-border innovations, national federations and UEFA vigorously oppose such strategies, defending the sovereignty of national leagues. Perhaps most decisively, the fans may also oppose the creation of such leagues for whom this kind of competition might be artificial.

Although better positioned than a club like Ajax, the biggest clubs have adopted very interesting strategies in the face of new pressures which illuminate the new geography of European football. In particular, almost all have recognised the importance of developing youth schemes in order to suppress wages and to maximise income from transfer fees:

> We can't compete with Real Madrid financially. We can't just throw money around. We operate on an entirely different basis. We cannot run up debts of £100 million in the knowledge that no bank is ever going to put Real Madrid out of business or that the Spanish government will at some stage bale them out. We are not on that playing field. So it is actually quite refreshing this – it forces you to be smarter and focused on the football stage in terms of the development of talent which is really about getting back to basics. Produce outstanding young players and be smarter in terms of the identification of young talent elsewhere. [Rick Parry, chief executive, Liverpool Football Club, personal interview, 9 February 2000]

> I think what Bosman forced you to do was to widen the net and spend a awful lot more on trying to get talent younger and develop it. [Peter Kenyon, chief executive, Manchester United Plc, personal interview, 3 March 2000]

> It is very difficult for a big club to produce talent. Man United are based on certain talent they found in-house, with the Neville brothers, Beckham, Scholes and Giggs and so on. We are still based on Maldini, and Albertini and Costacurta, we raised ten, fifteen years ago. We don't have anybody in between. It is not so easy ... I think it is very difficult to develop young talent within your own system. [Umberto Gandini, organisational director, AC Milan, personal interview, 15 March 2000]

While the Bosman ruling has subverted national borders by introducing a transnational market for players, a key element of the clubs' new strategy is the development of local talent. Thus, paradoxically while the top European teams are increasingly international, simultaneously there has been a growing emphasis on local talent by the big clubs. At Manchester United, for instance, under the management of Alex Ferguson, the club produced a crop of outstanding young players in the mid-1990s, as Gandini noted, who went on to be an important part of the club's success: Ryan Giggs, David Beckham, Paul Scholes, Gary and Phil Neville and Nicky Butt. Except for Beckham, these players, all of whom have had regular places in the United team, were brought up in parts of Greater Manchester within ten miles of the club. The use of local talent has been cited as one of the central reasons for the levels of success enjoyed by the club in the late 1990s. (The full significance of this is discussed in Chapter 9.) The in-house training of these individuals, most of whom supported the club as boys, instilled an unparalleled commitment to the club and produced a level of motivation noticeably higher than the players of other teams who had been gathered by the other possible strategy in the post-Bosman era, that is, transnational transfers. Consequently, in the late 1990s the localism of Manchester United's team was often compared favourably with the diverse origins of the very cosmopolitan Chelsea team, whose motivation was often questionable. As Gandini reveals, clubs across Europe have tried to imitate Manchester United and to develop local partisan talent which is then strengthened by foreign imports. We are seeing the emergence of new concentrations in metropolitan centres which have strengthened their connections to the local area in order to prevent other clubs poaching valuable local playing resources.

This localism is quite different to the strategies clubs once employed to recruit talent, although localism is often read back into this past. In the past, players were recruited on a mainly national basis. Thus, Busby's teams were not primarily recruited from the local Manchester area but from the whole of Britain. Indeed, none of the most famous post-war Manchester United players were from the local area: Duncan Edwards was from Birmingham, Denis Law was Scottish, George Best was from Belfast and Bobby Charlton was from Newcastle. Thus, the 1968 and 1999 Manchester United teams capture the different recruitment and training strategies of the international and transnational era exactly. United's 1968 team was British but its 1999 team consisted of a core of local Mancunian players as part of a transnational squad. Likewise, as we have already noted in Chapter 4, Liverpool's great teams of the 1970s and 1980s were British in constitution, relying in particular on outstanding Scottish players such as Sounness, Hansen and Dalgleish. Local talent was present at both Manchester United and Liverpool during this period, Brian Kidd and Phil Thompson being obvious examples, but the local origins of these players were weighted with no special significance. In the international era, then, the geography of European football was characterised by national hierarchies, in which the big clubs acted as focal points, recruiting talent from more or less isolated national economies. The national economies have now been penetrated and webs of recruitment extend transnationally from key clubs, which are simultaneously increasingly committed to their local area. As clubs broaden their range, the local area becomes invested with much more significance.

It is interesting that this emphasis on the development of local talent is not simply an economic strategy but has important cultural and political implications. Manchester United fans have taken pride in the development of local talent but it is important to recognise that this pride in local talent is also a new phenomenon. The presence or absence of significant local talent in United's teams in the past was more or less irrelevant and the national recruitment of talent from across Britain was regarded as wholly legitimate. It is interesting that a similar promotion of local talent is detectable at other major clubs in Europe. At Barcelona for instance, many fans were disillusioned with Louis van Gaal's employment of an excessive quantity of non-Catalan and particularly Dutch players under his management between 1997 and 2000. Fans complained about the de-Catalanisation of Barcelona Football Club (Burns 1999: 27; King, J. 2000a:). In an interview with the leaders of *L'Elefant Blau*, the politically active fan group at Barcelona, Alfons Godall and Armando Caraben rejected this de-Catalanisation of the football team regarding it as a threat to the identification of the fans with the club and as a corruption of the ideal of Barcelona Football Club. However, while the Catalonianism of Barcelona Football Club has always been important, the origins of the players themselves do not seem to have been as significant to the fans as they have now become. For instance, before the ruling in the early 1960s outlawing the use of foreign players, Barcelona had twenty internationals from seven countries on their books while most of the other players – especially the important ones – came from other parts of Spain (Radnedge 1997c: 109). During this period, Barcelona was without question a very important symbol of Catalan identity, especially since Castilian and Francoist hegemony was at its most repressive, but the development of local talent was regarded as irrelevant. The Catalan pride of Barcelona Football Club was demonstrated by their victories on the field (especially over Real Madrid) but players represented Catalonia merely by wearing the famous blue and maroon stripes of the club, whatever their origins. Even Cruyff, who has come to be regarded as the embodiment of Catalan autonomy by Barcelona fans, was most successful as Barcelona's manager when he did not field Catalan-based teams. For instance, his European Cup team of 1992 contained only two home-grown players, Guardiola and Ferrer (King, J. 2000a: 235) and, ironically, when he did introduce Catalan players to the first team in significant numbers in the 1995–96 season, mainly due to the failure of his foreign signings (ibid.: 238), the club won nothing and he was sacked (ibid.: 2). Localism has become important to the directors and the fans in the post-Bosman era. There is now a new emphasis on the connection between the club and the city in which it is situated. This new transnational order centred on the big clubs is a paradoxical phenomenon, however, for while this regime breaks down the borders which characterised the international era, it also encourages a growing emphasis by both directors and fans on the production of local talent.

Not only has the development of youth schemes involved the institution of in-house training programmes but it has also involved the growing vertical integration between the biggest clubs and smaller European clubs. These clubs are used as feeders for talent and as places where young talent can gain experience in their earlier years: 'We are going in the direction which is close to the American system where you have the top clubs and the farm teams. It depends on the philosophy of the club. I personally think that it would be very useful for big clubs to have a system of farm teams because you cannot do certain activities yourself' (Umberto Gandini, organisational director, AC Milan, personal interview, 15 March 2000).

Significantly, this vertical integration between bigger and smaller clubs has not taken place at the national level. A transnational network tying smaller clubs to the growing big city giants of European football has begun to emerge. Thus, Manchester United has formal links with Royal Antwerp, Shelbourne FC in Ireland, and FC Fortune in South Africa, as well as two clubs in Sweden; these clubs gather local talent and serve as nurseries for young reserve team players.[6] In 1998 Arsenal arranged a five-year agreement with St. Etienne in which the London club has invested 3.5 million francs in return for first choice of promising stars, whom St. Etienne have had a good record in producing (Eastham 1999: 72). Similarly, in 1999, Ajax bought a 51 per cent stake in Obuassi Goldfields FC of Ghana, which club was renamed Goldfields Sporting Club after the attempt to set up Cape Town Ajax failed. The South African Football Association prohibited the merger of the two local clubs which would create a farm team for Ajax there (*Soccer Investor* 2000b). The major European clubs are in a process of developing vertically integrated transnational networks which allow these clubs to compete more effectively in the global market for players. Significantly, the new networks extending from big clubs constitute a new system of redistribution at the transnational level which is likely to sustain smaller clubs economically, just as the old redistributive mechanisms used to sustain the smaller teams within the national league. As Rick Parry noted, the clubs are not redistributing their wealth out of charity or implementing the kind of utopian schemes advocated by Lenz. In the transnational era, the integration of smaller clubs over a wide geographical area is a rational strategy since the big clubs benefit directly from their investment. It constitutes a very different form of corporatism from the league-based solidarity of the international era but it is nevertheless a recognisable redistributive system.

The kinds of networks which the biggest European football clubs are developing accords with the wider strategy of capitalist companies noted by Sassen (1991). Her work reveals that company headquarters are still usually situated in the major metropolitan areas but that many of the subsidiary activities of these companies have been moved away from the metropoles to smaller centres where rent and labour is cheaper. A paradoxical process of centralisation and dispersion is occurring simultaneously. As the outlets become more diverse, the centres are becoming more important as they control and administer a wider network of subsidiaries. In European football, the development of these dispersed but centralised networks is also evident. We are seeing the emergence of transnational networks for the development, training and transfer of football players focused on the various major football clubs in Europe which subvert old national boundaries. This process amounts to the emergence of a new geography of European football. The national leagues and national television markets remain important, determining which are the major clubs but those clubs are now operating in a new environment. The once unified and sovereign national leagues with their own internal hierarchies have been transformed as new transnational webs emerge. Whereas the big city clubs were dominant in previously isolated national economies, they now form a new pan-European network which is increasingly important in structuring the sport.

Reactions to Bosman

The Bosman ruling has created a new transnational geography. As individuals like Kenyon make clear, this has created certain problems for the clubs but the post-Bosman situation can scarcely be described as chaotic. Yet, this is exactly how UEFA and the national federations have looked upon the ruling:

> The Bosman ruling and its consequences have destabilised European football. Contracts, transfers, competitions, rights sales – everything has been called into question, and the criteria used as a reference point have often been only of an economic nature, thereby creating the danger of a concentration of power and, consequently, a loss of the desired balance. [Gerhard Aigner, UEFA secretary, UEFAflash 2000]

Aigner usefully highlights the reasons why institutions like UEFA fear the liberalisation of the game. The Bosman ruling is an application of the free market to football – its criteria are only of an 'economic nature' – with the effect that new centres of power, the major clubs, are emerging to challenge the dominance of UEFA. The Bosman ruling does not threaten the viability of professional football *per se* but it does undermine the political economic regime in which UEFA enjoyed a position of pre-eminence. The national federations have been similarly concerned by the ruling so that while Adam Crozier, the chief executive of the FA, regarded the post-Bosman emphasis on youth development as beneficial, ultimately he dismissed the ruling: 'It has created havoc for people really' (personal interview, 11 April 2000). This hyperbolic view of the Bosman ruling is echoed elsewhere by representatives of national organisations. For instance, Gordon Taylor, while supporting the Bosman case as president of FIFPro, has emphasised the problems which the ruling posed for the development of native English players in his role as the chairman of the English Professional Footballers' Association:

> We were very much aware of the Bosman judgment and we supported him, both financially and morally, though we knew in England, it could disrupt our system – and was probably bound to. We thought we had a pretty fair system. We also had built into the system a 5 per cent levy on every fee that goes to a player's pension scheme that gives them a tax-free sum on retirement at age 35; that is for all players. In a strange way, those who are loyal do better than those who move. FIFPro knew that the problem it could create was freeing up the movement of labour. There should be no restrictions. Also the challenge was, of course – which Bosman's lawyers threw in – the limit on the number of foreign players. This was almost as a side issue but it was that side issue that we would worry about because we knew it would free up labour, but particularly cross-border, and that they would look at the restrictions because we had a maximum of three foreign players. All the players' associations were uneasy about that because, particularly countries like ourselves, Italy, Spain and Germany, knew that there would be a gravitation to their countries because they are high-economy football countries. That is a fair description. That is exactly what happened. It made it a lot easier. You suddenly had players like your Zolas coming over etc. ... It really increased a flow that had started as a bit of a trickle with non-EU players in 1978 with Villa and Ardiles, coming into a stream now ... You've got a situation where Chelsea play a side without one United Kingdom player which would have been unheard of in the past. There is a feeling from the players' body that we should try and stop this movement of youngsters. [Gordon Taylor, personal interview, 10 February 2000]

There are very significant concerns about the new transnational market for players, such as the exploitation of young players, especially from Africa, but Taylor's ultimate objection to the post-Bosman situation is that it poses a threat to the employment opportunities of native players in England; he is notably critical of Chelsea's foreign side. Yet, in the past, English club teams have often featured players from Scotland, Wales, Northern Ireland and the Republic of Ireland. While those players were not regarded as a threat to the development of national talent even though these players did not represent England, the influx of other European nationalities is now arbitrarily regarded as a threat to the production of national talent. In fact, the liberalisation of the European market for players increases the employment opportunities of British players who are now free to play anywhere in the EU, as Owen Hargreaves' career at Bayern Munich demonstrates. The Bosman ruling does not limit player opportunities *per se* but it does curtail the power of nationally based players' unions and, as chairman of the English players' union, Gordon Taylor's objections to the Bosman ruling are finally a defence of that institution which is threatened by the transnationalisation of the game. Reflecting Taylor's concerns about the Bosman ruling from his perspective as the chairman of a national players' union, the Spanish players' union threatened to strike in November 1998 over the influx of foreign players into the Spanish League. Before Bosman, foreign imports accounted for 14.5 per cent of the First Division workforce in Spain but by 1998 they accounted for 38.5 per cent and for the first time ever, the number of Spaniards registered as players fell below 300. In fact, the number of imports who have actually played has risen to nearly 45 per cent of the total footballers appearing in the league. If Atletico Bilboa, which fields only Basque players, is removed, the proportion of foreigners playing in the Spanish league is even higher (Turner 1998: 32). Nationally-based institutions like the players' unions and the federations reject the Bosman ruling because it constitutes a profound blow to the international order in which they had prospered. Significantly, the meltdown of European football predicted by the representatives of the international regime simply has not happened since the Bosman case. Certainly, there have been very significant changes to European football since 1995 but chaos has not descended. On the contrary, following the Bosman ruling, the transfer market was more active than ever; in the three years after the Court's ruling 'the nine most expensive transfers in world football have been recorded' (Radnedge 1999: 4). The Bosman ruling has not marked the end of European football but only the end of the international era. We are now entering a transnational era in which the big European clubs are emerging as the dominant force and which concentration is reconfiguring the geography of European football.

Given that the biggest clubs are the emergent force in the transnational era, it is significant that the directors of these clubs view the Bosman ruling very differently to the representatives of UEFA and the national federations. Although Rick Parry regarded the Bosman ruling as a poor judgment because it posited utopian forms of redistribution, many of the big European clubs recognise the legitimacy of the ruling. The very institutions whose authority has grown in this transnational era and who constitute the heart of European football now regard the legislation which frames this new order as legitimate:

> I don't agree that the Bosman ruling was good or not or a problem or not for football. But it was totally logical. Football has to understand – and everyone involved in football – we have to accept the rules of the countries and the rules of the European Community. I think it is stupid to try and exclude football all the time from the general rules. It is impossible. The Bosman rule, in my opinion, is very important but it is neither good nor bad. It is logical. It is understandable. We have to live with this. I don't feel that the Bosman ruling has been bad for professional clubs. [Juan Onieva, vice-president Real Madrid, personal interview, 19 April 2000]

> In origin, everyone thought it was a very bad move which came because there was not enough communication between the different parties and we just let the thing

happen. It was perceived as a disaster and I don't think it has been a disaster. I think that the Bosman ruling was somehow inevitable. There are some adjustments that it will bring in. But for the time being if that is the rule, we will just go with it. I don't think clubs have been affected so heavily as expected. Yes, it was problematic for the first two or three years but at the end of the day, the result is that the players are richer, the transfer market has increased in terms of prices and in terms of movement. Everybody was expecting no transfers at all because of the end of contract freedom of movement and I think we'd be in a situation where there would be a total freeze of transfers. I don't think it has created big negative aspects. [Umberto Gandini, organisational director, AC Milan, personal interview, 15 March 2000]

Bosman cannot be seen as good or bad, it is what it is: EU legislation. [Jaume Sobriques, FC Barcelona, personal interview, 22 May 2000]

Not only did the directors of these major clubs accept the Bosman ruling as legitimate but some of them approved of the fundamental principles of European integration which lay behind it:

This concept of national and foreigner. For me, I have never liked it. It is not a concept or idea of Europe that we should be thinking. I don't agree that the French is a foreigner and the German is a foreigner and the English is a foreigner. We have been in Europe for fifty years. The idea of Europe – we have to accept the idea that there is no difference between us. Why if I am a doctor, I can come to this country and work. If I am anything I can move all over Europe. Why if you are a football player, are you not allowed to do exactly the same? It is stupid, it is silly, trying to live with this idea. But in the end, identities in Europe are changing. What the Europe Union wants is the concept of a nationality of Europe. That means that we are going to lose the concept of English or Spanish or German or Italian. In line with this idea, professional football clubs and national teams will develop. [Juan Onieva, vice-president Real Madrid, personal interview, 19 April 2000]

Although Onieva may overstate the decline of nationalism as an identity, his point is important because it shows a profound commitment to the transnational European market beyond mere economic logic. His statement contrasts interestingly with Gordon Taylor's defence of national sovereignty, the two standing as reflections of alternative political economic regimes.

The Perugia Case

The Bosman ruling transformed the political economy of European football. Significantly, this transnational order has been affirmed by the recent 'Perugia case'. In 1998, Perugia were interested in signing Massimo Lombardo who was coming to the end of his contract at the Swiss club, Grasshoppers Zurich.

Lombardo had dual Swiss and Italian nationality and consequently Perugia argued that no transfer fee was required on the expiration of his contract; he was an EU national. Grasshoppers insisted that since he was Swiss, he was not subject to the Bosman rule and a transfer fee was necessary. Perugia complained to the Commission and the case initiated a major investigation of the European transfer system (Cohen-Tanugi and Rush 2000; Butler and Nunns: 13). The Perugia case was brought before the European Court of Justice in July 2000 and UEFA were given until the end of August to propose a new system. In the event, there were a series of negotiations between UEFA, FIFA, FIFPro and the Commission between August 2000 and March 2001 when the Commission belatedly made its final ruling on the Perugia case. UEFA seemed to have learnt from the Bosman case and their negotiations with the Commission had some impact on the final ruling, for the transfer system was not abolished outright as originally advocated by the Commission. Transfer fees for players under contract were preserved in order to ensure the redistribution of wealth in the leagues. (Butler and Nunns 2001). Indeed, 5 per cent of the transfer fees of a player over the age of 23 was to be cascaded down to the club that developed and trained him. Further restrictive measures were put in place to stabilise the market. During the season, transfers were limited to two windows and the contract was structured to hinder player movement. The minimum contract length is one year, while contracts will be protected up to three years for players under 28 and two years for players over 28. Players risk sanctions if they breach these protected contract periods (Butler and Nunns 2001; Cohen-Tanugi and Rush 2000). Players risk bans of up to four months and fines if they breach their contracts by transferring elsewhere without their club's consent.

The Perugia case is far less radical than the Bosman case. Indeed, the new contract system limits player movement more than was previously the case. Denoting their displeasure at the new system, FIFPro walked out on talks before they were concluded, alleging connivance between the clubs, UEFA and the Commission:

> The principles are ambiguous and open to different interpretations. In claiming to allow players greater freedom it appears players can leave clubs, but all the 'exits' have been blocked up by various measures. As a result, it is difficult to see any particular benefits for players compared to our present situation, and there are clear instances where it is worse. [Gordon Taylor, chief executive, FIFPro, *World Soccer* 2001, p.13].

Jean-Jacques Amorfini, the French players' union vice-president was more vitriolic: 'They are treating the players like imbeciles. We have been taken for turkeys' (*World Soccer* 2001). Given the exit of FIFPro from talks and their evident dissatisfaction with the result, the durability of the Perugia ruling seems unlikely. It is probable that FIFPro will stage another test-case like Bosman to challenge the ruling and, given the priority of Article 48 in European law, it seems highly unlikely that they would not be able to demonstrate that the proposed contract system is restrictive. It is entirely possible that within five years, employment conditions in European football will have been completely liberalised, concentrating power in the hands of the big clubs and diminishing the authority of national federations yet further. It is possible that the Commission, aware of the political costs of intervening in football, may have played a subtle game, whereby they have given the players the clear opportunity to initiate potentially unpopular proceedings by challenging the legality of present arrangements. The Commission may eventually achieve the desired legal outcome without incurring the negative publicity which might follow a radical intervention into football.

The Bosman ruling has had profound economic effects on European football, which are likely to be exacerbated by the repurcussions of the Perugia case in the future. Neither the Bosman nor the Perugia ruling have meant the end of football but they do mark its reorganisation with the emergence of new networks of power. However, although the Bosman ruling was a key moment in European football, it has only had profound effects because the biggest clubs in Europe have, in the late 1990s, been wealthy enough to exploit the transnational market which it has introduced. Although gate revenue remains the single most important revenue for all major European football clubs, in the 1990s, television revenue was the fastest growing income stream. This expansion in television income has been the prime factor enabling the biggest clubs to exploit the post-Bosman market. As Lorenzo Sanz, the president of Real Madrid from 1996 to 2000, noted: 'Bosman broke down the national barriers but without the money from television, no-one could have taken such advantage' (Lorenzo Sanz, President Real Madrid, in Radnedge 1997b: 22). In order to comprehend the transnationalisation of European football, it is essential that the new relationship between television and football is examined since it is developments in the media sector that have driven the changes to European football.

Notes

1 Interestingly, Rick Parry noted that Van Miert, the commissioner for competition, was 'quite taken' with the English transfer system which was liberal but also allowed for compensation (personal interview, 9 February 2000).
2 Marcel Benz, a secretary at UEFA, defended the organisation's strategy in the Bosman case, citing the 'three plus two' arrangement, and claiming that 'at the end it was the decision of the court' about which UEFA could do nothing (personal interview, 12 April 2000).

3 Richard Worth, managing director of Television Event and Media Marketing (TEAM), suggested the relations have improved between UEFA and the Commission since that time; 'Now of course, they are very much hand in hand with them, actually talking to them daily at the moment (Richard Working, TEAM, 2 March 2000). Gerhard Aigner affirmed this new relationship: 'Football's authorities are pleased to have found among the political authorities of the European Union ears that are willing to listen to their problems as well as a readiness to work together to resolve them. The new European Commissioner for Sport, Viviane Reding, has set an example in terms of this attitude' (Aigner 1999: 1). UEFA's new relationship to the Commission suggests that the institution recognised the effects of their arrogance during the Bosman case.

4 Big clubs are defined by four factors: attendances, their television audience figures, turnover and success. Together these determine a club's status. Clearly, the status of a big club is neither absolute nor objective. Clubs can lose or gain this status if there is a general decline in the four factors.

5 In his recent work on football, Richard Giulianotti has argued that teams have become post-Fordist because the tactics and players they use are more flexible than in the past (1999: 134). It is not clear that this is true since Ajax's Total Football of the early 1970s was certainly as flexible as anything that has appeared in the 1990s. Rather the post-Fordism of contemporary football seems to lie in the accumulation of playing squads which allow the big clubs to be flexible at the strategic rather than tactical level, resting players for games during the course of the season so that they are better able to compete in both domestic and European competitions.

6 One of the reasons why Manchester United has had to extend its operations abroad is that in the late 1990s, football academies were set up in each area to which local boys were affiliated. With the establishment of the academies, clubs could no longer sign boys who lived more than an hour-and-a-half's travel away. As Eric Harrison, the former youth coach at the club, has noted, it would only take one parent to challenge this ruling with the European Court of Justice for it to be abolished as restrictive: 'Young players have to live within 90 minutes travelling time of the training centre and it causes problems. There are a lot of obstacles put in our way to signing a player from, say Gloucester and I think it's wrong, if any parent challenged it in the European Court they would win hands down. Players are being restricted' (*United We Stand* 2001b).

Chapter 6
The Television

The Deregulation of Broadcasting in Europe

From the 1930s to the 1980s, broadcasting in European was organised on a public service basis; television was funded by a licence fee and closely controlled by the state.[1] Public service broadcasting was hegemonic in Europe at the time because nation-states recognised the political importance of the new media and were powerful enough to take control of this new sector of the economy. Consequently, the form of European broadcasting in the post-War period reflected the wider Keynesian political consensus (see King 1998b). From the 1970s, new forms of broadcasting were being developed which threatened to undermine the technological basis of public service broadcasting. Cable and satellite television, already in use in the United States, promised to increase the number of channels which would be transmittable in analogue and, in the light of this technological expansion, the strict limitations imposed by public service broadcasting began to look untenable. Certainly, the technological development of cable and satellite delivery systems was very important to the collapse of the public service system but, as with the public service broadcasting regime itself, the introduction of this technology cannot in and of itself explain the deregulation of broadcasting in the 1980s. The introduction of new technology is, as Williams has shown (1990), never automatic but presupposes a particular social situation in which certain groups regard technological developments as useful and appropriate. (See also Collins 1979 and 1990 for the same argument.)

From the 1970s, the development of satellite and cable technology was regarded as desirable because certain private companies – and states themselves – recognised the economic potential of these new transmission systems. This new technology promised to transform an underperforming sector, funded primarily by pre-paid licences, into a dynamic and highly profitable new market. In fact, only in the 1980s were new media consortiums of sufficient size to exploit the technological opportunity presented by satellite and cable transmission. Rupert Murdoch's News Corporation is one of the most important and interesting examples of these new media companies, which emerged in the 1970s through a series of takeovers and mergers to become a key player in the emergent satellite market of the 1980s. At the same time,

Murdoch has promoted a free market paradigm. Against the old public service system, Murdoch has persistently prioritised the free market against public sector monopolists who 'distort the market' (*The Economist* 1998b). For Murdoch, television broadcasting should not be administered by the state but its structure and content should, given available technological capabilities, be determined by market forces: 'Why should television be exempt from the laws of supply and demand, any more than newspapers, journals, magazines, books or feature films?' (Murdoch 1989: 8). Murdoch has summarised his position economically: '[private] competition is much to be preferred to [state] monopoly' (ibid.). Recently, Murdoch has advocated these free market views at a European level in a speech at the 1998 European Audiovisual Conference in Birmingham. There he announced his support for the European Commission Green Paper on regulation and applauded the efforts of Jacques Santer and Karel Van Miert, the competitions commissioner, to 'eliminate barriers to the free flow of capital, labour and talent among member states' and 'to break down the barriers to competition' (*The Economist* 1998b). For Murdoch, the liberalisation of the media markets has been essential to his entrepreneurial operations since it allowed him to enter new media markets. In fact, Murdoch's appeals to liberalisation did not ultimately introduce a genuinely free market into broadcasting but rather legitimated the replacement of an inconveniently obstructive state monopoly, with a private oligopoly or even monopoly. In this way, Murdoch is the embodiment of Schumpeter's entrepreneur who produces profit by creating a new market in which he enjoys a temporary monopoly (see Collins 1990: 124–33). However, Murdoch's free market rhetoric has served an important role. Not only has it influenced government policy but it has sensitised the public to the development of corporate media power, emphasising the advantages of being a consumer of media services rather than a citizen who pays a licence fee. It has altered the public's expectation of the media in line with the kinds of economic and cultural reforms which Murdoch has advocated.

Although media moguls and their new media conglomerates were crucial to the transformation of the media in western Europe from the 1980s, the deregulation of broadcasting was not forced upon unwilling governments. On the contrary, in the early to mid-1980s, governments deregulated television themselves to exploit the economic opportunities presented by the new technologies. Thus, in 1983, the British government issued a second independent broadcasting licence to Channel 4 and, later in the decade, it eventually gave a broadcasting licence to two competing satellite companies, British Satellite Broadcasting and Murdoch's Sky Television. After vast initial losses, the two companies were forced to merge. The merger was, in fact, a victory for Murdoch as he took the majority of the shares in the new company, now called BSkyB, and his staff and infrastructure remained in place (see Chippendale and Franks 1992). In the other major markets in Europe, similar transformations have occurred. These were particularly notable in France. Under President Giscard d'Estaing, the French public service system was liberalised in the 1970s by dismantling the *Office de Radiodiffusion Télévision Française* (OTRF). This liberalisation was carried even further by President Mitterand when, in 1982, the first public service channel was fully privatised to become TF1 (Kuhn 1995). In 1983, Canal Plus, the first subscription station in Europe, was established. After an initially slow take-up of subscribers, this company established itself very successfully in a niche, focusing on films and sports, including French League football. As we shall see, from these small beginnings, Canal Plus (eventually integrated into the utilities giant Vivendi) became a major force in the European media in the 1990s.

In Germany, a similar process was also taking place. There were extensive debates in the Federal Republic from the late 1970s onwards about the validity of the public service monopoly and gradually the pressure for deregulation became overwhelming (Humphreys 1990: 193). In 1982, the public service monopoly was finally broken and the new marketised regime of broadcasting was introduced with the licensing of SAT 1, West Germany's first private commercial satellite consortium, which was owned by the global media giants Bertelsmann and the smaller, but nevertheless important, Kirch Group. SAT 1 started broadcasting in 1984 and was later joined by other private satellite broadcasters, the most significant of which was RTL Plus, owned by CLT. New privatised platforms – some of them delivered by satellite or cable – also appeared in Italy and Spain. In Italy, the three-channel public service monopoly was broken in the late 1970s by four nationwide commercial networks owned by Silvio Berlusconi and the publishers Rizzoli, Mondodori and Rusconi. This period of Italian broadcasting was chaotic with excessive deregulation leading to an overly crowded and confused marketplace, though this situation was somewhat resolved by the emergence of Berlusconi's Mediaset network. In 1983–84, Berlusconi's new Mediaset station bought up two other channels which were in financial difficulty with the result that he owned the three major private channels with three others remaining public. His domination in the television sector, especially after his subsequent purchase of Italy's largest publisher Mondodori, have raised concerns about his monopoly position, while the low-budget content of his channels has also been criticised. In Spain, deregulation began in 1983, with a law which established a regional channel alongside existing public TVE channels and, in 1988, three private channels were allowed to broadcast nationally, eventually leading to the establishment of Antena 3, Tele 5 and Canal Plus which, as in France, broadcast as a pay-TV channel.

Digital Television

By the 1990s, the new private networks such as Canal Plus, BSkyB and SAT 1 had consolidated but, in the middle of the 1990s, by eliminating the band limitations of the analogue system, the introduction of digital broadcasting has facilitated further deregulation of the system. The digitalisation of broadcasting in the 1990s has complicated the map of the European media. The broadcasting systems in each country have become increasingly Byzantine, especially compared with the two- or three-channel systems which characterised the public service era. However, certain broad outlines are detectable, especially the transnational integration of the European media conglomerates. Even the very biggest consortiums, like Bertelsmann and News Corporation, have had to merge and ally with other firms in the risky and expensive development of digital television, while smaller media companies have been simultaneously absorbed by larger ones. Thus CLT-UFA, which was a very important network in Germany and Holland, was purchased by Bertelsmann in the 1990s. Consequently, since the late 1990s five companies – Bertelsmann, News Corporation (normally in the form of BSkyB), Canal Plus (owned by the utilities giant Vivendi), the Kirch Group and Mediaset (as a subsidiary of Fininvest) – have been involved in a complex and unstable series of alliances and oppositions. Each new digital venture has been supported by an alliance between two or more of these companies, and opponents over certain ventures have allied with each other in other markets. Thus, Berlusconi opposed Murdoch's entry into the Italian market and refused to give Murdoch shares in Mediaset (Betts 1998: 5) but he was allied with Murdoch as a joint share holder in Kirch (Betts and Studemann 1998: 24). Similarly, in February 1999, Murdoch's News Corporation and Canal Plus were exploring the possibility of pooling their European pay-TV interests to create a dominant player in the sector (Betts and Gapper 1999: 29) but, later in the year, Vivendi (the owners of Canal Plus) bought a 25 per cent stake in Murdoch's BSkyB (Newman, 1999) which threatened Murdoch's control over his own satellite venture. Since the late 1990s, then, the European media scene has been characterised by a series of strategic bouts between these groups as each vies for advantage over the others, using different partners at different times. In 2002, the Kirch Group succumbed to the pressures of this marketplace and was in the process of liquidation. Its various assets were integrated into the four remaining giants. The four remaining companies (Bertelsmann, News Corporation, Mediaset and Canal Plus) are now the key players in the new media markets in Europe and are bound together in competition and cooperation with each other. The future structure of European broadcasting will emerge from the eventual consolidation of the currently unstable alliances between these groups, though its exact form remains as yet unclear.

Significantly, the European Commission has recognised the importance of these transnational links in the development of a genuinely European media market which will ensure that Europe is competitive in the digital age. European media consortiums are presently of insufficient size to deter global and particularly US competition and the Commission has employed liberalisation to promote concentration. This approach was demonstrated when, for instance, the Commission ruled against a merger of Bertelsmann and Kirch over the development of Germany's first digital system DF1 in 1998 (Studemann 1998a). For the Commission, such a merger was unconscionable because it would have rendered the German digital market impenetrable to any external competition, closing off this key European market. Rupert Murdoch, who by the mid-1990s was very conscious of his absence from the European market, publicly supported this EU ruling against the Bertelsmann and Kirch digital merger since it prevented the closure of the German market to him (Studemann 1998b). Murdoch's relief at the ruling and his intense activity on the European front in the 1990s has demonstrated that European media entrepreneurs are increasingly looking to European rather than national markets to exploit the potential of the new digital media: 'There are two great markets in the world – one is North America and the other is Europe. They are almost equal in size and you cannot globalise a company without having some major activities in Europe' (Rupert Murdoch, cited in Betts and Gapper 1998: 33). It is unclear what blocks of interest will emerge out of the cross-cutting ownership ties between the four key players or whether a single international pay television consortium will ever develop (Bell 1998). However, the development of digital broadcasting and the cross-ownerships between the four key players mark a profound liberalisation of the former national public service system, which was still intact across Europe only twenty years ago.

This new media environment had a critical impact on the transformation of football in the 1990s as the financial imperatives of these companies have transformed the economic structure of the game: 'The global de-regulation of all media means that the whole basis for the way football is presented has altered beyond recognition over the past decade' (Guest and Law 1997: 14). There are obvious reasons why these companies have invested in football. The viability of these new satellite, cable and digital networks is dependent on content, that is, on the programmes which these networks broadcast: 'The moral is: first you win the content, then you win the customer' (CIT 1999: 4). In the intensely competitive digital market, content will determine the chances of a network's success just as it did in the development of satellite and cable channels. This struggle for content between the new networks has been a critical factor in the transformation of European football in the 1990s, since sport is a prime form of content: 'Sport absolutely overpowers film and everything else in the entertainment genre [and] football, of all sports, is number one' (Rupert Murdoch, cited in Guest and Law 1997: 24). Sport is then, to use Murdoch's term, a 'battering ram' by which new networks can break into and indeed create new markets (Harveson 1996). Murdoch himself had direct personal experience of the importance of sport and football to the development of new media networks. Even after the merger of BSB and Sky Television in 1990, BSkyB was still making vast losses until it secured the exclusive rights to broadcast the new English Premier League (see Chippendale and Franks 1992; MMC 1999: 62–6). On the back of its coverage of Premier League football, BSkyB has become a profitable and very significant network on the European scene.

The power of sports programming lies in certain obvious characteristics of sport. Sport is compelling viewing because the outcome is always uncertain. Dramatic and unpredictable events do occur and, unlike film, they are unplanned by the programme producers. The final minutes of the 1999 European Cup Final encapsulate exactly why sport is the most significant form of programming. In addition, football has some specific advantages over other sports since its rules are very simple, with minimal stoppages. Rugby League and Rugby Union even more so are seriously disadvantaged in this way. Moreover, since the pace of football is determined by the ball which is passed from player to player, rather than carried as in rugby, the game is free-flowing. It might also be noted that the sheer size of the ball, which is plainly visible at all times to the viewer (and attending crowd), renders the game particularly compelling in comparison to games like hockey, ice-hockey and cricket where the ball or puck disappear from view at certain moments because they are small and travel so fast. In his history of football in the 1950s, Geoffrey Green has noted the significance of the visibility of the football, especially under floodlights: 'Football under floodlights was highly theatrical; the use of the white ball made play easier to follow and the movements themselves gave the impression of greater speed and excitement' (Green 1974d: 26). Football has certain intrinsic characteristics which make it particularly appropriate for television, then, but it would be wrong to argue that these features were the ultimate reason for the new networks' emphasis on football. For instance, in the Asian subcontinent, cricket rather than football captures the imagination of the public and constitutes the most important sport programming there. The particular attraction of football to broadcasters and viewers in Europe lies in the position of football in European culture. Football is powerful programming because it has established itself in the urban cultural traditions of Europe. In the final instance, this social and cultural context rather than any essential qualities of the game has ensured the compelling power of football as a form of programming which the new media companies have sought to exploit in the 1990s. The deregulation of television has affected European football directly because live football coverage is critical to new media networks and in pursuing that content, these networks have altered the sport.

The Deregulation of Domestic League Broadcasting

As football has become a key form of programming, recorded highlights on the public channels have been replaced by live games on new private subscription channels. In comparison with live transmission, recorded highlights are weak programming. Consequently, by the mid-1990s, the rights for live league matches in France, Germany, Britain, Spain and Italy, the five major European markets, were all owned by new private companies and, towards the end of the 1990s, increasingly broadcast digitally. France was the first major European market in which this transformation in the broadcasting of football took place. In 1985, the newly formed subscription channel, Canal Plus, won the contract for live French First Division Football, initially paying the French League 250,000 francs for each match it broadcast. Canal Plus has remained the sole broadcaster of league football for over a decade, though the value of the games has risen steeply. In 1997, for instance, the company paid the league 6 million francs a game (*Ligue Nationale de Football*, personal communication, 23 February 2000). During the early 1990s Canal Plus eventually converted their satellite network to digital transmission (Hare 1999: 309–10) and, in competition with this development, TF1 set up their own digital satellite consortium in the mid-1990s called TPS (*Télévision par Satellite*). As a result, a new contract was signed for First Division French football in July 1999, with TPS and Canal Plus splitting the digital rights to the league between them, though the channels, France Télévision, Eurosport and TF1 have also bought various highlight and other rights packages. TPS has bought the rights to six pay-per-view games.

The purchase of exclusive rights to the English Premier League has already been mentioned (see King 1998c) but it is worth noting that the deregulatory pattern demonstrated in France was replicated in England. Under the public service system, the price of English football was suppressed by an informal cartel between the BBC and ITV. However, in 1988, as ITV came under pressure from new satellite and cable networks, this company broke the cartel and broadcast thirty live games a season from then until 1992. Any vestiges of the old public service system were finally broken when BSkyB won the subsequent contract in 1992, removing live top division league football from free-to-air television. Given that BSkyB won the next contract in 1996 and a further three-year contract in 2000, it is unlikely that live English Premier League football will ever be shown on free-to-air in Britain again. In retrospect, ITV's contract can be seen as marking a transition to this new free market and now digitalised system.

Similarly in Germany, the Bundesliga was broadcast by the ARD and ZDF, the two public service channels, from 1965 until 1988 but from then on the rights for live football have been held by new private subscription channels. From 1988 to 1992, UFA and RTL held the rights for the Bundesliga and they were succeeded by SAT 1 and ISPR until the most recent deal, when Premiere, a digital subscription channel, owned by Kirch, Bertelsmann and BSkyB, have taken the rights until the 2003–04 season. Significantly, Premiere have introduced a pay-per-view facility as well as offering differently priced season tickets depending on the matches a viewer wants to see.

Although the television contract for football was deregulated by the 1990s in France, Germany and England, in all three countries collectivist principles still hold. Neither Canal Plus, BSkyB nor Premiere pay the clubs directly; the contract is paid to the league in each of these countries which then redistribute this revenue to the clubs. Certainly, the revenue is not shared completely evenly since clubs are rewarded for finishing in higher positions in the league in France and England but even in England, which is a highly marketised league, the biggest clubs still support this collective redistribution of television income:

> Most people would assume we would [support individual television contracts]. Our view is that there has to be a healthy Premier League that supports football in the UK and that supports everybody's economy that is associated with it. So that the Italian model whereby four people get three times more than somebody else; I am sure we would not agree to that. So we think there has to be a core funding that benefits the Premier League. [Peter Kenyon, personal interview, 3 March 2000]

> Even as a big club we support the principle of the collective selling of TV rights. [Rick Parry, personal interview, 9 February 2000]

By contrast, in Italy and Spain, the deregulation of television has been more radical, since the collective contracts in these markets has been fragmented into group or even individual deals with the clubs. In Italy, as in the other countries, the old public service system had broadcast highlights of Serie A until 1994, when pay-TV was introduced (James and Sturgess 1997: 6). Following this, in 1996, state-owned RAI temporarily lost a three-year contract to broadcast the league to Vittoria Cecchi Gori's Telemontecarlo network though, in the event, Telemontecarlo was unable to service the contract and it was returned to RAI (Guest and Law 1997a: 15). Telemontecarlo's failed attempt to win the rights to Serie A was the beginning of the transformation in Italy. In the same year Telepiu, a Canal Plus subsidiary (part-owned by Berlusconi and Kirch) began to screen all Serie A games live on pay-TV (James and Sturgess 1997: 6; Guest and Law 1997a: 15). In 1998, when the contract for Serie A was renewed, the collective Serie A deal with the RAI was replaced by a series of packages to digital channels. Telepiu Digital Plus signed up three of the 'big seven' clubs – Milan, Juventus, Inter – and the smaller southern club Napoli for its pay-per-view contract (Morrow 1999: 24) while Stream, a new network owned by News Corporation (marking the very significant entry of Rupert Murdoch into the Italian marketplace) and Telecom Italia, signed up the remaining four 'big seven' clubs, Fiorentina, Lazio, Roma and Parma (*Soccer Investor* 2000e).[2] The directors of the clubs are fully aware of the market situation which has produced this explosion in rights value:

> We have a situation of two digital broadcasters on the market and that has obviously been the driving force behind the sky-rocketing of the prices. As long as there are two competitors, I think that football clubs will be safe. I am unable to rule out the possibility that they won't merge in the future and in that case, then certain amounts won't be paid again. [Umberto Gandini, organisational director, AC Milan, personal interview, 15 March 2000]

These directors have also argued strongly against collective television contracts:

> We broke the league because the revenue sharing system was not acceptable any more because the solidarity costs were at too high a level. We were funding the others too much. We also took the responsibility of understanding that we are the product which people are interested in. And, thank God, the legislator in Italy thought the same way and it seems that at the European level, they think the same way. There must be ways and means to protect other things. For instance, in Italy, we pay 18 per cent of our TV revenue to the visiting club. Why 18 and not 15 or 13 – because 18 was already in place as a way to share revenues from the gate receipts. Since we consider pay-per-view as an extension of the stadium, as a virtual stadium on top of a real audience, then if we are applying 18 per cent on the tickets, we should apply 18 per cent on the TV rights because we are talking about electronic tickets anywhere. So that is the system we put in place. Naturally, there are clubs which are benefiting much more than others but then we have a system within the League for rebalancing certain differences among the big clubs and the smaller clubs. [Umberto Gandini, organisational director, AC Milan, personal interview, 15 March 2000]

Gandini's argument against collective television contracts is interesting. Since Milan commands a large market on its own merits, it has a right to exploit its own commercial potential without being forced to redistribute its income: 'we are the product which people are interested in.' This is an important statement of liberal principles which differs from the national corporatist solidarities imposed in the international era. Gandini is not alone is denigrating collectivist arrangements and highlighting the injustice of this extraction of revenue from those clubs which earn it. Roberto Bettega, vice-president of Juventus, has confirmed this position:

> It is not just it was successful or was a good contract. The main thing is that for the first time the clubs, not just Juventus, Milan or Inter but Roma, Lazio, Piacenza, Fiorentina, Parma or Venezia – we have an agreement in our league that we could sell alone our TV rights, pay TV or pay-per-view worldwide. This is the first time in our history. Until last year, all the rights were sold together through the league. I am not saying that now is a better deal with bigger money. The Anti-Trust law in Italy

says that the distribution of TV rights are subject to the people driving the game. [Roberta Bettega, personal interview, 14 March 2000]

While Bettega might highlight the ethical dimension of the television contract in Italy in which all are now free to make their own deals, this situation plainly benefits Juventus, Milan and Inter more than Piacenza or Venezia. These big clubs, of course, are 'the people driving the game'. In Italy, the big clubs recognise that they are the attractive teams for television companies and, not unreasonably, question the collectivisation of television money. Since they earn the television revenue, they should also be the recipients of it. In the public service era, the problem of the equity of redistributing television revenue never arose because income from television was minimal and the limitation of player movement in that era necessarily reduced competition between the clubs, allowing clubs to adopt a less proprietorial attitude to the income they had generated. Such a position is untenable in the transnational era. The attitudes of Gandini and Bettega at Milan and Juventus, where they emphasise the entrepreneurial independence of the clubs, only reflect the wider economic situation in which clubs now find themselves. In 2002, the Italian situation became even more concentrated. The contract for the league as a whole collapsed when the broadcaster recognised that the rights were overvalued. The beginning of the season was delayed by a week as a result of new negotiations between the league and the broadcasting company. The situation was extremely serious for Italian professional football and various commentators suggested that this was the predicted nemesis of European football. In fact, no such nemesis followed. A new contract was signed with the league which seriously disadvantaged the smaller Serie A clubs whose television revenue with RAI was practically halved, from 88 million euros to just over 40 million euros; pay-per-view coverage was similarly reduced from 10 million euros to approximately 5 million euros (see *World Soccer* webpage <www.countryfile.co.uk/worldsoccer/newssept02/it0409html>). However, the 'big three' clubs, Inter, Milan and Juventus, retained their lucrative contract with Telepiu and have not been damaged seriously by this problem at all. Juventus, for instance, will receive approximately 60 million euros from the Telepiu contract in the 2002–03 season (see ibid.). Indeed, internally the rights dispute served only to accelerate the concentration of power in their hands.

The extreme deregulation demonstrated in Italy has also occurred in Spain where a complex distribution of rights has persisted. Nevertheless, while complex, the broad outlines of developments in Spain are clear. Telefonica and Sogecable own the rights to the Primera Liga until 2003 through their joint venture, Audiovisual. The Commission has expressed concern about this situation which it regards as potentially anti-competitive and, certainly, it does seem that the two networks have operated an informal cartel to reduce the cost of football rights. It is significant that the directors of the major clubs recognise that the current situation has not been beneficial to them. Juan Onieva noted that Real Madrid were 'going to suffer' in comparison with the Italian clubs as a result of this collective deal for the next few years (Juan Onieva, vice-president, Real Madrid, personal interview, 19 April 2000). Interestingly, Onieva made the same liberal argument proposed by Gandini and Bettega, that the clubs who created the television revenue by driving audience figures should be appropriately rewarded:

> Probably in the contract which is running now, the TV channels has paid too much. Not to all the clubs but to some clubs because when we look at audience figures, the situation is very clear. I'm talking here about pay-per-view which is like a supermarket ticket. Real Madrid takes almost 50 per cent. Barcelona reaches about 25 to 30 per cent. Atletico Madrid which is the third team gets 8 per cent. The others are 2, 3 per cent. [Juan Onieva, personal interview, 19 April 2000]

The implication of Onieva's statement is clear. Given that Real Madrid attracts the audiences, they should receive their dues from the television-generated revenue. Real are 'suffering' at present because the financial independence of each club has not been sufficiently recognised by the Spanish League. Any present disadvantages will certainly be erased with the new television deal for football which has already been signed. From 2003 through 2008, Via Digital will broadcast all of Barcelona's matches digitally while Canalsatellite Digital will broadcast Real Madrid's games. Consequently, from that date, there will be radical deregulation of Spanish football with the two top clubs making individual contracts with major television networks. Clearly, this deal is likely to establish Real Madrid and Barcelona in an unassailable position with regard to the rest of the Spanish League. Spain and Italy are extreme examples of the deregulation of television rights; not only are the rights held by newly privatized media companies but the contracts are drawn up between individual clubs or groups of clubs and these companies.

Although collective deals persist in England, France and Germany, it is not certain that such collectivism will necessarily endure in the face of transnational competition. There is already significant pressure on clubs in countries with collective deals. It is notable that Peter Kenyon added a significant caveat to his defence of the collective television contract: 'Having said that we then think there should be outside of that the opportunities for each club to exploit what it needs to exploit. It is a much more of a balanced approach than the Spanish or Italian model' (Peter Kenyon, chief executive, Manchester United, personal interview, 3 March 2000).[3] Rick Parry highlighted the dilemma which those clubs in collectivist leagues find themselves, where a genuine commitment to sporting equilibrium has become increasingly difficult to sustain:

> Liverpool's view is that the Premier League is enormously strong. We are entirely happy with the domestic league. We have a fundamental view that membership of football competitions should be driven by performance on the field and merit. *It is getting harder to sustain* with the revenues that are flowing in and with the consequences of not being in the Champions League but we are still very, very firm believers. [Rick Parry, chief executive, Liverpool Football Club, personal interview, 9 February 2000, emphasis added]

Consequently, although Parry and Kenyon are committed to collectivist television deals at the moment, the transnational context in which they now find themselves forces them to take a pragmatic line. It is clear that they could envisage a future in which collective deals became untenable because they jeopardised the European competitiveness of these clubs. In particular, with extreme deregulation in Italy and Spain, collective deals are becoming less tenable in other European markets.

Increasingly, national and European legislatory bodies are also opposed to collective deals, which are seen as restrictions of trade. Gandini revealed that the Italian legislator supported the deregulation of the contract for Serie A and similar legal pressure has been applied elsewhere. In 1999, the collective Premier League deal was challenged in the Restrictive Practices Court by the Office of Fair Trading in England. The OFT claimed that the Premier League deal was restrictive since it involved an exclusivity clause. This clause stated that only the company which held the rights to the Premier League could broadcast live matches; another broadcaster could not televise a Premier League game even if the central contract holder had no intention of broadcasting that game. The exclusivity clause in the contract certainly constituted a monopoly that limited access to rights and thereby falsely inflated the market value of the Premier League. However, despite the manifest restrictiveness of the exclusivity clause, the OFT case failed (see Szymanski 2000). The Restrictive Practices Court was persuaded that the public good produced by the collective sales of rights outweighed the formal illegality of this restrictive practice; sporting equilibrium was maintained through the collective sale and the increased value of the exclusive deal allowed English clubs to buy players otherwise unaffordable to them. However, following this case, the European Commission announced that it was concerned about the uncompetitiveness of the Premier League contract and threatened to examine its legality. Partially in response to this threat of European intervention, the new Premier League contract in 2000 included a pay-per-view package which went some way to rectifying the potentially anti-competitive exclusivity of the Premier League. That pay-per-view package, which was finally bought at a much reduced price by NTL, will be profitable only if NTL broadcasts the big clubs since only these clubs can attract a sufficient audience. Consequently, even in the English League where the principle of redistribution is recognised, the pressure for deregulation and concentration is growing.

In Germany, although the collectivist principles are enforced more rigorously, there has been sustained public criticism of this redistribution by the biggest three clubs, Bayern Munich, Borussia Dortmund and Bayer Leverkusen (Schaffrath 1999: 65). For instance, Micheal Meier, the general manager of Borussia Dortmund, predicted the demise of the strong centralism of the Bundesliga:

> We are decentralists by conviction. We had a vote in the Bundesliga where it was decided to negotiate TV deals centrally, and the German cartel court has decided that football has a privilege in this regard. But when Brussels decides that this is not the case, then this is not the case. This will happen – the question is when. [*Soccer Analyst* 2000c: 16]

The deregulation in Germany was initiated by the German Federal Court when it ruled against the German Football Federation that clubs could retain the television revenue from their European games (Demsey and Reilly 1998: 120; Bowley 1998b). Given the intentions of the biggest German clubs, it seems almost certain that the collectivised selling of football rights in Germany will undergo further fragmentation. In all the major European markets, football rights have been transformed by deregulation and, in each case, this has involved concentration at the biggest clubs.

Concentration

The deregulation of television has introduced ferocious competition into the once moribund market for football rights, as companies vie with each other for this essential content. This competition has increased the value of football astronomically. For instance, the BBC and ITV paid £1.5 million for the second half of the 1986 football league season between them. In 1992, BSkyB (with the BBC) paid £302 million for the exclusive rights to the Premier League for four years, but by 2000 the rights for only three years' live coverage was worth over £1 billion. Assuming that the BBC and ITV would have paid around £4 million for the 1985–86 season rights (had the Heysel disaster not dissuaded them from transmitting football until the second half of the season in January 1986), this increase in value constitutes an 830 per cent rise. This explosion is replicated elsewhere. As already mentioned, the cost of the French League rose from 250,000 francs a match in 1985 to 6 million francs in 1997 and the most recent deal has increased that price substantially. In 2000, in the light of the declining competitiveness of the French League, the negotiations over the television schedule for 2001 were brought forward to 1999 and packaged more imaginatively: nine lots were allocated over a three-year period and valued at a total of 800 million francs. The major lot was won by TPS which outbid Canal Plus with a 2 billion-franc contract (Glendinning 2000: 6; see also McKeever 1999: 167). In Germany, Bundesliga rights were sold for 12 million DM in the 1985–86 season but the most recent contract for 1999–2000 valued live and exclusive coverage of the same league at 175 million DM a season (*Stern* 1999). The new Premiere contract from 2000 to the 2003–04 season, is worth £893 million in total or nearly £300 million a season (*Soccer Investor* 2000e). In Italy, the Telemontecarlo's £90 million bid for Serie A forced RAI to pay £85 million a season. The digitalisation of Italian television and the development of pay-per-view has further increased the value of Italian football as Juventus' 60 million-euro contract for 2002–03 demonstrates.

In Spain, the same explosion in value has occurred. In 1985, TVE held the monopoly and paid £3.5 million to broadcast one weekly live game, international matches, the final of the King's Cup and a Sunday night highlights programme (Radnedge 1995b: 34). The deregulation of the early 1990s expanded both the number of matches shown on television and the number of companies broadcasting them; TVE1 and 2, Antena 3, Tele 5 and the pay-channel Canal Plus all broadcast football and together showed 512 live matches (ibid.). The overall fee paid for league football in the 1994–95 season was £26 million but this was dwarfed by the contracts which Barcelona and Real Madrid signed for 2003–08. Barcelona signed a contract with Via Digital for this five-year period worth £50 million a year (£240 million in total), while Real Madrid have a comparable contract with Canal Satellite Digital worth £259 million over the four-year period (Butler 1999; also *Soccer Investor* 2000f).

Although in Germany, France and England, a collective deal persists, the explosion in the value of the broadcasting rights to football has not benefited football clubs in each national league equally. On the contrary, the primary result of this hyperinflation of broadcasting rights in the 1990s has been to increase the wealth differentials between the biggest clubs and the rest. It is important here not to exaggerate this growing inequality since there has always been serious inequality in each national league, especially in the post-war period. The biggest city clubs, as the 1968 Chester report noted (Chester 1968), always tended to dominate even in the 1950s and 1960s and the history of the European Cup demonstrates that this was the case right across Europe. Nevertheless, although it is necessary to avoid overstatement, the deregulation of television has set a definable process in motion. The biggest city clubs in each country are now pulling decisively away from the others in their respective league since they benefit the most from deregulated television deals. For instance, in Italy, in 1996–97, the top seven clubs received 51.7 per cent of the encrypted pay-per-view revenue; in 1997–98 that figure had reached 59.4 per cent but in 1999–2000, those clubs received 76.1 per cent of all pay-per-view revenue (Jay Stewart, investment analyst, personal communication, 11 November 1999). The arrangement where Telepiu owned rights to the matches of Inter, Milan, Juventus and Napoli, while Stream broadcast the matches of Fiorentina, Parma, Roma and Lazio consolidated their financial position. The other clubs are limited to revenue from less lucrative sources and from their share of games when they play these big seven teams. After the difficulties with the television contract in 2002, the concentration of television revenue at the biggest clubs has increased while television revenue received by the smaller clubs has declined dramatically. The Barcelona and Real Madrid contracts with Via Digital and Canal Satellite Digital are perhaps the most dramatic example of this concentration of television revenue at the biggest clubs.

Even in those countries where the collective deal has persisted, the biggest clubs have still benefited the most. Although all the clubs in the Premier League receive a basic payment, Manchester United, Liverpool and Arsenal are advantaged in the distribution of Premier League television revenue because of the public interest in them. They have appeared more often on the television than other clubs and have also been able to earn the additional revenue attached to higher league positions. Over its first six years, between 1992–93 and 1997–98, the Premier League earned a total income of £361.32 million of which Manchester United, Liverpool and Arsenal received the highest proportion of the collective monies: 7.41, 6.42 and 6.31 per cent respectively (MMC 1999: 119, para 4.149). It is interesting that Liverpool have remained popular (like Manchester United between 1967 and 1993) even though they have not won the Football League since 1990. Significantly, apart from Blackburn who were relegated at the end of the 1998 season, the next biggest portion of television fees has been allotted to Chelsea but this club has received 5.37 per cent of television revenue – a full percentage point or about £3 million behind Arsenal (ibid.). The latest contract signed in the summer of 2000 is likely to exacerbate this division in English football because the division of the £1 billion will again be uneven while the pay-per-view revenue will go to the biggest clubs since they provide the only viable content. Clearly, the Champions League has been important in increasing this divide and its effects on the revenues of clubs will be discussed in Chapter 9, but many commentators in England now talk of a league within a league when discussing the Premier League, pointing to the financial gulf between the top clubs (Manchester United, Arsenal and Liverpool) and the rest. Although Germany remains far more collectivist than England, even there the redistribution of revenue to the lower division has been reduced; the first division of the Bundesliga now claims 70 per cent of the broadcasting revenue, surrendering only 30 per cent to the second division and Bayern Munich and Borussia have been able to claim a greater proportion of this money as a result of their popularity. In 2001, in response to the negotiations about a new contract, a nationwide fan group called 15:30 (after the starting time of Saturday

Bundesliga matches) protested for the preservation of the collective television contract against the criticisms of Bayern and Borussia Dortmund. It was the first time that fans had been seriously concerned that the collective deal was under threat.

The competition between new media consortia has inflated the market value of European football, concentrating financial power in the hands of the biggest clubs. In this way, the deregulation of European football broadcasting constitutes a prime example of uneven development. Against the national regimes of the Fordist era, which attempted to sustain at least a base level of equality within each sovereign territory, multinational corporations invest in specific sites which offer good investment opportunity. Certain strategic sites within each country benefit from this foreign investment while other contiguous cities and regions, once sustained under a unified political economic regime, languish. In European football, the investment of emergent media multinationals in football has promoted the big city clubs of Europe and effectively lifted them out of their national context to operate at a wider transnational level. These clubs are promoted by vast virtual audiences. Along with the deregulation of player contracts, the new television revenue has transformed the geography of European football, instituting a new transnational order.

Vertical Integration

Increasingly, media consortia have not merely favoured particular clubs in their transmissions but the mutual dependencies between the biggest clubs and media networks in the deregulated era has been formalised. Clubs have been vertically integrated into media corporations. The first example of vertical integration was Silvio Berlusconi's acquisition of the ailing AC Milan which he promptly transformed by investing money from his Fininvest and Mediaset operations. In 1995, Canal Plus followed suit buying Paris Saint-Germain, while Cecchi Gori, owner of Telemontecarlo, also became the owner of Fiorentina. By purchasing clubs, media companies gain leverage over their content. As owners, they are party to discussions between the clubs about the structure of the league, the number and timings of fixtures as well as the selection of teams for transmission. In addition, the purchase of a club provides the media company with rights to content which they can broadcast themselves or sell to a third party. Although blocked by the Monopolies and Mergers Commission in April 1999, BSkyB's bid for Manchester United illuminates the rationale behind this strategy of vertical integration. In 1998 there was a strong possibility of a breakaway European Superleague and since Manchester United was party to those talks from the outset, the purchase of the club would automatically give Murdoch political leverage over the format of any new

European competition which might emerge, as well as direct access to the proposed league's television rights. In addition, in 1998, the Office of Fair Trading had mounted its case against the exclusive collective Premier League deal. This case was a serious threat to BSkyB which had thrived on the exclusivity clause in the Premier League contract. The purchase of Manchester United would have protected BSkyB even if the Restrictive Practices Court had ruled in favour of the OFT. Murdoch would still have owned the most important rights in English football even if he had lost exclusive rights to the rest of the Premier League.

Although Murdoch's attempt to purchase Manchester United failed, his bid initiated a round of vertical integration between media consortia and football clubs in England. Soon after the Monopolies and Mergers Commission blocked the merger, Murdoch began to buy up 9.9 per cent stakes in various strategically placed clubs in the Premier League. The FA had belatedly ruled that a media company could not hold more than 10 per cent of the shares in any one club. BSkyB's holding in United was reduced to 11.1 per cent (which made the company the club's majority shareholder) (Brown 2000: 84) but it also bought stakes into Leeds Sporting, Manchester City (correctly predicting this club's promotion to the top flight), Sunderland and Chelsea. NTL and Granada have adopted a similar strategy. NTL bought into Newcastle United and Aston Villa, while Granada bought shares in Liverpool. All of this activity took place before the contract for the new Premier League rights from 2001–03 were negotiated and the intention behind the strategy seems clear. The media companies bought shares in the clubs so that they could influence the clubs' decision about the Premier League television contract. It has been plausibly claimed that 'the nature of the deal [with Leeds] leaves no doubt as to BSkyB's expectations to be *centrally* involved in the negotiations for TV rights' (ibid.: emphasis added) and that 'it is clear that BSkyB's roles at Manchester City and Leeds United will be to negotiate media deals on behalf of each club' (ibid.: 85). In the Premier League each club has an equal vote and in order to pass any motion a two-thirds majority is required. Consequently, seven votes constitutes an effective veto. Given this voting procedure, BSkyB would have only had 14 per cent of the blocking votes if it had purchased Manchester United. With shares in four clubs, BSkyB had effectively guaranteed itself 70 per cent of the votes it would require to veto any decision and about 30 per cent of the vote for a new contract. BSkyB were in a better position than if the planned merger with Manchester United had gone ahead, having almost guaranteed that no television contract signed by the Premier League would be against their interests. This new strategy of multiple vertical integration has, if anything, been more effective than the original bid for Manchester United because it has given the company greater political leverage at league meetings without the political backlash which would almost certainly have followed their purchase of Manchester United. The vertical integration of clubs into media consortia affirms the process of concentration initiated by the deregulation of television. Across Europe, major media companies are strategically allying with the major European football clubs to guarantee powerful content for themselves while simultaneously strengthening these clubs.

The attitude of Adam Crozier, the chief executive of the FA, to these critical developments was interesting:

> The general view whether it is in the City or anywhere else is that when the shareholding is under 10 per cent it is very difficult to exercise any real control. I am also not sure that media companies want to run football clubs. I don't think they do want to run football clubs in the main. I think what it is all about in the new digital age with more and more channels available, in the end, what people are interested in is content. It is not who owns the channel but who owns the content. So I think that is why they are trying to get into bed with football and I think they are playing a very long game there as well rather than a short-term game. I don't think that the issue is really about that and obviously we are looking into what some of those things may hold in the future. [Adam Crozier, personal interview, 11 April 2000]

However, as Adam Brown had made clear, it seems almost certain that BSkyB heavily influenced the clubs in which it held shares in voting for the new 2001 contract and this was one of their prime motivations for investing in them. Given the political threat which vertical integration poses to the authority of national federations, Crozier's *laissez-faire* approach is curious especially since this multiple ownership is in breach of FA rules.[4] Adam Brown has argued that 'it is absolutely essential to the credibility of the football authorities' regulatory functions that they uphold their own rules regarding the dual ownership of clubs' (Brown 2000: 91). The FA's lax approach to this issue has allowed the very developments which were blocked by the Monopolies and Mergers Commission to occur informally. Crozier's stance towards this new centralisation of power in the deregulated era does not only demonstrate poor judgement on the FA's behalf but it categorically denotes the declining authority of the national federations. It seems highly likely that Crozier refuses to recognise that certain FA rules have been significantly breached because he knows that the FA no longer have the authority to enforce these rules. It is simply inconceivable that the FA could force BSkyB and the other media companies to relinquish their multiple investments. In place of the authority of national federations, market forces increasingly determine the game's development, concentrating power among the biggest clubs who are ever more closely allied to privatised media corporations.[5]

The New Competitive Balance

The deregulation of television in Europe and the subsequent transformation in the broadcasting of football constitutes a very important moment of concentration in European football. The big clubs are certainly becoming more dominant but, against the jeremiads which are frequently made about the game by fans and commentators who claim they are 'saving soccer from itself' (Dempsey and Reilly 1998) or describe how 'egotism and greed are destroying football' (Freeman 2000; also Conn 1997), the game is not dying, only transforming. Many of those who are emotionally tied to the international regime which existed in the post-war decades find these changes objectionable but, as Chapters 3 and 4 demonstrated, their criticisms of contemporary transformations often falsely romanticise the international era. The international era was also an economic regime, though its structure was different to that which is currently emerging. The deregulation of football is having radical and very rapid effects on the game, but the transnational trajectory of the European game does not threaten the existence of the game *per se*, merely the way it has been known since the 1950s. Critics who insist that the game is dying are ultimately only protesting against the supersession of a regime with which they are familiar (and in which they may have interests).

These critics reject the deregulation of television rights for football on the grounds that the competitive balance of the league – and, therefore the sport itself – will be ruined (for example, Restrictive Practices Court 1999: 35, para 101). It is undeniable that the concentration of television revenue at the biggest clubs has put them in a very favourable position in the market for players, allowing them to dominate domestic and European competitions. The biggest clubs now have access to a transnational market in players and sufficient resources to exploit that advantageous position to the full. It is unlikely that one of the smaller teams in Europe such as Ipswich, Nottingham Forest, St. Etienne or Napoli could ever win their domestic leagues again and it is inconceivable that they would ever challenge for the European Cup. The old competitive balance of the post-war era is being replaced in the era of transnational, deregulated markets. Yet, that does not imply the end of all competitive equality. On the contrary, a new balance is emerging between the clubs of Europe which is drawing the giants of each national league together in an increasingly ferocious and evenly matched struggle for transnational supremacy. Thus, while the old struggles within the national leagues are becoming more predictable, the competition is becoming more and more uncertain at the European level. Certainly, the smaller clubs who have won the European Cup in the past are not excluded from this new form of competition but the deregulation of the player market and television contracts in European football has produced a new phenomenon at this top level. In the past, a strong club team which included a few international-class players from the national team was sufficient to win and indeed to dominate the European Cup; Real Madrid, Ajax, Bayern Munich and Liverpool are all examples of such teams. In the present marketised era, the top clubs require squads of transnational quality if they are to win the European Cup or even to reach its final stages. In the light of this increasing standard, the chances of winning the Cup consecutively are receding. In the mid-1990s, Juventus reached the Final three times in a row but only won the competition once. Real Madrid won the European Cup in 1998, 2000 and 2002, a level of success which reflects the club's unusual flexible approach to financial management, but it is unlikely that they could ever repeat their original domination of this competition. Reporting the words of Karl Heinz Rummenige, the vice-president of Bayern Munich, Liam Brady has highlighted the increasing uncertainty of outcome at the top level of European football:

> It's getting really tough. The Spanish in particular are coming on strong, really strong, searching for players. There is a lot of competition for the best players now, a lot of money and a lot of clubs. The last to really dominant was AC Milan but it is going to be hard for anyone to emulate them. There is more strength widely spread. [Holt 1997: 40]

The kind of domination by a single club which was a feature of the European Cup in the past was possible when football was organised on an international basis. In the late 1970s and early 1980s, that regulatory framework also allowed smaller clubs to win the competition. It is perhaps regrettable that it will be increasingly difficult for those smaller teams to win the competition in the future, though it might be noted that the period in which these smaller teams were successful in the tournament is not remembered fondly as the triumph of romance and democracy, but as a negation of the qualities of the competition; 'oh the longueurs and the mediocrity of such dire games' (Glanville 1991: 10–11). The other side of this concentration of financial power is increasingly unpredictable competition between the biggest clubs of Europe. European football is changing, not dying, and indeed, since the most democratic period of the European Cup coincided with the worst standards of play, the new competitive balance may produce better football which is more attractive to fans. Even so, while the deregulation of television has concentrated financial resources at the biggest clubs they will remain in a market position which is a long way short of monopoly. Smaller clubs will always have access to talent even though they are disadvantaged in the current era. Moreover, there are so many imponderables in football that even if the big clubs monopolised all the serious talent in Europe, their dominance would not be entirely certain. The arch-free marketeer of European football, Rodolfo Hecht Lucari, whose company Media Partners attempted to create a European Superleague in 1998, has described this uncertainty:

Look at football. Football as a sport is a truly barbaric sport. There is no other field in sports where technical talent pays off so little. You go out and buy the twenty best guys, indisputably the best, and you then for three years consistently lose every fucking competition you are in and you don't have to say anything. That is football. Welcome. [Rodolfo Hecht Lucari, Media Partners, personal interview, 17 May 2000]

The deregulation of television has transformed football from an international sport into a transnational spectacle. The big clubs are emerging as the dominant force in European football, but this does not mean that other clubs will become entirely irrelevant in the future. They too will remain significant actors in this transnational context.

Notes

1 For the history of public service in Europe see, Herman and McChesney 1997; Kuhn 1995; Humphreys 1990; Frachon and Vargaftig 1995; Ostergaard 1993; Robillard 1995; Drummond et al. 1993; Weymouth and Lamizet, 1999. The following account of broadcasting de-regulation is taken from these sources.
2 Rupert Murdoch initially bought the rights to Serie A through his majority ownership of Stream (Betts 1998a; 1998b) but the Italian government quickly introduced a new law which stated that no single company could own more than a third of the broadcasting rights to live Serie A football (Blitz 1999; Potter 1999). Given Berlusconi's prominence in Italian politics with his party *Forza Italia*, it seems unlikely that at least some of the impetus for this protectionist law did not come from him.
3 Kenyon revealed that Manchester United's collectivist principles were perhaps even more limited: 'We have gone on record continually, believing that the domestic league is too big. We would certainly like a reduction to 18 and if that went to 16 we would not be disappointed but certainly if it went to 18 – that would be important. It is about quality' (Peter Kenyon, personal interview, 3 March 2000).
4 It is significant that the Court of Sports Arbitration in Lausanne ruled against ENIC's ownership of a number of European clubs agreeing with UEFA that it jeopardised the integrity of the sport.
5 Adam Crozier's resignation from the FA in November 2002 demonstrates the new power of the biggest clubs which are now effectively able to dictate policy to the national federation.

Chapter 7
The New Business of Football

In his widely read critique of the commercialisation of English football, David Conn (1997) has proposed an individualistic account of this historic transformation. For him, the commercialisation of English football was the result of the opportunistic intervention of a handful of entrepreneurs motivated solely by personal greed, such as Martin Edwards at Manchester United, Alan Sugar at Tottenham, Sir John Hall at Newcastle United, Jack Walker at Blackburn and Doug Ellis at Aston Villa.[1] In each case, he highlights the amount of money which these figures have earned from listing their clubs to prove his point. Certainly, personal motivations are central to historical explanations but individual motivations such as greed are only relevant to historical transformation given a wider social context which render particular forms of personal motivations significant. In the case of the commercialisation of football, once this wider context is taken into account, the personalised and moralising tone of Conn's work becomes inadequate. Although individuals like Edwards and Hall were undoubtedly concerned with personal profiteering, the commercialisation of their clubs was not simply a matter of personal preference nor was the profit they gained from this commercialisation more than a case of serendipity for them. The value of club shares increased rapidly at this time primarily as a result of the explosion in the value of television rights. This was not the product of the actions of a few moderately able club directors. Moreover, in the light of increasingly ferocious transnational competition, commercialisation was imperative if these clubs were to remain significant forces in the transfer market. While personal fortunes were a convenient corollary of commercialisation for certain directors, this historic restructuring of European football clubs cannot be comprehended by reference to the legendary avarice of Martin Edwards et al. alone. The transformation of European football clubs is of too great a historical significance to be reduced to the vices of a handful of businessmen. Rather, transnational competition has demanded new strategies from the clubs. In the face of increasing competition, clubs have been forced to increase the traditional income from gate revenue, while developing new forms of revenue streams, such as merchandising, stadium reconstruction, sponsorship, flotation on the stock exchange and the exploitation of new internet rights.[2] The windfalls which some of the directors received as a result of flotation was not the driving force behind this economic transformation but only a contingent side-effect of it.

While flotation has been an important means for certain clubs to raise revenue, the transformation of the business structure of clubs has served another essential purpose. As a result of deregulation, the turnover of all major European clubs has grown exponentially in the 1990s, necessitating new business structures. The private and often irregular management of clubs which has been a consistent feature of European football has become an inadequate mode of financial administration in the contemporary context. The sums involved are simply too large – and the risks of error too great – to allow for the persistence of *ad hoc* management which characterised most European football clubs in the past. It is certainly true that some major clubs around Europe still operate in arcane ways. Real Madrid with its £170 million debt is the primary example while, in the late 1980s and early 1990s, Tapie's Marseille employed systematically corrupt techniques of financial management. Nevertheless, there is a clear shift towards accountable financial management, where even those clubs which have not floated or do not intend to float have restructured their management practices and structures in line with public limited companies.

Even Real Madrid has gone some way to transform itself. After his election as the new president in July 2000, Florentino Perez insisted that the club could not continue in the manner that it had and that the £170 million debt had to be cleared. This announcement was somewhat ironic considering he had just fulfilled his election promise of bringing Luis Figo to the club from Barcelona for £37 million, though some restructuring appears to have taken place. Real Madrid directors now claim to have shown profits in certain areas and, although the directors of the club do not see the club as primarily profit-making (in contrast to the owners of English clubs), profit has in fact become increasingly important to them:

> Most of the clubs today in Europe are companies. Real Madrid is not a company, it is a sports club. Of course, one of the objectives of company is to get money, to obtain profits. At Real Madrid, that is not the idea. At Real Madrid the only thing we have to do is to balance the budget and to put the best we can on the field. We say, 'We don't need the money in the bank, we need the money on the field.' It is what the supporters want but of course this is easy to say but sometimes difficult to do. We have balanced the budget. In the last four years, Real Madrid have obtained profits. We are emphasising the need to balance the budget. I think we have been getting almost 3 or 4 million dollars per year. [Juan Onieva, vice-president, Real Madrid, personal interview, 19 April 2000]

Indeed, in a convenient initiative worth £180 million, the city council of Madrid are planning to purchase Real Madrid's training ground, thereby eliminating its debts.[3] As Florentino Perez commented; 'With the sale of our sports ground, we will cancel our debt for good and this will allow Real

Madrid to live under normal economic conditions for the coming decades' (Schafer and Owen 2001). The business structure of European football clubs is transforming in response to new transnational competition and even those clubs like Real Madrid and Barcelona that formally retain their old mutual structures have, in fact, outgrown that form of financial organisation.

Floating

The strategy of floating was first developed by English clubs. Tottenham Hotspur was the first European club to float in 1983, followed in 1989 by Millwall and in 1991 by Manchester United. From 1995, there was a spate of flotations so that by 2000, 16 other English clubs or their holding companies had gone public: Aston Villa (1997), Chelsea (1996), Leeds (1996), Leicester (1997), Newcastle United (1997), Sunderland (1996), Southampton (1997), Charlton (1997), Birmingham City (1997), Bolton Wanderers (1997), Queens Park Rangers (1996), Nottingham Forest (1997), Sheffield United (1997), West Bromwich Albion (1997), Gillingham (2000) and Preston North End (1995) (Sturgess et al. 2001: 4). Moreover, between 1 January 1993 and 31 January 1997, overall shares in the football sector rose 774 per cent, outperforming the Stock Market as a whole by a factor of ten (Morrow 1999: 91). There were several reasons for this post-1995 spate of flotations in England. The inflation of television revenue necessitated the formalisation of clubs' business administrations for which modernisation flotation was a convenient method. It is notable that 'listed clubs are, generally, better at controlling their total wage bills and transfer spending than their unlisted brethren' (Boon 1999: 8). In addition, the growth in television revenue attracted investors. In effect, by floating, clubs could exploit the expansion in their television revenue twice-over by attracting the secondary investment of stock-market speculators.

The success of Manchester United and its sound performance on the stock exchange after an initially shaky start has also promoted flotation as a business strategy. Manchester United floated in 1991 in order to fund the rebuilding of the Stretford End in line with the Taylor Report requirements but, unlike any other club, Manchester United has been able to sustain and indeed increase its turnover and profit even in years when it has won nothing. Thus, at the end of the 1997–98 season, when they were knocked out of the quarter-final of the European Cup by Monaco and lost the Championship to Arsenal, their turnover still rose by 19 per cent. Manchester United's flotation has become the European archetype, described by Franz Beckenbauer, the president of Bayern Munich, for instance, as the ideal which Bayern should follow. Following United's example, Lazio, Ajax, Borussia Dortmund and FC Porto have all gone public and more Italian clubs are likely to follow when conditions are favourable:

> We have one club in Italy that has floated, Lazio, but maybe a few more will follow them. This is a question of the strategy of the owner. If the Agnelli family wants to go public. We think in our opinion, myself and Giraudo [Antonio Giraudo, club secretary] and Moggi [Luciano Moggi, general manager], we are here together – it could be the right way or should be the right way but at the right moment. When we are not just a football team but when we have a stadium, training facilities, the commercial side which we are trying to build. So when we sell something more than just the notion of the club. So you know you are buying a company that is on the stock market but not just because it is a football team but because it is something more and bigger. Then it is up to them [the investors]. [Roberto Bettega, vice-president, Juventus, personal interview, 14 March 2000]
>
> Floating is an opportunity but we won't float until we reach our maximum value. Our shareholders do not need us to float. We are financially very solid. We don't have the need to raise capital. We will if the conditions were exceptional. Others are going into a market which is not sophisticated enough. I think the example that you have in England where everyone is floating but only two, three if not one really succeeded but the rest were just fashion. Lazio went through the fashion, they are the first, and so have received the benefits of being the first. We do not control the stadium. We will from July 1. So we are trying to bring their group within the company. Now everybody talks about the internet. Our website is developing fast and we think that is another development which is important to us. There will be better times for flotation. [Umberto Gandini, organisational direction, AC Milan, personal interview, 15 March 2000; see also Adriano Galliani, *Soccer Analyst* 2(3) 2000c: 14–15)

Although clubs have a choice about when is the best time for them to float, increasing transnational competition pushes them inexorably towards flotation. The directors' prime motivation is not that they may receive a windfall following floatation, as Conn insists, but that their investments in the clubs will decline in value if the club becomes uncompetitive. New shares are not offered to increase personal profit directly but to sustain the club's general financial position. This rationale is clearly revealed by Adriano Galliani, the vice-president of AC Milan:

> I personally think that if Milan want to keep the edge over its competitors, then it needs to have the financial structure of the biggest European clubs, otherwise, it won't be possible to win in the future. In others words, if Barcelona have a turnover of L. 100 bn (£31.2 million) higher than Milan's, it means that it will have L. 100 bn more to invest in new players. And the US experience teaches us that revenues are in an almost one-to-one correspondence with sporting results. [Adriano Galliani, *Soccer Analyst* 2000b: 13]

The competitive pressure on European clubs is compelling them to adopt the business strategies of their transnational rivals and so the strategy of listing publicly has spread rapidly from clubs in England across Europe. The often informal business structures which persisted in the international economic regime have become outmoded as transnational market forces have become more dominant.

Demonstrating the importance of business structure to competitiveness, clubs in the French league are severely disadvantaged by their anachronistic business structures. Due to the relative underurbanisation of France, professional football, as an urban form of entertainment, has always been weak in comparison to the other major nations of Europe. In addition, the French state has the strongest involvement in sport of all countries in western Europe prioritising public good over private profit (Eastham 1999: 58).[4] Consequently, from their inception, football clubs were established as non-profit-making organisation under 'Association 1901' or *'association a but non-lucratif'* which prevented elected adminstrators making money from the club (ibid.: 59). Even when clubs subsequently turned professional, the 1901 law still remained in force and it was unknown for the *Société Anonyme* (Limited Company) model to be adopted by professional football clubs. In 1984, the *Loi Avice* forced professional sports clubs with annual turnover of more than 2.5 million francs to constitute themselves into a *Société Anonyme a object sportif* or a *Société Anonyme d'Economie Mixte Sportif* but even under these modifications professional clubs were still bound by the Association 1901. The new legal status of professional clubs allowed clubs to conform with the basic principles of commercial enterprise but neither of these statutes allowed profit (ibid.: 60), although Jean-Luc Lagardiere at Racing Club de Paris and Bernard Tapie at Marseilles both breached these statutes. It might be argued that only by engaging in illegal practices could Tapie overcome the inherent disadvantages of French football, allowing Marseilles, alone among French clubs, to win the European Cup. There has been a reformation of business practices in French football since Tapie and Lagardiere, but many of the larger clubs are straining under the restrictions of Association 1901 which severely limits the possibility of attracting investment to compete with their European rivals. Moreover, the heavy taxation of football clubs by local authorities is also seen as an obstacle to the competitiveness of French clubs in Europe. In the light of the disadvantageous regulatory regime, the government has reconsidered the legal status of French football clubs (ibid.: 74) and from 1999, clubs have been allowed to transform themselves into public limited companies. Following this decision, Robert Louis Dreyfus, President of Olympic Marseilles, has announced that he intends to float Marseilles while Paris Saint-Germain and Strasbourg are also keen to list themselves, although given the level of restructuring required it will probably be about five or six years before even the biggest French clubs like Marseilles are in a position to go public (ibid.). Listing will provide much needed investment for the clubs but flotation will also enforce more rigorous financial management.

A similar process of transformation is evident in Germany where clubs were amateur until 1963. As in France, clubs retained the same legal status after professionalisation and were registered as sporting or mutual associations. These clubs were non-profit-making institutions with the status of private social clubs owned by the members. However, as clubs have found it increasingly difficult to compete, especially after Bosman, the Deutsche Fussball Bund (DFB) was pressurised into allowing the clubs to transform their legal status into joint-stock companies (Kipker 2000b). In October 1998, the DFB sanctioned that transformation, and Bayer Leverkusen were the first to convert to a Plc in March 1999. Borussia Dortmund transformed themselves into a *Kommanditgesellschaft auf Aktien* rather than a full Plc in the autumn of 1999 which meant that the board of directors was elected by the old private social club and the stockholders had less rights than in a normal stock company (ibid.: 6–7). The stockmarket has been less enthusiastic about this status since investors' control of the club and its profits have been curtailed but it still constitutes an important transformation. Borussia Moenchengladbach, FC Bayern Munich, Hertha Berlin and VFL Wolfsburg have all mooted possible flotations and Franz Beckenbauer, president of Bayern Munich, has said that flotation will be essential to fund a new stadium (Bowley 1998b).

While German, Italian and French clubs are all responding to the new competitive pressures of a post-Bosman Europe, only the Spanish clubs have no plans to transform their legal status into Plcs. The opposition to floating is particularly notable at FC Barcelona where both Lluis Nunez and the new Barcelona president, Joan Gaspart, have insisted that flotation is antithetical to the club's cultural standing. Nevertheless, the club developed a private bond scheme under Nunez, called 'The Foundation', whereby 105 companies pledged themselves to the club. The Foundation involves three forms of membership. A company can become an 'Honorary Member' by contributing between £40,000 and £60,000 per year to the Foundation. Each member then receives eight seats in a new box, two seats in a professional box, two parking spaces, tickets to watch Barcelona, and the use of the clubs' facilities once a year as well as other unspecified privileges. There are 25 Honorary Memberships available. In addition, there are 48 Associate Memberships which raise £14,000 each per year, giving those sponsoring company similar entitlements. Finally, companies can become a 'patron' for £4,000 per annum, receiving tickets in the front row. Individuals can also make a personal contribution for £38 in return for which their name is engraved on the wall of the Nou Camp; 22,700 individuals have contributed to this scheme. While Barcelona remains adamant that it will not go public, it has effectively implemented a private flotation in order to raise money and, while this private flotation scheme might avoid the manifest loss of independence which follows listing, the club has necessarily forfeited some of its autonomy by allowing itself to become indebted to the companies which have become Honorary Members.[5] It is not clear whether these companies have any formal say in club policy but it seems unlikely that Honorary Membership would not involve at least some informal influence over the club.

The Brand

European clubs are being mutually forced to undergo a profound transformation as a response to increased competition between them. The floating of clubs in the 1990s has been one of the most striking developments but it is only one of several other new strategies which the clubs have been forced to adopt. From the early 1990s, English clubs and especially Manchester United developed merchandising in order to create new sources of revenue. Before the 1990s, Manchester United had had a small souvenir shop located on the stadium forecourt by the Warwick Road but after the club's flotation, it became necessary to increase the club's revenue in order to sustain the share-price. To that end, Edward Freedman, who had developed Tottenham Hotspur's merchandising, was appointed as commercial director of the club. As he revealed in a personal interview on 19 November 1999, his strategy was to exploit the 'brand' of Manchester United as fully as possible and under his stewardship, the merchandising revenue at Manchester United jumped from a negligible sum to a major part of the club's revenue, reaching a figure of over £30 million.

It is worth considering what exactly is meant by the term 'brand' – while it is used almost ubiquitously by individuals like Freedman, its exact significance is not always specified. The brand refers to the marketability of a commodity and, therefore, to the particular quality which make people buy the commodity. To exploit a brand means emphasising that quality in order to improve a commodity's sales. Sometime the brand refers to tangible qualities. For instance, a spade is sold very substantially on its usefulness; the brand is its function. However, many other commodities do not have such obvious 'use-value' and, indeed, Lash and Urry have argued that the most important commodities now have 'sign value' (Lash and Urry 1993). By this they mean that in post-Fordist capitalism, many of the most important commodities are not bought primarily for their use but because they are central to the creation of identity and social standing. In fact, all commodities have 'sign-value' since even the most functional presuppose some social understanding about what they will be used for. Even spades reveal something about the social identity of their users. However, Lash and Urry's concept of 'sign-value' usefully illuminates what Freedman means when he calls a football club a brand. In football, the brand refers to the kinds of identifications which individuals make with their team. A football club has sign-value for the fans because through their support of the club, their consumption of this brand, they are able to express their identities and social status. Consequently, to exploit the brand of a football club refers to the process whereby products are marketed which facilitate the expression of identifications and affections.

With regard to football, according to Freedman, there are two sides to the brand: the club itself and the players. The club refers to the whole institution, the fans, the ground, the history and the teams while the players, self-evidently, refers to individual footballers. Of course, the two are very closely related because the club primarily exists for the fans as a series of teams featuring certain players, while the players are part of the club's brand because they have played for the club; they are part of this institution. The two sides of the brand are inseparable, therefore. Significantly, Freedman noted that not all the players contributed to the brand, although they might be very effective on the field. Thus, while Cantona and Beckham have been major assets for the brand since their charisma has been highly marketable, Roy Keane and Jaap Stam, while essential on the field, have been of modest value to the 'brand'; neither players, particularly Stam, could be marketed (Freedman, personal interview, 19 November 1999). Few individuals would want a picture of a bald Dutchman on their wall. By contrast, a player like Eric Cantona who was both skilful on the pitch and a central symbol for the fans, was an extremely powerful addition to the brand. Many fans viewed him as the embodiment of their understanding of Manchester United; he was regarded as cosmopolitan, creative and independent and, therefore, explicitly opposed to the inanities of the football authorities. Given these exceptional personal qualities and his association with the new success of the club in the 1990s, Freedman was particularly aggressive in his exploitation of Eric Cantona for he was plainly an individual with whom fans wanted to identify (see Bose 1999: 198).[6] In addition to developing a range of commodities which fans would purchase, Freedman blocked the leakage of revenue to independent sellers by copyrighting the club's name and crest. Consequently, only sellers licensed by the club and selling official club merchandise could legally exploit the 'brand', Manchester United. After Freedman's controversial departure from the club following an argument with Peter Kenyon, the club's merchandising revenue dropped by 30 per cent and Freedman, clearly bitter about his ejection from the club, claimed that 'errors' had been made (Edward Freedman, personal interview, 19 November 1999). It is difficult to establish whether the club really has made mistakes with its merchandising or whether, in fact, the market has reached saturation. It is notable that the decline in merchandising revenue also coincided with the retirement of Eric Cantona in May 1997. Nevertheless, in 1999, merchandising still brought in some £24.1 million to the club and constituted some 27 per cent of its total revenue (Deloitte and Touche 2000). Manchester United are well ahead of their English rivals but all English clubs have adopted merchandising strategies similar to United's and have raised significant revenue from their operations in this sphere. German clubs have also been able to develop merchandising because German fans traditionally wear club shirts, scarves, and denim waistcosts called *Kutte*, onto which various badges are sewn.

By contrast, in Italy and Spain, the merchandising operations of the clubs are almost negligible. Fan culture does not prioritise wearing colours though, perhaps more significantly, there is no copyrighting of club names or badges so anyone can produce club merchandise with the result that potential revenue leaks out to independent sources. Thus, while 39 per cent of Manchester United's revenue was from 'other sources' (merchandising and catering) in 1996–97, only 14 per cent of the average Italian club's revenue comes from these sources (Marchesi 1998: 28). Yet, while Italian and Spanish clubs have not developed merchandising to the levels of English clubs, through its contract with Nike, Barcelona have an impressive and stylish club shop which contrasts markedly with Manchester United's 'mega-store'. Moreover, Real Madrid have announced that they intend to boost their merchandising arm dramatically:

> We have studied Manchester United very carefully but I am convinced that in a short time, we will be the club that raises most money from merchandising, ahead of Manchester. We are going to open shops in almost every country in the world and licence our products. With that, soon we will have international sales with the prestige and the brand name of the club. [Florentino Perez, cited in Shafer and Owen 2001]

The exploitation of the brand has become an important strategy for European football clubs and, as clubs like Real Madrid realise the potential of merchandising, Manchester United, the initial pace-setters, will be forced to reinvigorate their strategies. The commercialisation of the clubs is a self-perpetuating process driven by transnational competition which has increased the financial inequalities between the biggest clubs and other teams in Europe. The biggest clubs are best able to exploit these new forms of revenue since their market is the biggest and they do not have to redistribute revenue earned from exploiting their brands.

Sponsorship

While southern European clubs may not have developed the kinds of merchandising strategies which have been typical of English clubs, it would be wrong to claim that these clubs lack commercial acumen. On the contrary, these clubs demonstrate a highly sophisticated awareness of how to exploit the 'brand' of a football club to its full potential:

We think we produce movies every Sunday. The way a game is – it is a movie. It is a 90-minute show. The exploitation of it is very similar to what you do with a Hollywood movie. You have the theatre, you have the home video, you have the CD-ROMs, you have pay-TV, pay-per-view TV, video on demand whatever. The same for a football match. To produce a movie you need stars and you need actors and actresses. The same applies when putting together a football club; the stars – regardless of where they come – and a backbone of local players, at least that is the strategy we would like to implement. [Umberto Gandini, organisational director, AC Milan, personal interview, 15 March 2000]

Umberto Gandini's understanding of the club's brand suggests that the apparent under-exploitation of club merchandising has not been an oversight. Instead, the management of AC Milan wanted to project a certain image of the club. Rather than focusing on merchandising, Gandini's statement reveals that Milan prefer to exploit the deregulation of television in Italy. Perhaps, unlike Manchester United, they did not want the 'brand' of AC Milan to become 'a byword for crass commercialism' (*The Economist* 1998a). In place of such commercialism, as Gandini reveals, the Italian clubs exploit the images of their star players in rather more sophisticated ways, as Roberto Baggio's transfer to AC Milan in September 1995 reveals: 'Baggio is an investment. From the point of view of his image, he will generate a lot of cash. 50 per cent of our takings come from sources other than gate receipts and sponsors were asking us to land a big name' (Agnew, 1995). Similarly, when Ronaldo signed for Internazionale in 1997, season ticket sales rose to 48,000 (Deloitte and Touche 2000) and by himself he added significant value to the club in terms of sponsorship and television rights.

European clubs outside England may not have developed such strong merchandising wings but the most successful of these clubs understand how to market themselves in order to exploit old and new revenue streams. The sponsorship deals in Germany are significantly larger than those generally offered to English clubs mainly because of Germany's larger population. Bayern Munich's sponsorship by Opel is worth £6.5 to £7 million per year while Borussia Dortmund's shirt sponsorship with s'Oliver is worth £5 million a year (ibid.). Juventus also have a very large contract with Telepiu Digital worth 9,720,000 euros (£6.5 million) a year (*Soccer Investor* 2000c) and it is typical for Italian clubs to earn more from sponsorship than English clubs (Marchesi, 1998: 4, 6).[7] By contrast, Arsenal's shirt sponsorship with Dreamcast was worth only £2.84 million a year (*Soccer Investor* 2000). Predictably, Manchester United are an exception to this. In January 2000, Manchester United signed a new four-year shirt sponsorship deal with Vodafone worth over £30 million including various potentially important subclauses about future Internet rights. It was a big deal but it went beyond traditional shirt sponsorship agreement because it was also a commercial and strategic alliance linking Manchester United with Vodafone, one of the world's biggest companies. In addition, in September 2000, Manchester United signed a new shirt contract with Nike, replacing the Umbro contract which had persisted for many years. The Nike contract is worth £300 million over 13 years. In signing the deal, Nike noted Manchester United's inability to compete with Real Madrid, Barcelona and the major Italian clubs for players. By financing player transfers, Nike will strengthen the 'brand' of a club by funding the transfer of world stars but Nike will also receive tangible benefits from the relationship. The club has already made a significant entry into the Chinese and the Far Eastern markets where it has many fans. This region is currently becoming Nike's most important market.[8] By associating itself with Manchester United, Nike will open these markets to its own products. Through sponsorship, international capital is allying itself with certain major football clubs, lifting them out of the national markets in which they used to operate. The emergence of the big city football clubs in Europe is a prime example of the uneven effects of market forces.

The Ground

English clubs have serious advantage over their European rivals in one significant area: they own their grounds. In the rest of Europe, the grounds are typically owned by the local council, which leases the facility to the clubs. This was not a particularly significant fact before the 1990s, since English grounds were largely characterised by inadequate and often dangerous facilities and of little market value. After the Taylor Report (Taylor 1990), English football clubs were forced to rebuild their grounds, replacing standing terraces with all-seater stands. This had a number of important social and cultural effects on English football (see King 1998c) but, in terms of the European competitiveness of English clubs, the installation of seats has also been important: it has increased gate revenues. By contrast, in Italy, Germany and Spain, tickets are still relatively cheap. For instance, a Juventus season ticket in the 'Curva' at the Stadia delle Alpi costs under £100. Similarly, at Bayern Munich a standing season ticket in the Sud Kurve at the Olympic Stadium costs only 100 DM or about £35 (including free admission to the first three home matches of the Champions League), while a season ticket in the stands only cost 520 DM or about £170 (with the same concessions for the Champions League) (fieldnotes, 18 September 2000). This contrasts with England where the average season ticket in the Premier League cost over £380 in 2000 (Chaudhary 2001: 7).

Yet, it is not simply that English clubs have been able to increase the value of the gate through improving their facilities. Through their ownership of the ground, English clubs have been able to exploit the ground for catering, conference and entertainment revenue unavailable to many of their European rivals. In Italy, especially, the directors of the major clubs are conscious of their competitive disadvantage in this area. Milan took over the running of the San Siro in July 2000 (Umberto Gandini, personal interview, 15 March 2000) and Juventus have been similarly concerned to develop the unpopular Stadia delle Alpi or build a new stadium elsewhere in Turin:

> We are living in a small city if we compare it to Madrid, London, Rome or Milan. So we are losing in comparison with these teams, a lot of money – I am talking about the stadium – because the average attendance of Barcelona every game is 88,000, for Juventus it is 45 [thousand]. This is significant. We have to find new ways where we can. Why do the English clubs own their grounds? For them it is a money-maker. For us, it is just a cost. So we have to try to find new avenues in areas where we are losing out. We have a project on the stadium. In Italy just one team owns its own stadium; it is a third division club. But Inter and Milan are talking with their municipality to have their stadium for thirty or fifty years. So not just Inter and Milan but Bologna also has an agreement with its city. If we want to invest, to put money into the stadium, to make it better, to make it nicer, make it a meeting point for the supporters, you have to do it in a place you know is yours or is yours for the next thirty or forty years. Why invest money in a stadium now when you don't know whether you will be playing in it next year? [Roberto Bettega, vice-president, Juventus, personal interview, 14 March 2000]

It is becoming uncompetitive not to own the stadium. As Bettega's statement reveals, ownership is essential because it is not sensible to invest the private income of a club in a public facility which the club may not even be using in a few years' time. In order to maximise income from their grounds, clubs need to own them so that they are able to recoup the investments which they make in them.

This ownership allows the club to transform a public facility into a cultural home. The club can express its identity through its ground, demonstrating its international standing. The ground itself becomes a symbol of the club's status. The international standing of clubs like Real Madrid or Barcelona are physically demonstrated by the Bernabeu and Nou Camp stadiums. The total rebuilding of Old Trafford during the 1990s illustrates the potential benefits of ground ownership. In 1993, the ground was turned into a 44,000-seat, two-tier bowl with a single cantilever roof which fulfilled Busby's original vision; he had presided over the erection of the first section of the cantilever over the main stand in the 1960s (Inglis 1991: 59). Almost immediately upon the completion of the all-seater stadium for the 1993–94 season, the demand for tickets far outstripped the size of the ground and the board decided to increase the capacity by rebuilding the United Road stand. That stand was replaced in 1997 by a 15,000-seat, three-tier stand, renamed the North Stand, followed by the rebuilding of the K-Stand and the West Stand (the old Stretford End) into matching three-tier stands which eventually raised the capacity to 67,000 for the 2000–01 season. There are suggestions that the old main stand, which the original Busby cantilever covered, may be similarly rebuilt into a matching three-tier stand, though the presence of the railway immediately behind the stand presents a problem for the architects. The rebuilding of Old Trafford has increased match day receipts considerably as well as producing new sources of revenue through expanded catering operations.

However, just as important as the increase in revenue is the symbolic significance of the new stadium. While some criticism has been levelled at the architecture of the New North Stand, whose exterior is bland and functional, the façade of the new East Stand (the old K-Stand) is striking. This façade consists of large panes of reinforced glass which run from ground level to the very top of the stand, above which towers a white steel structure supporting the new roof. Apart from the inconspicuous steel frames which hold each oblong pane in place, the façade is transparent. The internal structure of the new stand and some of the club's office space is visible to the outside world. In his famous analysis of the Bonaventure Hotel, Frederick Jameson discusses the use of glass facades as a central element in the new postmodern archectural style.[9] Like the new façade at Old Trafford, the Bonaventure Hotel reflects the buildings around it, undermining its own autonomy as an edifice (Jameson 1991: 42). In contrast to the stark rationality of modernist structures, it does not stand as a discrete monolith but is unstable and illusory, reflecting different images depending on the viewpoint of the onlooker. There is a confusion of spatial categories since the outside and inside of the edifice are no longer separated but permeate each other to produce a bewildering but inspiring architectural form (Jameson 1991). Jameson defines this illusory and disorientating quality of postmodern architecture as 'hyperspace'. Crucially, Jameson links these new structures to the emergence of the multinational stage of capitalism, whose logic they reflect culturally. For Jameson, a structure like the Bonaventure Hotel symbolises the pursuit of individual gratification through commodity (brand) consumption. The glassy façade, a characteristic feature of postmodern architecture, reflects the relentless flow of ever-changing global capital and has become the architectural symbol of the post-Fordist capitalism. Norman Foster, in particular, has exploited it in numerous important projects, such as the ITN headquarters in London, the new Reichstag in Berlin, the Agiplan in Mulheim and the Commerzbank Headquarters in Frankfurt. In all these designs the glass façade has been a prime element in his work, opening the interior of his buildings to external view.[10] The decision by Manchester United to construct a postmodern façade denotes the club's position as a dominant force in this new transnational order. It is appropriate that it should occupy a building of the same style as other key institutions in the era of global capitalism because the club itself is closely allied with the commanding heights of post-Fordist capitalism. Like Jameson's Bonaventure, this building communicates the restlessness of global capital.

The façade carries other significant connotations. One of the key forces in deregulated global capitalism is the television, the cultural and political importance of which the prominent French social theorist, Jean Baudrillard, has highlighted.[11] Baudrillard has developed a series of metaphors to describe the television and its effects. In particular, he invests the notion of 'the screen' with great significance: 'The media are not a scene, a prospective space, or something that's performed, but a screen without depth' (Baudrillard 1990: 65) For Baudrillard, 'the screen' denotes the way television has transformed western culture today. The screen has become the central object in contemporary culture, effacing all genuine social reality. In place of actual social interaction, we are now confronted by hyperreality. We live in a world in which we are dominated by compelling images which are more vivid than normal reality. These images do not represent any original reality but have become the reality themselves. In hyperreality the screen is the reality and this reality imposes political subordination on the masses which passively consume its compelling images. They have no reality against who to verify these images. The glassy postmodern façade is the appropriate architectural embodiment of post-Fordist capitalism because it transforms buildings precisely into television screens. Entire city blocks have been transformed into screens broadcasting reflected images to the outer world. While the old K-Stand façade consisted only of bland concrete and functional corrugated cladding with narrow turnstiles, the new façade opens up the interior to view. It becomes like a television screen at which pedestrians gaze. The new façade reflects the surrounding environment of the Trafford quays and even the fans themselves as they walk across the concourse. The new ground architecturally embodies a critical contemporary transformation. The entire stand is open to constant and total viewing, emphasising the most powerful aspect of the club in the post-Fordist age; it constitutes indispensable programming in the New Europe. The façade represents the priority of television in contemporary European football and the way it has thoroughly transformed Manchester United.

However, while the K-Stand façade symbolises the club's absorption into the flows of global capital, it also emphasises the club's attachment to its locale. In this way the ground symbolically echoes the club's policy of recruiting players transnationally while simultaneously developing local talent. To commemorate the Munich disaster, a clock and memorial listing the dead were placed prominently in the middle of the old K-Stand in the late 1950s. With the erection of the new stand, the Munich clock and memorial were re-sited (with some significant opposition) to the corner of the North Stand. In their place, a new bronze statue of Matt Busby was positioned at the centre-point of the new façade above the portico. This statue is the focal point of the new edifice. The new Busby statue emphasises the historical legacy of the club, pointing to the long connection between Manchester United and its specific location in the western part of the city. Yet, it does so at precisely the time when the club's relationship to this plot of land near the Manchester Ship Canal has changed radically. The statue appeals to a notion of the locale at the very time of its most radical transformation. The land and the stadium are no longer owned by local members of the bourgeoisie but are a point of convergence for global forces of transnational capital, in the form of deregulated television, the financial markets and multinational sponsors. The stadium is directly connected to those forces and an expression of their interests. The fans' relationship to this local space is now insuperably mediated by these global forces but the very prominence of Busby's statue attempts to emphasise continuity at a moment of rupture in order to sustain the transformed social relations between the club and its fans. Old Trafford is a focal point in the New Europe through which these global flows course but this transformation is legitimated by continued emphasis on the past. Manchester United has remained true to the Busby legacy even in the era of deregulation. The new ground denotes a new relationship between the club and its locale in the post-Fordist era. It symbolically connects the club to the flows of global capital but simultaneously emphasises the connection of the club to this particular locale. The club is both an increasingly globalised and localised institution.

The same transformation of the club's locale is demonstrated in Italy where Internazionale and AC Milan have bought the San Siro from the Milan council. In the past these clubs' relationship to their locale was mediated by the local council and, by extension, the Italian state. The purchase of the San Siro denotes a privatisation of these clubs' relationship to their locale. The clubs are now the site not of private and public partnership but rather they are points at which the forces of transnational capital realise themselves, colonising a key public ritual. By buying the San Siro, AC Milan has linked this locale directly to Berlusconi's Fininvest corporation which itself is closely related to the major European media consortiums such as News Corporation, Bertelsmann and Canal Plus. While Berlusconi's motivation in purchasing the San Siro was only to increase certain revenue streams, this policy has simultaneously rooted powerful global forces into that site with potentially profound results for the fans. Solidarity will not be impossible in this new era but the kinds of solidarity which emerge will differ to those sustained in the international period. Across Europe global flows are coalescing and germinating at key locales, radically transforming these sites and the ritual creation of social relations which occur there. A match day at Old Trafford is now directly connected to the highest levels of global capital and has become an expression of relations between hegemonic corporations and new groups of consumers.

Fan Pressure

As transnational European competition has become ever more ferocious in the 1990s, clubs are streamlining their business structures to make themselves more competitive. This transformation of business structure is a self-propelling process whereby clubs increase the competitive pressures on each other, mutually demanding continued transformation. Consequently, the business structures and strategies of the major European football clubs are converging on a privatised business model which is transforming their relationship to their locales. It is entirely conceivable that within the next decade the majority of major clubs will have floated, that they will have developed sophisticated merchandising, sponsorship and internet operations, and that they will all own their own grounds which they exploit for commercial value. Football is moving rapidly and inexorably from a Keynesian model of corporatism and public-private initiatives toward a privatised and competitive model. Increasingly, in the deregulated post-Fordist era, transnational corporations often through the mediation of the markets have allied with the major clubs in order to expand their markets, thereby creating new hierarchies within the sport and transforming the solidarities of fan groups. This is a profound transformation of ritual form.

It is important to recognise that the pressure for the commercialisation of the game has not come merely from the new directors at the clubs, hungry for increased profits, or television executives who want better 'content' to broadcast. The fans themselves constitute an important part of this competitive pressure. The fans themselves demand success, which is wholly understandable since football support is very substantially concerned with gaining recognition from rivals through success on the field:

> This cup [the European Cup] which we haven't won since 1976. I want to win it again. I would like to see Bayern winning this Cup. That is what I want to see. Afterwards, the Bundeliga may become as important as the Champions League or the European Cup but at the moment at Bayern as they have lost three finals ... [Dominik Müller, Club Nummer 12, Bayern Munich FC, personal interview, 3 July 2000]

However, this demand for success necessitates the employment of the best players which a club can afford and places a potentially limitless demand on the finances of the club. In the attempt to satisfy fans – and therefore sustain the attractiveness of the club at least partially – the directors themselves must concede to a greater or lesser extent to the demands from the fans for expenditure on players. At Manchester United, for instance, it was all but universally agreed that Roy Keane had to be given a new contract and the fans pressurised the board through various forms of public protest. Of course, the board could have ignored these protests, as it has done over many other issues, but the unacknowledged, persistent and organic ability of fans to influence club policy should not be dismissed. Fans may not be able to influence particular policy decisions directly but they do have an informal veto, whereby the board of a club will avoid certain courses of action for fear of provoking public protest. The fans' desire for success demands certain commercial structures which enable the club to buy playing talent even though the fans might object to aspects of this commercial development at other moments.

The new business of football whereby football clubs have established radically new relations with the institutions of post-Fordist capitalism has not simply been imposed from above. The transformation of European football is the product of both the elites who run the game and the fans who consume it. Consequently, even those who deplore the emergence of a new transnational order contribute to it by watching television, attending games or purchasing the club shirt and, more generally, by their persistent desire that their club is successful. The new transnational order in which the big European clubs have become ever more dominant has not been unilaterally imposed from above by a handful of individuals motivated by personal greed – Martin Edwards himself is simply not that historically significant – nor even by a few demonised corporations such as BSkyB. Rather, the new order has emerged out of a gradual and complex organic dialectic between deregulated global capital and the fans who constitute its market. Certainly, global capital has manipulated this market through rebranding football but it has not merely imposed a new ritual form on passive consumers.

Notes

1 In point of fact, the new directors of football clubs have not generally taken excessive amounts of money out of clubs and in some cases the dividend payments on shares have been derisory.
2 Internet rights are not considered here as there is very little data about their economic importance. However, it seems clear that they will have the same economic effect on football as the other deregulatory measures; they will concentrate capital among the biggest clubs who are able to attract the greatest Internet audiences.
3 It seems that Real Madrid's political links have been extremely useful to them once again.
4 Interestingly, Pierre Bourdieu, the prominent French sociologist, has polemically defended the role of the state in sport, rejecting commercialisation as intrinsically corrupting (Bourdieu 1999). His position is an interesting example of the habitus of the state nobility in France committed to Keynesian interventionism rather than an accurate account of contemporary transformations of European football.

5   For details of the foundation see FC Barcelona's website: <http//www.fcbarcelona.com>.
6   It is notable that there is some evidence to suggest that Cantona was unhappy about the extent to which the club exploited his image.
7   In Spain sponsorship is underdeveloped; Real Madrid receive only 2,103,530 euros a year from Teka, while Barcelona refuse to put the name of a sponsor on their shirt for reasons of cultural pride.
8   'The fastest-growing locale [for Nike] was the Asia Pacific region, which turned in 20% revenue growth for the quarter. The Americas came in with 14% growth, while Europe logged a mere 2%' <http://www.fool.com/news/2000/nke001220.htm>.
9   In his famous comments on the relevance of the architecture of Las Vegas to postmodern design, Venturi similarly emphasises the importance of the façade in postmodern architecture although he stresses the relevance of pastiche and parody rather than the use of impermeable glass membranes (Venturi et al. 1977).
10 For extensive details on Foster's architecture see: <http://www.fosterandpartners.com/projectsmenu.html>.
11 Baudrillard's criticisms of the television are philosophically and politically untenable (see King 1998a; 1999b).

Chapter 8
The League of Champions

Antecedents of the Champions League

Gabriel Hanot had originally envisaged the European Cup as a league competition but due to various difficulties, not least the objections of the national federations, a European league was impossible in the 1950s. Yet, from the outset, the biggest clubs regularly advocated the development of a league or quasi-league competition. In March 1967, the top clubs of Europe, including Manchester United, AC Milan, Juventus, Real Madrid, Barcelona, Benfica, Anderlecht, Feyenoord and Dukla Prague met in Monto Carlo with the approval of UEFA and FIFA to discuss the possibility of a European Superleague (Green 1967a). Interestingly, although the last four clubs' importance had waned by the 1990s, the major clubs which attended this conference were the same as those who would subsequently drive the transformation of the European Cup in the 1990s: 'As a first step the delegates suggested that the European Cup should be reorganised into pools for the early rounds, divided into groups of four with each team meeting the others home and away' (ibid.). It is interesting that the format proposed by the clubs at Monte Carlo anticipated the eventual structure of the so-called Champions League in the 1990s. Significantly, the proposals for a European Superleague which were ratified at this meeting were never implemented: 'As I see it, there is one major obstacle to the reality of any European Superleague of the future. The fears of the loss of sovereignty by the national ruling bodies must be overcome' (ibid.). The national federations would not allow this infringement of their sovereignty. A European league would undermine the national leagues by giving the big clubs excessive financial advantages and distracting attention from domestic fixtures. In the late 1960s, the clubs did not have the economic or political strength to challenge the federations. Nevertheless, even after the failure of the Monte Carlo conference, the major European clubs continued to consider the possibility of expanding the European Cup.

On 9 November 1977, there was an informal meeting of club, national and UEFA representatives in London to discuss the possibility of creating a European league once again:

The idea basically – the concept of David Miller, football correspondent of the *Daily Mirror* – is to expand the UEFA Cup into a European league and that the number of teams who now compete for the UEFA Cup, should be divided into two groups – Group A and Group B – to bring in a league competition. By this method, there will be more matches and more money for the clubs involved. With graded opposition there could be better competition and perhaps better crowds. [Green 1977]

The divide which emerged in this meeting about the possible transformation of the UEFA Cup highlighted the battlelines in professional European football at that time. The national federations defended the autonomy of their leagues against any increase in European club competition: 'There were of course adversaries to the idea, like Mr Bangerter, Mr Hardaker and Mr Croker. All of these are secretaries of their organisations. They talked about the complications of these fixtures and the other commitments of the World Cup, the European Nations Cup and the rest' (ibid.). By contrast, the big European clubs advocated increased European competition as the solution to their economic difficulties. Matt Busby promoted the development of European competition strongly: 'We are now living in a different era. This is an age for progress. The problem of fixtures should be nothing compared to the opportunities that it offers to others' (ibid.). Yet, the clubs were too weak in the 1970s to implement their proposals and the London meeting was rapidly forgotten. The UEFA Cup and the other European competitions remained unchanged, though Green's article concluded with a prophetic sentence: 'As Busby says, there must be progress and one day, though most of us will be gone, it will come to pass' (ibid.). In fact, the conditions for the development of a European league appeared sooner than Green anticipated.

Seeding and European League Proposals

In 1986, Juventus and Real Madrid were paired against each other in the second round of the European Cup ensuring the elimination of at least one of these giants from the competition. In the event, Juventus were knocked out, while Brondby, Anderlecht and Besiktas playing in other ties all went through to the next round. Highlighting the weakness of these clubs, the latter two clubs conceded seven goals in their respective games against Bayern Munich and Dynamo Kiev in the quarter-finals, both being beaten in the first leg 5–0 (Macwilliam 2000: 97). The Juventus president, Giampiero Boniperti, publicly recommended that a seeding system be introduced after the elimination of his team: 'It's a pity that one of us [Real Madrid or Juventus] will not reach the quarter-finals. They should change the way the Champions' Cup is organised. Something more like the World Cup seeding system is needed' (Boniperti, cited by Radnedge 1986: 4) In the following season, having paid £1 million to broadcast their European games, RAI had to watch as Napoli led by Maradona was eliminated in the very first round by Real Madrid. 'It was an expensive lesson ... which led to seeding' (Fynn 1992). It might be noted that the elimination of major teams early in the competition was an expensive lesson for UEFA itself which had lost considerable revenue in two consecutive years as a result of early exit of the attractive teams.

As a result of these eliminations, UEFA introduced a seeding system which sought to give some weight to the relative size of clubs and, later in the 1990s, they developed a system of coefficients which ranked every club on the basis of its performance in European competitions. A club received two points for a win and one for a draw and its coefficient was calculated by dividing the total by the number of games it had played in Europe.[1] In addition, each league had its own coefficient calculated by aggregating all the results of its clubs in European competition. The club's individual coefficient was then added onto the coefficient of its league to create a ranking system for every single club under UEFA's jurisdiction. UEFA's coefficients are as accurate and fair as any seeding system is likely to be. Yet, the coefficient system necessarily involves a gradual but determinant shift in favour of the clubs in the biggest markets in Europe. The biggest clubs in Europe are themselves likely to have better personal coefficients than small clubs but, more particularly, whatever their own performance, the strongest leagues of which the biggest clubs are part inevitably have far better coefficients than small market leagues. The occasional exceptional result by a smaller club becomes statistically unimportant when the performance of leagues as a whole is taken into account. The bias towards the major leagues implicit in the seeding system became apparent by the mid-1990s. In 1995, Ajax beat Milan in the European Cup Final and they were consequently automatically selected for the next year's competition. However, had they lost that Final, they would have had to qualify for the competition while the English champions, Blackburn, a far poorer team who subsequently performed abysmally in the tournament qualified automatically. The English league had a higher coefficient than the Dutch league, even though Ajax as a club had an outstanding European pedigree:

> Had they lost, the best team in Europe would have been downgraded in favour of Blackburn, this despite the fact that they have retained their Dutch title by a distance, and thrashed Bayern Munich 5–2, as well as beating Milan twice, en route to the final. The logic? Entirely commercial. Dutch TV has a smaller audience than the 10 million ITV averaged for Manchester United's European games this season, and contribute much less to the overall pot of £200 million. [Lovejoy 1995]

The seeding system was a conscious concession to the big clubs in the biggest markets. This system certainly created anomalies but so did the previous system in which there were no seeds. While it was strange that Blackburn were favoured over the manifestly superior Ajax in the 1995–96 season, it was not particularly fair that Juventus should have been eliminated in 1986 while Brondby, Anderlecht and Besiktas all went through when they were much weaker teams. Neither system is objectively fair but were compromises which reflected contemporary political and economic realities. Each produces its own anomalies and injustices. Seeding and, later, the coefficient system recognised the new power of certain clubs to the disadvantage of smaller clubs in lesser markets. Between the 1950s and 1980s, the situation was reversed; champion clubs from smaller leagues were favoured.

Significantly, the early elimination of Juventus and Napoli coincided with the takeover of AC Milan by Silvio Berlusconi who wanted to exploit the commercial broadcasting value of his newly acquired team. However, he viewed the format of the European Cup as a serious obstacle. Berlusconi insisted that structural changes were essential to the European Cup: 'The European Cup has become a historical anachronism. It is economic nonsense that a club such as Milan might be eliminated in the first round. It is not modern thinking' (Hughes 1993; Fynn 1992). Although the statement was typically hyperbolic, Berlusconi's argument reflected the changing economic realities of European football. From the mid-1980s, European television companies were investing increasingly large sums of money into football from which both UEFA and the clubs benefited but, the value of these television rights depended on the most famous clubs. Only these clubs constituted powerful enough programming to attract large European television audiences. Consequently, the early elimination of the big European clubs was not in the interests of television companies, the biggest clubs or UEFA itself. As Berlusconi's statement suggests, seeding was only a preparatory step towards the transformation of the structure of European competition itself.

In 1988, supported by Ramon Mendoza, the Real Madrid president, Berlusconi proposed that eight, four-group mini-leagues should replace the early rounds of the tournament with the winner of each group moving into a knock-out quarter-final stage. UEFA rejected the plan (Macwilliam 2000: 104) but this did not discourage Berlusconi who employed Alex Fynn of Saatchi and Saatchi to develop a blueprint for a European Superleague. Alex Fynn had helped Irving Scholar to exploit the commercial potential of Tottenham Hotspur in the mid-1980s (see Scholar 1992). This was the beginning of a long relationship which Fynn has had with professional football, including the publication of several books about the problems and opportunities presented by commercialisation (for example, Fynn 1999; Fynn and Guest 1999; Fynn and Guest 1994). In 1988, following his involvement with Tottenham, Fynn gave a speech at the annual launch of the Rothman Football Yearbook which proposed a ten-point plan for the modernisation of professional football, including the development of a European Superleague (Fynn 1992, also personal interview, 2 November 1999). Fynn's ideas came to the attention of

Berlusconi who was a client of Saatchi and Saatchi and it was out of this connection that Berlusconi commissioned Fynn to develop a full blueprint for European football. Fynn's original plan proposed the creation of two regional leagues of nine or ten teams from northern and southern Europe, the winners of which would go forward to a deciding final (Fynn 1992). The three existing European competitions, including the European Cup would be unaffected: 'We realised that the plan stood little chance of becoming short-term reality. But Berlusconi and I wanted to begin the debate' (ibid.). Although Fynn's plan, sponsored by Berlusconi, was not implemented, the format of the European Cup was changed soon after this intervention and, as Fynn has subsequently noted: 'my blueprint set the ball rolling' (personal interview, 2 November 1999). The blueprint illuminated ways in which the competition format might be realigned with the emergent geography of European football.

The Champions League

In 1990, Rangers' chairman David Murray, supported by Ramon Mendoza, submitted another blueprint written by Rangers' secretary Campbell Ogilvie to UEFA which proposed the creation of a mini-league in the European Cup (Forsyth 1993; Fynn 1992, and personal interview, 2 November 1999).[2] As a result of this intervention, the European Cup was reformed for the 1991–92 season by UEFA. The quarter and semi-final of the European Cup was replaced with two mini-leagues of four teams, the winners of which went on to the Final. According to reports at the time, Berlusconi had no direct influence over the introduction of these mini-leagues into the European Cup, though it is possible that he employed Mendoza and Murray as stalking-horses who would not attract the level of political censure which would inevitably follow his own involvement. This seems particularly likely since Berlusconi and Mendoza worked closely together on the 1988 initiative and it seems an unlikely coincidence that Ogilvie's proposals happen to have a similar format as Berlusconi's 1988 plan. Yet, even if Berlusconi had nothing to do with the Rangers-Real initiative, he had played a crucial role in creating an environment in which this reformation was possible. He had highlighted the need for structural change to the European Cup.

Although UEFA introduced the first mini-league format to the European Cup as a result of the pressure imposed upon them by Rangers and Real Madrid, there were substantial benefits for UEFA in adopting this new format. By introducing more matches, UEFA stood to increase its income from the European Cup dramatically and the organisation was fully aware of this fact. On their own initiative, UEFA commissioned its marketing wing, Television Event and Media Marketing (TEAM)[3] to develop new methods of marketing the mini-league in order to maximise its financial value, a very substantial portion of which would go to UEFA itself. As a result of TEAM's work, the new mini-league system which had been initially introduced in 1991–92 was renamed as 'The Champions League' for the 1992–93 season. The development of the Champions League did not initially involve structural changes to the European Cup – the mini-league system had been implemented in the previous season – but it did involve three revolutionary marketing initiatives. Instead of sponsors being signed up for each match, UEFA sold the sponsorship rights in a unified package to eight and, from 2000, four exclusive sponsors. Similarly, the television rights were sold not to individual rounds but as a complete and exclusive package to free-to-air national broadcasters from the first mini-league match to the Final. The larger the television market, the larger the fee, so that the German, Italian, English, Spanish and French television companies contributed the most to the total Champions League revenue. In return, UEFA rewarded the clubs from those big television markets with the largest appearance fees. Finally, TEAM developed a Champions League brand which highlighted the distinctiveness of this tournament for viewers through the creation of three key symbols; black, silver and white house colours, the 'starball' and a rearranged version of Handel's 'Zadok the Priest' anthem.

Under pressure from the clubs but also recognising their own financial interests, UEFA have altered the format of the Champions League a number of times since its inception in the 1992–93 season. Originally, clubs played in two knock-out rounds before qualifying for the Champions League which replaced the quarter and semi-finals. This format was problematic because if a single team dominated a group, the other games in that group became academic and, therefore, unattractive. In the very first season of the Champions League, AC Milan's dominance undermined the significance of the games between IFK Gothenburg, Porto and PSV Eindhoven in the same group (Macwilliam 2000: 117). Consequently, in the following 1993–94 season, the first and second rounds remained the same but two clubs now qualified from the group phase to play in a knock-out semi-final (ibid.: 122). There was effectively an extra round in the competition. In 1994–95, the competition was altered quite dramatically as the first and second rounds were replaced by an expanded Champions League format of four mini-leagues. The winners of the competition, AC Milan, were joined by 15 other teams: the top seven seeded European sides according to the UEFA coefficient system, and eight qualifiers from a preliminary round between clubs ranked 8th to 23rd (ibid.: 25). For the 1997–98 season, the group phase was expanded to six groups of four from which the top teams and the two best runners-up qualified for the quarter-finals. This expansion involved the inclusion of certain second-placed teams from those countries ranked highest according to UEFA's coefficient system (ibid.: 140).

The major European clubs have gained significant financial benefits from the restructuring of the European Cup. For instance, when the Champions League was first introduced for the 1992–93 season, a team competing in the league would share a pool of £15 million pounds with the other eight teams (White 1992). Thus, the clubs in the Champions League received approximately £3 million that year (ibid.). This sum steadily increased as the competition expanded so that when United won the competition in 1999, they earned approximately £15 million from the event. Although winning the competition was valuable, the most decisive fact in Champions League earnings was determined by the television market in which a club was situated. Clubs in the biggest five television markets received decisively larger amounts for their appearance in the competition than those in the smaller market leagues. For instance in 1999, although both Barcelona and Brondy FC were eliminated from the same group simultaneously, Barcelona received a 3 million Swiss francs (CHF) (*c.* £1.2 million) appearance fee to Brondby's CHF 500,000 (£200,000) reward. Barcelona earned six times as much as the Danish club because it was in a bigger television market. The financial implications of playing in a small market were starkly demonstrated by Ajax since, despite its status in footballing terms, it received only CHF 1.1 million (£400,000) for competing in the group stage, a third of Barcelona's fee (TEAM 1999: 65). As these figures reveal, the big clubs situated in the biggest markets have received an increasing proportion of the rapidly expending revenue produced by this competition:

> You have an elite within the Premier League. You have exactly the same in the other countries. The Champions League is exacerbating it. There is a huge gulf between clubs in the Champions League and those that are not. So it is bound to be the case that those clubs will basically stay in the Champions League. It is very difficult to break into as we are finding. Once you are in it, the stakes are so high that you have to develop your commercial basis rapidly in order to sustain it. There will be twelve to sixteen global brands – bound to be. [Rick Parry, personal interview, 9 February 2000]

The Champions League has initiated a self-propelling process of concentration.

The clubs have not only benefited financially. Although the Champions League was an UEFA initiative, it has ultimately undermined the political authority of UEFA. The success of the league is dependent upon the participation of the biggest clubs and this competition has become an increasingly important part of UEFA's operations: 82 per cent of UEFA's revenue comes from it. Consequently, as UEFA has become more reliant on the big clubs, 'the power of clubs has changed dramatically in the last few years' (Richard Worth, TEAM, personal interview, 2 March 2000). The chairman of the biggest clubs are also well aware of this shift in political gravity: 'Fundamentally, the way that football has been structured with FIFA and UEFA, the clubs did not have any say. So this was a question of saying, "Excuse me, without the clubs there is no competition." Therefore, there has to be a dialogue' (Peter Kenyon, chief executive, personal interview, 3 March 2000). UEFA has been increasingly forced into a dialogue with the biggest clubs and ultimately compelled to acquiesce to the demands of these clubs. It is widely recognised that it would be possible for the clubs to organise a European competition away from the auspices of UEFA. UEFA's predicament in the face of the growing influence of the big clubs has been accurately captured by TEAM's Richard Worth:

> Do we feel under threat, yes, in a way of course, because at the end of the day it wouldn't be very difficult for any marketing agency if they have got a proper strategy to sit down with a group of top clubs and say, 'Do you fancy giving this a go?' and they will say, 'Yes'. And then the political fall-out will happen, the same as it did with Kerry Packer. Of course it can happen. If someone can say to a club, we will double or treble your money, it does not take a genius to work out that soon someone will say, 'All right, we'll give that a go.' Yes, there is a threat. [Richard Worth, TEAM, personal interview, 2 March 2000]

The Champions League has empowered the biggest clubs financially and politically. In the course of the 1990s, they, rather than UEFA or the national federations, have been increasingly able to determine the organisation of European football. In 1998, the threat posed by the big clubs' new independence was realised to the full.

The Media Partners Project

In July 1998, news emerged that a media rights group based in Milan, called Media Partners, had approached the biggest clubs in Europe with a proposal for a 'European Football League'. The chairman of Media Partners and the individual behind this radical proposal was Rodolfo Hecht Lucari, an expert in the field of sports rights who had worked under Silvio Berlusconi for 15 years. He applied free market principles to create a radical blueprint for European football. Hecht's plan was to create a league of 16 of the most famous teams in Europe which would compete throughout the season in order to exploit the value of these clubs' broadcasting rights to the full. Given the risks attached to the project, the 16 teams were selected to play in the new league for three years with no promotion or relegation in this period. This competition would be organised independently of UEFA and the sticking point of the proposal was that it offered the selected clubs far higher financial remunerations than they had received from the Champions League. The Champions League had earned about £180 million in the 1997–98 season of which 55 per cent went to the clubs. The biggest share by contrast went to UEFA and, according to Media Partners, £30 million went to TEAM (Curry

1998). By contrast, Media Partners promised the clubs involved that their proposed competition would produce five times the revenue of the Champions League. Indeed, some clubs suggested that their share under this project could be £160 million (ibid.). Media Partners exploited the clubs' discontent about the disproportionate amount which UEFA and TEAM in particular extracted from the Champions League. These bodies only organised and marketed the competition after all, whereas the biggest clubs actually brought value to the competition. The clubs demanded a share of the revenue which reflected their contribution more accurately.

The Champions League was a reformulation of European football along transnational lines. The format of the competition reflected the new dominance of the big clubs but under UEFA's administration certain international elements persisted. Revenue was redistributed to even the smallest national federations from the Champions League and the champions of each one had a formal right to enter the competition. UEFA weighted the competition in favour of the biggest clubs in the biggest markets but national sovereignty remained relevant, if not primary. The Media Partners project overturned the international basis of organisation entirely. The Media Partners project was a radical attempt to apply pure market logic to the format of European football, irrespective of national boundaries and traditions: 'I think the game has a problem in terms of rules [regulation]. I wanted to address that though I was told to avoid raising that issue but I insisted upon it. I think the game is bad because it is still structured according to realities and capacities which existed a century ago' (Rodolfo Hecht, Media Partners, personal interview, 17 May 2000).

Hecht exaggerates the longevity of the rules which regulate football but he usefully highlights the obstructiveness of the international regime to the free market. In place of arbitrary and obsolete regulations imposed by vested interests which had structured European football in its international era, Hecht insisted that the best way to organise European football was simply by allowing the market to decide who should prosper and who should fail. Football had to organise itself according to present economic realities:

> So if you are the owner of a big club you have huge pressure from the fans to go on investing in talent but also in names, there is a blend here. You don't only have to win, to play well but you also have to attract players that have some kind of flair which is not so rational. If you are one of those big brands because you have won a lot in football, you have this huge pressure. You have this predictable revenue coming from your domestic activity because now we call it 'competitions' because it is a nice, reassuring name. But now you have invested a zillion in players suddenly you have a bad referee or it doesn't pay off in the first year and you're fucked. You're truly fucked. It is a world that starts imploding because all this potential of support and show is there. It is a system that cannot work. De Coubertin is fun up to a point.

> It is a matter of scale. Of course it is fun, when it is you and I running on a field to see who is the fastest. There is no infrastructure required. But when you are now running an investment of a billion dollars, you cannot decide that it is not honourable to look into the obvious business side of this. Either you want gangsters to come in for some secondary reason or you want guys who can come in and get out in twenty years' time or three years' time because it made economic sense. [Rodolfo Hecht, personal interview, 17 May 2000]

Hecht accepted the theoretical attractiveness of sporting principles of solidarity but in the light of a competitive transnational market for players, such an approach was obsolete. In this new deregulated context in which the major clubs were under very serious financial pressure, a free market approach was the only conceivable approach. Although notably more vivid, Hecht's argument accords precisely with that proffered by Advocate General Lenz. European football should be ordered only by market competition:

> If people love Man U more than they love Leeds, what can you do? And therefore, they win more. Isn't that logical? Yeah. What should I do? And why should we do something? Because it is not the way it was. Of course, it will never be – nothing is ever the way it was. It is an illusion of our minds. Yes of course, it will amplify differences. [Rodolfo Hecht, personal interview, 17 May 2000][4]

Unlike Lenz, Hecht did not point to the economic inefficiency of smaller clubs but he does fully vindicate the ultimate effects of free market competition; the big clubs will become more dominant. For Hecht it is not only logically necessary to accept this fact but by embracing this new reality, new opportunities for profit-making would be realised. His commitment to profit was fundamental:

> I can sell this for three times as much as you sell it ... Is it immoral to make three times as much? No. It is immoral not to, in my view. It is totally immoral not to. Football is – or could be – for Europe what Hollywood is for the USA. It is our Hollywood and look what we are doing with it. $500 million revenue? Are we joking? 150 million families are mesmerised by it and don't look at anything else. The UK has a multicultural sports culture but it is an exception. You have mitigants. But where are the mitigants here? Where are they all over? There is only football ... And what do we make? Half a billion. It is a joke. [Rodolfo Hecht, personal interview, 17 May 2000]

The Media Partners project constituted a radical deregulation of European football competition, regardless of institutional interest, national sovereignty and historic precedent. The only significant factor was the economic potential of the clubs.

The big clubs were understandably interested in the project. Echoing Santiago Bernabeu's enthusiasm for the European Cup in 1955, Lorenzo Sanz, the president of Real Madrid, expressed public support for the project since the massive increase in revenue offered by the Media Partners project promised to alleviate the club's £170 million debts. By contrast, although definitive evidence is lacking, it seems highly likely that many of the other clubs took an instrumental attitude towards Hecht's proposals. They were never seriously committed to the creation of a new European league outside UEFA's jurisdiction but used the Media Partners project to demand financial concessions from UEFA over the distribution of television revenue. The Media Partners initiative was a way of rectifying certain injustices in the distribution of Champions League revenue. For instance, of all the revenue created by the Champions League in 1998, 83 per cent came from the biggest five television nations but the clubs from these countries received only 23 per cent of this income (Bose 1998). Yet, while other clubs wanted to increase their European revenue, they were adamant that domestic competition remained their core activity. For instance, AC Milan, which were always looked upon as the chief instigator of the project because of Berlusconi's connections to Hecht, were particularly committed to their domestic league:

> Certain English clubs were very involved in the project, much more than the Italians. Everybody thought that the project was Italian driven which it was not. We were called by the independent company [Media Partners] when the others were on board already. The others went on board because they thought we were ... Media Partners people are people who have been working with me and Mr Galliani for the past ten or fifteen years so it is a common assumption that since you know each other, it is natural that it is assumed that you would do things together. But in this case, it is not true. In fact, I think we – and I mean especially Milan and Juventus – we were the two clubs who created the most problems to the Media Partners project because we were more cautious than the others. We were slower than the others. We were realistic, I should say. We never thought that the European League could overtake the importance of the national league. That has never been in our thoughts. We just understand that we are in a system and the system is based on mutual respect. There are rules starting with FIFA down to UEFA then to the FAs. Breaking the system is not so easy. I'm not saying the system is correct but since you are in the system for a century, you cannot simply say, 'OK now I am fed up. We don't want to do it anymore. We go our own way – regardless of transfers, national teams, FIFA rules. We'll just go our own way.' It was too much. I am not saying that we are not going to that place but for the time being it was too much. [Umberto Gandini, AC Milan, personal interview, 15 March 2000]

Significantly, given the assertions of this connection between Milan and Media Partners, whose offices are located less than a mile from each other in central Milan, Hecht also confirmed the diffidence of the Italian clubs when it finally came to breaking with the established national and international structures: 'If I had had the support of the Italian clubs, UEFA would be history' (Rodolfo Hecht, personal interview, 17 May 2000). Interestingly, although both Gandini and Hecht pointed to the enthusiasm of certain English clubs (especially Manchester United) for the project, in fact, even that club was committed to the English domestic league:

> Certainly, Manchester United's position on this is that the domestic league is your number one priority and will always remain so. The right format for European competition we feel has to be – it has to be formatted right, the transparency needs to be right … Now we do not want to live outside of the sport – outside of the structure. What we want is a seat at the table. Now quite clearly the constitution of FIFA or UEFA does not allow for a club with a grievance to take it up directly with that organisation. [Peter Kenyon, chief executive, personal interview, 3 March 2000]

Hecht's initiative demonstrated UEFA's dependence upon the biggest European clubs but the primary basis of most of these clubs remained their domestic leagues.[5] Consequently, although it is not inconceivable that clubs would have participated in the Media Partners project, it seems likely that for most clubs, except perhaps Real Madrid, the Media Partners initiative was attractive because it allowed the clubs political leverage over UEFA. It threatened UEFA with the loss of its most important competition and, faced with this dire prospect, UEFA was obliged to concede to the clubs. The Media Partners project allowed the clubs to earn a greater part of the value which they themselves created. This was an optimal situation for the clubs since it allowed them to increase their revenue while avoiding political repercussions at the domestic level. The national federations threatened clubs with exclusion from domestic competition should they participate in the European Football League.

The debate between UEFA, Media Partners and the big clubs continued from July 1998 until the end of the year. Facing the threat of losing the vast bulk of their income, UEFA had no choice but to acquiesce to the demands of the biggest clubs and to restructure the Champions League in favour of these clubs. On 11 December 1998, UEFA and the clubs agreed to the new format of the Champions League. The competition was expanded to two group stages the first of which would consist of eight four-team mini-leagues, featuring 32 teams. The selection of the 32 demonstrated a further bias towards the clubs in the biggest markets. The holders would go into the first group phase and would be joined by a further 15 top-seeded clubs, the league winners from the nine highest ranked countries and the runners-up from the six highest ranked countries. More strikingly, the third-placed teams of countries (England, France and Germany) ranked third to fifth on the coefficient system had the opportunity to enter the Champions League itself if they won qualifying rounds against the teams of the smallest federations, as did the fourth-placed teams from the top and second-rank nations (Spain and Italy). Assuming that the current champion who qualifies automatically comes from the major television markets (which has been the case every year but 1995 when Ajax won), half the 32 clubs competing in this competition are now from the major markets. The competition has turned decisively against its international selection procedure in which only champions were selected to market-oriented and transnational criteria. The teams in the first group stage played each other in their mini-league in the autumn, the top two teams going through to the next group phase which consisted of four further mini-leagues of four teams. From then on the competition proceeded as it had done in the previous two years, the top two teams of each group qualifying for knock-out quarter finals. However, the third-place team from the first group entered the new, expanded UEFA Cup which had replaced the now abandoned Cup-Winners' Cup. This seemed to guarantee the biggest clubs European football even if they failed at the first group stage, though, highlighting the uncertainty of the game, some of the biggest clubs have failed to reach this stage; in 1999–2000, AC Milan came bottom of their group and were eliminated from Europe as were Juventus and Barcelona in the following year. Despite these inevitable contingencies, the new structure of the competition reflected and promoted the power of the biggest clubs. In this format, the Champions League was certainly no longer an anachronism.

Revenue for the reformed competition was increased dramatically by broadcasting additional games on pay-TV digital channels. The clubs themselves were guaranteed a larger share of this income partly because UEFA reduced the proportion which it allotted to itself. In 1999–2000, the new competition produced CHF 611 million (*c.* £240 million) as opposed to CHF 205 million (£82 million) under the old format in 1998–99 with Real Madrid, the winners receiving CHF 44 million (£18 million). The redistribution of revenue was skewed even more heavily in favour of the teams in the biggest television markets. For instance, although Borussia Dortmund, Rangers and Spartak Moscow were all eliminated at the first group stage, the differential between the respective remunerations was notable. In 1999–2000, Borussia received over CHF 15.1 million (£6 million) as opposed to Spartak's CHF 6.6 million (£2.6 million) and Ranger's CHF 10.7 million (£4 million). The increased revenue widened the divide between those clubs in the biggest markets and those outside them. Indeed, there was some evidence that even within the big market leagues, the clubs which could attract the biggest television audience were rewarded proportionately. While Barcelona received CHF 37.8 million (£15 million) for reaching the semi-finals in 1999–2000, Valencia, although the defeated finalists, received almost exactly the same amount, CHF 37.7 million. Indeed, Manchester United, although eliminated in the quarter-final stage, received CHF 35.4 million (£14 million). By the

2000–01 season, the revenue had increased considerably. The competition as a whole produced CHF 730 million (£300 million) with the winners Bayern Munich receiving over CHF 70 million (£30 million). Overall the competition revenue grew by 19 per cent, but the winner's share has increased by 60 per cent. Indeed, at every stage of the competition, the differentials between the revenue received by clubs in big and small markets had expanded. This can be demonstrated by comparing the respective representatives from the German league with those of Russian and Scottish leagues. For instance, in 2001–01 Bayer Leverkusen, eliminated at the first group stage, received CHF 27.8 million in comparison with Rangers who received CHF 13.5 million. Although Rangers received over CHF 3 million more than in the previous year, they had fallen behind clubs in the German league proportionately. In the 1999–2000 season, they received 70 per cent of Borussia Dortmund's CHF 15 million' fee but in 2000–01, the CHF 13.5 million which they earned was only 48.5 per cent of Bayer Leverkusen's fee (UEFAflash 2001). Even more strikingly, Spartak Moscow, who played in both group stages, received only CHF 12.6 million, or 45 per cent of Leverkusen's fee in 2000–01, but in the previous year when they had played the same number of games as Borussia Dortmund they received 43 per cent of their German club's fee (ibid.). Spartak's share of the revenue had effectively halved in a year for they received almost the same proportionate fee in relation to German clubs in 2000–01 as they had in the previous year even though they played twice as many games. Even before the Media Partners initiative, the Champions League favoured the biggest clubs in the biggest markets but with increasingly large remunerations on offer, the current redistribution of revenue has accelerated the inequalities in European football.

Even so, some of the more radical clubs, such as Real Madrid are still dissatisfied with this distribution of revenue:

> We negotiated a new format which was the best thing which we could obtain. But I think that we think that the Champions League has exactly the same problems as UEFA has internally. UEFA is an association of associations and it needs the approval of all the members of all the associations to make a decision. That means that the vote of England or Italy or Spain is equal to that of Lichtenstein. These countries have to be kept happy and this occurs with the Champions League. There are many many clubs involved, many many countries involved in the Champions League that give nothing to the competition. It is just a matter of giving money to clubs – what do they give to the competition? Nothing. The money they make from the Champions League has to be given to a lot of people. But who produces the money? There are not many clubs: there are five countries. There is something that not many people know; in the Champions League, five countries, Italy, England, Spain, Germany and France, produce 92 per cent of the income. And we receive less than 40 per cent. This is wrong. Everyone has to understand that we are professional clubs. If we produce 92 per cent, we have to receive – I don't say all – but a majority

of it. This is the problem with the Champions League at the moment. [Juan Onieva, personal interview, 19 April 2000][6]

Real Madrid were still unhappy about the distribution of revenue which they regarded as still overly biased towards the smaller clubs and federations. Onieva's comments suggest that the pressures which have propelled structural changes in the 1990s will continue to necessitate further change in the near future. In the deregulated era of increased live television coverage, the biggest clubs are producing more and more revenue and, in line with the wider liberal paradigm, they are demanding that they should receive a greater share of this new income which they effectively produce. This is a self-perpetuating process: as the biggest clubs demand more income, they are able to accumulate more playing talent, thereby becoming even more attractive to television companies. There is a spiralling concentration of economic and political power. Despite the economic forces which may demand change in the future, the other major clubs seem to support the current format and, although the new competition seems unwieldy, it has met with general approval from them:

> We are having some problems with the format [of the Champions League] because there is no global calendar. Because the schedule for the league, cup and international games is already there, you have to play four weeks in a row. FIFA and the national federations have to sit down with a clear piece of paper and work out a new calendar. We would like to play the Champions League every 16 days. [Roberta Bettega, personal interview, 14 March 2000]

Umberto Gandini confirmed that the scheduling of the event was a problem:

> I cannot talk on behalf of the entire group – I can only talk for AC Milan who may have a different view. We pushed for 32 clubs and two round-robins and then quarters and semis. We agreed upon that for the next four seasons. I don't think it is complicated. The problem is the calendar with the games following each other. We are satisfied with the format of the Champions League. [Umberto Gandini, personal interview, 15 March 2000]

Nevetheless, despite the satisfaction of AC Milan and Juventus with the post-Media Partners format, it was clear even in December 1998 when the new format was agreed that further alterations are inevitable. The spiral of concentration on the biggest clubs in the biggest markets demands further structural alteration.

The G14

The Champions League and the Media Partners initiative were responses to the growing power of the big clubs and the demand for programming by new television companies. In the course of the debates about the possibility of a European Superleague, the big European clubs formally recognised their new power. In November 1998, as an adjunct to one of the meetings with Media Partners, the top European clubs established themselves as a lobby group, which they named the G14. The G14 consisted, in the first instance, of the clubs which had been most successful in European competition (Juventus, Liverpool, Real Madrid, Milan, Barcelona, Inter, Bayern Munich, Ajax) but also included other obvious or strategically located clubs (Manchester United, PSV Eindhoven, Porto, Paris Saint-Germain, Marseilles, Borussia Dortmund). Nottingham Forest and Benfica (both of which had won the European Cup twice), Hamburg, Aston Villa, Steaua Bucherest, Red Star Belgrade and Celtic were all notable by their absence from this group even though they had all won the European Cup once. Umberto Gandini has provided a detailed account of how this group came into being and how, in particular, the clubs which are part of it were selected:

> AC Milan became involved because it was one of the founders actually. The idea of creating a group of selected teams which had historical reasons and sporting merit to be together came along with the discussions a couple of years ago. With UEFA we found out that there are eight teams which have won at least three European trophies and the eight teams are: the three major Italians, Milan, Juventus and Inter, Real Madrid and Barcelona, Liverpool, Ajax and Bayern Munich. So these eight clubs were considered special, the founders of European football both by UEFA and the other clubs. So we decided on the verge of discussions with Media Partners on the Superleague project to get together these eight clubs and start talking about our mutual interest. In European football, you have the association of associations [UEFA], the national associations, you have the leagues but you don't have an association of owners, I should say, the clubs. You have player unions but you don't have the owners. Also, during the Bosman case discussions, the Commission made it very clear that they wanted to talk to the owners not the associations: the ones who do the business. So we decided to get together and the idea was to have a meeting in Milan. We looked at the eight members and talking among ourselves we said that we must have Manchester United because Manchester United is the best club now, the most important club now as far as brand and potential and financial aspects are concerned. We invited Man United so we got to nine. We didn't have a French club so we said, considering France is an important country, it is an important territory, we invited Olympic Marseilles because they won the Champions Cup – not discussing the manner – so we got to ten. So then, Lorenzo Sanz, President of Real Madrid, said 'Well there is my good friend from Porto which is a historical club' which is true – they won the Champions Cup. So they invited Porto so we went to that point. And then, Germany with only Bayern Munich being such an important

territory but with only one club, so Bayern said 'Well let's invite Borussia Dortmund, they also are a former winner of the Champions Cup.' So we started with twelve clubs. The meeting went on all day and the point was to make clear to UEFA that we wanted to be part of the decision-making process ... At that moment, the focus was the restructuring of the European competitions. We were not satisfied with the way financially the Champions League had been administered. We wanted to be more involved. We wanted a bigger slice of the cake instead of funding all the national associations, all the eliminated teams, all the small countries and so on because we are the ones who make the show and therefore we are the ones who should get the profit. Then we extended it to 14 clubs by extending it to PSV Einhoven from Holland and Paris St Germain from France for their size, and their importance in their own market. [Umberto Gandini, personal interview, 15 March 2000]

It is interesting that in the selection of clubs, historical precedent was important. Although all the clubs in the G14 are economically important powers in European football, their European pedigree is in almost all cases a defining characteristic. Only Paris Saint-Germain has been selected on purely economic grounds; the G14 required two representatives in France since the television market there is large.

Gandini's statement is also interesting since Hecht claimed that his initiative was crucial to the creation of the G14: 'I am the dad of the G14. The G14 was put together by Media Partners. They did not know each other before. They were not allowed, they were afraid, there was no contact' (Rodolfo Hecht, personal interview, 17 May 2000). Clearly, the Media Partners project was very important to the creation of the G14 and it certainly seems to have accelerated the formation of this group, but progress towards this alliance was already underway before Hecht's project appeared. This is further confirmed by the fact that while Arsenal were involved in talks with Media Partners, they are not members of the G14. David Dein, the chief executive of Arsenal, is also the chair of several UEFA committees and this conflict of interest resulted in Arsenal withdrawing from discussion with Media Partners and prevented the club from joining the G14. The G14 was primarily created by a self-selecting group of clubs and, demonstrating its autonomy, it has strengthened itself since the Media Partners project. It has established itself on a formal legal footing and now has permanent and strategically situated offices in Brussels, so that it is in a better position to lobby the European Commission, whose free market principles best suit the interests of these clubs.

The importance of the G14 is clearly recognised by the participants who regard its new-found political power as both legitimate and essential:

> To go back to how the G14 emerged: the important thing to recognise is that the major economic players in the game are, increasingly, the clubs, the major clubs ... I'm not going into a battle about club v. country but I am just stating basic economic fact; the major clubs are the big drivers ... The economic power is shifting to the

major clubs. And it is actually then, in my view, an inevitability that that will be reflected at the European level as well. If the clubs domestically are pretty much in control of their own destiny. They manage their own competitions, they negotiate their own television deals, they are in control of their own commercial destiny. Why then should that not be reflected on the European stage? It is actually perfectly logical. There is nothing sinister. It is nothing to do with covert political groupings. If Liverpool, Manchester United, Arsenal, Newcastle and Chelsea have a dialogue and manage their destiny then when it comes to the stage when it's Liverpool and Manchester United, and Real Madrid and Barcelona and AC Milan, particularly post-Bosman with increased freedom of movement, there is nothing wrong with that. It is absolutely inevitable and the initial UEFA response 'Sorry, we don't talk to clubs, you have to go via your own national association' is actually bizarre because you are going through your own national association for things that you wouldn't dream of talking to them about on a domestic front ... If we want a dialogue with Milan and Madrid and Bayern Munich, then what is wrong with that? [Rick Parry, Liverpool FC, personal interview, 2 February 2000]

Although Rick Parry's intentions are clear when he says that the G14 is not 'sinister' or a 'covert' political grouping – he wants to emphasise the legitimacy and indeed necessity of this group in the light of economic changes – the G14 is self-evidently a political body. Rick Parry, in fact, recognises it as such. It is a forum in which the big European clubs are able to mobilise themselves to their best advantage especially in relation to UEFA. The dialogue with Milan, Madrid and Bayern Munich may be inevitable given the transnational reality of the sport today but this dialogue transforms formally autonomous clubs in separate markets beneath the sovereignty of a national federation into a coherent, unified group. Through this dialogue these clubs recognise their shared interests and challenges. Significantly, the G14 has been formally recognised in the political arena. In the debates over the Perugia case, the G14 played an important role in the discussions with the Commission, UEFA, FIFA and FIFPro. Crucially, the Commission regards the body as entirely legitimate and consults with it openly. As Gandini noted, the Commission itself explicitly wanted an association of the clubs, 'the ones who do the business'. The rise of the G14 is a key moment in the emergence of a transnational regime. The group is a prominent feature in the new European geography characterised not only by a concentration of financial and playing capital but also the steady accumulation of political power as well.

Although individuals like Rick Parry and Umberto Gandini see the development of the G14 as necessary and legitimate, the opposition to it by both UEFA and the national federations is understandable. It constitutes a manifest erosion of their sovereignty and UEFA and the national federations have tried to minimise the G14's political power by simply ignoring it:

To be honest, we don't recognise it in any shape or form. All clubs are represented through their football associations. UEFA has actually put a great deal of work into getting the clubs forums where they can raise any issues that they have: club committees and all sorts of things. So, I don't spend too much of my time worrying about it or thinking about it. I'm not being naive or sticking my head in the sand ... You cannot let any individual or any set of individuals derail the process. [Adam Crozier, chief executive, The Football Association, personal interview, 11 April 2000]

The G14 is not recognised by anybody in UEFA, the national associations or by the leagues. They are not a constituted association. They hold informal meetings but we do not recognise them because we have, inside our structure, committees which are responsible for this and in relation to the Champions League we have set up as a consequence of the new structure an advisory board and in there there are a lot of clubs involved who are part of the G14 but not exclusively. So we have allowed other clubs to get involved and give their input. [Marcel Benz, UEFA, personal interview, 12 April 2000]

In the light of the very real threat which the G14 pose to their federations, Adam Crozier's and Marcel Benz's views are perhaps understandable but they are also unrealistic despite their claims to the contrary. Given the dependence of UEFA on the clubs who are members of the G14 clubs, this group is an ultimately unignorable force in contemporary football. Indeed, the club committees which Benz mentions were established after the Media Partners initiative and thus UEFA have in fact been forced into a dialogue with these clubs even if they do not admit to it. As already noted, in formal discussions over the Perugia case, UEFA were ultimately forced to recognise the legitimacy of the G14. Minimally, the G14 have an effective veto on any proposed developments since they will simply threaten to create their own superleague should UEFA attempt to introduce regulations or redistributive measures which are against their interests. At best, the non-recognition of the G14 by the federations is a temporary measure designed to reduce this group's influence. Just as UEFA emerged at the beginning of the international era of European football to regulate that regime, the G14 has emerged at the inception of the transnational regime and it does not seem fanciful to suggest that this institution is likely to become as significant in the current era as national federations were in the past.

Romance

The development of the Champions League and the emergence of the G14 are among the most radical developments to have occurred in European football. It is understandable, then, that they have stimulated intense commentary in the media as journalists, players, clubs and federations try to come to an understanding of the significance of these transformations. They had to accommodate themselves to these changes and their commentaries should be understood as the attempt of various individuals and groups to readjust to a transformed social context. In the 1950s and 1960s, as Chapter 3 revealed, no division between financial and sporting imperatives was recognised; the commercial benefits of European competition was regarded as valid. The revenue earned from competition paid players' wages and transfer fees. In the 1970s and 1980s, there were worries that the obsession with money had corrupted the sport by encouraging foul play. In the 1990s, as the Champions League developed and became more lucrative for the clubs, a new critical tone appeared in the press which denigrated this pursuit of wealth by the clubs *per se*. The argument was not that the pursuit of financial gain led players to cheat or clubs to bribe referees as had been the case in the 1970s, but that the increasing wealth of the big clubs intrinsically corrupted the sport. The new power of the big clubs was itself antithetical to the sport. Thus, in the early 1990s, *The Times* journalist David Miller described Milan as a '£20 million team' but whereas in the past this had been taken as a vindication of the quality of a team, the term now had distinctively negative connotations. Entitled 'Choking on their Champagne', the expense of the team had become a reason for resenting it (Miller 1991). The big clubs themselves now became the focus of critique and vitriol. In a critical article on the Champions League and the seeding of the competition, Robert Hughes of *The Times* rejected the attitude of the big clubs where they 'have to be indemnified against failure' (Hughes 1993). In his criticisms, Hughes similarly claimed that the financial power of the big clubs had undermined the validity of European football. Hughes illustrated this inversion of values by citing a comment by Lennart Johansson, the president of UEFA: ' "In such a situation as we have today, you have to see things from a financial and sporting point of view". Note the priority' (ibid.). For these commentators, the new power of the big clubs was ruining European competitions.

In rejecting the dominance of the big clubs, these commentaries drew frequently on the concept of 'romance' or 'glory': 'When sport begins counting the takings ahead of glory, we have problems. When money means more than the integrity of the competition, who can doubt that sport itself is devalued and that the disease will spread to the minds of the players?' (Hughes 1996a). Earlier, Hughes had commented' 'The whole affair debases a wonderful tournament, the European Cup, that has been built up over 40 years ... The logic is finance at the cost of merit ... The marketing men who devised this bastardisation of European events will be the first to bale out when the price drops, as it will when customers see the devaluation' (Hughes 1996b).

These criticisms reached a furious pitch with the announcement of the Media Partners proposals for a European Superleague in 1998. A long critical article on the Media Partners project by Roy Collins was titled 'High and mighty put the boot into romance' (Collins 1998a). Alan Shearer, the England captain from 1996 to 1998, reiterated the criticism: 'From what I gather there wouldn't be any relegation or promotion yet that's what football is all about. The uncertainty of how the season unfolds is the great thing about football. I think if the Super League was created then a lot of that romance would be taken away' (Shearer, cited in Walker 1998). Other commentators made similar points. 'Let's not be mealy-mouthed, as the proponents of the new hybrid would have it. This latest putative breakaway, like the last, is all about greed, nothing remotely to do with glory' (Lovejoy 1998a). Romance and glory referred to the sporting uncertainty of the European Cup when smaller clubs could defeat larger ones because economic considerations were putatively secondary to sporting values. For these commentators, the romance and the glory of the European Cup is antithetical to the self-interested manoeuvrings of the big clubs in the 1990s. For them, the Champions League and the Hecht initiative in particular were motivated only by money whereas the old European Cup embodied sporting principles. It prioritised romance and glory above financial imperatives and consequently, while the European Cup was legitimate, the Champions League was an aberration. In the Champions League, the romance of uncertain outcome has been stifled by a growing emphasis on financial power. Yet, this account of the European Cup is inaccurate. As Chapter 3 demonstrated, that competition never took the form of a genuine knock-out competition where 'glorious' or 'romantic' uncertainty was unquestionably prioritised. The two-legged ties were instituted for primarily financial reasons and they always favoured the bigger teams. The format of the European Cup was not *a priori* the embodiment of sporting principles but a political compromise which reflected the balance of power in Europe at the time. The competition was the contingent and ultimately *ad hoc* result of negotiations between sovereign national federations and UEFA, on the one hand, and subordinate clubs, on the other. Consequently, when these commentators mobilise the concepts of romance, glory or tradition to reject the Champions League, they do not point to some timeless principles of sporting excellence but simply to the kind of competition which existed in the past when European football was organised on an international basis.

That these critics defend only the previous competition format – rather than any objective sporting principles themselves – becomes clear if their criticisms are examined more carefully. Many critics of the Champions League cite the selection of teams who are not national champions as irrefutable evidence of the corruption of sporting standards. The runners-up in the big market were allowed into the Champions League from 1997 but, after the 1998 reforms, third and even fourth-placed teams from Italy, Germany, Spain and England qualified for the competition. The entry of non-champions into a tournament originally called the Champions Cup and now called the Champions League was regarded as nonsensical: 'the moneymen have bastardised the most famous club tournament of them all, turning it into a misnomer by admitting runners-up' (Lovejoy 1998b). Commentators like Lovejoy or Hughes regarded the selection of clubs by means of a coefficient system as intrinsically inferior to the selection of national champions alone. For them, it was self-evident that only national champions should be in the European Cup. Yet, national champions did not necessarily produce better football. Indeed, as the elimination of Juventus in 1986 demonstrated, there were clear instances when it could produce inferior football. In this case, a competition which was apparently organised with only sporting considerations in mind knowingly produced weaker competition. In defending the selection system which persisted in the era when European football was organised on an international basis, critics are not appealing to self-evidently superior principles. On the contrary, they are simply defending the format of a competition which existed under a particular regime of regulation when the national federations were dominant and when national leagues were more autonomous. Commentators are mistaken when they assume that the selection of national champions automatically embodies the highest sporting ethics. With typical vividness, Rodolfo Hecht has illustrated the contingency of selection procedures:

> But isn't any selection criterion cultural? So any line we draw is cultural. There is nothing obvious. In the Olympics the fourth Austrian downhiller cannot compete because he is number 4 in his country but he may be number 4 in the world and watching the event on TV. Is that fair? It is fucking unfair but we draw a line which is due to the interaction of many factors. [Rodolfo Hecht, personal interview, 17 May 2000]

Selection criteria are never pure. They reflect only the political realities of any sport at any particular time. Certain criteria become normalised over a period of time and they are then taken as self-evidently fair and proper as participants in the sport become emotionally wedded to them, but this normalisation does not mean that a competition actually embodies pure sporting principles. The critics of the Champions League originally became attached to a competition in which all the teams in it were *national* Champions. The European Cup was romantic for them because it was an international competition between the representatives of the nations of Europe. The concept of romance is not an appeal to objective standards of sporting quality but only to the kind of sports competition which has existed and with which these commentators are familiar. The appeal to romance is finally a defence of the old European Cup organised on an international basis. Romance values this kind of international tournament over the transnational spectacle which the Champions League has become.

The Importance of Romance

The most attractive aspect of the Champions League 'brand' for sponsors and television companies is plainly the quality of the competition. However, the mere presence of top players does not automatically make a sporting competition attractive unless the competition itself is regarded as authentic. Matches have meaning when there is a historical context which fans and players recognise. If there is no historical context, then matches are artificial; they become meaningless displays of virtuosity like the Harlem Globetrotters. As Kerry Packer's 1970s World Series Cricket reveals (when Packer signed most of the best cricketers in the world for contrived spectaculars), such artificial competitions do not sustain supporter interest for long. Consequently, they become valueless for both promoters and sponsors because they do not attract consumers. The crucial aspect of all sporting competition is that they are regarded as real; they genuinely reflect the affiliations of the fans. Each new encounter is part of a long-term relationship between the teams in a recognised competition; new games are part of a sequence recognised by all involved. They have a social context and consequently have a meaning. Although the concept of romance is untenable when it is used to essentialise the selection criteria of the European Cup, when romance refers to these collective memories which fans share, it is an unignorable part of football as a ritual. As collective memory, romance gives each game a context in which it is meaningful. It is notable that Hecht has rejected any attachment to the past, prioritising only market logic: 'This attachment to the past is something that I truly cannot understand. I cannot share it. I don't understand it intellectually. There is no such thing as the past, only the present' (Rodolfo Hecht, personal interview, 17 May 2000). Hecht rejects the concept of 'romance' as mere irrationality. Umberto Gandini has similarly noted: 'Romance doesn't pay the bills' (personal interview, 15 March 2000).[7] Yet their rejection of romance is misplaced. The financial value of the European Cup depends on the memories and traditions which fans have of this tournament.

The importance of collective memory is demonstrated by the fact that certain games in the Champions League between even very well-known clubs have been played out in front of almost empty stadiums. For instance, during the 1997–98 season, Newcastle United played Barcelona in the penultimate match of the group stages. Having only won one point from the previous three games, Barcelona were already eliminated from the competition and only 2000 Barcelona fans attended the game in a stadium whose capacity is 100,000. With no historical relationship between the fans, the game was insignificant and without a crowd to create an atmosphere, the television coverage lost much of its attractiveness. The point here is that unlike domestic league games where the relationship between the two sets of fans and the common memories (and enmities between them) give even technically meaningless games significance, this is not yet the case in Europe. Barcelona fans simply do not have a sufficiently strong relationship with Newcastle United and its fans to render a meaningless mid-table game attractive to them. Since there was no shared past, there was no honour at stake between the fans beyond qualification to the next round of the Champions League and once that is impossible, as it was in 1997–98, then the games become pointless. The key problem with Hecht's proposal for a European Superleague was that it threatened to introduce a large number of games which were simply not meaningful to the fans:

> There would inevitably be teams in the middle of that league [the European Superleague] as there are in any league and that much of the season for them would become uncompetitive. They would be in the comfort zone of the Media Partners Superleague or whatever it was called and only the teams at the top and perhaps at the bottom would really have something to play for. As we've seen the past, when there has been a game in the Champions League that hasn't really mattered to the home side and I give you Barcelona against Newcastle as a perfect example, where the Nou Camp was almost ghostly on that night – one of the world football's great theatres with 2000 people in it because Barcelona couldn't stay in the competition. With a league, there is always a chance that that kind of game is going to be repeated – not on a regular – but on more than an occasional basis. [Jeff Farmer, Carlton Television, personal interview, 18 January 2000]

Richard Worth of TEAM also recognised the importance of 'romance' and tradition to the viability of the Champions League:

> The problem I see is that if Manchester United are in a 16-team European League and after 10 games, they are 13th playing AC Milan who are 14th, nobody cares. They will say: 'We are not all that interested in this anymore. We would rather be back playing Everton.' The teams at the top will think it is wonderful but I am not sure that the social structure is mature enough to say, 'Yes a European League is definitely going to work.' [Richard Worth, TEAM, personal interview, 2 March 2000]

European football is commercially viable only in the context of the common traditions and memories of fans. Without these shared understandings and relations, games are empty. Romance does, in fact, pay the bills.

The recent reactions to the transformed format of the Champions League following the Media Partners intervention are significant because they demonstrate exactly the importance of collective memory to the viability of these competitions. The first group stage, in particular, has been seen by most fans as artificial, as the decline in viewing audiences and attendances in both 1999–2000 and 2000–01 confirmed:

> Last year, the one we've just been through, was shite. The year before, I missed Brondby and Juventus and that was it because they were all important games.

Whereas this time, Graz doesn't matter ... There was just too many [games]. Look at the home games – it was like a League match. You know you go to a league match like Coventry and no one's arsed. It was like that for a European game. Eight years ago, we were never in European Cup and Gothenburg was an amazing thing. The games just don't matter, you know we are going to win. [Luke, Manchester United fan, personal interview, 27 June 2000]

Dominik Müller: It is the greatest bullshit football has ever seen. What do you expect?

Lutz Hepperle: It is merely commercial. It is too big. [Club Nummer 12, 3 July 2000]

Indeed, at Bayern Munich, Dominik Müller and Club Nummer 12 are not the only individuals who are unconvinced by the present format. Bayern's president, Franz Beckenbauer, has publicly expressed doubt about the current competition on the very grounds that it is reducing the attractiveness of the competition. His criticisms are particularly apposite since he himself played at the highest level.[8] As individuals like Beckenbauer recognise, the current format of the Champions League stretches the meaningfulness of the tournament. It is highly likely that a completely new European Football League, as envisaged by Hecht, would be alien to fan affiliations and that the games would be seen as purely artificial. Consequently, although we are in a period of rapid transition in which a new transnational regime is emerging quickly, the collective memories of the fans prevent the immediate imposition of a transnational competition on purely free market lines of the kind which Hecht envisaged. Such a competition could only emerge when the understandings of the fans, reflecting the social reality which confronts them, saw such an event as meaningful. In domestic leagues, even a technically academic game between two mid-table teams is meaningful because the fans who have built up relations with each other over decades have their pride at stake. Their final position in the table is always significant to local rivalries where it becomes a weapon by which one set of fans asserts its status over another. Thus, even games against socially insignificant domestic opposition become important. These decades-old relations provide the context which render extrinsically meaningless games intrinsically valuable. The viability of a European League would depend upon the development of these social relations.

Nevertheless, although a genuinely new European Superleague is unlikely to attract the allegiance of fans yet, the development of the Champions League has transformed fan traditions. Romance, the collective memories of the fans, is not an essential unchanging entity but adapts along with the development of fan groups. Collective memories are manipulated to reflect the reality of contemporary social relations. Thus, while a full European league might be rejected by the fans, a return to the former structure of the European Cup involving only a series of knock-out ties would not be supported by the fans. Thus, although the United fan, Stan, regarded the present format as unsatisfactory, he did not advocate a return to the original structure of the European Cup but only to the Champions League format before the Media Partners project. The mutability of collective memory was demonstrated by Chelsea fans in the 1999–2000 season when Chelsea played in the Champions League after coming third in the Premier League:

> We have very mixed emotions about the Champions League. A lot of Chelsea fans didn't really think we should have been there because there was a feeling that you should earn the right to be there; you should win your league to be there. Before we kicked the ball in the competition, there was a lot of Chelsea fans saying we should be in the UEFA Cup. They shouldn't have changed the format. That argument disappeared completely as soon as AC Milan had played at Stamford Bridge. Nobody questioned that it wasn't a great idea anymore. Emotionally, I think the Champions League should be just for Champions of each country. I don't think it is right that the champions of Estonia should be routinely knocked out by a team that finished third in Portugal. That makes a nonsense of the competition. But if you're in it and you are lucky enough to jet off to Milan or Turin, it is just too good to be true so you wouldn't want to change it. It is a bit of a dilemma. [James Edwards, personal interview, 10 August 2000]

As fans find themselves in new social relations, they begin to understand themselves and their relations differently. Their memories transform in line with the situation which confronts them. Collective memory, reflecting the actual social relations between people, limits change but it does not prevent it. Collective memory is malleable and groups can agree on new memories in the face of new demands. European competition is going through a period of rapid transition and the memories of old competition and the relations which were established in the past still persist. However, as Edwards reveals, while Chelsea fans formally supported the old international criterion of selection, in practice, no supporter of a team which qualified for the Champions League as a runner-up seriously advocated that their team should not compete. The fans' views of what is valid and invalid changes in the light of altered circumstances. Romance is a key element to the success of European sport but the collective memory of European football – its romance – is shifting. Fans are adapting their collective memories and are inventing new traditions of support which acknowledge and recognise the deregulation of European football. As they gain more experience of European football and play more games against European opposition, new relations with other clubs are developed which render future games between them meaningful. The romance of the old international European Cup is being superseded by a new tradition – a new form of romance. In this emergent transnational reality – and against many of the purely dismissive and, in fact, reactionary critiques – new sporting 'romances' in the form of highly charged memories are developing:

> How could you watch what Manchester United did in the Champions League last year [1998–99], and I was at every game, and say that the Champions League has ruined the excitement and adventure of football? It was pure drama all the way through. They were out of the competition so often, it had to been seen to be believed, ending up with a climax to a game that you will never see again, irrespective of a game of that importance. In answer to those who say that it has ruined the romance, and the excitement and the adventure of the normal two-leg European football: it hasn't. [Jeff Farmer, Carlton Television, personal interview, 18 January 2000]

> Manchester United–Barcelona 3–3. It would never have happened in the old system which did not always mean that the best sides were there. [*The Independent*, 27 November 1998]

Reflecting the growing frequency of encounters between clubs, new memories or new forms of 'romance' are emerging which provide a context for future games and which, in fact, make a further expansion of European football possible. The transnational regime cannot implement free market logic at a stroke ignoring the realities of fan culture, but this regime has set certain processes in motion which are likely to render increasingly pure transnational competition meaningful and desirable for the fans.

Towards a European League

In 2002, UEFA decided to reform the Champions League once again. The double mini-league format had reduced spectator interest and attendances at ground and television viewing figures had declined. The average viewing figure for the Champions League in the major television markets fell from over 5.5 million in 1998–99 to 4.8 million in 1999–2000. In response to this decline, UEFA have replaced the second mini-league with eliminating, quarter and semi-final rounds played over two legs and culminating in a final. For the first time since its inauguration, the number of fixtures in the Champions League has been reduced. This reduction should not be taken as evidence of a return to a system of international regulation. The competition still involves 32 teams and the finalists will play twelve matches, which is as many as Bayern Munich and Manchester United played in 1998–99. Although smaller than the present unwieldy format, it is still bigger than the 1998 format featuring an extra eliminating round and since it is likely to be more popular, it will ultimately strengthen the Champions League. It will consolidate the competition in European fan culture even more, though it is unlikely that this format will remain in place for long as the economic forces propelling structural transformation are becoming stronger. Although the G14 have accepted this new format, there were serious criticisms of it. The competition will produce less revenue for the clubs because there are fewer games, especially for those clubs eliminated early in the knock-out rounds. Under the old format, they would have been guaranteed six games in the second group stage. The G14 were also affronted that they were not consulted about the new format before its announcement:

> We are very surprised by the decision ... We wish to express disappointment and disapproval with regards to the form in which UEFA proceeded in changing the format of the most important European club competition ... With the congested international calendar indicated by UEFA as the main reason justifying the change, the G14 reiterates that an alleviation of the fixture list may not be conducted on the back of club football only ... G14 therefore request a comparable reduction of dates reserved for national team matches, friendly matches in particular. [G14 statement cited at <www.countryfile.co.uk/worldsoccer/newsdec02>]

Given the discontent of the G14, it is extremely unlikely that this format will remain for longer than two to three years. Further development of the Champions League, which may or may not take the form of a more regular European League, is almost certain:

> The Champions League is developing slowly but constantly towards a league system. In order to get to a European Championship for clubs there are two ways: either a breakaway situation or a development. I think that we are now following the development route. The fact that there are countries with four teams, countries with three, countries with two, means that the strength of those countries is respected by opening access to their teams and the fact that certain champions do not make it any more means that they are not good enough to make it because they have the chance ... The Champions League's development reflects reality. We want a European League one way or the other to take place. We want a league which would not be detrimental to the national leagues and national associations. I think they can be complementary. They don't have to be alternatives. And the aim of our activities is to get to that point. The fact that there is also political integration occuring in Europe. It is not a mystery that UEFA are controlling 51 federations but there are different speeds among these federations. The easiest thing is to find out whether there is a speed for European Community countries and the rest of Europe. I wouldn't be surprised to see the European Community call for a European Championship among their countries. [Umberto Gandini, personal interview, 15 March 2000]

Even David Dein who has been as committed as any of the club directors to UEFA, recognises the trajectory of current developments: 'I think a European league system will evolve in due course' (David Dein, chief executive, Arsenal

Football Club, cited in Moore 1996). Whatever form the evolution of the Champions League takes, the big European clubs and the G14 above all will increasingly have a decisive say in the direction of change. It is highly likely that in this new era, UEFA will lose even more of its current authority and become a forum not for the national federations but for European clubs. Although some commentators regard the Champions League as an abomination and view the future negatively as the corruption of European football by commercialisation, the new foci of power in Europe and the new marketised networks in football have not and will not ruin all competitive balance nor will they obliterate the possibility of fan solidarity and allegiance. Fans have developed new relations with each other and reinvented their understanding of themselves in the light of the deregulation of the sport. They are creating new solidarities in the face of the new environment which now confronts them. New forms of identification are emerging which reflect emergent transnational reality.

Notes

1 In 1999, UEFA altered this system so that clubs received one point for a win and half a point for a draw – see <http://www.xs4all.nl/~kassiesa/bert/uefa/rank99.html>.
2 Rangers and Real Madrid seem to have been motivated by financial need. Rangers was seriously disadvantaged by operating in a relatively weak league while Real Madrid was in debt and therefore supportive of any initiative which might ease their financial problems.
3 TEAM was founded by Klaus Hempel and Jurgen Lenz who had worked for the Adidas' owner Horst Dassler's marketing company ISL until his death in 1987 (see Sugden and Tomlinson 1998: 93).
4 Even UEFA's representatives recognised the logic of the market: 'It is life. You can take a lot of different modern institutions – let's take the broadcasting world. The Rupert Murdochs of this world, the big guys are taking over all the small ones and they are all becoming much bigger and stronger. Some of us don't like it, we would prefer for that not to happen but it is a fact of life' (Richard Worth, TEAM, personal interview, 2 March 2000).
5 See Kipker (2001) for a good discussion of the viability of alternative European leagues and the political pressure on UEFA.
6 Gandini highlighted one other problem: 'There could be some adjustment with the drawing procedures, maybe, because we have to take into consideration the strength of the club not by its performance in Europe in the last five years but the strength of the actual club the moment they gain the first or the third place in an important league. There should be a system by which the groups should be a little more balanced. The coefficients need to be more balanced than they are. Talking about our experience; we went into a group where we have the third team from England (Chelsea), the first team from Italy (Milan) and the first team from Turkey

(Galatasaray) and the third team from Germany (Hertha Berlin) so Italy, Germany and England were in the same group and Hertha Berlin was considered a weak club because they didn't have any historical background in European competition. Since they made third place in the German league, they must have had something. They weren't a better team than us, but we lost. But that is the idea. On the other hand, we had a group with Sparta Prague and Spartak Moscow and very different size of teams. That probably is the only adjustment I would like to see' (Umberto Gandini, personal interview, 15 March 2000).

7 Hecht emphasised the point: 'I don't argue with people that don't like sunsets. There are people who believe in something they call "conservatism". There is no such thing in nature. I am sorry. It is just ignorance. Of course, romance is getting out of our lives. Sorry. I hate it. I suffer as much as anyone. Is the Internet bringing romance into our lives? Potentially and potentially not. Romance is disappearing because we are animals of that sort. Nostalgia is something that leads to nothing. We have to love what we are losing but accept we cannot keep it. The world changes, the game has a future. I think it has to change for structural reasons' (Rodolfo Hecht, personal interview, 17 May 2000).

8 Rick Parry confirmed the legitimacy of Beckenbauer's view: 'At some of the G14 meetings, you have got people like Beckenbauer, you've got people like Rummenige, you've got people like Bettega, you've got people like Frank Arnason. You've got players. People who actually played the game and understood the game. It is not just the media barons by any stretch of the imagination. It is people who really understand international football and have played international football at the highest level in the World Cup. If they haven't got a balanced view then no one else will have' (Rick Parry, personal interview, 9 February 2000).

PART IV
FOOTBALL FANS IN THE NEW EUROPE

Chapter 9

The Politics of Football

Independent Supporters' Associations

Although football has a different cultural position in each European country, a similar form of supporting culture has emerged and become dominant across Europe since the 1960s or 1970s. For the last thirty to forty years, the core support for European clubs has consisted of active and dedicated groups of white men. It is true that a small minority of women have become part of these groups, especially in the 1990s, and that at some clubs, the dedicated support has included members of ethnic minorities whose presence is also significant but these fan cultures has been overwhelmingly dominated by white men. Since the 1960s in Britain and a decade later in most of the rest of Europe, groups of dedicated male supporters have gathered behind the goal at one end of the ground. These fans have colonised the ends or 'kurva' at grounds across Europe, developing their own distinctive style of supporter culture in these spaces. This culture includes vociferous, boisterous and potentially violent support of their team. Especially in Italy, it has involved elaborate displays before games to intimidate the opposition and to express the identity and solidarity of the fan group. In Italy and Spain, these groups have become extremely well organised, forming themselves into so-called 'ultra' groups which organise displays and chants during games as well as ticketing and travel arrangements for the fans. In northern Europe, these masculine groups have been less formally ordered, although they have been no less significant. Although not all these individuals in these group have been committed hooligans, hooliganism has been a feature of this style of support. Hooliganism has constituted an element of this masculine style of support and there are reasons why fan violence has been a consistent feature of this masculine fan culture.

Masculine fan culture of the ends or kurvas has prioritised the honour of the fans. The fans gain status from their support of their team and from the team's success in relation to other fan groups. In this struggle for status, these men have regarded violence as an appropriate instrument by which they demonstrate their superiority. In his recent book, *Morbo: the story of Spanish football*, Phil Ball highlights the central role which this status struggle between these masculine fan groups has played in Spanish football since the 1970s, although his historical survey extends back to the origins of the professional clubs at the turn of the century. He notes that Spanish football is dominated by the 'morbo' or rivalry which has more recently been promoted by these masculine fan groups (Ball 2002). The organisation of European football since the 1960s with its large open terraces, cheap ticket prices and generally lenient policing, has facilitated the development of this distinctive terrace or kurva culture. Consequently, these fan groups have constituted a very important element of European football, creating an unmistakable atmosphere in the grounds and, especially from the mid-1970s onwards, creating crowd problems for the clubs and the authorities. These masculine fan groups have been a prominent part of European society, and are an unignorable aspect of the new geography of Europe. In the 1990s, they have remained extremely important but they have had to transform themselves in the light of the commercialisation of the game. Commercialisation and the transformation of European football over the last decade has forced these groups to renegotiate their relations to the club and to develop defensive strategies to protect their supporting practices. As clubs have been transformed by the deregulation of European football, these fans have had to adapt themselves to the transformed space in which they find themselves inside the football ground. In the light of these changes, the relation between fans and clubs has become more overtly political since the 1990s.

The politicisation of the relationship between fans and clubs has been most advanced in England. There, unlike the rest of Europe, there has been a dramatic increase in ticket prices and crowd control in the new all-seater stadia. This transformation has been characterised as an attempt to turn football fans into customers. The term 'customer' has been mobilised by the new directors in England to describe the remarketing of the game away from the 'traditional' masculine supporters to a new familial audience which is more lucrative and disciplined than the masculine fan culture (see King 1998c: 138–43). The increase in ticket prices and the new relationship which clubs have imposed upon their fans in order to turn them into customers has had a profound effect on fan culture:

> Converting people who are supporters into customers – that is a problem – because it changes the whole point of it. It destroys loyalty which a lot of people think is important about football. Everyone will just become floating customers. It destroys the whole point of it. The whole point was about supporting a club of which you were a member. It was just like a maintenance thing. The loyalty was that you all turned up. I am not sure that it feels the same everywhere exactly; other clubs have different feelings or the fans do. At United, it always felt to me that we've got to keep the numbers up, partly because we weren't winning. Your attendances were something to be proud of. I think that is exactly why City had such good attendances when they went down – it was to compete with United ... As soon as it becomes too

expensive for someone who is unemployed, then you realise that it is becoming a significant amount of money whereas it was almost a token gesture. It was a token gesture. Pretty much anyone could afford to go to football. You would have supported anything they did; you'd be happy to pay into the lottery or super-pools but now you say, 'Bollocks you're not having anything off me.' It is a very strange attitude to your club but it is because you don't feel it is a club anymore. It is a money-making exercise. We're almost there. We're all customers now and that is why so many people feel negative. That has been taken away from them. [Duncan Drasdo, IMUSA and SU committee member, personal interview, 13 June 2000]

Before the commercialisation of football in the 1990s, fans looked upon themselves not as customers but as members of their club which they supported through active participation. The season ticket was not regarded as an onerous expense but rather as a subscription fee which sustained an institution of which the fans were active members. The club was ultimately supported not financially but by fans' regular and vociferous attendance at games. The ticket price was a maintenance fee for use of an institution of which a fan was a member. Fans contributed to the very public good from which they benefited. The rapid increase of ticket prices in the 1990s has transformed this membership model radically. Fans are no longer members who happily pay a nominal subscription fee to the club which they sustain through active demonstrations of loyalty; they have become mere consumers whose mode of support is now purely financial.

The rebranding of certain symbols which had become very important for masculine fan culture across Europe from the 1960s has signified the marketisation of the relationship between these fans and their clubs. Apparently minor changes to these symbols, for example, badges, have been invested with great significance by these masculine fan groups. For instance, in 1997 Manchester United removed the words 'Football Club' from its badge on the grounds that these words detracted from its primary brand name, 'Manchester United'. Market research had revealed that fans identified with the name 'Manchester United' to which the words 'Football Club' were superfluous and, following the logic Freedman outlined in Chapter 7, the club decided to strengthen this brand identity by dispensing with the words 'Football Club'. This appears to be an apparently small alteration but it symbolises a quite profound change. The club badge, along with various other cultural artifacts, such as songs or key players, constitute the symbols which represents the fans' collective identity and their social solidarity. From the early 1970s, the club's crest, featuring a trident-carrying devil and the words 'Manchester United Football Club', became an important symbol of the masculine fan culture which was dominant at that time. This symbol represented the shared memories of this group, denoting, for them, their relationship to each other and to the club. The commercialisation of the club has primarily aimed to restrict this group's access to the ground and to expand the market for football to a wider, possibly more affluent, but certainly more restrained familial form of support (see King 1998c). The transformation of the club badge symbolises a renegotiation of the relations between fans and club. The new badge denotes that the fans are now just customers of Manchester United rather than supporters of a football club. Moreover, the new badge brands the club differently in order to attract a different kind of fan. While the old badge symbolised the masculine culture which was a central part of the club's support from the 1960s to 1990s, the new badge denotes the new relationship which the club is trying to establish with its fans. In particular, it denotes the fact that the club is trying to attract new kinds of fans – customers – to the club and to reduce the dominance which masculine fan culture has enjoyed since the 1960s.

Similarly, in the late 1990s, Bayern Munich have also altered their badge. The edge of Bayern's crest originally consisted of two concentric red circles, in between which the words 'Bayern Muenchen FC e.v.' were inscribed: 'e.v.' stands for 'einiger Verein' or 'mutual club'. The middle of the crest consisted of the blue and white diamonds of the Bavarian flag. Since the Bayern shirt is also red, the outer red circle of the badge did not stand out from the shirt. Consequently, the outer circle of their club badge was changed from its original red to blue. Many long-standing masculine Bayern fans reject the new badge as an aberration. The alteration of the outer circle is an artificial marketing ploy which neglects the traditions of the club. These fans have adopted the badges which were in existence when they first formed into fan groups, as symbols of their social groups. For them, these badges are authentic; they reflect the traditions of the club but, more specifically, they reflect the relations which they have developed with this club since the 1970s. This new badge does not represent the masculine fan group nor its relationship with the club. The transformation of these seemingly trivial aspect of the clubs' operations undermines those common symbols of the fan culture denoting a profound transformation of relations between the club and these fans. The privileged position which these fans once enjoyed in relation to their club has been altered as clubs have become more commercial and, in response to these changes, new forms of politics have developed around football.

Since English clubs have been commercialised most radically in terms of their stadia and merchandising, the masculine fan groups have been most affected and consequently the new politics of football has been most pronounced in England. In response to the radical transformation of the grounds and supporter culture therein, club-based Independent Supporters' Associations have developed strongly in England. These groups have emerged in the mid- to late 1990s at many of the major clubs in England as a direct response to increases in ticket prices and the changes in the practice of support in the new stadia. For instance, since the transformation of Old Trafford to an all-seater ground, masculine fans at the club were aggrieved by the dispersal of their informal fan groups which made it very difficult to produce an atmosphere in the ground. In addition, through its use of new professional stewards, the club had taken an increasingly draconian line on even apparently innocuous practices like standing for prolonged periods. In April 1995, during an important League game against Arsenal, large sections of the K-Stand, where much of the masculine support was concentrated, stood for most of the game in an attempt to support the team. A loud announcement was made over the public address system which instructed the fans to sit down or to face ejection from the ground. Masculine fans were incensed by this announcement which starkly illustrated the divide between themselves and the newly commercialised club. Soon after the game, the Independent Manchester United Supporters' Association was established. Similarly, contingent events gave rise to independent supporters' associations (ISAs) at other clubs, such as Southampton:

> When Ian Branfoot was manager, he brought a long ball style of football to the game. Le Tissier, who was just coming into the first stage of his prime at that point, was being left out. The fans who had been submitted to long ball football all the time were booing the team. It got to the point where they were booing the team even when they beat Newcastle and Le Tissier scored one of the best goals I've ever seen. Even after that match and after that result when Branfoot brought him back into the team after pressure you still had 2000 fans staying behind in the ground after the match chanting: 'We want Branfoot out.' So the formation of SISA was not based in anything to do with politics or economics but it was based purely and utterly in a footballing issue. Which meant that the original committee of our independent supporters association apart from one or two guys was actually very naïve – decent enough guys, well-intentioned but they didn't understand the concept. [Richard Chorley, SISA, personal interview, 26 June 2000]

While local factors precipitated the rise of particular ISAs, the underlying cause of this movement was broadly the same at every club. Each of these new organisations opposed increased ticket prices and the unreasonable restriction of masculine forms of support. These new groups sought to protect the distinctive masculine fan culture from commercialisation.

The constitution of these ISAs demonstrates that these groups represent the politicisation of masculine fans. Richard Chorley highlighted the significance of this link between old hooligan networks and the new ISAs:

> This is another thing which I am on about: the difference in infrastructure [between IMUSA and SISA]. The difference here would be that we would have more members of the old hooli brigade; we would have more than they have. That is the sector of most solid support and that has come on from a sense of trust. We just trust these guys. It does help us that a couple of us were actually quite notorious hooligans in

the late '70s, early '80s. We are now grown-up fathers and adults. We have more members who are old hooli brigade than IMUSA. [Richard Chorley, SISA, personal interview, 26 June 2000]

In fact, although there are no ex-hooligans on the IMUSA committee, some prominent members of the organisation have connections to United's hooligan gang. This is only to be expected because English football culture between 1960s and 1990s was heavily informed by hooligan rivalries, which were an organic part of football support at the time. Although the presence of hooligans or ex-hooligans demonstrates that these groups defend a masculine form of fandom, it would be wrong to say that these organisations are primarily organised by ex-hooligans. They draw their main support from the wider committed masculine fans who were a key part of the clubs' support from the 1960s. Moreover, the strength of these organisations lies in the kinds of individuals who have come to the fore among them. In most cases, especially at those clubs where the independent groups have been effective, the leadership has been assumed not only by charismatic and intelligent individuals who have credibility with the masculine fans (including the hooligans) but who also often have long experience of union activity and a strong commitment to formal leftist politics. Thus, the ex-chair of the Independent Manchester United Supporter's Association (IMUSA), Andy Walsh, was a union representative at the bank where he worked in the 1980s and was a prominent leader of anti-poll tax protests in Manchester. The chair of the Independent Newcastle United Supporter's Association (INUSA), Kevin Miles, has been similarly active in union politics, as has Richard Chorley of the Southampton Independent Supporters' Association (SISA). All three are committed members of Militant through which organisation they have developed close personal relations which have been important to the development of the ISAs in England.

Significantly, the independent supporters' movement has been strengthened by the allegiance of professional individuals who have given these nascent groups unusually high levels of expertise:

> Because of the width of the United fan base – the bigger the fan base you have the more likely you are to find the quality of components you need to arrange a major campaign like they did against Murdoch. You will have people like Adam Brown, who comes from Durham originally but has been a Man United fan since he was a kid and went to Manchester University because he is a United fan and didn't want to go to the University of Kent. Then he got a job and then stayed in Manchester. So you've got your guys like that. You've got your Olivers and Rogers. You've got your Jonathan Michies. You've got people in professional positions, who when it comes to situations like that, can galvanise all of those things. It's a sheer numerical thing. Their fan base compared to ours is huge. I said when the Murdoch thing was on that if they could find amongst their whole fan base 25 to 30 people who they could rely on and who could all perform good functions in various areas, we would be lucky to

field a five-a-side team relatively. [Richard Chorley, SISA, personal interview, 26 June 2000]

As discussed in Chapter 6, BSkyB attempted to purchase Manchester United in 1998. There was widespread opposition to the merger and IMUSA played a prominent part in these protests. In particular, IMUSA conducted a sophisticated campaign which targeted media and political figures. Andy Walsh, with his expertise in public campaigning, was instrumental in the success of this campaign (see Brown and Walsh 1999) but he was supported by individuals who held useful professional positions. As Chorley notes, Walsh was able to draw upon academic expertise from Adam Brown, a sociologist specialising in football and a member of the Football Task Force, and Professor Jonathan Michie of Birkbeck College, while he found adept media advisers in journalists Michael Crick and Jim White and the actor, Roger Brierley. Interestingly, Walsh noted that old-boy connections at Manchester Grammar School created a credible interest group capable of opposing Murdoch. IMUSA's sister organisation Shareholders United Against Murdoch (which has subsequently become simply Shareholders United) was a Manchester Grammar School alumni initiative developed by two former pupils Michael Crick and Richard Hytner: 'This coalition of predominantly middle-class professional people, largely based in London, complemented IMUSA's strengths' (Brown and Walsh 1999: 77). It is important to recognise that these professionals are not the irrelevant appendages to authentic working-class groups. These professionals are valid members of these groups who contribute as significantly to group culture as those fans who might be more easily described as 'working class'. Individuals from a wide range of backgrounds, even professional ones, have coalesced at the ends of football grounds since the 1960s to produce a distinctive supporter culture.

The social composition of the ISAs is significant in understanding the nature of these masculine fan groups. While the fans themselves often define themselves as 'working class' and describe this masculine fan culture as 'working class', these groups may have a more complex social basis. It is likely that the political significance of ISAs themselves may be misunderstood if this rhetorical use of the term 'working class' is taken at face value. In order to comprehend the historical significance of masculine fan culture and the rise of new political engagements within it, it is necessary to consider the nature of these groups more carefully. Unfortunately, in recent accounts of masculine fan culture, commentators have generally failed to see the social complexity of the groups and have, instead, assumed them to be unproblematically working class. Indeed, recent accounts of masculine fan culture have tried to prove the assumption that the independent supporter movement can be explained by reference to the concept of class. Thus, Garry Robson provides an interesting account of contemporary Millwall fan culture, claiming that fans are enacting a habitus which is engrained into them by their class position: 'To be Millwall at this level is to draw in a heightened, actualizing and overwhelmingly implicit way, on the fundamental orientations of working-class, masculine solidarity. Bob, who is now past sixty, learned these patterns as a boy and he still lives in them in a *fundamentally unchanged* way' (Robson 2000: 147–8, emphasis added). Robson assumes that the fan culture at Millwall and therefore the class whose culture it represents has remained 'fundamentally unchanged' for over forty years. Yet, in the period to which Robson points, the English working class has experienced decisive transformation. Since the late 1950s, working-class culture originally underwent 'embourgeoisement' followed by the decline of mass manufacture and fragmentation in the post-Fordist era. It would be strange to describe the social groups which now work in different kinds of jobs, reside in different locations with transformed standards of living as 'fundamentally unchanged'. In the light of these changes, it seems extremely unlikely that fan culture at Millwall has remained the same. Of course, it is possible that it might have remained similar but evidence would be required to prove this immutability. The problem is that not only does Robson's own fieldwork – full of interesting material though it is – not provide this evidence but, in fact, it vitiates his central claim. It suggests a decisive transformation of Millwall masculine culture. On the very same page as asserting the existence of an essential working-class culture at Millwall, Robson describes one of his informants:

> David's successful career in the diplomatic service and resultant upward mobility would appear to be a classic example of the 'opportunities' afforded by the post-war loosening of the boundaries around class identity and occupational progress. His process up the diplomatic career ladder has been swift and sure. But he has not renounced an identity, and a sense of the world, forged in New Cross as a youngster. [ibid.: 148]

It is not clear how an individual who now lives in a six-bedroomed house in Kent (ibid.: 149) and works in the elite section of the civil service can be defined as working class. David's upward mobility does not invalidate his support – his allegiance is unquestionable – but it does undermine Robson's claim that the best way to understand these fan cultures is in simple class terms. Class determination is assumed rather than demonstrated here as is the claim that the class culture from which this support arises has remained unchanged. The example of David does not prove the enduring validity of class explanations but in fact undermines simplistic appeals to the concept of the working class when explaining football fandom. Robson's class explanation fails to reflect the complex social reality of football fandom which he himself highlights. In the light of the decomposition of the working class, masculine football culture cannot be explained simply by reference to some objective and essentialised class reality. Masculine fan culture is certainly not dominated by the professional middle classes and many of the individuals who are part of these fan groups are from non-professional social groups often with lower social and economic status, but to assume that masculine football fan culture in the 1990s is self-evidently working class is reductive. The reality of these groups is more interesting and diverse.

In a recent article on independent supporters' associations, Rex Nash makes a similar error. His data demonstrates that many of the individuals involved in these associations cannot be described as working class:

> Within class terms, the active elements of the ISAs [Independent Supporters' Assocations] were broadly confined to upper-working and middle-class fans, with a professional career element at the top. There appeared to be only one unemployed member active within any of these ISAs, and 45 of 64 activists in INUSA, BIFA and SISA said their attendance had been unaffected by ticket prices. [Nash 2001: 45]

It is clear from Nash's own data that class position is not an independent variable which determines participation in ISAs and, indeed, Nash accepts this: 'On the basis of this evidence, there is no essential unity of the class backgrounds of the ISA leadership, save that they were not from the excluded element of the crowd struggling to raise the prices of a ticket' (ibid.: 46). Having accepted that class is not the determining factor in the creation of ISAs, Nash goes on to make a convoluted argument which, against the evidence of his own data, attempts to defend class as an explanatory factor:

> These fans *considered* themselves to be working class or traditional and sought to defend such fandoms: of 53 activists, 45 said they were 'traditional' supporters with the class implications that flow from this ... Seventy-four members agreed that their ISA should campaign for 'traditional working-class values' at football, while 74 were ex-terrace fans, all of which locates ISAs within working-class *traditions* even if the actual demography of members is more within the upper-working and middle class. [ibid.: 46]

For Nash, ISAs represent authentic working-class *traditions* even if the individuals in the ISAs are not members of the working class itself. Nash assumes that masculine fan culture whatever its form can be described as traditionally working class. Yet, the traditions to which masculine fans appeal are not unchanging practices with a lengthy heritage. They are forms of actions which have been adopted relatively recently. The kind of terrace culture which Nash describes as working class can be traced back to the 1960s. Even then, these cultures have undergone significant reformation so that it would be dangerous to describe them as essentially traditional. For instance, most ISAs now eschew racism, xenophobia, sexism and violence which, even in the 1980s, were central elements of the fan culture out of which these groups have emerged. Consequently, while the ISAs claim to be defending 'working-class traditions', they have in fact renegotiated apparently timeless traditions in the light of new circumstances. Similarly, individuals in these fan groups overwhelmingly adopt a casual style of dress rather than wearing club colours. Yet, in the 1970s, wearing club colours as an expression of pride was regarded as a necessary part of this masculine culture. The change in the fashion sense of these fans appears trivial but it in fact denotes a quite profound transformation in the economic and social conditions of these groups and their relation to their club. The idea of working-class tradition is a concept which is mobilised by the group to define and redefine its contemporary constitution and practices. It is a normative concept which legitimates the activities of the group at the point in time when the term is mobilised. It is a description of this group's status honour or status lifestyle, as Weber would call it, which entails certain practices on behalf of group members. The term 'working class' or 'traditional' refers to a particular supporting culture and applies to all self-selecting members of this group whatever their social background and employment. It is the culture which fans adopt that finally determines their membership of these groups. Instead of asserting the existence of some essential working-class traditions, a claim only ever asserted through the demonstrative use of italics, it would have been easier for Nash to argue that these masculine fan groups have developed at football clubs since the 1960s as a result of the coalescence of a range of individuals, located across a quite broad social spectrum as a result of the decline of Fordism; they are unified not by any prior objective social factors but only by their mutual support of a football team. It is pertinent here that while individuals like Nash and Robson assume an unbroken tradition of authentic working-class support stretching across the decades, Gavin Mellor has demonstrated that during the 1960s as Manchester United became a 'super-club', as he calls it, there were debates between supporters about new and old fans which echo the debates in the 1990s: 'Interestingly, these were often invested with language of class distinction, and would criticize the perceived "respectability" of United's new fans' (Mellor 2000: 157). It is highly likely that many fans who were 'new' in the 1960s and 1970s went on to become a key part of the club's support and, in that way, became 'traditional' fans in the course of their supporting career. Their authenticity was not an essential property but was earned through regular participation in this particular ritual.

In prioritising and reifying class or tradition, Robson and Nash make the same error of which Melucci (1989; 1988) and Touraine (1971; 1981; 1988) have accused classical sociology. Classical sociology has typically reified class into a unified and durable actor. Against this essentialist vision, Melucci and Touraine have demonstrated the diversity and contingency of political groupings in contemporary society in their seminal work on new social movements. New social movements are not to be reified into unified actors which exist independently of the issue around which mobilisation takes place (Melucci 1989: 18); collective action does not follow on logically or automatically given certain prior economic conditions. On the contrary, Melucci and Touraine emphasise that collective action is achieved through a process of complex negotiation between individuals as they recognise and call upon certain shared interests emerging at specific sites of communal interaction. Collective action is not a given. It emerges out of specific forms of interaction between people who form coherent social groups. The prior social location of these individuals is not as important as the actual interaction of these people as they coalesce around certain sites. At that point, concepts of tradition are mobilised to engender and legitimate appropriate forms of practice among this new group. Although Melucci and Touraine do not recognise it, their sociology of new social movements closely echoes Weber's famous discussion of status groups. There, he insisted that the critical factor in the development of coherent social groups was 'intercourse which is not subvervient to economic or any other purpose' (Weber 1968: 932). According to Weber, the emergence of groups is not determined automatically by prior factors such as shared economic conditions. Rather, groups only emerge as individuals come together and create a shared lifestyle for themselves. Once the group has come into existence with a particular lifestyle, it comes to have economic interests which its members promote. Against Marxian class accounts, the economic interests do not precede the formation of the group but follow from the kinds of groups which emerge in interaction. The implications of Weber's analysis of status groups are radical because it ultimately undermines any appeal to class. Classes are really status groups which sociologists have misrecognised (see Collins 1990: 129). The theoretical significance of Weber's comments about status groups affirm the central point of Melucci and Touraine's discussion of new social movements. These groups can be simply read off an objective class background. Economic factors do not determine their creation. Rather, new social movements arise contingently at particular sites through social interaction between people of potentially diverse social origin. Melucci and Touraine (and, of course, Weber himself) allow us to recognise the reality of these groups without reifying them.

Significantly, for Melucci and Touraine, in post-industrial or programmed society, as they call it, the key issues around which individuals interact and out of which collective interests arise are in the area of lifestyle and consumption. The primary political issue in contemporary society is increasingly not between labour and capital but between consumers and corporations (Touraine 1971: 221). Prior class allegiance does not determine which groups will arise but rather contingent and diverse groups unify temporarily through their interaction around primary sites of consumption. The development of the ISAs is an important example of a new social movement wherein a socially diverse group becomes unified around one particular political issue concerned not with employment but consumption. This politicisation of consumption is particularly emphasised in the case of the ISAs since the key personnel in these new groups – Walsh, Chorley and Miles – have themselves shifted their political commitment from conventional workplace politics to an almost exclusive focus on football. The independent supporters' associations are new social movements which express the new collective interests of the masculine fans, who constituted the key part of the clubs' support between the 1960s and 1990s, in the face of transformations which threaten their social solidarity (see King 1998c: 188–90). Like other new social movements, such as feminism, gay rights, nuclear disarmament or anti-globalisation, independent supporters' assocations are important in Europe today. These movements arise out of the dense interactions which have occurred at football grounds over the last four decades and have produced recognisable social groups. These cultures cannot be explained by blunt reference to class. Clearly, it is important not to imply that social networks outside of football are irrelevant. Many fans have attended football games and become part of these groups as a result of their membership of other networks, as a result of their families, their schools, their friends or their work. These networks introduce them to masculine fan culture. However, even though prior networks are not dismissed, these networks themselves cannot be simply described as working class. In the light of deindustrialisation and post-Fordism, these networks from which football supporters at any particular club emerge have fragmented and diversified so that fans are drawn from more diverse geographical and social locations. The prior social networks of fans may in many cases be relevant to their participation in ISAs but all these various networks cannot be usefully described as working class. In the post-Fordist era, society consists of a complex hierarchy of status groups which have coalesced from older groups around changing or new forms of employment, housing and lifestyle. Former working-class status groups have been among the most dramatically affected by these changes, diversifying upwards into new forms of service employment and downwards into unemployment and underclass status, so that the usefulness of the concept of 'the working class' is even more problematic than it was in the past. It is more sustainable to argue that masculine fan culture and ISAs arise out of diverse social groups unifying at particular football clubs to develop particular fan cultures. These cultures do not embody 'traditional working-class' values but are the expression of new identities and new solidarities which are themselves the product of a transformed society.

Independent Strategies

Independent supporters' associations have aimed at defending masculine fan culture against commercialisation and, in England, these new fan groups have developed important new strategies to promote their collective interests; fans have organised demonstrations in the ground, contacted the media to communicate their grievances or, in the case of Newcastle United, taken the club (unsuccessfully) to court. One of the most significant of these strategies has been the political use of share-ownership. From its inception in 1995, IMUSA had always advocated the purchase of shares by United fans as a way of exerting influence upon the board at Annual General Meetings. In the late 1990s, many of these AGMs became heated when the board and Martin Edwards, in particular, were berated for their policies by minority shareholding fans. In response to the Murdoch bid, this strategy was formalised by the organisation of a group called Shareholders United Against Murdoch. After the bid, the renamed organisation, Shareholders United, has continued to promote this strategy, unifying diverse fan shareholders into a more coherent lobby group. The use of shares for political ends is a powerful strategy against the commercialisation of the clubs because it recognises contemporary economic realities. The clubs are commercial enterprises operating in an increasingly competitive transnational market and this strategy employs that commercial reality for political ends. It politicises the very economic principles and rights by which these clubs now operate. The board of a club like Manchester United have to recognise this politicisation because their own commercial enterprise is predicated upon the same rights.

This strategy of employing the newly privatized economic structure of the sport to democratise football has gained recent academic legitimation. In the late 1990s, following his intervention against Murdoch's bid for Manchester United, Professor Michie established an academic group, the Football Governance Research Centre in the School of Management at Birkbeck. The Research Centre has become increasingly influential by organising conferences which provide an arena for emergent fan groups and by producing publications for the ISAs. In particular, the Research Centre has provided academic support for the strategic use of shares to increase the democratic accountability of the clubs. Michie has promoted the idea of full mutual ownership of football clubs by the fans through a restructuring of share-ownership (Michie and Ramalingam 1999: 161–6). Michie's prominent position at Birkbeck College has allowed him to raise the issue onto the political agenda, especially since New Labour has been keen to exploit populist issues like football. As a result of Michie's intervention, the government developed a 'Supporters Direct' initiative which will collect fan shares together into fan trusts, allowing them a democratic say in their clubs: 'Put in simple terms, if 5,000 fans donate £1,000 each then the Trust will raise £5 million. Once we have raised a substantial amount of money then the Trust will enter into negotiations to buy additional shares and invest in the club. The more money we raise, the more influence and impact the Trust can have' (Roy Hattersley cited in *Supporters Direct* 2001).

Recently, Michie has similarly used the very business laws by which Manchester United operates to criticise the club and to promote democracy. He has publicised the fact that the club is in breach of trading regulations since it does not declare all its shareholders and, therefore, all those who have an interest in the club and might be able to influence club policy.[1] Of course, the strategy of buying up shares is a 'weapon of the weak' which can alter the commercial courses of the clubs in only small ways, but the influence of fan shareholders is real. Moreover, this influence is enshrined in the very legal principles of ownership on which these publicly limited companies are founded. The use of newly privatised structures to increase the democratic representation of the fans is an ingenious strategy. It is also important to recognise its novelty, despite the frequent appeals of a return to a putatively democratic past before commercialisation which fan groups and commentators like Michie or Conn (1997) often make. In the past, clubs were no more democratic than they are now. It was simply that up until the 1990s, the consumption of the game itself was not a political issue. This is even the case at clubs like Barcelona whose structure was formally democratic. In fact, in the past, there was almost total political apathy on the part of the *socios* (members) and benevolent despotism on the part of the presidents. Independent fan groups have emerged in response to the deregulation of European football in the last decade, protesting against the threat which commercialisation has posed to masculine fan groups. They are a part of the new geography of European football.

Significantly, reflecting that geography, ISAs are club-based movements. After the Hillsborough disaster, a group of Liverpool fans led by Rogan Taylor created a national association of fans called the Football Supporters' Association which was opposed principally to the proposed introduction of identity cards for all football fans. Initially, the FSA was able to attract a very large membership, but once the identity card scheme had been rejected, the FSA membership scheme dwindled drastically. By the mid-1990s, the FSA had a membership of less than a thousand and it is more or less defunct as a political organisation. By contrast, the ISAs have become more and more significant because masculine fans at the same club are unified by years of close association and share the same interests in regard to their club. The FSA is unable to mobilise fans because in an increasingly deregulated environment there are few national issues. Fans at different clubs have different interests reflecting uneven economic development. ISAs are therefore a coherent response to altered social and economic realities:

> People don't seem to be able to accept that the FSA and the National Federation are going to have to lose sovereignty to this bigger body. I think it should have gone the other way, in fact, which was to ignore the FSA if they were not cooperative and basically get an IMUSA at every club, an ISA at every club, and then you can say; 'Look we have an Independent Supporter's Associations from every club in the

country. Therefore, talk to us.' That would be a reasonable basis. If you could do that in terms of Britain, England and Wales in terms of our league and Scotland and then all the European clubs, then you can lobby the European Parliament. Then you can change things. The European Parliament is the only thing that can stand up to the television companies and the big clubs. Otherwise it can all be done by saying, 'You're disadvantaging us in Europe.' United are going to say that: 'It's not fair that we're getting penalised by the way you operated the television deal.' It has got to be done on a European level. [Duncan Drasdo, personal interview, 12 June 2000]

In the new geography of European football, club-based ISAs constitute a logical and coherent response. As Duncan Drasdo reveals, it may be possible for these ISAs to align together in relation to supranational authorities but their effectiveness lies in their situation at specific locations. ISAs are the logical reflection of deregulation in which the local is taken partly out of its national context and reconnected into a transnational one.

European Fan Movements

Although the ISA movement is the most developed in England, similar developments are underway in other European countries particularly in Germany, where the commercial forces and the masculine fan culture of the fans – involving heavy drinking and large-scale away attendance – are similar to England. The most important of these new groups at a national level is the Bundniss Aktiver Fussball Fans (BAFF, Association of Active Fans). It was particularly active in the protest against the possible introduction of all-seater stadia which would be mandatory if Germany won the World Cup bid for 2006 (see Aschenbeck 2000):

> We used to be anti-fascist but we weren't just anti-fascist, when we started off it consisted of anti-racist fanzines and groupings. We got together and discovered we were all doing this and this and this against racism in the grounds but then we soon realised that the all-seater stadia thing was coming up and we were campaigning against that. But we soon realised that with a name like that we weren't reflecting what we were actually doing so we decided to change it. If you say you're anti-something, it tends to put people off. Once we announced that we were campaigning against the German FA staging the World Cup that is when the German FA agreed to meet us. They were obviously worried about how much influence we might have. Obviously there were one or two interviews in the British press at that time. The main issue again was the all-seater stadia issue. That was the main issue and then the side issue was the amount of money that was going to be spent on it. A lot of it was coming from the left-wing of the political scene. It was a difficult campaign because most football fans want the World Cup or, now they have got it, are happy that the World Cup is going to be staged in Germany and cannot understand why you should be against it. As far as we at Schalke were concerned we just concentrated on the all-

seater issue. But that campaign died a death. We had all the meetings with the German FA and they came and then they ignored us. I think they had satisfied themselves that we weren't really powerful. [Stuart Dykes, BAFF committee and Schalke Fan Initiative, personal interview, 17 July 2000; see also Aschenbeck 1998: 169–86]

BAFF faces a similar problem in Germany that the FSA faced in England. While it is possible that fans can be mobilised on a national level for certain critical developments such as the introduction of all-seater stadiums, it is almost impossible to sustain national fan groups beyond a period of crisis. While Stuart Dykes (who is also a Manchester United fan and a member of IMUSA), and other members of BAFF believe that they can see the direction of developments in Germany and want to oppose them in their initial stages, most German fans, content that all-seater stadia will not be introduced, have lost interest in BAFF:

BAFF is an organisation ahead of its time. Because you haven't had the extreme situation which you've had in England. We are waiting for something to happen. While we had the all-seater campaign, we had one of our most successful times but as soon as that sort of question faded away because with one or two exceptions, we still haven't got all-seater stadia. That is all going to change again with the World Cup. Once fans realise we are not going to have all-seater stadia tomorrow, even the interest in that campaign waned. We are an organisation without any real campaigning. We are constantly reminding fans of the situation in England and pointing to the possible developments ahead but people just can't see it. It is all right talking about all these things that might happen but ... I am constantly hammering this message home when I was at United last season the cheapest ticket was £31 and we are constantly writing these things in the fanzines but people say 'That is in England, though, it is not here. You can still get in for four quid here and that is for adults.' [Stuart Dykes, personal interview, 17 July 2000]

German apathy towards the issue of commercialisation is understandable because the fans are not immediately affected by the stadium developments and this apathy demonstrates Touraine's and Melucci's point that the collective action is not given by prior economic factors but only arises in contingent ways in relation to issues. Since the issue of German fans are not immediately threatened by it, no collective mobilisation has taken place, even though it is possible that fans may confront the issue of commercialisation later. Although Stuart Dykes may be right that the situation in England illustrates the future, it is equally possible that in Germany football will not be commercialised so ferociously and, therefore, the inactivity of German fans may be entirely appropriate. In the light of the German apathy towards commercialisation, BAFF has recently returned to its original remit of anti-fascist and particularly anti-racist action. It is possible that in this limited anti-racist role, it may be a viable national organisation but it is also possible and even likely that it will experience the same decline which befell the FSA. Fans simply cannot mobilise at a national level because clubs and their fans do not share the same interests in the transnational era. In the light of the growing economic divide between them, it is difficult to unify fans into a coherent protest group.

However, while BAFF itself has receded in significance, club-based fan movements have become more important in Germany, as in England. One of the most important groups of these club-based activists is Club Nummer 12 at Bayern Munich which consists of a network of 'traditional' Bayern fans. The name refers to the fact that the fan group is the twelfth player for the team. The group emerged in 1996 to organise the 'choreographies' (orchestrated fan displays) before the UEFA Cup Final and from that time has consisted of a hard core of about 300 activists who claim to be concerned with defending 'the traditions of the club' against commercialism (Dominik, personal interview, 3 July 2000).[2] While these fans are deeply knowledgeable about the history of the club as their new fanzine, *Vorspiel* featuring an article on Franz John, the founder of the club, reveals, the style of support which they promote, in fact, emerged in the 1970s. Club Nummer 12 consists of prominent members of Bayern's 'Sud Kurve', the terrace behind the goal in the Olympic Stadium, where the most vociferous and dedicated (masculine) supporters have gathered since the club first moved to the ground in 1973. These fans, like their English counterparts, also travel most frequently to both domestic and European away games. By 'traditions', this group refers to their collective experience of supporting the club since the 1970s and the key symbols which have become associated with that group's experiences since that time. In particular, they are the fans who reject the new Bayern badge most forcefully.

In the late 1990s, a prominent independent group has also emerged at Barcelona, called '*L'Elefant Blau*', organised by Armand Caraben, Joan La Porta and Alfons Godall. The explicit objective was to oppose the presidency of Nunez which was regarded as a corruption of the traditions of Barcelona Football Club. The strange name meaning 'blue elephant' denotes the traditionalism of this group. Like an elephant, it has a long memory and the elephant is blue, of course, because one of Barcelona's club colours is blue:

> The people of *L'Elephant Blau* are people that had been following the clubs' affairs for a great many years, and are all against the Nunez regime mainly due to the formation of great debts in the financial side since Nunez came to power. We all arrived at the conclusion that the statutes of the club can help us present a vote of censure. In short, *L'Elephant Blau* was born as a group of individuals to promote a vote of censure. [Godall, *L'Elephant Blau*, personal interview, 26 April 2000]

In its opposition to Nunez, *L'Elephant Blau* is similar to the other independent supporters' associations which have emerged around Europe. *L'Elephant Blau* defends the 'traditions' of Barcelona Football Club, including particular styles of support. However, Armand Caraben, Alfons Godall and Joan La Porta are white-collar professionals and, indeed, in the 1970s Armand Caraben held senior positions at Barcelona Football Club including club secretary, organising the transfer of Johan Cruyff from Ajax. Consequently, *L'Elephant Blau* is a similar organisation to Shareholders United, IMUSA's sister group. Like the English groups, *L'Elephant Blau* is primarily concerned with the exclusionary and undemocratic implications of the commercialisation of football.

The Development of Transnational Relations between Fan Groups

Significantly, just as increasing transnational competition has driven the biggest clubs into ever closer relations, so has commercialisation propelled these independent groups into increasingly close contact with one another. The proposed Sky takeover of Manchester United brought IMUSA into close contact with both *L'Elephant Blau* and Club Nummer 12. The relationship between Club Nummer 12 and IMUSA is particularly close because the issues which confront the fans at Bayern are recognised by them to be very similar to those at Manchester United, despite the trauma of the 1999 European Cup Final. For instance, in October 2000, Jon Leigh, a member of IMUSA, visited Bayern Munich to investigate the administration of standing areas in the Olympic Stadium to further IMUSA's return to standing campaign. Since his retirement as the chair of IMUSA, Andy Walsh has been concerned with building up a European network of independent fan groups (Winton 2001). Under his leadership, IMUSA has developed a 'Eurofans Initiative' run by Oli Winton and Brian Kavanagh, which is a 'fledgling group of fans' representatives, [which] aims to lobby UEFA for all European match-going fans ... IMUSA, Barcelona's *Elephant Blau* and Bayern Munich's Club Nr. 12 are the founders' (Winton 2001). Other key members of IMUSA were well aware of the importance of these new European networks – but also the difficulty and potential danger of establishing them:

> IMUSA was formed basically to address problems at Man United three years ago. Andy Walsh said to me that IMUSA's got two years to go and then they'll be nothing left for us to campaign about because it will be on a national level. I agree with him there but our board's argument against any club-based argument we put to them is that we can't do anything about it unless Liverpool or Arsenal do it. But it is bigger than that. It is a Europe-wide thing now. There is a groundswell of opinion among the supporters of all clubs around European countries, like Barcelona fans have railed against going Plc. I got a thing through from this guy who is a Wycombe Wanderers supporter whose name is Andreotti and who supports Udinese. He has

now gone back to Italy. They had a fans' charter in the fanzine which was basically saying the same as we are saying in the UK except they weren't complaining about ticket prices because their ticket prices are reasonable but it was concerned about TV's influence, merchandising. Exactly the same things to us. What we are trying to do now is get a Europe-wide fans' group going of traditional fans who go to the match who want to see rivalries with the local teams continuing. We are trying to get those people together to say, 'You must be joking we don't want a European Super League.' Attendance figures will tell you that. It is very difficult to find the right people to speak to. We met with some Real fans. We played with them. But effectively we were meeting a bunch of students. All right, they go and watch Real week in, week out but they weren't the *lads* behind the goal with the big banner. They're the people we want to get to. They're the people whom IMUSA represents. This Udinese lad reckons he knows fanzines editors who can get things out through Italian fanzines – to the hardcore. We have contact with loads of people over the Internet. [Mark Longden, Chair IMUSA, personal interview, 13 June 2000, emphasis added]

For important figures at IMUSA, like Duncan Drasdo and Mark Longden, the new chair, there is an explicit recognition that political activity at a European level is required and both recognise that commercialisation has produced similar effects right across Europe. Interestingly, *L'Elephant Blau* have recognised transnational links as their connections with IMUSA show but they are also wary of the potential dangers of these links:

Caraben: With the Champions League, football is a European phenomenon but we are just at the beginning. Talking about the new links and relationships between cities, it is too early to speak about relationships between groups like IMUSA. Well, we know the people at IMUSA, they are excellent people and we have every confidence in them. We are talking with them but there are times when you have to think.
Godall: If you are using the Internet, you have to know about other groups – who they are, what they want, who they have relationships with, because it may be dangerous. I went to Manchester to visit IMUSA. I didn't know them but we were looking at the question of Murdoch's bid for Manchester United. I went to an IMUSA meeting but nobody knew I was there so that I saw that it was the same questions, the same feelings, the same concern with the well-being of football and of the supporters. And then, in this situation, this kind of relationship is going to grow in the future, not only with people from England but also with people from other countries. But you need to be careful before you make a link. [Armand Caraben, Alfons Godall, *L'Elephant Blau*, personal interview, 26 April 2000]

Caraben and Godall are concerned that they might unwittingly align themselves with an extremist political grouping. Despite that, there are nascent links between European fans groups. For instance, the Newcastle Independent Supporters' Association, through its chair Kevin Miles, has developed links with the fan group of the similarly-sized German club, Schalke 04, from

Gelsenkirchen near Cologne. The development of links between the activist fan groups are tentative at the moment and there is certainly no European-wide response to the commercialisation of football. However, these relationships are growing and through them these groups can mutually assist each other in their various projects of resistance. As such, they echo at the level of the fans, the growing connections which are emerging at the level of the boards between these clubs and are significant developments in themselves; they are a new phenomenon specific to the 1990s. Significantly, the politicisation of fan movements has occurred primarily at the local and not national level. These shadowy outlines are likely to be increasingly significant in the new Europe as groups of consumers, mobilised at club level in particular European cities, come into ever greater contact.[3]

Reflecting the new hierarchical network of clubs in the transnational era, these connections are highly differentiated. Consequently, while connections are being developed between the fans of those clubs who are competing with each other at this transnational level and who therefore face similar threats, the fans of smaller clubs do not recognise these transnational connections as valid. The development of independent supporters' associations as a new social movement has not produced a unified transnational movement. On the contrary, these groups emerge at specific locales with particular agendas reflecting the uneven development of deregulated European football. Richard Chorley has illuminated the very different position of independent fans at Southampton in the new European order:

> If those who are initiating towards Barcelona and Bayern Munich are coming from Manchester United, one of the overriding reactions from a lot of grass-roots fans is: 'There they go, well now they've got their own elite fucking European supporters' organisation. What the fuck has that got to do with us here. Sod them.' How do I sell the concept that we must be working closely with IMUSA and these others when they are looking all the time to Barcelona? I couldn't begin to sell the stuff that Andy [Walsh] touched in his book [*Not for Sale*] about all that stuff and the photographs with those guys [from Club Nummer 12, Bayern Munich]. I haven't even got past the first base and to try and sell that idea would be met with derision. I understand it. I understand it perfectly why it would be a wonderful idea to have a proper organised federation of European supporters but the principle has to be; you cannot move before your mass. If you move before your mass, all you are is a little isolated thing. [Richard Chorley, SISA, personal interview, 22 June 2000]

It is important to recognise that Southampton fans' decision to remain local is not a continuation of the past, but it is an active response to the transnationalisation of football. Whereas in the past, Southampton were unself-consciously focused on their local issues in a national context, Southampton fans now recognise the changes which are occurring at the European level but see these developments as irrelevant to their club. For them, protest against that marginalisation is not to be furthered by creating links with other European groups but by emphasising the distinctiveness of Southampton from those flows. The significance of SISA's emphasis on local issues has altered because they promote these issues independently in full knowledge of wider European developments and of the growing connection between supporter groups across Europe. New networks of fans are emerging across Europe which are likely to be increasingly significant in the future and even at those clubs where these European connections are eschewed, such as at Southampton, the fans have emphasised local connections against transnational flows. Consequently, even those fans who have not actively sought new alliances in the transnational era have been profoundly affected by the new business of football.

Notes

1 Michie's radical mutual ownership strategy where the fans own the club completely is implausible. At clubs of even a reasonable size, there will always be significant economic interests which are able to buy up more shares than the fans and which do not have the problem faced by the fans of coordinating multiple small-holdings. Reflecting this idealism, Michie and others often cite Northampton Town as the ideal which should be replicated at the biggest clubs. David Conn, for instance, describes Lomax's supporters' trust as 'a ray of light in the exploitative profanity that is modern football business' (Conn 1997: 241; Lomax 1999). While the Northampton case is interesting in itself and the motivations of those involved such as Brian Lomax admirably democratic, the Northampton model is simply inappropriate since the fan trust persists there only because the club is in an extremely weak market position with few fans and little commercial value (Michie and Walsh 1999; Frampton et al. 2001).
2 As both Stuart Dykes and Dominik Müller confirmed there is a political divide between BAFF and Club Nummer 12. According to Dykes, BAFF are seen by Club Nummer 12 'as being a left-wing, drug-taking rabble which in many ways it is' and this was confirmed in discussions with Müller, who explicitly stated that he thought BAFF were trying to use football as a vehicle for their own external political agendas. For him, the only legitimate political interest which fans could protest about were issues which directly related to their relationship to their clubs and the game.
3 In France and Italy, activist fan groups (primarily organised as ultra groups) are generally concerned not so much with the issue of commercialisation – which has not effected the fans in these countries as the clubs have introduced few radical changes to the ground – but with the issue of racism and fascism. Ultra groups are either opposed openly to fascism or in the cases of Lazio's *Irriducibili* ultras and various other groups promote it wholeheartedly. The issue of racism and anti-racism in European football will be discussed in Chapter 11.

Chapter 10

Localism

The New Hatred of the Big Clubs

Rivalries between clubs in their national leagues are of long-standing and, with the development of hooliganism in the 1960s in Britain and the 'ultra' movement in the 1970s across Europe, these rivalries have become more serious and vitriolic. The chant 'We only hate Man United' was prevalent among the supporters of Manchester City, Leeds, Liverpool and other clubs in the 1970s and 1980s (Redhead 1986: 43).[1] However, while the hatred of Manchester United might have been of long-standing among the committed fans of rival clubs, the club was certainly popular among neutrals and was not the object of general derision (see Mellor 2000):

> I always find it quite funny because when I used to go to watch United regularly when I lived in England, we [Manchester United] were the most popular team in British football. Say that to anyone under twenty and they wouldn't believe you. [Stuart Dykes, Schalke Fans Initiative, personal interview, 17 July 2000]
>
> One of the saddest things that this whole commercialisation has brought is the levels of resentment – it is not just resentment, in reality it is hatred – between the clubs that fall in a certain money bracket. Obviously, United epitomise it. For one football club in England to become so universally hated and despised, is ugly. It is not what football is about ... People talk about the death of hooliganism. We have a new type of hooliganism now. What used to be a punch-up in the streets has been replaced by a type of – though it is the wrong phrase – it is an intellectual hooliganism against United fuelled by the papers and media, who all at the same time maximise the coverage of United's games to sell papers but at the same time, fuel the hatred and resentment. Every magazine you buy – your *Loaded* magazine or your glossy football magazine – constantly, constantly, constantly reinforce it because they know there is this latent hatred out there. It is not latent, is it? My first memories of football come in about 1968/9. In those days, when you used to go to the park to play football there was no such culture of wearing the replica shirt of the team you supported. You used to go down the park and lads bought the football shirt whose design they liked. At Christmas, you go to play football on Boxing Day. You'd see someone in a Man United shirt, someone in a Celtic shirt, someone in a Wolves shirt, someone in an Aston Villa shirt and they'd be a little craze at school. 'Have you seen the new Villa shirt?' 'Yeah, it's really smart.' These days, children cannot do that. You cannot buy a Manchester United shirt because you like the shirt. You go into the school

playground as an eight or nine-year-old, you will be pilloried in a place like this [Southampton] for having a United shirt on. Well, there are some big social questions to be asked with these types of things going on. When Manchester United won the European Cup in 1968, every English football fan in this country, I can remember it clearly, watching it and everyone going beserk in the room. That carried on right through the way through the Liverpool years, right the way through to the mid-1980s. That is one of the saddest things and it has happened for one reason: money. Manchester United is obviously at the zenith of it but it does exist and will flourish whereby more and more of these top clubs are allowed into these top competition. If that becomes a regular thing and we see clubs like Chelsea, Arsenal, Manchester United, Liverpool, maybe that hatred of Manchester United will be developed into a wider hatred and it will be concentrated on those clubs. Once people consciously grasp what is going on that sense of disenfranchisement will only lead to resentment. That is the natural progression: resentment and hatred. [Richard Chorley, SISA, personal interview, 22 June 2000]

Not only does Richard Chorley highlight that this general antipathy towards Manchester United is new but that its origins are commercial, the result of its economic dominance. Other commentators have made similar arguments: 'One of the consequences of Freedman's marketing revolution and United's success on the field, was that the club everybody loved and regarded as their second club if they did not already support United, became one of the most hated clubs in the country' (Bose 1999: 201). Bose may overstate the case when he claims that United was loved by everybody but his general point is sustainable. Expressions of antipathy towards Manchester United were not absent in English football from the 1960s onwards among the committed fans of other clubs, but they were not so frequent as they have become and, crucially, they remained unreported by the media. Groups of committed fans might have detested Manchester United as a playing rival but the widespread revulsion of the club as a public institution is new. This new hatred was expressed in the commentary on the 1999 European Cup Final.

Although the hatred of Manchester United is perhaps the most extreme example of the fissuring effects of commercialisation on fan cultures, Manchester United is not alone in Europe in being the object of national hatred: both Bayern Munich and Juventus face similar vilification in Germany and Italy. Unlike Manchester United, these clubs were never popular nationally before the 1990s, perhaps because, unlike United they were consistently successful throughout this period. For instance, Bayern Munich, the contempt for whose economic power was summed up in the club's moniker 'FC Hollywood', was seen as a club which bought success by suborning the best players of its competitors:

Bayern have always been hated. I say always, they only came to prominence in the late '60s. Ever since then they have been hated. They have always been seen as the club with all the money who weakens their opponents by buying their best players. That has been around for decades. Bayern are the anti-team just like United are in England, or rather what United have become. [Stuart Dykes, Schalke Fans Initiative, personal interview, 17 July 2000]

Reflecting this view of the commercial power of Bayern, there is a popular badge which the fans of other German clubs sew onto their *Kutte*. This depicts Uli Hoeness, Bayern's general manager holding a large magnet towards which deutschmarks and dollars are being pulled, above which are written the words, 'Hoeness? Nein Danke [no thank you]'. The point was confirmed in an interaction which occurred on a tram returning from Schalke's ground in Gelsenkirchen after a league game against Bayern Munich in November 2000, in which Bayern had been beaten 3–2. A well-known Schalke fan started singing a popular song which denigrated Uli Hoeness to the initial amusement of the crowded tram. However, a masculine Bayern Munich supporter who also happened to be on the tram standing next to the Schalke fan took exception to the song. He mockingly dismissed the idea that the success of Bayern Munich was bad for German football or that it was appropriate to lay the blame for Bayern's dominance on Uli Hoeness. He concluded by warning the Schalke fan that had they not been on a crowded tram, he would have hit the Schalke fan for singing this song. This tense and somewhat embarrassing interaction highlights the way in which transformations at seemingly abstract levels of the economy filter down into specific social interactions.

Although the hatred of Bayern might be long-standing in origin, in the 1990s, this hatred of Bayern Munich was raised to a new level and widely publicised beyond the sphere of football, just as the resentment of United has been communicated across the media in Britain. In 1999, a punk band called *Die Tote Hose* (literally the 'Dead Trousers' but idiomatically meaning 'there is nothing going on') released a single entitled 'We will never go to Bayern Munich'. Although the song was not allowed to be played on the radio due to its lyrics which described the Bavarian club as a 'scheiss Verein' (a 'shit club'), the record reached the top ten in the German charts. Moreover, on the last day of the 1999–2000 season, the band organised for a huge airborne banner which read 'Congratulations to Bayern' to be displayed above Leverkusen's last game of the season at Unterhaching. Leverkusen only needed to draw at Unterhaching, who were weak opponents, while Bayern Munich needed to win their last game if they were to be champions. Since everyone assumed that Leverkusen were going to be the new champions, *Die Tote Hose*'s banner was intended ironically congratulating Bayern for coming second in the Bundesliga (Dominik Müller, Club Nummer 12, personal interview, 3 July 2000). To the delight of Bayern fans, it backfired rather badly: Leverkusen lost and Bayern were champions.

Like Bayern, Juventus have also been reviled for many years for their economic power and success, as Domineco Lo Forte, the president of the Milan-based Juventus fan club, revealed:

> Juve's power is historic. Football history is longer than our Republic ... and in 100 years of football, Juve has won four times what all the other teams have and this is annoying. Moreover, Juve has always been competitive. And it belongs to the Agnelli family who've got enormous political and economic power in Italy. Juve's always been the subject of much controversy and I'm wondering whether it lost the championship because of its unpopularity. [Domineco Lo Forte, personal interview, 17 May 2000]

Lo Forte's statement is important because although he cites historic reasons for Juventus' long-standing unpopularity, he also refers to the now infamous way in which Juventus lost the 1999–2000 championship to Lazio. Juventus' last game of the season was against the small club of Perugia whom they had to beat to win the championship. During the first half there was a torrential downpour which flooded the pitch, rendering it unplayable and, by all reasonable standards, the game should have been abandoned. Yet, after a brief delay the game continued in farcical conditions in which Juventus were only able to draw the game. Significantly, this decision against Juventus seemed to have been motivated by the league's desire to offset a dubious decision in the club's favour the week before, when a last-minute headed goal by Parma's Fabio Cannovaro, which would have cost Juventus two crucial points, was disallowed by the referee. That disallowed goal had caused outrage in Italy where there was public protest against the prospect of Juventus winning another championship. With television evidence backing Cannavaro's claim that the goal should have stood, a wave of anti-Juventus feeling swept the country and the authorities themselves were accused of being biased towards Juventus. As Lo Forte's statement reveals, Juventus fans widely believed that they were the victims of a national conspiracy which wanted them to fail. The significant point here is not that Juventus were cheated at Perugia nor that they had been favoured against Parma but that the prospect of another Juventus championship provoked such extreme reactions among opposition fans and that Juventus fans, in turn, have seen themselves as the victims of a national conspiracy. Interestingly, masculine fans in the 1990s at Manchester United have also conceived themselves to be victims of a national conspiracy. They describe people who are part of this conspiracy as ABUs (anyone but United).

The new hatred provoked by football's commercialisation is demonstrated by the vitriol directed at the players of the biggest clubs by opposing fans. Eric Cantona was an early example of the new resentment which players could inspire in fans. During the 1991–92 season, Cantona led Leeds to their first League Championship since the early 1970s and, during the victory parade, declared to the Leeds fans, 'I don't know why I love you but I do.' Despite his undying affection for the club, Cantona was, however, transferred from Leeds United to Manchester United in November 1992. Given his profession of allegiance, his subsequent transfer to Manchester United, Leeds' most hated rivals, less than six months later understandably angered Leeds fans. However, the abuse which Cantona received was interesting since, besides certain xenophobic elements, it focused on the wealth of Manchester United. For instance, on the back of the main Leeds fanzine, a cartoon called 'The Temptation of Cantona', pictured Leeds' pride (in the form of Gary Speed, a key midfield player at the time) being crucified while in the foreground, Cantona is led away by 'Beelezebub' Ferguson, clutching thirty pieces of silver (*The Square Ball* 1992). For Leeds fans, the transfer demonstrated the corrupting power of Manchester United's commercial dominance. Yet, Cantona's transfer fee was set at only £1.1 million, his wages were within United's relatively modest pay structures and various personal reasons later emerged which explained the transfer. Yet even given this evidence of which Leeds fans were aware, they still regarded this transfer as evidence of the corrupting influence of United's financial power.

The outrage at Cantona's transfer to Manchester United illustrates that by the 1990s, antagonism between fans had increased decisively as a result of new economic pressures. However, some of these pressures were beginning to be felt in England before the 1990s. In particular, the abolition of the maximum wage in 1961 had increased the competition between clubs for players within the national market. Anticipating the furious reaction to Cantona's transfer in 1992, Leeds fans had been angered by the transfer of Gordon McQueen to Manchester United in 1978 for £495,000. However, the levels of outrage were not as extreme and, equally significantly, the dissatisfaction of the Leeds fans remained unreported. *The Times*, for instance, does not record the response of the fans at all. The transfer of Cantona was an early example of the kinds of hatred which the new commercialisation of football is capable of creating. Demonstrating the point, in 2002, after the transfer of Rio Ferdinand from Leeds for £31 million, United fans have chanted 'Leeds are our feeder club' (Brewin 2002). The economic power of Manchester United has become an explicit means by which its fans could assert their superiority over their rivals. As economic competition has intensified, the rivalry between local fans has increased. In fact, the way in which fans now appeal to the economic power of their clubs to denigrate rivals facilitates a possible reinterpretation of fan culture before the 1990s.

In 1971, Ian Taylor proposed that football hooliganism was the protest of a working-class 'sub-cultural rump' against their alienation from their football clubs as a result of commercialisation (Taylor 1971). He may have been correct to highlight commercialisation as a major cause of fan violence but it seems unlikely that fans felt alienated from their clubs as a result of it. Certainly, he provides insufficient evidence to prove it. It seems rather more likely that as economic competition increased between football clubs, the fans became embroiled in ever more intense status competitions which paralleled these economic struggles. Hooliganism may not have been so much a reaction against commercialisation as a product of it especially since these same economic forces were transforming the fans' lives away from football. Commercialisation and deregulation fissured older social solidarities within football and wider society creating new forms of local rivalry between fans. Hooliganism was a product of new social groups who created in and out groups through the use of violence in the face of uneven development. The aggression with which fans now respond to unfavourable player transfers is likely to be an intensification of a long-standing process, in England at least. Nevertheless, it is an intensification of such an extreme nature that its contemporary social importance has to be recognised.

The growing economic rivalry between fans can be detected in other parts of Europe. In Spain, Luis Figo's transfer from Barcelona to Real Madrid in the summer of 2000 has induced a ferocious reaction from Barcelona fans. Given the historical significance of the two clubs, transfers between them have always been problematic. For instance, when Michael Laudrup transferred to Real in the mid-1990s, the Barcelona president, Nunez, publicly stated that while he wished Laudrup every possible success as an individual, he wished him all possible disaster as a player. Laudrup described his return to the Nou Camp in 1995 as the worst day of his life (King, J. 2000a). The reception for renegades was always uncomfortable in the Nou Camp but Luis Figo's reception at the Nou Camp for his first game in October 2000 was extraordinary even by Barcelona's standards. The chant 'Figo dies' echoed around the ground for the entire game and he was subjected to a barrage of fruit, vegetables, plastic bottles, fake banknotes, lighters, lollipops and even mobile phones. Despite being a winger, he avoided the touchlines throughout the game, drifting into the middle of the pitch and he did not take a single corner, in order to escape the worst of the abuse, the bombardment and the threat of physical assault (ibid.).

Perhaps the most obvious example of the powerful effects of commercialisation is the extraordinary levels of abuse which the Manchester United player David Beckham has received in the 1990s. David Beckham is a particularly useful example here because the treatment he has received from the press and fans contrasts with that of George Best who attained a similar cultural position before the commercialisation of the game. Both Beckham and Best were brought to Manchester United as boys from other cities in the United Kingdom, London and Belfast respectively; both were outstanding right-wingers for Manchester United winning the European Cup with the club and, while George Best won the European player of the year award in 1966, Beckham was runner-up in this same competition in 2000. Moreover, both were handsome and stylish individuals, embodying contemporary masculine ideals, as a result of which they have been able to transcend their role as footballers to become international celebrities. In both cases, this entry into a wider media world has been assisted by their choice of partners. Best famously had a series of relationships with famous models and actresses, while Beckham married Victoria Adams, a member of the successful pop group the Spice Girls. However, while there are parallels between the two players, there are also important differences. Although Manchester United's 1968 team was not universally popular in England at the time, Best himself was singled out for no special or concerted abuse from the fans of other clubs in the 1960s. It is true that he was abused by some fans on his return after his temporary retirement and Glanville, for instance, records a case of this abuse at Queens Park Rangers:

> He suddenly and impulsively retired, stayed out long enough to put on weight, then came back, but was never the same again; with United, with Fulham or in America. The dazzling pace had gone. I remember one Christmas at Loftus Road, the Queens Park Rangers crowd cruelly and viciously booing him when a god seemed mortal. What envy builds up, in the mass psyche, of the brilliant maverick; and how much more so when to his professional success is added success with women. [Glanville 1991: 54]

Although Glanville's description must be treated with care, the abuse which he describes seems to have been motivated by the self-evident decline of the once brilliant winger, mocking Best for his decline as a player. By contrast, Beckham was the object of almost universal derision which was continually highlighted (and, indeed, aggravated) by the media. The vitriol which Beckham faced at every ground in England first escalated after he was sent off in the World Cup quarter-final in 1998 against Argentina for kicking Simeone. From that moment, he was castigated by the fans of other clubs. His effigy was hung from a lamp-post by West Ham fans before the first game of the 1998–99 season. However, as the abuse which Beckham received in Euro 2000 (where he was undoubtedly England's best player) revealed, his vilification now detached itself from the particular incident in the World Cup in 1998: he was now routinely denigrated by the fans of other club teams and even by England supporters when he played for England. In the important qualifying game against Finland on 24 March 2001 which was played at Anfield, a significant portion of the game's previews focused on the issue of whether Beckham, as captain, would be barracked by England fans.[2]

Fans rejected Beckham because he played for Manchester United. It was notable that his abuse was normally accompanied by the chants of 'Stand up if you hate Man U'. Yet, the abuse also focused specifically on his international celebrity status and his extreme personal wealth. A large part of the abuse was directed not at Beckham himself but at his wife, Victoria Adams. In particular, the obscene chant 'Does she [Adams] take it up the arse?' established itself at the heart of the repertoire of opposition fans. Marking a profound contrast to the standards of British television under the Reithian era, this song became standard fare on comedy shows and television interviews in Britain. The song was significant, for the imputation of this sexual practice to Beckham's wife was intended to demean her, reducing her to the status of a whore. While a respectable woman would never submit willingly to this form of sexual intercourse, the chant implied that a prostitute might consent to this practice. Emphasising the point of the song, much of the random abuse shouted at Beckham during games explicitly referred to her as a whore. The attempt to denigrate her was significant because it highlighted that her financial status was objectionable to some fans; that she had attained a position of prominence and power by shamelessly selling herself rather than through respectable feminine initiative. Beckham was denigrated because he had married someone who had earned a fortune illegitimately. By focusing on Victoria Adams, the fans revealed their main objection to David Beckham was his wealth and celebrity. This objection was radicalised because Beckham represented a club which is itself viewed in a similar way to Victoria Adams. Manchester United is seen to have prostituted itself through commercialism to attain dominance in England. The commercialised glamour of Manchester United is now broadcast unremittingly through the television, tabloids and magazines to a global audience, provoking resentment on the part of other fans:

> A lot of fans get pissed off with Man United not because they are Man United but because of the media's attitude ... That [hatred] follows the sycophantic media treatment which they've been getting over the last few years since they won the European Cup. I think you just get exasperated. If you watched the European Cup Final this year, Manchester United were mentioned more often by name than Valencia were. That shows how much the media are obsessed with Manchester United when they weren't even taking part. And yet the commentator still felt it necessary to mention them. If you watched a lot of the European Championship coverage, the commentator didn't feel able to mention Fabian Barthez without mentioning that he was a Manchester United player. That builds up in people. [James Edwards, editor, *Chelsea Independent*, personal interview, 10 August 2000]

The revulsion which Manchester United now provokes is not simply because the club is more visible in the media, as James Edwards claims, but also because United fans are prominent in every town. The increasingly visible presence of supporters of the biggest clubs in cities and towns with ostensibly adequate teams has become offensive to the fans of other clubs. It demonstrates that the big city clubs are undermining the local support of these smaller clubs. Clearly, this is a process which has been occurring since the 1950s, with the development of car and television ownership which enabled individuals to familiarise themselves with the biggest clubs and allowed them to travel easily to support these teams (Bale 1989: 93, 96; 1982: 29), but it has been accelerated in the contemporary transnational era. The global flows of capital have been channelled into certain focal points like Manchester United in a process of uneven development which has initiated protests in the form of vitriolic abuse of particular individuals who represent those favoured locales.

The new geography of European football has given risen to new hatreds and new social fissures. The new transnational reality has exacerbated local rivalries. In his analysis of the construction of identity in the post-Fordist world, Appadurai has usefully described the disjunctures and differences which appear in the global cultural economy:

> The central feature of global culture today is the politics of the mutual effort of sameness and difference to cannibalise one another and thus to proclaim their successful hijacking of twin Enlightenment ideas of triumphantly universal and resiliently particular. This mutual cannibalization shows its ugly face in riots, in refugee-flows, in state-sponsored torture and in ethnocide (with or without state support). Its brighter face is in the expansion of many individual horizons of hope and fantasy, in the global spread of oral re-hydration therapy and other low-tech instruments of well-being, in the susceptibility of South Africa to the force of global opinion, in the inability of the Polish state to repress its own working class and in the growth of a wide range of progressive, transnational alliances. [Appadurai 1996: 42–3]

For Appaduria, the post-Fordist world offers opportunities for the emergence of new forms of imagined communities sited at particular points in the emergent global network. While these solidarities can provide support and even liberation for those within them, their boundaries are guarded by hatred and violence, excluding outsiders. The abuse of David Beckham is one of the ugly sides of globalisation, reflecting new lines of solidarity and exclusion. Globalised market forces are producing new forms of solidarity centred especially on those locations which have been successful in attracting multinational capital but this concentration simultaneously involves aggressive responses from marginalised groups. The coalescence of the forces of global capital at a site like Old Trafford has had very serious social effects on less favoured locations and has stimulated a new hatred of this institution. In turn, the masculine fans at Manchester United have begun to transform themselves in the face of this increased antipathy, drawing on the idea of the locale and specifically of Manchester to reconstitute themselves as a social group in a changed landscape.

The Locale

Appadurai has drawn upon and expanded Anderson's notion of 'imagined community' (1990) to consider the different ways in which communities – and not only national ones – are currently brought into being.[3] In particular, Appadurai discusses the significance of the concept of locality in this globalised world. Interestingly, Appadurai claims that the fetishism of the commodity which was typical in the modern industrial period has been replaced by new forms of product and consumer fetishism in the global, post-Fordist period (Appadurai 1994: 306; also 1996: 41–2). For Appadurai, product fetishism refers to 'an illusion created by contemporary transnational production loci, which masks translocal capital, transnational-earning flows – in the idiom and spectacle of the local' (Appadurai, 1994: 306). Multinational capital situates itself in certain localities and draws identity from those localities in order to hide its global anonymity. Although Appadurai might overemphasise the conspiratorial nature of global forces which have to conceal themselves as local, his analysis is illuminating because he demonstrates, following Anderson and Hobsbawm and Ranger (1983), that communities are continually reinvented or reimagined in the face of new developments. Locales should not be thought of as self-evident places. Apparently obvious geographic space – like a city – does not determine the kinds of social networks which arise in it. The locale is not prior. Rather, a geographic space becomes a locale when members of a particular social network invest that place with significance. The 'locale' becomes the symbol of the social network; it is a shared understanding developed by a particular group about the nature of their social group which is employed by members of the group to maintain and regulate their relations with each other and to denote appropriate forms of conduct. The locale embodies the central understandings of the group and acts as a common cultural resource by which members of the group are called to order. The emergence of new forms of local consciousness is connected to the growing importance of regions and cities in the New Europe as global capital bypasses nation-states to reconfigure European geography into a new transnational network of increasingly autonomous cities.

As already mentioned in the previous chapter, since about the 1960s, European football fan culture has been dominated by groups of masculine fans who have colonised the 'ends' or 'curvas' of the grounds. In England, these groups have taken a distinctive form, although the practices of the English masculine fan groups have drawn upon and been imitated by other European groups. These fans also display their masculine 'pride' (or status) by singing in the ground and potentially fighting to protect their honour (see King' 1997a, 1998a). Arising out of the so-called 'fashion-wars' between certain British hooligan groups in the 1980s (see Redhead 1991a, 1991b; Allan 1989), it has become normal for masculine fans to wear expensive 'casual' designer clothing rather than replica kits or club colours. Among the masculine fan group at Manchester United, this practice has become the norm as replica shirts have become synonymous with the new fans being attracted to football in the 1990s (see King 1998a). Consequently, denoting their different long-standing relation to the club, the masculine fan group rarely wear club colours. In addition to wearing these expensive casual clothes, as discussed in Chapter 9, there is a common rejection of the commercialisation of the game which is stifling the ability of these men to express their masculine solidarities by communal singing and celebration in the ground. This group of football fans consist of an almost exclusively male network most of whom live in or around Manchester and who have been a prominent element in United's support. They are the producers and key consumers of the two major fan magazines (fanzines), *United We Stand* and *Red Issue*, and have been central to the creation of the Independent Manchester United Supporters' Club (IMUSA), described in Chapter 9.[4] It would be wrong to overemphasise the homogeneity of this network: tensions exist between different loose groupings since there is a blurred divide within this masculine group between more politically committed fans and those who are part of or closer to United's hooligan firm. However, despite potential differences which surface on certain issues, there are substantial areas of shared culture and understanding between these men.

Following Appadurai and Anderson, the notion of the locale of Manchester, to which the masculine Manchester United fans now appeal, has emerged in the specific context of the 1990s. The locale has become particularly significant in the light of the new transnational geography of football and the new hatred directed towards Manchester United in this context. The locale refers not primarily to birth or residence in Manchester, though they are certainly not irrelevant, but rather to the adoption of the central forms of practice of this group such as the wearing of designer clothing which are seen as properly Mancunian. Thus, there are many fans who live in Manchester but are not part of the 'locale' for these masculine individuals because they do not accord with the forms of consumption which this group has adopted in the 1990s. Moreover, there are many other fans who are not Mancunian – by birth or residence – but who are part of this network because they do adopt these masculine practices and, through supporting the team, have become part of this network. The increasing place which Manchester has in the imagination of these men means that the city is frequently employed as a common symbol which the fans invoke to define appropriate behaviour in their relations to others; this is intrinsically connected to the transformed economic circumstances in the 1990s in football and in society more widely. Consequently, in Manchester's growing importance to these men, the outlines of an emergent identity which highlights regional or local urban interests and affiliations above national ones can begin to be traced.

The Development of European Consciousness

The deregulation of European club football in the 1990s has provided these Manchester United fans with the opportunity to travel in Europe more frequently. This has been particularly important for masculine fans since the European away trip is regarded as the best form of football trip available and has been central to this group's support. The European away trip provides these fans with several days together in an unknown and potentially exciting foreign city in which their celebrations can be extended. Indeed, one fan commented on a trip to Munich that many of the masculine supporters of United who had been prominent to the club's support in the 1980s, due partly to their violent conduct, went to no games except European aways because they found Old Trafford intolerably restrained and restrictive (Chris, fieldnotes, 30 September 1998).[5] Consequently, masculine fans look upon European trips as the best 'craic' available to them and emphasise 'the buzz you receive from each trip' (Chilton et al. 1997: 3–4): 'Following your team in Europe is an education and what's more, is like a drug ... you just want more and more, visiting countries where licensing laws mean you can only drink for twenty-four hours a day' (ibid.: 5). Since the European away trip is viewed as the best supporting experience available to the fans, masculine United fans have taken the opportunity provided by the expansion of the Champions League and United's playing success to travel extensively in Europe. As a result, these masculine United fans have become more familiar with many of the major cities in Europe, a familiarity not very much in evidence during the 1970s and 1980s, although Liverpool fans travelled extensively at that time (despite the knock-out format of the European Cup) due to the extraordinary success of the team. The knowledge which these current United fans have of Europe may be directed at a narrow range of masculine interests, revolving around bars and clubs, though this is certainly not universally the case; several fans said that they liked to see the sights of the cities they were visiting, and not just spend their time inside bars. Yet there is nevertheless a growing awareness of Europe and its cities among the fans, as well as a sophisticated knowledge of the transport system in Europe:

> The fans go out there and in three days in a foreign city, you cannot help but pick up certain things. And those who go to every game, they have racked up a really good list of away trips. They have become what we would now call European citizens. They are at ease in all the capitals, they know the different culture, what you can do with a woman in one place, what you can't in another. That is a socialization process and that is very new. [Richard Kurt,[6] personal interview, 12 May 1998][7]

Furthermore, as a result of the increase in the number of matches, fans are beginning to develop contacts with other fans. For instance, Kurt noted that

United fans were developing the beginnings of a violent rivalry with the fans of some clubs, such as Juventus, while Mike Adams suggested that a similar relationship was developing with Feyenoord (Mike Adams, IMUSA committee, personal interview, 15 May 1998).

For some fans among this network, the extension of European travel had meant that they had become almost too familiar with certain cities in Europe. Andy Mitten emphasised that originally he could only dream of seeing United play Juventus or Barcelona in the Nou Camp, but having played these teams several times in the last few seasons, the 'buzz' of going to Barcelona or Turin had worn off; he concluded that 'familiarity breeds contempt' (personal interview, 30 April 1998). If fans are to spend substantial amounts of money travelling to see their team, they would rather visit new cities than return to familiar destinations. Despite the claim that familiarity has bred contempt in relation to certain destinations, these masculine fans still look upon the European away trip as an 'oasis in a desert of mediocrity' (Mike Adams, 15 May 1998). Although a trip to Barcelona may not inspire the excitement it once did, it is certainly regarded as substantially more attractive than an away trip to a domestic league ground, not least because it simply offers the fans more time to celebrate with each other. Other fans suggested that it was not simply the expanded opportunities for travel which had increased these United fans' familiarity with Europe but the increased prominence of European football on television had produced greater interest in European leagues than was formerly the case (Richard Kurt, 12 May 1998; Andy Walsh, 30 May 1998). Many United fans now know the positions of clubs in other European leagues, their players and those clubs' main domestic rivals.

This familiarity with Europe is significant because it could potentially play a part in the development of a supranational European identity, where these United fans genuinely begin to see themselves as primarily Europeans rather than as British. There seemed to be some evidence that this extensive travel across Europe had had an effect on the attitudes of this group of fans towards Europe. In interviews and in the fanzines, a recurrent theme is that these United fans have begun to see themselves as more European and have more substantial knowledge of other European countries than previously:

> The little Englander resides in every single one of us – that islander. It is only through education, through experience that it is driven out of you but I think it is inbuilt, inbred within every single one of us, that Englander, that islander, that isolationist. The more you go and experience the taste and absorb different culture, the more you do become a European, a Europhile. [Mike Adams, personal interview, 15 May 1998]

> Among the fans you will find few Eurosceptics, they've enjoyed some great times on the continent indulging in the delights of fine cities like Barcelona. [*United We Stand* 1996: 8, also Chilton et al. 1997: 98].

However, although these United fans are certainly more familiar with Europe, and employ the terms 'Europhile' and 'Eurosceptic' which refer to specific political positions in relation to monetary union, their use of these terms and specifically their notion of themselves as Europhiles cannot be taken as evidence that they think of themselves as distinctively European in the supranational way that the Commission or a theorist like Chryssochoou envisage. They do not draw on a common cultural heritage with other European fans, with whom they do not interact sufficiently to develop intimate rivalries on a par with their relationship to Liverpool or Leeds fans.[8] They feel no bond of supranationhood with these other European fans and they have not transferred their political and cultural allegiances to some ill-defined entity called Europe or some little-known supranational institution like the European Commission. Indeed, the fans explicitly rejected the suggestion that any such supranational identity might be emerging among them. Richard Kurt echoed the point made by many sociologists (for example, Delanty 1995), that Europe could never constitute a coherent identity because there is 'no external opposition' to it. Without that common other, Europe could never be the source of identity in the way that nations have sometimes been. Mike Adams, echoing many cultural critics, added that not only was there no evidence of a genuine pan-European identity among United fans but the emergence of such an identity was unwanted: 'God forbid if there was any Euronationalism because any rampant nationalism that gets out of control is dangerous. It would be too much of a leap. Too presumptuous on my part to believe that United supporters saw themselves as being in the vanguard of some pan-European movement' (personal interview, 15 May 1998).

Yet, while rejecting a notion of pan-European nationalism, Adams did comment that 'a lot of United fans I know and speak to, see themselves as being or would want to see themselves as being European before British or English – I would, certainly.' Given that he and other fans have rejected the notion of pan-Europeanism and the emergence of some homogenous cultural identity, this claim that United fans see themselves as Europeans first, then British, and see themselves as Europhiles because they are increasingly familiar with Europe, seems strange and even contradictory. It is peculiar to claim to be European and, yet have no idea of the common cultural traditions, experiences and interests which would constitute a European identity – and, indeed, if anything, to reject any idea of homogenised and exclusive supranationalism.

However, this apparent contradiction between a growing integration into European relations and familiarity with Europe without the development of any kind of supranational cultural consciousness can be reconciled by understanding the significance of the appeals to Manchester United and Manchester by these fans. For these fans, European integration has begun to raise the importance of Manchester above the nation and their Europeanness lies only in the fact that they now increasingly want the city of Manchester and

Manchester United to be fully integrated into the flows of capital and culture in this New Europe. They want Manchester and Manchester United to compete at this emergent transnational level so that the city and club can be recognised as the equal of the other great clubs or cities in Europe. These men have not elevated their identities and interests to a supranational level but, on the contrary, have emphasised local affiliations. This local identity repositions the club, its fans and the city in a new transnational context.

The Emergence of Mancunian Identity

One of the major effects of the concentration of power among the biggest clubs has been the growing antipathy which fans of other clubs direct towards them. Thus, Bayern Munich, Juventus, Real Madrid and Barcelona are all the objects of vilification by opposition fans in their respective leagues, but the radical commercialisation of Manchester United and its dominance over domestic competitions in England has provoked levels of unmatched hatred. As already noted, opposition fans have vilified the clubs and its fans in various ways including directing obscene abuse at David Beckham and his wife. However, one of the most effective ways in which these fans have expressed their hatred of the club has been through the widespread use of the chant 'Do you come from Manchester?'. This chant asserts that the commercialisation of Manchester United has rendered the club inauthentic since it is supported not by the local working-class but by middle-class fans from outside Manchester who only attend because the club is successful. This rejection of Manchester United (and the vitriol directed at Beckham and his wife) is a half-articulated resistance to the new global forces which are reconfiguring Europe, marginalising some cities and regions while favouring others. Whatever the rationale behind the claim that Manchester United is an inauthentic club, it has seriously threatened the status of this network of masculine fans organised around *Red Issue, United We Stand* and IMUSA because at the very moment of the club's superiority, their support has not been recognised by their rivals at other clubs. Local rivalries have transformed the consciousness of Manchester United fans, precipitating an increased emphasis on the locale and on European competition.

In the face of these local rivalries and the accusation of inauthenticity, this network of masculine United fans have re-emphasised their Mancunian identity in order to reassert their status. Certainly since the 1960s at least, with the development of large away followings and hooliganism, Manchester United fans have often expressed some allegiance to Manchester, particularly in their songs, which have overwhelmingly directed abuse at their rivals such as Liverpool and Leeds. However, these fans now emphasise the importance of being Mancunian, which was never a particularly important issue while United were unsuccessful in the 1970 and 1980s and before commercialism had seemed to favour out-of-town supporters and encouraged other fans to question the authenticity of United. For instance, the heated and extensive debate over the importance of United fans being from Manchester only became a topic of discussion in informal conversations and in the fanzines in 1993, after Manchester United won the Championship for the first time in 26 years and were first subjected to the chant, 'Do you come from Manchester?'. This so-called 'out-of-town' debate then became a dominant theme in the fanzines for the following two years and is still a point of discussion. In the course of this 'out-of-town' debate, the issue of Mancunian identity has gained a new self-conscious significance for this network of fans which was never the case in the past, where their Mancunian identity was merely taken for granted and had no special significance. Different fans have now adopted different positions with regard to the out-of-town debate so that many Mancunian fans see any non-local support as inauthentic. For other local masculine fans in the 1990s, it was possible to be a United fan without being a Mancunian but the Mancunian identity was increasingly highlighted. In particular, it is better to be a Mancunian United fan because a Mancunian fan's understanding of the club and its relationship to the city is deeper. Thus, for instance, a contributor to *United We Stand*, significantly calling himself 'Abbey Hey', after a district in the city from which this writer presumably comes to denote his authentic attachment to this network, writes:

> The Manchester in MU means so much more to Mancunian Reds and there for me is the difference – Manchester is not just the love of the club in the west of the City, it's our home, it enlivens our experience, it forms our ways, it loves you back. East-Central Manchester is the J-Stand of Manchester – quiet, unassuming but beats with a deep heart. [*United We Stand* 1995]

However, although many United fans might concur with this ecumenical view of the club's out-of-town support, during the 1999–2000 season, a more negative view of non-Mancunian support has been commonly expressed. As terraces have disappeared at away grounds, the allocation for away supporters has become smaller and smaller and given the size of United's travelling support and their attraction to the fans of opposing teams (who pressurise their own club to maximise tickets for home supporters when United visit), the availability of tickets has become scarce for United fans. Significantly, the lines of distinction and debate about who should get these tickets has been drawn between Mancunian United fans and out-of-town fans:

> Really quite often at away matches, I hear people [Mancunian United fans] slagging off United fans, saying, 'Fuck off if you're not from Manchester.' I've never seen it get really aggressive but there is definitely a feeling that has grown – especially at

away matches – because the tickets are in limited supply. You're getting your tickets through a branch so my mates can't go and I only get to go to one in three matches. [Duncan Drasdo, personal interview, 13 June 2000]

This increasingly overt and, indeed, aggressive attitude to non-Mancunian United fans was demonstrated very vividly on the night before United played Bordeaux in the second group phase of the Champions League in March 2000. A group of about 15 Mancunian fans stood outside the Irish Bar in which large numbers of fans were gathered and, with increasingly ferocity, sang a song which they had invented and which repeated the simple refrain, 'So proud we're from Manchester', for nearly half an hour. The meaning of the song – the denigration of non-Mancunian fans – was clear and led to a discussion in the fanzines after the event which generally rejected the aggressive assertion of Mancunian identity by this song.

> 'So proud, we're from Manchester'. Just what the fuck is all that about then? The biggest load of shit if ever I heard it and rivalling only 'we're Leeds and we're proud of it' and the pathetic 'City till I die' for the most cringeworthy song ever. The last thing anyone who is from Manchester and proud of the fact has to do is sing about it. [Team Manchester 2000]

> 'We're proud we're from Manchester!' There is a time and a place for everything but Bordeaux's Irish Bar was neither the time nor the place to make this stunning declaration. What its intention was, I'm not sure, but if it was aimed at pissing off every non-Manc in the bar then it certainly succeeded. [Dave 2000]

However, while overt and aggressive expressions of Mancunian identity which deliberately distinguish between Mancunian and out-of-town support are increasingly legitimate to many United fans (such as those who sung outside the Irish Bar in Bordeaux), the debate about this particular song was interesting in that even those who rejected the song itself, in fact, supported the notion of Mancunian distinctiveness. The letter, significantly signed 'Team Manchester', did not really dispute that Mancunian origins were not now significant nor that they were not a source of pride, only that truly Mancunian fans did not have to announce this publicly. This overt statement of identity was regarded as being the preserve of inauthentic and unmanly groups like Leeds or City fans. Similarly, 'Dave' legitimated his rejection of this song by describing himself as writing from 'Glasgow near Failsworth', which is a district in North-east Manchester. He was well aware that any commentary on this song from 'out-of-towners' would not have the validity of a Mancunian fan and so while he admitting he no longer lived in Manchester, he highlighted the fact that he was originally from the city. Thus, although fans might explicitly accept out-of-towners as true fans, in the late 1990s a hierarchy which did not exist before this time has come into being, where Mancunian origins are not only of increasing relevance but are also, to many, definitively superior.

Significantly, this same theme of the Bordeaux song was taken up in an article in *United We Stand* at the end of the season written by the self-styled '061' (Manchester's former phone code):

> Travel broadens the mind as we all know but less celebrated are the adverse effects trekking round European can have on the old grey matter. These are clearly evidenced in the quantity of ridiculous songs spawned on many a foreign jaunt although few attract such polarised opinion as the recently debuted 'So proud we're from Manchester'. Now despite hailing from the fair city in question and yes, being quite full of myself at the fact, I immediately took exception to this particular ditty. [061, *United We Stand* 2000c]

Like 'Team Manchester' he saw the song as un-Mancunian: 'I'm fairly certain that standing in a bar in a far-off land drunkenly slurring "So proud I'm from Manchester" ain't what being a proud Manc is all about.' On the contrary, for 061, 'there is no "Mancunian" way to behave but the laid-back understated attitude has always been there.' Significantly, however, while 061 – unlike the singers of the Bordeaux song – recognised proper out-of-town supporters who accorded with the masculine norms of the Mancunian fans and were, therefore, 'sound lads' who became 'adopted Mancs', he rejected those fans who advertised the fact that they were not from Manchester by displaying flags at European games with the place-name of their disparate origins emblazoned on them:

> There are those who get upset at being singled out as a non-Manc and then turn up in the grounds and expect to have their 'No-markville Reds' flag in prime position over the fence. One minute they expect to be accepted as a non-Manc and the next they are distinguishing themselves from the majority with their own label. They aren't a 'Shittytown Red' because United don't play in Shittytown. If they want to be a United supporter then that's the end of the matter – United don't represent any crappy little towns or cities – Manchester United represent Manchester and Salford if anywhere at all. [061, *United We Stand* 2000c]

The rejection of flags which advertise out-of-town locations has been similarly rejected elsewhere in the fanzines:

> Whatever the reasoning behind the, ahem, 'Chelmsford Reds' banner it still looks shite and out of place on the curva Stretford alongside genuinely original smart banners of Serie A quality ... Your allegiance to your home town ended with your support of a club formed in Newton Heath, Manchester, so why is there this bizarre need to advertise your home town? ... If your home town is such a matter of local pride, surely that pride finds its identity with the local football club, it's clearly not

compatible with supporting a club from miles away. [*Red Issue* 2000d; see also *Red Issue* 2001]

The author signed the letter as 'Partisan Moston, People's Republic of Northern Mancunia' to highlight his own connection to the city and, significantly, one of the banners which the 'Chelmsford Reds' flag threatened to cover read 'The People's Republic of Mancunia'. It is interesting that the Chelmsfords Reds banner also undermines these masculine fans' attempts to equate themselves with the most important Italian fan movements. Given that United are denigrated for their nationwide support and that the public evidence of these flags provides opposing fans with ammunition to undermine the status of United fans, it is understandable why these fans should object to their presence. However, this is a decisive transformation from the past, when the presence of diverse fans and their flags was either an irrelevance or even a source of pride to Mancunian United fans. From the 1990s, however, Mancunian United fans have emphasised the locale of Manchester as a key site of identification and this locale is situated in a transnational rather than merely a national context.

The Rejection of England

In addition to this new emphasis on the locale of Manchester, there is a widespread rejection of England among these masculine fans. Clearly, there were fans in the past who would have been uninterested in the England team but the difference at Manchester United in the 1990s is the extent to which this disconnection from the England national team has been emphasised, paralleling the growing significance of Manchester to these fans. In the past, whether fans supported or did not support the England team was irrelevant to their support of United but it has now become a contentious issue, where fans either self-consciously reject or consciously continue to support the England team. Increasingly, however, many reject allegiance to the English national team:

> I said, 'I'm being totally honest; I hope England get sent home after the first round so that our players can get a rest before next season.' And he said, 'Do you mean that?' And I said, 'I mean it.' For United in Europe, the cause is a lot greater than England's. We pay the wages, they're our players. If they can get a rest before next season, that will be a bonus. [Gordon, personal interview, 30 April 1998][9]

Gordon highlights that the financial pressures introduced by deregulation of European football has divided the interest of club and national teams. In addition to this increasing recognition of the separation of economic interests between the national and clubs teams, Gordon further explained his rejection of England: '"Stand up if you hate Man U" at England games – that's happened this year, hasn't it?' (Gordon, personal interview, 30 April 1998).[10] In rejecting the England football team, these United fans make an interesting and potentially important critique of English nationalism which they no longer see as a universal identity which encompasses all English people but rather only an expression of the particular interests of regionally located groups. For these United fans, English nationalism is the appropriate identity of the South (which has benefited from the free market policies of national governments, particularly under Thatcher) or of those small clubs (also often in the South) whose fans' only hope of foreign travel (and status) is with the England team: 'Most cities in the north of England have got less reason to feel a national identity than down south' (Gordon, personal interview, 30 April 1998):

> The national team is there to give supporters of small time crap little clubs – West Ham, Millwall, Leeds, City etc – the chance to lord it up abroad watching a team that at least has a chance of winning, unlike their own tin-pot lowly outfit. This is the view the majority of United fans and indeed supporters of other big clubs, usually in the North (Liverpool and Everton), subscribe to firmly. [*United We Stand* 1998c]

It should be noted that these United fans are not rejecting appeals to all forms of nationalism or allegiance to the British state but rather they are specifically withdrawing themselves from relationships with masculine football fans from other clubs who support the England team. These fans specifically reject English and not a broader British nationalism and are, consequently, rejecting a group of identified individuals – the supporters of smaller and especially southern teams – with whom they no longer wish to be associated through following England.[11] Clearly, it is necessary to be very careful here, as nationalism (as we shall see in Chapter 12) remains an important force in European football culture, but it might be tentatively suggested that the new localism demonstrated by United fans involves certain 'post-national' elements. This consciousness does not refer to a total rejection of the nation but rather the development of overlapping and competing allegiances to the nation, the city or region and supranation where different forms of solidarity are called forth at different moments. The nation is certainly not irrelevant but neither is it the primary solidarity around which social action was mobilised in the past. The idea of the nation has itself undergone renegotiation under the pressures of globalisation. For instance, while these Mancunian fans may reject nationalism as a particularistic identity of the south, those fans who vilify Manchester United and its players at England games are simultaneously transforming their own once universalist nationalist ideas into an avowedly particularistic one, for their allegiance to England now excludes Manchester United and its fans. Thus, even those fans who continue to espouse nationalism and, therefore, seem to affirm long-standing, universal traditions have in fact quite radically altered the form which their nationalism takes. It is a nationalism which has become increasingly regional in orientation and which now sees parts of England as alien to the nation; Manchester United and its supporters are seen as being outside the imagined community of men to whom these fans commit themselves when they support the England team.

Given United fans' rejection of the English national team, its fans and, at some moments, English nationalism more generally, the question of the appropriate conduct in Europe has become a central concern for United fans, especially in the light of the prominent coverage given to the often violent and xenophobic conduct of England fans abroad. It is increasingly important for these United fans that they distinguish themselves from England fans abroad by their behaviour if they are to establish themselves as distinctively Mancunian:

> You're going away. You're taking your club. You're taking your city to a foreign field. That sort of theory's been espoused on behalf of why England supporters cause trouble. United fans don't necessarily not cause trouble but they don't take their national identity abroad, they take their identity as Man United fans abroad. They are more cosmopolitan, more clued up, they're more hospitable and less antagonistic to foreign supporters. They go over in big numbers, they drink lots of beer, they sing lots of songs but they get on with the locals. [Mike Adams, personal interview, 15 May 1998]

However, since many United fans still appeal to national affiliations when abroad, often singing songs associated with England such as the national anthem, this 'local' network of United fans have had to distinguish themselves from a significant body of United fans if they are to sustain their distinctively Mancunian identity. Consequently, the rejection of nationalist United fans is often ferocious: 'Why do certain United fans feel they have to behave like cretinous arseholes every time they step foot on foreign soil? All this chanting "Engerland, Engerland" and "No surrender to the IRA" etc has no place on a United away trip' (*Red Issue* 1997). Significantly, the fans who inappropriately sing nationalistic songs are also seen to be those who wear replica shirts rather than 'casual' clothing, thereby demonstrating a double inauthenticity: they are English nationalists rather than Mancunians and are the creation of commercialisation. For instance, an article in *United We Stand* called 'Men Behaving Badly', which complained about the increasing presence of fans who threaten the reputation of Manchester United, featured a photograph of a replica shirt-wearing United fan cavorting with a belly dancer. The picture demonstrated the kind of embarrassing practices which the author regarded as inappropriate for true (Mancunian) fans (*United We Stand* 1998c). This linkage between inappropriate behaviour abroad and the commercialisation of the club is significant: throughout the 1990s, as Manchester United converted itself into a very successful leisure company, the masculine fans, who constituted the dedicated part of United's following from the 1960s onwards, increasingly sought to differentiate themselves from 'new' fans attracted by the club's success (see King 1997a; 1998c). These 'new' fans, symbolically identified by wearing the replica shirt, are seen as a threat to the masculine fans since they are taking the place of masculine fans in the ground and ruining the atmosphere by not singing. The same individuals who are seen as emblematic of the commercialisation of the club which the masculine fans reject are now seen as threatening the status of these masculine fans abroad. Typically, these nationalist, commercialised fans are also seen as not properly masculine:

> Yet it's the other end of the spectrum where arguably the biggest lesson in United conduct abroad is required. The lot who actually believe that they are somehow the true Reds abroad. The lot whose first whiff of foreign air reduces them to absolute arseholes. Acting up as Jack Large in a foreign bar doesn't mark you down as a leading face [a well-known hooligan], likewise ripping [off] Italian cab driver's doesn't mark you down as jib master general.[12] [*United We Stand* 1999a]

These non-Mancunian fans have adopted specious forms of masculine practice which they believe give them status in foreign cities but which, in fact, only demonstrate their backward insularity.

By contrast, for the Mancunian network of masculine fans, demonstrating their anti-English, Mancunian masculinity involves potentially more considerate behaviour in Europe or, at least, it requires restrained and inconspicuous behaviour when there is no significant threat to the status of these men. By behaving more casually in Europe, Mancunian United fans seek to denote their distinction from English fans but also to demonstrate that they are thoroughly familiar with the Continent and do not feel the need to assert themselves publicly when in foreign cities. However, while these United fans prefer inconspicuousness for the most part, highly visible forms of public disorder in the form of confrontations with the police or with opposing fans are certainly condoned if it is necessary for the defence of their masculine status:

> As Feyenoord last season showed we can still tear it up a bit when the need calls for it. But there is a time and a place, and Milan wasn't the place, just as Barcelona wasn't and Porto wasn't. We are talking about the great cities of Europe here, playing the great clubs of Europe and yet an increasing number of Reds insist on playing the village idiot that we accuse so many of our rivals of being. [*United We Stand* 1999a]

For masculine fans, the mark of a true Mancunian United fan is one who is able to fight but will only do so if it is unavoidable or, in the case of the hooligan elite, if the opposition is worthy of attack. This network of United fans claim that they are not interested in asserting their masculine status on a parochial and insular level like nationalist fans by abusing all foreigners, but want to establish their status as representatives of Manchester United by acting in a way which demands the respect of the locals, not merely their hatred. Random abuse of innocents is dishonourable and brings Manchester United into disrepute.[13] Of course, it is not clear whether the locals see these fans in this way.[14] Moreover, there is no objective standard of when it is the appropriate time to 'tear it up'. Rather the appropriately masculine and Mancunian place to fight is often determined, in fact, when the masculine fans who are recognised as part of this group – and especially the members of this group associated with United's hooligan firm – engage in fighting. As Mike Adams commented, United fans do not necessarily not fight but, it might be inferred, when they do, their violence is interpreted as being in the name of Manchester rather than a nationalist assault on foreigners and it is justified by the provocation of opposing fans. It is, therefore, legitimately masculine and Mancunian rather than nationalistic. Inhabitants of foreign cities may well miss that distinction but to this network of United fans, this definition of violence is crucial to them; it constitutes the basis of a newly imagined community grounded in the reinvented 'locale' of Manchester.

Thus, these United fans reject England and see themselves as European but this notion of Europeanhood has nothing to do with any putatively common cultures and histories shared with the other nations of Europe. Rather these United fans want Manchester United to be recognised as the equal of the biggest European clubs and they want themselves to be seen as the equals of the fans of these clubs. For these fans, European integration involves ever greater competition with the largest and most famous clubs in Europe. Increased European competition has expanded the horizons of these United fans so that they now situate Manchester United in a specifically European context rather than a merely national one. They see that European context as the crucial arena in which to assert their status in their relations with other fans both domestic and European. Consequently, the putative Europhilism of these fans ironically involves an increasing sense of their difference from other European clubs and other European fans and, indeed, in the case of Feyenoord and Juventus, a growing and increasingly intimate hatred of them. The 'other' against which they are beginning to develop a European consciousness is not an 'other' which is external to Europe, which has concerned philosophers such as Habermas and Derrida, but an internal European other – the great clubs of Europe and their fans: 'United's real rivals are now in Europe. The standard of English football has declined sharply and United are getting so much bigger than every other English club that we are miles ahead of our domestic opponents both on and off the pitch' (*United We Stand* 2000a). These fans are repositioning Manchester United and themselves in a transnational competition with the other big clubs of Europe which is gradually becoming more significant than international or domestic competition – especially against the smaller teams in the League.

In line with these tentative new rivalries, United fans are developing a more sophisticated understanding of the fan cultures of other European teams so that national stereotypes are being gradually eroded in favour of more differentiated and locally specific understandings. For instance, United's hooligan firm itself had close links with the hooligans from the small Dutch club of Den Haag who have joined the United fans on several trips abroad. On one occasion, a few members of the Den Haag group were present at United's match against Anderlecht in October 2000 which prompted one leading individual in United's firm to joke, 'What an international mob we have' (fieldnotes, 25 October 2000). In addition, many fans were increasingly familiar with the specific urban cultures of fan groups: 'The fans in Bordeaux, I didn't go to Marseilles, but I would imagine that they were different to the fans in Marseilles. They were apologising for themselves in a way. They were the nicest people you'd ever meet. I'd like to think I don't think of them as "Krauts", "Itis" or "Frogs"' (Dan, personal interview, 21 June 2000). However, any erosion of these national stereotypes is certainly still partial. Mancunian fans themselves often employed nationalistic stereotypes of 'Krauts', 'Spics', 'Itis' and 'Frogs'. However, there seems a determinate though not complete shift in the core of this masculine group away from simplistic national stereotypes to a more differentiated understanding of specific fan cultures (though these can be equally dismissive).

The contrast with Liverpool fans in the 1970s and 1980s is instructive here. Although travelling Liverpool fans at this time showed some of the features of the new European consciousness demonstrated by United fans in the 1990s, these fans' understanding of foreign fans was overwhelmingly nationalistic.[15] In the 1980s, Liverpool fans demonstrated their cosmopolitanism by wearing the latest European designer fashions, sometimes stolen from shops while abroad on football trips (Redhead 1986: 99–100). For instance, in 1984–85, bobble hats became fashionable among 'casual' fans and the 'style war' between fans was won by the possession of obscure hats (ibid.: 19). The introduction of these new styles was intended not only to demonstrate privileged access to the products of affluent consumer society but also highlighted the success of Liverpool Football Club which allowed its fans to travel to European games every year for over twenty years. However, while a nascent European consciousness seems to have been present in Liverpool casual culture from the late 1970s, in other key ways, the consciousness of these fans seems to have remained unremittingly nationalist, in line with the international structure of competition at the time. A popular terrace chant of the 1980s demonstrated the salience of this nationalist consciousness:

> He's only a poor little wop
> His face all tattered and torn
> He made me feel sick
> So I hit him with a brick
> And now he don't sing anymore [ibid.: 100]

Commenting on the part which the assaults on Liverpool fans by Roma fans in 1984 played in the Heysel disaster the following year, Glanville also noted the nationalist consciousness of the Liverpool fans in the 1980s.

> Italy is still less a country than a collection of mutually suspicious city-states, but it would be of little use to tell a Scouser how much difference there was between a plebeian Roman and a supercilious Torinese. All were simply 'Italians' and I am convinced that this misconception played a part in what so tragically happened at Heysel, a year later. [Glanville 1991: 154]

Clearly, this evidence is fragmentary but it does suggest that Liverpool fans remained wedded to nationalist understandings. By contrast, although it is important not to overstate the case, from the 1990s onwards, United fans are less likely to appeal to nationalistic stereotypes. These fans are now more familiar with the diversity of fan culture in Europe and reject English xenophobia. New relations with and alternative understandings of other fan cultures seem to be emerging slowly among United's travelling support, reflecting the transnational regime in which fans now exist.

Europe and the City of Manchester

Echoing the rejection of nationalistic practices by certain inauthentic United fans, this network increasingly reimagines the city in line with their anti-English and cosmopolitan sentiments. Thus, the Abbey Hey contributor, cited earlier, was specific that the greatest source of pride which he had in Manchester was its celebration of diversity: 'I'm proud of the city's diversity, it's no surprise the gay village in Manchester is so vibrant ... I'm proud of my Dad and Lenny Johnson (a famous Beswick boxer of the thirties) who went down to Belle Vue in 1962 to give it to Oswald Mosley when he attempted to march' (*United We Stand* 1995).

This theme of Manchester's diversity was repeated both elsewhere in the fanzines and in interviews:

> Manchester has never been about boundaries, never been about lines on the map or about local authority bureaucracy. Manchester is not so much a city, as a state of mind. The whole history is one of progress and one of change but more importantly one of people. People who refuse to accept the boundaries of the mind. The least

English city in the country, a city that drew influence from all over the world. To deny that is to deny your history, to deny the essence of Manchester. That's the Manchester that [Manchester] City fans seek to deny as they increasingly resemble small-town hicks, little-Englander mancs, insular, backward and decidely non-mancunian. [*United We Stand* 1996]

In line with these claims, Richard Kurt also emphasised this Mancunian diversity referring to Manchester as a 'Celtic and immigrant city' (personal interview, 12 May 1998). Significantly, the fans have redescribed the city in accordance with the new self-understandings which have emerged in this group. Since they see themselves as cosmopolitan, they have reinvented the city as a diverse place so that it can stand as an appropriate symbol for their network, informing the fans' actions. The locale has been renegotiated to embody the common values of this group. This notion of Manchester as a diverse, Celtic city and of Mancunian United fans being unconcerned with national identity or open towards foreigners is an imagined claim which deliberately illuminates those features of Manchester which these fans now find politically and culturally meaningful but which in the past were irrelevant. Even in the present, they are by no means the whole truth about United or Manchester. There is no evidence, for instance, that City fans are 'little Englanders'. However, the statement is important for it denotes an attempt by the United fans to create a locale which enjoins certain actions on behalf of group members; they should be cosmopolitan, open and liberal and opposed to the narrow xenophobia of English nationalism.

Not only do fans among this network emphasise the cosmopolitanism and diversity of Manchester, but these fans have become increasingly aware of the economic development of the city from a formerly decaying industrial city into a post-Fordist, service-oriented city of international significance which is capable of competing with the major cities of Europe. In a vitriolic piece in *United We Stand*, a regular contributor called 'Manky' John, produced a piece entitled 'A Tale of One City' in which the contributor vilified Bolton (which he termed a 'parochial hill-billy hick town'). This piece was the third in a series, called 'A Tale of Two Cities', in the previous parts of which the author had sought to demonstrate the superiority of Manchester over Birmingham in Part One (*United We Stand* 1999: 22–23) and Leeds in Part Two (*United We Stand* 1999: 16–17). Although by no means all United fans in this network would subscribe to the contributor's views about Bolton itself, the interesting point of the article was 'Manky' John's complaints about the media representation of Manchester as a city. He complained that the image of Manchester was created by the well-known Boddington's adverts produced by 'London based, ex-Thatcher loving Saatchi and Saatchi' (*United We Stand* 1999: 28) and is, consequently, a false and damaging image of Manchester produced by outsiders. Echoing the fans, cited above, who see English nationalism as the expression of southern interests, 'Manky' John, highlighted the way in which London and the South (which often employs universalistic nationalist rhetoric) in fact threatened the interests of other cities and regions in Britain. Significantly, John blamed Bolton for communicating false and damaging images on Manchester:

> The media image of Coronation Street should have ceased to represent Manchester years ago, but until our surrounding pie-towns learn the meaning of progression the stereotype ain't going anywhere. And it won't matter what image of the city we try to paint in the meantime, there'll still be some Bolton mill-chimney defacing the skyline like an ugly cousin in a wedding photo. [*United We Stand* 1999a]

Although it is a mere assertion that Bolton threatens Manchester's attempts to reposition itself in global networks, the significant point about the contributor's complaint is that he views the architectural legacy of the cotton industry on which Manchester's initial wealth was founded as a threat to Manchester's current economic position. The author rejects the industrial image of Manchester and promotes the post-Fordist, service-oriented transformation of Manchester, which is reconfiguring the cityscape. Crucially, as far as this fan is concerned, Manchester can only renovate itself successfully if it was allowed to operate autonomously without interference from the exploiting South or from regressive areas in the North.[16] Interestingly, in a more recent article in *United We Stand*, the author compared Manchester to other European cities and came to the conclusion that European fans visiting Manchester might regard the city unfavourably (*United We Stand* 2001c).

The independent transformation of Manchester into an 'informational' city, as Castells would call it (1996), was also emphasised by other fans. Although less vitriolic than the contributor to his fanzine, Andy Mitten, the editor of *United We Stand*, also confirmed the importance of transforming Manchester and its image. Significantly, he regards the football club as having an important role in this renovation:

> There is no doubt that Manchester United has raised the profile of Manchester as a city. There's been features done on Manchester as a city which would never have been done if it wasn't for Manchester United and it is good to be given a chance to shatter this dirty northern, industrial, smoking chimney-stacks image which Manchester has been typecast with – and it has. [Andy Mitten, personal interview, 30 April 1998]

He was not alone among the fans in connecting the development of Manchester United and the city as a whole:

> Sport has generated an enormous amount of business activity, economic activity, cultural activity, tourist activity. It's tremendous now. Manchester is unrecognisable to ten years ago. Certainly from a business point of view, economically, tourist-wise, cultural-wise; there's a different culture now, a '90s culture which started or seemed to start from the bid [for the 2000 Olympics]. We knew we were never going to win the Olympic bid but the belief that the Olympic bid subconsciously gave the city ... I think there are a lot of far-sighted and innovative people in Manchester. I actually look at it sometimes in the cold light of day – certainly from a business point of view – it's booming. [Ray Ekersley, personal interview, 13 May 1998]

Although Ray Ekersley does not specifically talk about football here, he notes like Andy Mitten the symbolic importance of sporting success such as the staging of a major event in a city or the possession of a major team, like Manchester United, in raising the international profile of the city and in encouraging development. The success of Manchester United is seen as part of the economic development of the city of Manchester by these fans; both developments are increasingly situated at a transnational, European level in which Manchester and Manchester United must detach themselves from hobbling national ties to compete for status and economic rewards at the highest level.

In the light of the growing importance of Europe to this network of fans, their recognition of the connection between the city's economic renovation and the success of Manchester United is significant. For just as they are concerned that Manchester United competes with the best clubs in Europe and that they as fans gain recognition in the great cities of Europe, these fans are beginning to recognise the increasing economic competition between the major cities in Europe. They want Manchester to be part of the '90s culture', as Ray Ekersley puts it; that is, part of the entrepreneurial, informational and service-oriented economy so that Manchester can compete with other cities across Europe. For these fans, European integration means increasing competition with other European clubs and cities and a gradual disarticulation from the national context. Just as they view competition with clubs like Coventry as of little significance in comparison with games against the likes of Juventus and Feyenoord (*United We Stand* 1997), so has Manchester's standing as a major city in Europe in relation to other European cities has become an increasing concern to these fans. Mirroring the process of globalisation which undermines national sovereignty, these United fans are not becoming supranationalist, as various theorists have discussed, but are emphasising the local and urban; they demonstrate a new localism. Their consciousness matches the complex processes of globalisation which is cutting across national boundaries to produce new transnational networks of inclusion and exclusion and of success and failure. Through their support of Manchester United, these fans reveal the way that these complex globalising processes are reconfiguring social

Localism

interactions and solidarities at the everyday level to highlight the new salience of local or regional affiliations in an increasingly transnational context.

Localism Among Other Fan Groups

It would be wrong to overstate the significance of the emergence of a new localism among this group of United fans. The Manchester United fan group is a relatively small network and the emphasis on Manchester among United fans is neither fully established nor completely universal among this group. However, the attempts by these Manchester United fans to assert the status of Manchester United and the city of Manchester in the context of European competition at least provides some ethnographic evidence to suggest that the emergent transnational order has initiated a transformation of everyday social relations and identities. Moreover, although the reinvention of Manchester in this group cannot be generalised to the other clubs, there are differentiated parallels in Europe to developments in Manchester. The biggest clubs in Europe are the victims of increasingly public vilification and, even though the fans of these clubs may not demonstrate the self-conscious localism of Manchester United fans, their identifications are changing. As discussed in Chapter 5, although Barcelona has always been a symbol of Catalan identity, Barcelona fans have recently begun to stress the importance of the Catalan origin of their players which was irrelevant in the past. There have also been interesting developments among Bayern fans which point to a growth in transnational rivalries. In their fan club located in southern Munich in a disused railway-yard, they have the emblems of about twenty European clubs against whom they have played in the 1990s on a wall in the bar. Certain clubs with whom they have bad relations have been defaced with words like 'Hass' (hate) or 'Tod' (death) or simply crossed through. Borussia Dortmund's crest is defaced in this way but so are the crests of Galatasaray and PSV Eindhoven. Manchester United's emblem is simply inverted to symbolise the 1999 European Cup Final defeat. Moreover, any public mention of this team is met with derision. When Champions League results are announced in the Olympic Stadium, the name of Manchester United is inevitably jeered and its defeats celebrated (fieldnotes, 19 September 2000). These new hatreds suggest the development of certain transnational rivalries and a new horizon of competition for Bayern fans, although their significance should not be overstated. Local rivalries with 1860 Munich remain the most important. Indeed, the increasing competitiveness of European football has intensified local rivalries. In order to gain recognition from local rivals, masculine fan groups at the biggest clubs demand success at the European level. These fans employ European competition as a way of demonstrating their superiority over these local rivals. The transnationalisation of football intensifies the significance of the local context and strengthens the solidarity of groups at that level and their opposition to other local groups. These local rivalries which involve constant face-to-face interaction are likely to be more significant in creating a cultural context or a collective memory (romance) for developing European competition rather than still distant transnational rivalries.

Interestingly, although the evidence cannot be pushed too far, the outlines of a new localism might be discernible among some smaller clubs. Echoing his statement about their rejection of any European fan movement, Richard Chorley noted a reappraisal of the relationship to national team by some Southampton fans:

> More and more people are saying, 'I hope England win but I care more about Saints.' I found it incredible. I was watching the Germany game. I was sat with a good friend of mine in a big club. I said to him, 'I feel sick, I feel like I'm playing, you don't look upset.' He said, 'I want them to win but, to tell you the truth, I'd rather see Saints win the Littlewood Cup. I'd rather sacrifice England losing tonight.' I said, 'You're joking.' He said, 'No, I'm not.' Now what that tells you is that those elitist clubs are accelerating into a position where trophies are becoming monopolised, success is becoming monopolised, football supporters in general from the lower clubs – that club orientation and that need to feel some kind of communal success themselves. The English team is not going to give it to them because of the exact situation that exists. They cannot find it in the English team anyway and more and more, they don't care about England. They want to see their club win something. For Leicester City fans going to win the League Cup at Wembley is the equivalent of United doing the treble, emotionally. That is an enormously sad and worrying factor to me because what you are doing in the desperation for some type of emotional identification with success, you are not thinking anymore whatsoever about the overall period, the welfare of the game, the structure, what football really means, what it is about. You are not. Everyone's viewpoint is becoming polarised. And when that polarisation takes place it becomes ever more difficult to put the pressure on those who are taking advantage of that polarisation. [Richard Chorley, personal interview, 22 June 2000]

While Chorley himself defends the international regime, he reveals that some Southampton fans are increasingly concerned with local success. Extreme care needs to be taken here, but Chorley's comments suggest that uneven development has led to increasing localism on the part of some Southampton fans. Interestingly, this emphasis on local success echoes Southampton fans' rejection of the developing transnational links between independent fan groups. Just as they reject those European moves as irrelevant to them, Richard Chorley's statement illuminates a parallel focus on exclusively local success. Southampton fans recognise the development of transnational forces but their response is to concentrate ever more closely on their own club and its local and domestic context, demanding success at this level.

The exclusiveness of this nascent local identity, even among those individuals who demonstrate this localism, must not be exaggerated. Although in their participation in this social practice, certain fans increasingly highlight Manchester and its place in Europe, there are many cross-cutting relations in the lives of these individuals which link them to England and to Britain. When the occasion arises, these relations may be more important than their relations to the network of fans which they have established through following United. At that moment, appeals to Englishness may become important to them. To insist that this local affiliation is essential and primary to all others and to ignore the other networks in which these individuals are bound is to maintain an anachronistically monolithic concept of social life. In this 'neo-medieval' order, social allegiances are likely to be increasingly divided between the three levels of region or city, nation and supranation in which none has automatic priority but where mobilisation occurs at the different levels in different contexts. As the international structure of European football is superseded by a transnational regime, fan culture and solidarities have been reformulated in the face of new realities. Although great care must be taken not to exaggerate, in different ways localism is beginning to become a more significant element in the way that fan groups understand themselves. Few other football fans except perhaps Barcelona fans demonstrate the advanced localism of Manchester United fans but as the new geography of European football becomes more apparent, fans at every club are being forced to reconsider their social relations. In this work of re-creation, the sense of locale is likely to become increasingly important in the next decades.

Notes

1 There is further evidence of pre-1990s hatred of Manchester United: 'I was speaking to Dave Kirkwood in the pub last night and he was saying that he hates England – I support England.' And he said, "I went to Spain in '82 and I spent the whole time trying to avoid getting battered because people found out I was a United fan. I told the wrong people and I was ducking and diving trying to avoid getting beaten up." I said, "I can't believe that: 1982. I wouldn't have thought there would be that feeling against United fans." "Oh yeah" he said, "It was all the cockneys, West Ham and that" (Duncan Drasdo, personal interview, 13 June 2000).
2 With the success of the English team under new manager Sven Goran Erickson, Beckham's taunting has diminished when playing for the national team.
3 Appadurai has postulated five 'scapes' in which differing, overlapping and potentially contradictory communities are imagined in the contemporary world: ethnoscapes, mediascapes, technoscapes, financescapes and ideoscapes (Appadurai 1994: 296; 1996: 33). For reasons of space and relevance, I omit discussion of these terms here.

4   Although *United We Stand* and *Red Issue* are sold to fans outside the network of Manchester-based fans, the majority are read and contributed to by local masculine supporters.
5   Chris was employed at a white-collar level at a Leeds fabric factory, until recently made redundant.
6   Richard Kurt has written several books on United and is a regular fanzine contributor to *Red Issue*.
7   As Steve Redhead has usefully pointed out, the kinds of transformations in consciousness which have been detectable among Manchester United fans since the 1990s as a result of travelling more in Europe, were also evident among Liverpool fans in the early 1980s as a result of similarly increased travel (Redhead 1986).
8   Several fans stated that the rivalries with European fans could never get to the level of those with certain English clubs such as Liverpool, City and Leeds because United fans simply did not interact with European fans enough (Andy Walsh, personal interview, 30 April 1998).
9   The growing conflict of interest between the national team and the clubs has been an increasing aspect of European football as player salaries have increased: 'Clubs are now paying players such enormous wages that it does not make business sense to pay them for a week or ten days when they are away with the national team' (Uli Hoeness, general manager, Bayern Munich, cited by Radnedge 1999b). See Chapter 12.
10 Gordon, an ex-crane driver, is now a mature student.
11 There is some evidence that English nationalism is rejected by other United fans. Anti-England chants were sung widely by crowds at Old Trafford in the 1998–99 season and, before the game against Croatia Zagreb, fans mainly from Wales and London spontaneously sang anti-English songs in a pub near Old Trafford (14 September 1999).
12 The term 'jib' means to gain entry without paying. In the 1980s, a section of United's hooligan firm called themselves the 'Inter-City Jibbers', a play on West Ham's famous ICF (Inter-City Firm), which referred to their avoidance of payment on trains to away games as well as any other event which required entrance fees.
13 Clearly, there are many United fans in this group that never fight.
14 In several interviews, fans (for example, Richard Kurt, Ray Ekersley) revealed that European fans may not recognise the distinctions which United fans are so careful to make in order to distinguish themselves from England fans. In the game against Juventus in Turin in 1999, there were many abusive signs displayed by Juventus fans, including some which referred to the Heysel disaster and which apportioned the blame to United, presumably on the grounds that they are English, even though it was Liverpool fans that had been involved. The United fans found this confusion of themselves for their most hated rivals extraordinary.
15 I am grateful to Steve Redhead for making this point.
16 It is interesting that in recognising the need for the city of Manchester to compete with other European cities, the fans reflected the views of many of the most important business and council leaders in the city of Manchester, the so-called 'Manchester Mafia', who have tried to place-market the city in order to improve its position in the global economy since the mid-1980s (see Peck and Tickell 1995; Peck 1995; Harding 1997; Cochrane et al. 1996).

Chapter 11
Racism

In their response to the new geography of European football, the masculine fans at Manchester United have increasingly reinvented an idea about the locale of Manchester. The locale of Manchester should not be seen as a prior and self-evident fact which has subsequently determined the nature of this fan group. Rather, the group itself, confronting new conditions, imaginatively draws upon the locale to reconstitute itself. The same social process occurs when individuals and groups draw upon 'race' as a biological category in order to create exclusive social groups, although the appeal to biology by these groups confuses many observers into thinking that biological facts are at the root of the social distinctions which are drawn. Yet, biology does not determine the character of social groups which happen to mobilise 'racial' definitions any more than geography determines the solidarity of Manchester United fans who use Manchester as a source of identification. Michael Banton has been an important figure in emphasising the sociology of 'race'. Banton does not deny the discriminatory practices which some groups have adopted when they have emphasised 'racial' characteristics but he is concerned that the social process by which this exclusion takes place is recognised:

> A crucial weakness associated with many of the words ending is 'ism' is that they single out of sets of beliefs, practices or relations and present them as if they have an existence apart from the beliefs, practices and relations of particular individuals in particular times and place. Once people slip into the assumption that racism or capitalism or communism exist in the sense that ... influenza exists ... they are led into one trap after another. [Banton, 1983: 3]

The social relations between groups, in which certain biological signifiers (such as skin colour) are employed, are assumed to be the outgrowth of those biological characteristics. Banton rejects biologically essentialist accounts of race:

> People do not perceive racial differences. They perceive phenotypical differences of colour ... first order abstractions. It is these differences which are used as role signs and they can be the bases for structures of inequality without society having any concept of race. It just so happens that Western European culture in a particular phase of its history has ordered phenotypical variations into what have been known as 'racial' classifications. [Banton 1983: 8]

Groups draw upon arbitrary distinctions such as skin colour to restrict access to certain social positions which these groups wish to monopolise for themselves. Biology itself does not determine the lines of social inclusion and exclusion which social groups will draw. Banton prefers the term 'racial discrimination' because it captures the social process of exclusion more accurately than the potentially essentialist terms 'racism' or 'race relations'. Racial discrimination is, therefore, simply one example of a general social process by which groups constitute themselves and exclude others, though it is no less exploitative or divisive for that, as Banton always emphasises. In arguing for racial discrimination in this way, Banton, of course, replicates Weber's position on the formation of status groups:

> Usually one group of competitors takes some externally identifiable characteristic of another group of (actual or potential) competitors – race, language, religion, local or social original, descent, residence etc. – as a pretext for attempting their exclusion. It does not matter which characteristic is chosen in the individual case: whatever suggests itself most easily is seized upon. [Weber 1968: 341–2]

Discriminating on racial grounds is simply a pretext where a random physical feature is used to create and maintain group solidarity.[1]

In discussing the rise of 'new' racism in Europe in the 1990s, Robert Miles has effectively promoted the same approach to 'racial discrimination' as Banton. Miles has expressed severe doubts about the usefulness of the concept of 'new European racism'. Like Banton, Miles has 'reservations about the holistic and totalising character that is often attributed to a notion of European racism' (Miles 1993: 39) Echoing Banton, Miles opposes essentialist notions of race and insists that 'what is new is the determinants and contents of that imagination' (ibid.: 38). For Miles, the 'new' racism of 1990s Europe must be understood in terms of its specific social context and by reference to the actual ways in which groups mobilise biological signs to exclude other groups. The transformation of the nation-state and the emergence of supranational economic and political structures in Europe are critical here in providing a context for new European racism (ibid.: 50).[2] Racism does not arise naturally out of biological factors but biological markers are mobilised by groups in the light of wider social circumstances. Racial discrimination is a cultural rather than a biological phenomenon which manifests itself according to the logic of the social situation not the biological facts.

Interestingly, in a recent work on racism among English fans, Back et al. (2001) have demonstrated the theoretical arguments of Banton and Miles empirically. They reveal that racist fans might appeal to ideas of racial purity but, in practice, individuals are included in their social group who should be formally excluded. Consequently, black fans are legitimate Millwall followers, even though many Millwall fans are explicitly racist or employ racist abuse unthinkingly. The most extreme example of this informal and pragmatic acceptance of formally excluded individuals and groups is demonstrated by Back et al. when they cite a black England fan's description of an interaction with a group of Combat 18 activitists before a match against Scotland in London:

> I'm on the kerb – this is mad – I'm right on the kerb [outside The Globe pub in London] and C18 are walking past. I'm with my mates and that, and then they just walked past me. But one guy stopped and clocked me, it was the wierdest thing – total skinhead as well, it was really weird, and he just looked at me and like he nods – I've got a little red rose, red rose lapel on and he looked at me, looked at my badge and just nods ... and goes: 'Yeah, right.' And I just held my own, it was just like eye contact and like: 'Today we're on the same team, yeah, England. Any other day it'd be different, but today it's about the fucking Jocks.' [Back et al. 2001: 301]

Even among the most committed racist groups, exclusion is not an *a priori* certainty determined in all circumstances by the putative logic of biological fact. Crucially, although groups often appeal to purified forms of discourse, group membership is finally determined by the more mundane fact of which individuals are regularly present during important periods of social interaction. Out of this interaction, the group emerges which may well include individuals who should be excluded on formal grounds. The temporary acceptance of a black England fan by this C18 skinhead when faced with a common Scottish enemy demonstrates Banton's argument about racial discrimination lucidly. Discrimination is a social process which utilizes apparently obvious biological facts to order social relations by creating in- and out-groups. The wider historical context provides the setting for the emergence of particular groups and the use of specific forms of racial discrimination. Since the 1990s, racial discrimination in Europe is most usefully understood as a reaction to the globalised deregulation involving transnational competition and migration. In this way, the increasing use of racial categories by various fans in Europe is another kind of response to the deregulation of football. They are new forms of imagined communities which Appadurai might describe as the 'ugly face of globalisation'.

Racism in the New Europe

In the post-war era, as large-scale immigration into Europe became a significant social phenomenon, especially in those European countries such as France and Britain with imperial histories, three broad models of integration – folk, republican or multicultural – have characterised the differing strategies of European nations towards their new populations. The folk or ethnic model is the expression of an ethnically homogenous society and emphasises parental nationality (*Jus Sanguinis*). Naturalisation is difficult because, under this model, the nation is seen in cultural, ethnic and even racial terms. Of European countries, Germany is the most important example of this model (Baldwin-Edwards and Schain 1994: 11–12). By contrast, the republican model defines the nation in political terms as a group of citizens unified by the law, in which immigrants can be 'assimilated' (certainly far more easily than the folk model) as long as they accept the political and, in fact, cultural norms of the nation. France is the prime example of this model where, as long as migrants assimilate the dominant culture, integration is possible. Finally, the multicultural model, like the republican model, highlights political citizenship and allegiance to the laws as the appropriate method of assimilation but recognition is made of cultural and ethnic differences to a far greater degree. In Europe, the Netherlands and, to a lesser extent, the United Kingdom are examples of the latter (ibid.: 12).

As the many criticisms of both the republican, multicultural and especially folk models have demonstrated, there are serious problems with the models as they never question the hegemonic culture, into which immigrants have to assimilate. Nevertheless, under these models, a degree of integration occurred between the 1950s and 1970s. Clearly, many commentators have demonstrated how the apparently reasonable consensus reached in this period was implicitly discriminatory. Nevertheless, extreme rightist views were consistently excluded from formal political representation under these paradigms, including the German one. Above all, notions of repatriation and, of course, the use of violence against ethnic minorities were rejected in the post-war period. This is not to say that extremist groups, such as the National Front in Britain, did not exist, but such organisations were politically irrelevant before the 1980s in Europe, though they did start to make their appearance in some countries in the 1970s.

From the 1980s, by contrast, these rightist groups have become more prominent in every European country and, more importantly, begun to attract formal political support of a size which is no longer negligible. The rise of Jean-Marie Le Pen's National Front in France was a definitive moment here. In 1984, his party emerged as a significant political force in the elections to the European Parliament, when it won 11 per cent of the votes and 10 of France's 81 seats (Fysh and Wolfreys 1992: 309). Le Pen's successes in France were not isolated. In Germany, from mid-1992, the extreme right-wing Republican Party had substantial success in state-wide elections, gaining 11.4 per cent of the votes in Baden-Wurttemberg and 6.4 per cent of the votes in Schleswig Holstein (Wilpert 1993: 80; see also Roberts 1992: 331–2). Although the National Democratic Party is currently in decline, the German People's Union (DVU) which is the most extreme of the parties has a substantial following (Roberts 1992: 334–5). Moreover, the growing salience of extreme right views in political debates is matched by the rapid growth in racist assaults on immigrants by gangs of generally young men, explicitly expressing neo-nazi allegiances. The first outbreak of this violence occurred in Hoyerswerda in the summer of 1991 with arson attacks on refugee hotels but this was followed by increasing levels of random violence towards immigrants. In 1992, 2600 racially motivated assaults were recorded in which 17 of the victims were killed (Baringhorst 1995: 225). Refugee hostels were often the target of these assaults because they were symbols of immigration opposed by extreme right-wing groups. In August 1992, there was a further attack on a refugee hostel in Rostock which met with little public response, but the death of three Turkish people in an arson attack in Molln in November 1992 provoked a candle-lit march in Munich which was attended by 400,000 (ibid.: 227). While such displays have been important in resisting extreme rightist views, such public renunciations did not in and of themselves stop further violence. A fatal arson attack on a hostel in Solingen followed these protests in 1993, after which there were further increases in racist violence (ibid.). The chief cause of this upsurge in racist violence in East Germany was unification with the West which has involved an influx of mainly Turkish immigrants at the same time as a rise in mass unemployment and a drop in real living standards. The incoming immigrant population has been blamed for the new insecurities and seen as a threat to the precarious position of jobs which were once guaranteed to the ethnically homogenous white population.

Similar developments have occurred in Spain. Before the mid-1980s, extreme right-wing political activity and violence was a minor problem in Spain. Although groups such as the *Frente Nacional* and the overtly neo-nazi *Círculo Español de Amigos de Europa* (CEDADE) existed, they attracted minimal support (Ellwood 1995: 145–6). However, from the middle of the 1980s, the situation began to change as economic recession in northern Europe turned Spain into a country of net immigration, particularly from Africa and from eastern Europe. In addition, Spain was eventually also affected by the recession in the late 1980s which brought with it unemployment that in 1993 remained at 17.5 per cent (ibid.: 149). The Spanish government attempted to update the Foreigners Law passed by the Cortes Parliament in July 1985 (ibid.: 150–53) but mass regularisation of illegal immigrants did not solve the political problem of the status of these immigrants as the flow into the country persisted. There was an increase in racially motivated violence in Spain in the 1990s. In 1992, a Guinean was seriously injured in Barcelona by a group of skinheads. In the following month a Dominican woman was shot dead by a racist gang in Madrid where a Moroccan was also beaten to death by skinheads. As the economic situation remained precarious and immigration continued, the incoming population has been blamed by the indigenous population, which has drawn upon biological differences to denote in- and out-groups.

In Italy, the same chronology is detectable. Before the 1980s, Italy was seen to be a country without 'racial' problems. Despite its fascist past, there was little formal rightist political activity between the end of the Second World War and the 1980s. Similarly, no significant acts of racially motivated violence were recorded. This changed quite dramatically in the 1990s. From the beginning of the 1970s, Italy became a country of immigration for the first time but, while the numbers of immigrants was certainly significant in that period, the figures increased exponentially in the late 1980s – in 1990, 781,000 recorded immigrants arrived (Melotti 1997: 86). Most of these new immigrants came from Africa and East Asia, although there were also many from eastern Europe, the Middle East and Central and South America. In 1991, a very large influx of Albanian immigrants presented severe problems for the state which rounded up many of them and flew them back across the Adriatic. However, there were further mass migrations of Albanians in 1997 (ibid.: 90). As in Spain, this sudden increase in immigrants has coincided with severe economic problems. Italy had an average unemployment rate of 12 per cent in the 1990s but in southern regions this figure reached 20 per cent (ibid.: 87). Similar violence has also followed. In 1984, the Commission of Enquiry of the European Parliament on Fascism and Racism concluded that 'Italy is one of the European countries where there is a very low number of racial incidents' but that is no longer the case and, following the murder of a Somali in Rome, there have been a series of violent attacks on immigrants (Campani 1994: 517).

The rise of formal extreme right politics has been demonstrated most clearly by the rise of Haider's Freedom Party in Austria and its eventual accession to power in 2000, to the anxiety of the rest of the European Union. Although Austria might be in the second division of European member states, it is nevertheless a very significant power in the Union, not least because of its historic connections to Germany. While the re-emergence of fascism is unlikely in western Germany where liberal capitalism is extremely strong, Haider's rise provides unwelcome encouragement and support for extremist parties. Although his party was defeated badly in elections in November 2002, it is likely that Haider and his Freedom Party will remain significant forces in Austrian politics. The election of Berlusconi as Italian Prime Minister in May 2001 raised further concerns since the political alliance on which his power was based included the explicitly racist Legia Nord. Although differentiated by the peculiar historical circumstances which persist in each nation-state, there are parallels between the development of racism across the major European nations. In particular, from near irrelevance between the end of the Second World War and the 1970s, far right parties have become a more significant part of formal politics in each European state and violent assaults on immigrants have become more frequent.

Local Racism

The rise of the new right in Europe can ultimately be traced to globalisation and the increasing dominance of the free market. Deregulation has opened borders and encouraged population movement as economic opportunities disappear in certain regions while appearing in others. The uncertainty created by economic liberalisation has encouraged the development of more exclusive social groupings which are better able to defend themselves from the dislocating forces of globalisation (Castles 1993: 17–29). Many social groups, especially those whose culture and livelihood were secured by the Fordist regime of regulation, have employed 'race' as a means of sustaining their group's cultural and economic position. They have often appealed to grand notions of a white Europe and ethnically pure nations. CEDADE is a prime example here which defines itself as the 'defender of biological and spiritual differences between peoples' with the objective of creating a 'Europe of ethnic groups' (Ellwood 1995: 157). Neo-nazis in Europe typically draw upon grand images of Europe. Thus, the Commission with its liberal economic policies is viewed by these groups as an arm of the Zionist Occupational Government (ZOG) and seen as threatening the integrity of the white race which is putatively 'on the brink of total extermination' (Bjorgo 1997: 62). The Scandinavian-based 'Blood and Honour' group, a small and disparate network of neo-nazi skinheads led by Max Hammer, have been at the forefront of this new supranational rhetoric:

> It is vital that the Movement operates on an international scale. Our enemies work worldwide and it's essential that we are organized as least on a pan-European level, though the ideal is naturally a pan-Aryan army with divisions wherever White people dwell. By now no real racial nationalist will oppose this idea. The days of pure patriotic xenophobia and imperialism are over. They have spilt enough Aryan blood to the joy of Mosaic merchants of war and destruction. The term 'No more brother wars' can only be achieved through international co-operation and understanding between white people, based on a common racial history and destiny while respecting each people and nation's right to self-determination. Big words? Perhaps. Impossible to achieve? I trust not. But if it proves to be just that, I'd rather scrap the whole idea of nationalism for the sake of White racialism. [Hammer n.d.][3]

Although Hammer's message seems to be supranational in intent and the 'Blood and Honour' group might have transnational links with other similarly-minded groups in Europe, this is not a supranational movement. Although they might have an ideal of a 'white' Europe, fascist groups reject any loss of national sovereignty. They may reject future wars between white brothers but, for them, the nation is the most valid and natural social unit. It is very significant that Hammer calls for *international* cooperation, for the nation is regarded by these groups as the most authentic unit of solidarity against the dangerous dissolution posed by integration and globalisation. It is notable that Hammer respects the 'nation's self-right to determination'. Fascist groups emphasise the ethnically homogeneous nation-state as the only legitimate social order and the defence of the 'white race' is, in fact, a defence of a racially cleansed international order.

Indeed, although nationalism is an important part of racist politics, racial discrimination in Europe increasingly mobilises local urban understandings. Extreme right groups arise out of local grievances using specific notions of 'race' to create group solidarity in specific cities in order to monopolise certain economic or cultural opportunities there. The references to pan-European whiteness and to false nationalist consciousness which has set white 'brothers' against each other, in fact, unify local extremist groups consisting of individuals who have often lived and worked with each other for long periods. Grand international rhetoric provides these groups with a sense of collective purpose for a different scale of reality: the intimidation of local immigrants. Racial discrimination in Europe cannot be understood without reference to the local context in which it is mobilized by particular groups. Overwhelmingly, political activity is directed at the local urban level against specific grievances and in defence of specific opportunities. They are the specific response to the presence of immigrants, often working publicly, hawking and begging in particular cities.

For instance, in May 1991, bus drivers in Milan held a strike in protest at a new hostel for immigrants which had opened near their depot (Campani 1994: 518). According to Campani, twenty years before, the same workers would have struck in the name of class solidarity. In the 1990s, the priority of national class solidarity has been superseded by local political issues of which this new racism is a salient part. The racial discrimination displayed by the Milan bus drivers reflected the increasing appeal of local solidarity from which immigrants and southerners were to be excluded (ibid.: 520). Campani has captured the local basis of racism in the new Europe well:

> In fact, in Italy, it is difficult to comprehend the complexity of circumstances, which underlie the hostility to immigration and 'racist' actions not least because it is different according to regions and local areas. A study carried out by the association Itali-Razzismo has shown that the image of immigrants is very different according to the geographical areas and level of urbanisation. [ibid.: 520]

Grand racist ideologies might be mobilised by groups but this ideology is the conduit for a more specific claim. The 'new racism' is not carried out in the name of the abstract concept of a white Europe but on the contrary refers to the immediate group and its members which feel threatened by new developments. Racism becomes a means by which threatened groups protect themselves from deregulated global forces. Uneven, post-Fordist development has given rise to uneven patterns of racial discrimination so that in different regions, cities and nations across Europe there are differential hierarchies of exclusion and inclusion depending on local circumstances. In particular, the economic, cultural and political situation of the indigenous population and the culture, origin and size of the immigrant populations will determine whether and how racial discrimination becomes an important political weapon between groups. The new geography of European racism is reflected in the new geography of European football.

Racism and Football

As new forms of racial discrimination appeared in Europe in the 1990s, the football ground became an important site at which racial discrimination has been publicly expressed primarily because a large section of football fans consists of those groups of young, white men who have been threatened by post-Fordist liberalisation. Appeals to 'racial discrimination' have been particularly appropriate for some of these groups and, consequently, the football grounds of Europe have been a fruitful recruiting ground for extreme right groups. This process is well-documented in England: 'Martin Wingfield, former leader of the National Front Flag Group, admitted in an interview with the London magazine *Time Out* that the group had encouraged its members to be active in football stadia and had reaped benefits from this both financially and in terms of new members' (Ford 1991: 47).

Similar processes have occurred in Italy since the 1970s, where political movements on both the right and left were instrumental in the creation of new 'ultra' fan groups. At Inter, Lazio and Verona, the extreme right-wing party, the Italian Social Movement which had been banned from public demonstrations, employed young male football supporters to create highly organised and prominent ultra groups. In Milan, the leading members of the young people's section of the Italian Social Movement founded the 'Inter-Boys' while a large number of middle-aged right-wing militants motivated and recruited younger supporters at Lazio (Podaliri and Balestri 1998: 153). This rightist emphasis persists at Lazio to the present time and has joined with wider currents in Italian society to become an increasingly significant social phenomenon.

However, although by the end of the 1990s there was a high level of organised and committed racism at particular football grounds in Europe, informal forms of racial discrimination were even more commonplace. Above all, in Italy and Spain, the monkey chant which denigrates players of African origin is very commonly used by fans, who are not committed racists, against opposing black players. Back et al. (1996) have discussed this phenomenon whereby racial discrimination is employed unthinkingly by fans, who are not politically committed racists, as a way of distracting the opposition. Back et al. call this uncommitted use of racial discrimination 'instrumental' since it is intended not primarily to stigmatise opposition players but merely to distract them. They reserve the term 'organic' for those groups and cultures in which racial discrimination has an explicit political purpose of excluding ethnic minorities. In fact, although Back et al.'s analysis is illuminating, their terminology may be problematic. It might be easier to employ the term 'organic' to refer to the everyday non-committed form of racial discrimination while reserving the term, 'instrumental', for the political activists. The latter are explicitly trying to achieve something by their use of racial abuse and therefore their actions are 'instrumental'; they try to exclude or subordinate ethnic minorities directly. By contrast, uncommitted racists draw instinctively upon taken-for-granted cultural resources in order to make interventions which are not primarily intended to enforce lines of racial discrimination. These fans draw on 'organic' and assumed understandings in order to make specific claims, the purpose of which may not be racist. In these cases, racial discrimination is merely a convenient vehicle for these other claims.

Organic Racial Discrimination

There is widespread organic discrimination in Europe. In particular, 'monkey' chants, which refer to the putatively close connection between black people and apes, are extremely common in southern Europe. Interestingly, Domenico Lo Forte, president of the Milan branch of the Juventus supporters' club, dismissed the significance of this kind of organic racism in Italian football. 'Racism is not an issue. The spark is always rivalry. Every team has at least one black player. Picking on a black player is just a way to denigrate the team. I wouldn't give it too much importance' (Lo Forte, personal interview, 17 May 2000).

For Lo Forte, since the fans who abuse opposing black players normally have black players in their own team whom they accept, these fans cannot be seen as racist. Certainly, as Back et al. argue, they do not display a form of racism which can be captured straightforwardly. The use of implicit forms of racial discrimination to emphasis social hierarchies does not diminish the political and social significance of this racial discrimination. It still assumes the general social inferiority of ethnic minorities. In their most recent work, Back et al. have illustrated the point, when discussing a racist chant which is commonly used in England, 'I'd rather be a Paki than a Scouse [or any other denigrated fan group]'. This chant assumes 'the hegemony of the white norm' which 'lies at the heart of English football culture' (Back et al. 2001: 100). The fans who sing this song and the fans to whom it is sung both assume the fact of white superiority; they agree upon this norm. Consequently, fans are shamed by being subordinated to an ethnic group which both sets of fans knowingly regard as inferior. Although these fans might well overtly accept black players in their own team, their abuse of black opposition players makes a clear point; black players might be acceptable but they necessarily have a subordinate status. They are not equal to the native white players even though they might be nominally accepted. Although Lo Forte himself is genuine in his argument – and he himself is no racist – his leniency towards this kind of abuse is problematic. Monkey chanting discourages the attendance of ethnic minorities at matches and it establishes an exclusive 'whiteness' as an ideal for the fan group, even though they might celebrate a particular black player on their own team. Moreover, it reinforces and legitimates the use of racial discrimination in everyday life. A football player is no threat to the specific economic and cultural position of white fans and, consequently, even though fans might engage in racial discrimination at the ground, fans can admire a black player. Their discrimination is directed not at elite professional footballers but towards ethnic minorities in similar economic circumstances in their own neighbourhoods who are seen as a threat. Black players are part of a different group to local immigrants and it is against the latter group – not against the biological fact of skin-colour – that racism is directed. As Banton noted, the social not the biological facts provoke racist abuse.

There are many other examples of this organic racism where those who commit these acts do not fully recognise that this abuse draws, often unwittingly, on an assumed racial hierarchy. In September 1997, in a Champions League game against the Turkish team Besiktas, Bayern Munich fans in the Sud Kurve parodied Italian ultra groups by staging a display before the game. The fans unfurled a banner which read 'Commando Aldi' (imitating Italian ultra groups which often use the name 'Commando'), brought plastic Aldi bags which they waved as flags and, changing the words to a common German terrace chant, sang, 'You can all go to Aldi', to the Turkish fans. Aldi is a German discount supermarket chain which is favoured by the large but poor immigrant Turkish population in Germany and it has consequently become a way of defining and denigrating Turkish immigrants among white Germans. The Commando Aldi episode drew on this widely recognised reference and the Bayern fans sought to mock the Besiktas fans by referring to their low economic status. The Commando Aldi display was not motivated primarily on the grounds of racial discrimination. It was intended ironically and certainly demonstrated more imagination than the monkey chants which are typical in Italian football. Moreover, although more elaborate, it was very similar to the standard denigration of opposition fans for their putative poverty by fans in England, especially by fans of London teams against northern teams but also by Manchester United fans against Liverpool fans. However, the Commando Aldi demonstration drew upon already highly sensitive divisions in German society between indigenous Germans and Turkish guest-workers which were primarily defined in racial terms. Consequently, although the Bayern fans did not intend their actions to be racist, the wider context of Turkish-German relations invested the Commando Aldi demonstration with greater significance than these fans themselves recognised. It necessarily drew upon more serious and overt racial discrimination against Turkish immigrants in wider German society.

The organic use of racial chants or displays cannot be dismissed for they draw upon very significant but taken-for-granted understandings about race and ethnicity, reinforcing the hierarchies created by racial discrimination. Moreover, tolerance to this kind of uncommitted racist abuse facilitates the infiltration of politically committed racists into the ground. This is demonstrated quite clearly in English football in the 1970s and 1980s, where casual abuse of ethnic minorities substantially aided the operations of groups like the National Front, in turn provoked an even more racist atmosphere. Indeed, it is clear that at some clubs such as Lazio or Fiorentina, monkey chanting is not merely a way of upsetting opponents through appeal to an unquestioned racial hierarchy. It is politically motivated or instrumental. In the 1990s, in Florence for instance, in an explicit response to the influx of immigrants especially from Africa who worked as street hawkers, there was a spate of racist graffiti and serious violence. In February 1990, two hundred masked individuals attacked blacks and gypsies in the city centre (Ford 1991: 65) and a survey indicated that 37 per cent of Florentines agreed that all immigrants should be repatriated. In the light of these facts, the monkey chants directed at Manchester United's Andy Cole and Dwight Yorke by large sections of the Fiorentina crowd when the two teams met in November 1999 for a Champions League game take on a more sinister aspect than Lo Forte's explanation allows. The 'organic' use of racial discrimination at the football ground is likely to be a sign that this form of discrimination is common and legitimate in wider social life. Significantly, organic racial discrimination highlights the local and specific nature of racism in European football. While monkey chanting has become typical in Italy because the immigration of Africans is high in that country and has given rise to new forms of discrimination, in Germany the largest immigrant population is Turkish and most racist activity is explicitly directed at Turkish immigrants. Although racist politics in most European countries focus on the issue of immigration, the issue is not the same across Europe. The different origins of immigrant populations and the different local conditions give rise to different forms of racial discrimination in the new Europe.

Instrumental Racial Discrimination

A growing emphasis on the locale is also evident among politically motivated fan groups whose racial discrimination is 'instrumental'. The rise of the ultra movement in Italy in the 1970s was closely associated with political movements on both the left and right but this association waned in the 1980s as groups adopted the more apolitical 'casual' style based on British hooliganism, where violence was a pleasurable end in and of itself (Podaliri and Balestri 1998: 162–3). The political neutralisation of ultra groups in the 1980s, in fact, favoured the re-emergence of extreme right groups in the grounds and from the end of the 1980s, racism against immigrants became increasingly common at Italian grounds. This was assisted by the development of xenophobic political groupings such as the Northern League, the National Alliance, the Lombard League and the Tricolour Flame, along with the growth of skinhead and other extreme right-wing groups at that time. Formal connections between these rightist parties and ultra groups soon developed. Thus, some of the National Alliance's Members of Parliament were originally recruited at Verona while, in Rome during the administrative elections of November 1993, a total of 13 elected right-wing representatives were from the Roma or Lazio curva supporters (ibid.: 166). The re-emergence of the new right was announced by the increasingly prominent display of fascist symbols and banners in the grounds supported by racist singing (ibid.: 164, 166). Significantly, at exactly this moment in the late 1980s, as the effects of globalisation were highlighting the disparity between the industrial North and the Mezzogiorno, racialised anti-southern chants became common. Atalanta ultra members adopted a common chant: 'Bergamo is a nation, all the rest is South' (ibid.: 165). The point here is similar to the chant which Back et al. noted, where other fans were equated to Pakistanis. At the bottom of every white northern fan's social hierarchy is the South. Significantly, the South is itself often understood in racial terms. Other fans have sung 'Africa begins at Rome', highlighting the economic backwards of the South. For racist fans in Italy, modernisation is conceived as a northern and white phenomenon from which both southern Italians and Africans are to be excluded.

The involvement of extreme right-wing political movements among some ultra groups continues to the present day. Recently, Lazio's *Irriducibili* ultra group have gained international attention. Since Mussolini's rise, Lazio has always had associations with fascism and was explicitly connected with Mussolini himself. However, from the late 1980s, this connection has been reinvigorated and re-emphasised by the volatile *Irriducibili* ultras. They have employed Lazio games as a means of expressing their extremist views on African, Albanian and other Balkan immigrants and refugees. It is, perhaps, significant that the increasingly politicised racism of this group emerged just as immigration to the region of Lazio itself increased. For instance, in 1988, 150–

200,000 illegal immigrants entered Italy, the majority concentrated in Lazio, Campania, Sicily and Lombardy (Vasta 1993: 86). Following the murder of Arkan, the indicted Serbian war criminal in February 2000, the *Irriducibili* displayed an extremely large banner in the ground which read 'Honour to the Tiger Arkan' (Agnew 2000: 52). This banner made an important intervention into local politics because it implied that Arkan's policy in the Balkans towards ethnic Albanians, who have formed a major part of Italy's immigrant population in the 1990s, was justified. The intention of the banner was to intimidate local Albanian refugees. The celebration of Arkan may also have been intended as a form of support for Lazio's Serb player Sinisa Mihajlovic who has publicly demonstrated the same views on ethnic minorities as his fans among the *Irriducibili*. He found himself under police investigation for the incitement of racial hatred after his persistent and extreme abuse of Patrick Viera during a Champions League tie against Arsenal in October 2000 (Agnew 2001: 53). The group has persistently employed songs suggesting that certain immigrant groups, specifically from Eastern Europe should be deported to Auschwitz. Similar references to the Final Solution have been a common theme among the neo-nazi groups who are increasingly taking hold of the grounds in eastern Germany. There migrant East Europeans and Turks are the main target of their abuse and assaults. Significantly, along with other racist groups, the *Irriducibili* have formed a link with the extreme rightist remnants of Chelsea's old hooligan gang, the Headhunters, since Lazio's games against Chelsea in the Champions League in the 1999–2000 season. The *Irriducibili* are a prominent example of a politically motivated racist ultra group. Certainly, in their banners and their chants, they draw on standard nationalistic and supranational notions of race and whiteness but, in fact, their actions are directed at the local level and specifically against the African and Albanian immigrants who have become a salient feature of Roman life.

In Spain, the development of this new but highly localised racism was demonstrated by the murder of a Real Sociedad fan on 8 December 1998 by an Atletico Madrid supporter, called Guerra, who belonged to the extremist Atletico ultra group, 'Bastion' (Ball 2000: 21–2). The murder was carried out at the second leg of a European away game, as 'revenge' for the stoning of an official Atletico supporters' bus by Real Sociedad fans. This act was itself a response to the provocation on behalf of Bastion who displayed a swastika in Sociedad's ground and sung offensive racist songs throughout. Bastion have displayed a number of neo-fascist symbols in Atletico's ground over the last decade and, emphasising the committed fascism of this group it was revealed at his trial that Guerra's heroes were Hitler, Mussolini and Franco; Guerra had even tried to learn German so that he could read *Mein Kampf* (ibid.: 22). One of their key chants, sung to the tune of the Spanish national anthem, declares: 'Get out, get out, queers, niggers, Basques and Catalans'. Although their neofascism draws rhetorically on the now supranational white supremacist myths of Hitler and Mussolini, both Basques and Catalans – whose European heritage is unquestionable and whom other fascist groups would never regard as aliens – are included in their list of undesirables. Bastion's racial discrimination is a response to the particular conditions which confront them in their local context. Neither this social grouping nor the lines of discrimination by which it establishes itself are universal, even though Guerra and his friends at Bastion might very well use similar language and symbols as the *Irriducibili* or the neo-nazis at East German clubs.

The emergence of these forms of racism may be local responses to the broader processes of globalisation but this does not detract from the seriousness of the activities of these individuals. The public expression of these extremist views not only excludes ethnic minorities from the grounds but the colonisation of the stadia by these groups normalises their views to the wider public (who can hear their chants and see their banners on the television). The emergence of these groups and their use of the stadium constitutes an unignorable political development which should not be dismissed as a pathological distortion of an essentially anti-discriminatory Europe. Racism is a social response to the dislocation created by globalisation and it is an unignorable part of contemporary social reality rather than an aberration of it. The activities of these groups in and around the stadium reveal the uneven, locally-based hierarchy in which different immigrant groups are excluded or included in different locations according to the local political, economic and cultural circumstances. The New Europe is and will be a complex patchwork of hierarchies produced by deregulated globalisation. Racial discrimination is an important factor in locating groups in this emergent hierarchy.

Anti-Racism and Football

The Commission is deeply concerned about the rise of racism and fascism in Europe, and since 1985 has published a number of reports analysing the problem, the most important of which were written by Evrigenis (1985) and Glyn Ford (1991). Evrigenis' report noted the activities of extremist British and Italian groups in the Heysel disaster and went on to discuss the problem of racism in football grounds in England at some length (Evrigenis 1985: 54). Similarly, Ford also considered the heavy involvement of fascists in European football (Ford 1991: 47). The concerns of the Commission have been reflected by the fans themselves and in the 1990s, a number of prominent anti-racist fan projects have developed across Europe. The first of these appeared in England because a large number of black players made appearances in professional football earlier there than elsewhere in Europe and the aggressive terrace culture of the time provided an ideal context for racism. Most of these initiatives have remained as club-based initiatives, such as Leeds Fans United Against Racism and Fascism, or the Charlton Athletic Race Equality initiative, but, by the second half of the 1990s, some had widened their remit beyond the specific club at which they started. Howard Holmes' 'Football Unites, Racism Divides' project in Sheffield originally started as a campaign against racist chanting at Sheffield United but has operated on a wider level more recently. Piara Power's 'Let's Kick Racism out of Football' was launched during the 1993–94 season (Power 2000: 220) and, more recently, the Newcastle-based scheme, 'Show Racism the Red Card' has also become prominent. Similarly, in Europe, there have been many club-based initiatives such as the Schalke 04 Fan-Initiative in Germany which is explicitly concerned with anti-racism and anti-fascism and whose logo pictures a footballer's leg (in Schalke socks) smashing a swastika. St Pauli has had a reputation for leftist activism since the 1970s and these groups feature prominently in BAFF.

The Bologna-based Progetto Ultra group run by Carlo Balestri is currently one of the most important European organisations. Progetto Ultra maintains contacts with many of the most important ultra groups including fascist ones like *Irriducibili* in an attempt to eliminate or, minimally, reduce the expression of racism in Italian grounds. For the past four years, the Progetto Ultra has staged the weekend-long 'Anti-Racist World Cup' in the province of Reggio Emilia, west of Bologna, in July. This 'World Cup' is an informal five-a-side tournament which is attended by large numbers of ultra groups from around Europe, including Germany, France, Italy, England and Austria, with the explicit purpose of building up connections between these disparate groups to strengthen the anti-racist movement. In fact, although the tournament has facilitated the creation of links between groups which may be useful in the future, the Anti-Racist World Cup illustrates the extent of the problem which confronts anti-racists in Europe. Although the tournament has included teams from ethnic minorities such as the Somali Dragons, representing the refugee Somali community in Cardiff, and all are agreed in principle upon diversity, few of the teams have actually been multi-ethnic in composition. Most of the teams have consisted of liberal white European fans with a small number of minority teams. Without the genuine integration of ethnic minorities into indigenous communities, it is easy for racist groups to draw upon certain biological signifiers to discriminate against individuals. As long as skin colour and ethnic status is, in fact, an important definition of group membership, racial discrimination will exist. Certainly an event like the Anti-Racist World Cup provides an arena of interaction where new genuinely multi-ethnic groups might emerge but the event also demonstrates that this process is a slow one.

On 7 June 2000, a new network based in Vienna, called 'Fans Against Racism in Europe' (FARE) was launched and through the internet this group is currently attempting to sustain and extend a European-wide group of fans by regular electronic reports about the activities of racist groups. A typical report was transmitted on 15 November 2000:

> 1. Pouring rain of bananas on Polish International Emmanuel Olisadebe (Interview with the top-striker of the Polish League in *African Soccer* Magazine, No. 61, November 2000)
> *African Soccer*: Yet you were the victim of a racist incident in a Polish league Match at Lodin at the end of September.
> Emmanuel Olisadebe: It was the most terrible thing I have ever seen because I have been in Poland for about three years and nothing like that had ever happened. Then I took Polish nationality, I played a couple of games for the national team and scored three goals, so I certainly wasn't expecting that kind of treatment. I was shocked.
> *African Soccer*: What happened?
> Emmanuel Olisadebe: I took the ball to the corner flag and all of a sudden it was as if it was raining bananas. Around 50 or so came pouring down on me. I was in shock, but the players from the other team were saying to me: 'Emmanuel, don't worry, they're hooligans, they're drunkards.' Afterwards the club sent me a letter of apology. [FARE email communication, 15 November 2000]

Interestingly, this communication from FARE confirms the significance of organic racial discrimination. So long as Olisadebe remained a foreigner, his ethnic inferiority in Poland, although assumed, was irrelevant. However, the moment that he became a Polish national and therefore formally the equal of the white Polish fans, it became necessary for them to demonstrate the racial hierarchy and the informal exclusion of ethnic minorities from full Polish citizenship. The communication went on to describe various other extreme incidents with the clear purpose of highlighting the seriousness of racism in football and providing a forum for European groups to establish links with each other.

The launching of FARE in June 2000 took place in the European Parliament Building in Brussels and was attended by senior representatives of the Parliament and Commission such as Enrique Baron Crespo, the leader of the Party of European Socialists (PES)-Group at the European Parliament, Johannes Swobada, MEP and vice-chairman of the PES-Group and Odile Quintin, director-general of Employment and Social Affairs at the Commission.[4] Highlighting the close political connection between anti-racist groups and the European Commission, the Commission sponsored the event. The panel of individuals drawn from the Parliament, the Commission, FARE and other anti-racist groupings such as Progetto Ultra emphasised the role football could play in combating discrimination. In promoting anti-racism, these individuals provided a clear insight into anti-racist politics, the speakers promoting an individualistic account of equality based on human rights. For instance, Odile Quintin equated racism with other forms of discrimination against the elderly, the handicapped and homosexuals and insisted that 'freedom from discrimination is a basic human right.' She cited Article 13 of the Amsterdam Treaty which opposed discrimination on the grounds of race. Similarly, Mathieu Sprengers, president of the Royal Netherlands Football Association, emphasised that 'people are equal' and that football was one of the ways of bringing them together. Bent Sorensen of the European Monitoring Centre on Racism and Xenophobia drew on exactly the same concepts, emphasising equal opportunity: 'Equality and diversity are key concepts in Europe'. For him, football was a universal language which was unique in its ability to integrate individuals. The appeal to the basic individual right of being treated equally regardless of colour or creed inverts the response of racist groups to globalisation. Anti-racist groups reject all group markings. They promote individual equality of opportunity before the global market as a way of unifying Europe. Cultural diversity should be tolerated and even celebrated, but group affiliations should not affect an individual's prospects, especially in the labour market.

Echoing the statements of the panel at the FARE launch, the Evrigenis report of 1985 defined fascism as 'discrimination between individuals and the denial of equal basic rights to all' (Evrigenis 1985: 19). By discriminating against people on the grounds of their group affiliation, fascism is directly opposed to the liberal principles which lie at the heart of the European Union and the Maastricht Treaty. Racial discrimination distorts the transnational free market. It is logical that the Commission should demand that markers of group status should be eliminated since they distort that emergent European market.[5] Racism is an informal barrier which is as pernicious to the European integration as the trade tariffs which were eliminated in the 1950s by the Treaty of Rome. The fan groups who engage in racial abuse are effectively monopolising the game for themselves and reducing its potential market.

However, although the Commission and the anti-racist groups demand equal opportunities and an unfettered European market, the obsolescence of racial markers will not produce a Europe that is equal. As we have seen in football, the liberalisation of labour markets leads not to equality but rather to new forms of inequality and, in particular, to a new hierarchy of cities and regions around which new social solidarities will emerge. The promotion of equal opportunity and cultural diversity is an important way of combating discrimination but this liberalism will not eliminate all exclusion in the New Europe. On the contrary, liberalisation will necessarily involve new forms of marginalisation though they may not be primarily determined by 'race'. Both the new racism of the 1990s and the new anti-racist groups which prioritise equal opportunities are responses to the liberalisation of Europe. While the racists mobilise notions of racial purity to resist the local effects of globalisation, the anti-racists embrace the transformations brought about by globalisation and attempt to extend the operations of the market. For them, equal access to the market will produce prosperity but will also render divisive forms of social solidarity unnecessary.

The Realities of Football

Starting in the 1990s, UEFA has also explicitly rejected racism and xenophobia. UEFA's anti-racism is closely related to their current marketing of the game where they want to increase rather than to limit the market. UEFA like the Commission want the game to include as many Europeans as possible but as long as racial discrimination is a significant feature of the game, its market is necessarily limited. The anti-racists demand total access to this ritual for all groups and they are engaged in a war against those informal methods against the entry of certain groups. Although there may be a connection between the logic of the market, which is central to the new European project, and equal opportunities, this does not mean that clubs and authorities in football have promoted anti-racism in practice. On the contrary, clubs and federations have consistently turned a blind eye to racist activity for fear that public campaigns against racism would tarnish the image of the game, reducing its marketability and commercial value. This reluctance to confront racist activity by the clubs and federations has been noted by many anti-racist activists:

> We also face another enemy and this enemy sits in the clubs, in the DFB [Deutsche Fussball Band] and in UEFA. It's these who don't take us seriously at all and who sabotage our campaigns all the time. I remember once we distributed leaflets with an anti-racist message and afterwards the club charged us for the costs of cleaning up the leaflets! Just one week later a supporter of my football club set fire to a home for asylum-seekers and was arrested. As a reaction to this the club asked us to distribute the very same leaflets they had rejected just one week before. [Bodo Berg, Schalke 04 Fan Initiative, Networking Against Racism 1999: 15]

> Initially, the first reaction of the authorities in England was a defensive one, to say: 'we don't have a problem with racism, it's not our fault, it's nothing to do with us'. We used to hear: 'It's society's problem' as an excuse for not addressing it in football. [Kevin Miles, FSA and INUSA, Networking against Racism 1999: 17]

In the light of the comments of Berg and Miles, it is notable that Sergio Cragnotti, Lazio's president has persistently apologised for the activities of the *Irriducibili* ultra group and has attempted to limit the excesses of this group after the 'Arkan' outrage:

> The stupidity of these people is beginning to exceed all reasonable bounds. All racist or political manipulation of soccer should be totally eliminated from grounds. This will not be easy but I'm preparing a series of innovative measures because Lazio wants to be a leader even when it comes to fans' behaviour. [Cragnotti, cited in Agnew 2000: 52]

However, while he might publicly reject the *Irriducibili*, there has been little systematic attempt to exclude this group or the leaders of this group from the ground. It seems likely that they constitute such an important part of Lazio's support, Cragnotti dare not alienate them for financial and political reasons. Indeed, it has been suggested that the public rejection of extremist fans by club directors is temporary, relations being resumed with these prominent fan groups only days later (Carlo Balestri, personal interview, 21 September 2000). Demonstrating their political and economic leverage over Cragnotti, the leaders of the *Irriducibili* have recently claimed that they will not stop their racist displays until Cragnotti concedes to the group's demands that the club make more match tickets and away match travel available to them. Other directors of major clubs have connived more closely with these extremist groups for their own political benefit. For instance, according to *L'Elephant Blau*, FC Barcelona's former president, Josep Nunez promoted the emergence of skinhead gangs such 'el Boixos Nois' who were given permission to roam freely around the stadium, enforcing appropriate forms of support for the club under the Nunez regime (Armand Caraben, personal interview, 26 April 2000). This relationship between the Nunez regime and this group is confirmed elsewhere:

> At best, the powers that be turn a blind eye to the ultras' antics. In August 1999, six crop-headed Boixos Nois, two of whom were under police investigation for dispatching a Moroccan teenager to hospital, were allowed to travel with Louis Van Gaal's team for a game in Santander and stay in the same hotel. [King 2000b: 44]

A similar phenomenon has been noted at Real Madrid where the board provide the politically extremist group, the Ultras Surs, with free tickets and expenses for away matches. In September 1999, the leader of this group was caught touting tickets which he had received from the club outside the Bernabeu (ibid.). There may be a logical connection between the neo-liberalism which is now becoming the dominant paradigm of social and economic activity and anti-racism informed by ideas of equal opportunities but in practice, football clubs and federations prefer to accept a potentially distorted and ethnically exclusive market. Consequently, the solidarities which are emerging at these locales in the transnational Europe are complex. These new solidarities may appeal to the local city, as many United fans do, but notions of race may also be mobilised at the local level to create new groups in response to globalisation. The uneven development of transnational Europe will produce a complex hierarchy of cities and regions, many of which will be internally structured by appeals to race to exclude and subordinate ethnic minorities and immigrants. Although anti-racist discourse is likely to become hegemonic in Europe because it has close affinities with the free market principles which are dominant in Europe, racial discrimination and racist politics will remain a very significant feature of European society and will, consequently, be a prominent factor in European football. The new geography of European football will be contoured by discrimination which will partly reflect the processes of uneven development engendered by deregulation.

Notes

1 In point of fact, Banton attempts to graft a theory of rational choice onto his sociology of racial discrimination to argue that individuals join these groups and stay loyal to them because they offer them certain benefits which are not available outside them. In fact, the emergence of these groups cannot be reduced to a rational theory model.
2 I use the term 'racism' throughout this chapter for the sake of brevity but the term stands throughout for 'racial discrimination'.
3 See <http://www.bloodandhonour.com/index2.html>, posted extract from Max Hammer's *Blood and Honour: The Way Forward*.
4 This description of the launch of FARE is taken from fieldnotes.
5 Suggesting this link between global capital and anti-racism, it is interesting that after the Solingen attack, Daimler Benz sponsored an advertising campaign which called for racial harmony, revealing a possible affinity between capitalist enterprise and anti-racism.

Chapter 12
The Contours of a New Europe

The End of International Football?

On the evening of Thursday, 29 July 2000, the streets and baroque arcades of Reggio Emilia, a small Italian town some fifty miles west of Bologna, were deserted and the city was quiet even though the evening was warm and limpid. Only occasional exclamations and exhortations echoed from opened windows out into the mysteriously emptied thoroughfares. Italy were playing Holland in the semi-final of the European Championships, which had, against all predictions, proved to be one of the most successful and entertaining football tournaments ever. This decisive game had imposed a voluntary curfew on the inhabitants of Reggio Emilia. At full time the game was still level and the hush from the windows became more intense, interrupted only by ever more fervent exclamations as the penalty shoot-out began. In a small pizza-parlour by the town's football ground, anxious eyes were transfixed to the decisive final moments of the shoot-out. Italy were ahead and should Holland's Paul Bosvelt miss the fourth penalty kick, Italy would be through to the final where they would meet World Cup winners, France. Bosvelt placed the ball, retreated to his mark and waited for the referee's whistle. His penalty was saved.

Instantly, the pizza parlour and the entire city of Reggio Emilia erupted in ecstasy. From every window and doorway came delirious screams and shouts. The once empty crossroads by the football ground was suddenly blocked with lines of cars, converging wildly from every direction in a cacophony of hooting. Italian flags and the famous shirt of the national team were waved by young men and women, hanging out of the opened car-windows and sun-roofs or clinging to the backs of unbaffled mopeds. This fervent demonstration of national pride continued for over an hour. Gradually as the azure sky darkened, the sound of car-horns and cries of triumph subsided, to be replaced by the contented hum, as the people of Reggio Emilia celebrated the national team's success into the night.

As a result of the deregulation of television and football itself in the 1990s, new transnational relations and new solidarities have developed. In response to these changes at the highest level of football, European football fans have renegotiated their relations with their clubs and created new forms of solidarity. New forms of political activity and identification are emerging.

However, while fans across Europe have become more politically active and have sometimes emphasised a new sense of localism, the growing significance of the big city clubs in Europe has not undermined the relevance of international football. The celebrations in Reggio Emilia which might have been any town in Italy on that evening were a testament to the enduring significance of nationalism and the nation-state represented by the national team. Indeed, the development of the Champions League was widely seen by many commentators as the key reasons for the success of Euro 2000 because it has allowed the best players, now concentrated at the major clubs in Europe to compete at the highest level far more frequently. Thus, the levels of skill and standard of play among European national teams has improved noticeably as a result of developments at club level. Of the 22 players in France's squad for the World Cup of 1998, 15 played in leagues outside France and the proportion of the squad playing outside France increased even further by 2000 (Mignon 2000: 232). France's eventual victory in Euro 2000 and their earlier success in the World Cup Final in 1998 highlights the way in which transnationalisation has ironically strengthened the national team. Indeed, a notable feature of the French team was how many players were drawn from France's former colonies. The definition of who is part of a nation has changed and in this case it has broadened to include individuals who would once not have been considered as genuine French nationals. Echoing this transnationalisation of the nation, there has been a developing trend in world football for national teams to be coached by foreign managers. England notably employed the Swede, Sven Goran Eriksson, after the failure of English managers, while Scotland hired the famous German coach Berti Vogts. Most successfully, South Korea employed the Dutch coach Guus Hiddink for the 2002 World Cup. National teams are becoming increasingly transnational.

The new geography of club football has not rendered the international game obsolete, despite Berlusconi's claims that the concept of the national team will, gradually become less and less important since it is the clubs with which the fans associate (*World Soccer* 1996). Yet, the new dominance of the big clubs is necessitating a transformation of the national teams. It is notable that while Berlusconi's views are normally somewhat hyperbolic, even the steady Franz Beckenbauer has envisaged a similar ascent in the importance of club football: 'I can see a time when a world championship of clubs will come into being and will, in time, take over the World Cup as the most important football tournament on earth' (Collins 1998). Other directors of the major European clubs have also noted this evolving relationship between club and international football:

> I saw Chelsea against AC Milan earlier this year in the Champions League and if you looked at the two teams on view, you would actually look at that and say, 'Well that is probably better quality than England against Italy. In truth.' Let's be grown up

about it. And with the increase in movement of players post-Bosman – and you only need cast ahead when there will be players post-Bosman who have never played in their home country. They will join a club at seventeen. There will be Africans or South Americans who join a club at seventeen and play their entire career in Europe. What will the relevance be? It sounds like heresy but you have to look at the practical reality. What will drive it is market forces and what supporters are interested in. [Rick Parry, personal interview, 9 February 2000]

International football will certainly not be redundant in the conceivable future but as the transnational regime becomes more established, club football, concentrated at the biggest clubs, will become relatively more important in relation to the international game than it has been in the past.

In football, as in the wider Europe, national solidarity will not disappear. Rather, football is likely to be characterised by a new 'mediaevalism', where overlapping and even contradictory groupings and affiliations between clubs and the national team exist to be drawn upon in different circumstances. One of the crucial changes in this now complex relationship between clubs and national teams is that, whereas in the past, fans would often subordinate their rivalry with other clubs from their own league when playing with European opposition, quite the opposite phenomenon has become the commonplace response in the 1990s. National solidarities are still valid when international events – such as games between national teams – occur but that framework is becoming irrelevant at the club level. The fans of other clubs want their local rivals to fail when they play European opposition while national affiliations have little relevance. At the European Cup Final of 1999 even those commentators and fans who appealed to national solidarity as the appropriate principle for interpreting that game recognised that nationalism was a contested category.

Moreover, although nationalism will remain an important imagined community for the foreseeable future, the kinds of communities invoked by nationalism are undergoing profound transformation. National communities have been commercialised in the post-Fordist era so that these communities are reformulated along lines consistent with deregulation and the growing power of the global market:

> The nationalization of sport intensified after 1918 particularly in totalitarian states which used it to prepare their peoples for war and which, in this respect as in so many others, merely went further than the rest. It probably peaked between 1950 and 1980 or so when, in the USSR under Stalin, to attribute success in sport to any but patriotic motives was to risk punishment. Since then things have changed as money has begun to play a larger role and nationality a lesser one. From the Olympic Games down, the most important competitions have become commercialized. While many events are still organized on national lines, in others both competitors and

teams are sponsored (if not owned outright) by corporations which use them for advertising purposes. [Van Creveld 1999: 411–12]

The sponsorship of national teams denotes the new relationship between nation-states and global capital since those who support the national team are now also aligning themselves with a group of multinational corporations. Indeed, under the uneven pressure of globalisation, formerly unified national identities have been increasingly fissured by new regionalised nationalities (Keating 1988; Jenkins and Sofos 1996). Apparently immutable nations have undergone rapid transformation. For instance, the concept of Britain, taken for granted by Geoffrey Green in 1968, has become a problematic solidarity in the 1990s. Britain is not an irrelevance at the turn of the millennium, but the conflation of England, Scotland, Wales and Northern Ireland is now a matter of dispute. As global forces are channelled towards different regions, former national solidarities have less importance as reinvented notions of the nation have come to the fore. It is not a coincidence that just as Britain is breaking up under the force of global markets (Nairn 1981), discussions about the nature of Englishness are becoming more evident (Scruton 2000; Paxman 1999). As Scotland, Wales and Northern Ireland devolve from England, the demand for a specifically English nationalism has become more pressing. It is notable that in English football supporting culture, this English nationalism often excludes Manchester United and its fans.

In football, national and supranational bodies like UEFA and the national federations will, of course, continue to exist but they will be increasingly dominated by the biggest clubs for which they will provide forums. In the late 1990s, we are not seeing the disappearance of the nation as a social solidarity or as an emotive form of identification in football, but the growing significance of the big clubs are transforming it. Thus, the sovereignty of the national and international federations is not completely irrelevant but it is undergoing rapid renegotiation. National communities are changing in the face of globalisation. As solidarities at local levels are becoming relatively more important than in the past, national identities and the cultural significance of national teams have begun to change.

The European Superleague

The premature announcement of the death of international football, often by those individuals who have every interest in promoting club football, is usually accompanied by an assertion about the imminent emergence of a European Superleague. For instance, in 1998, KPMG carried out a survey about the possibility of a European Superleague by canvassing the opinion of 35 individuals located in the clubs, financial institutions and the media. Of the

69 per cent of respondents who thought a superleague was likely, 75 per cent thought it would begin before 2001–02 while only 20 per cent thought it would emerge after 2005 (KPMG 1998: 5). The format of this league was conveniently unclarified but the 75 per cent who thought one was imminent were over-optimistic and it seems unlikely that a regular European league with no knock-out element could emerge much before 2020. It is inconceivable that this league could entirely replace domestic leagues. Even clubs like AC Milan, Manchester United and Real Madrid remain committed to their domestic leagues, as Umberto Gandini and Juan Onieva made clear. However, while the domestic leagues are certain to remain crucial to European football for the foreseeable future, it is also clear that European competition will evolve. For instance, Rodolfo Hecht's Media Partners has continued to lobby the European Commission since the initiative in 1998 and Hecht circulated a document, 'The European Scenario for Club Football', to the clubs in 2000 outlining future strategies for European competition. The document accused TEAM of failing to maximise European television revenues (Hecht 2000: 4–5):

> The first half of the European Football League game has ended over a year ago. That has been the first serious effort to create additional value in European football. Media Partners is currently preparing its strategy to be back on the playing field as soon as the EU Commission rules on our notification. We are expecting such a ruling from the EU Commission during the course of this year. We expect the ruling to be obviously one that opens the market of football to free competition, like any other area of enterprise. Following the ruling we will take the appropriate action. Please keep in mind that Media Partners is a Marketing Agency: our goal is to contribute in creating value in European Football and make money in the process. Therefore we do not consider UEFA as our competitor: we appreciate their role as a Regulator, a role that needs to be protected. So please be assured that when we return – and we will – we will try again hard to involve UEFA in the process. We do consider TEAM Marketing as our competitor and we will do our best to demonstrate their weakness. [ibid.: 2]

Hecht has not been alone in promoting a European Superleague. In September 2000, the Spanish media consortium Telefonica announced its own plans for a European Superleague. As yet, nothing has developed from the Media Partners or Telefonica initiatives, but they are, nevertheless, significant reminders to the clubs and to UEFA of the possible alternatives for European football. As such, these plans increase the clubs' political leverage over UEFA. Given these manifest pressures from the clubs and media, European football will develop in the next two decades in line with the trajectory of the 1990s. The primary European competition will expand to become increasingly concentrated on the biggest clubs in the largest television markets.

Significantly, a European football competition which comes closer and closer to representing a genuine competition of the European Union is conceivable. Indeed, although the Media Partners project was predicated on purely free market principles, Rodolfo Hecht was not unaware of the cultural and political aspects of his project: 'If you give Europe a great competition, number one you create a continent which is a nice by-product and number two you create a great competition for the fans; they would love it. And it would be for Europe, an incredible source of wealth. I cannot go on and say I want to unite Europe but that does not mean that one doesn't have ideas' (Rodolfo Hecht, personal interview, 17 May 2000). The Eastern European teams will be marginalised from the competition since there is little television revenue to be earned from them. Consequently, over the next two decades as fans become more familiar with foreign teams, European competition is likely to move to a more regular league structure involving the biggest clubs, reflecting the realities of the Union more closely. Although under the pressures of deregulation it is possible that a European league might emerge, a genuine European league which is competed over the whole season like a domestic league is a distant prospect even if it did not replace the domestic league. As Jeff Farmer noted in Chapter 9, there is currently little interest in an effectively academic game between even two giants like AC Milan and Manchester United if both were in mid-table positions by February. Yet, as the audience matures, the significance of apparently meaningless games in Europe may increase in a manner similar to domestic leagues. The G14 have proposed that the present two-tier structure of the Champions League be reduced into a single phase of group games but that the groups themselves be expanded from four to six teams. This proposal is significant because it reveals that the G14 clubs believe that transnational audiences are now sufficiently mature to find an expanded league attractive, even though the number of potentially academic games would be increased. It seems highly likely that UEFA will alter the structure of the Champions League again in 2005 or 2006 and it is possible that this proposal for enlarged mini-leagues would be adopted then. The development of European football is self-perpetuating because the greater the number of encounters between clubs, the greater the significance invested in them by the fans. Fans have an increasingly close relationship with other fan groups and a richer collective memory with which to contextualise these games.

Neither the current Champions League nor the possible development of the competition into some form of 'Superleague' will replace domestic league football. Because of the intense rivalries which it invokes, domestic football is the economic basis of even the biggest European clubs and even those clubs which recognise European football as an 'underperforming asset' cannot contemplate living outside the domestic league structure. However, as a result primarily of the Champions League, a slow process of transformation may be beginning to take place where the relevance of domestic football is eroding. This process is most advanced among the cup competitions in Europe and the 1999–2000 season demonstrated this decline most clearly. For instance, in

England, FA Cup-holders Manchester United withdrew from the competition in 1999–2000 on the grounds of excessive fixture congestion. Having won the European Cup, Manchester United were invited by FIFA to a new club competition to be held over a two-week period in Brazil in January 2000 called the World Champion Clubs' Cup. With the addition of six more Champions League matches as a result of the Media Partners initiative and the rescheduling of the third round of the FA Cup from the first week of January to 16 December, the club could not play in both the World Champion Clubs' Cup and the FA Cup. The FA Cup was regarded as dispensable and controversially the FA allowed Manchester United to withdraw from its own Cup competition as the FA believed that Manchester United's participation in FIFA's fledgling tournament would enhance England's chances of hosting the 2006 World Cup.[1] In the event, both the World Champions Clubs' Cup and England's bid itself were failures while the withdrawal of Manchester United from the competition devalued the FA Cup.

However, although Manchester United had opprobrium poured upon it, the devaluation of the FA Cup was by no means Manchester United's fault alone. On the contrary, the FA Cup has steadily declined in popularity over the past three decades. Before the 1970s, an FA Cup fixture attracted a 50 per cent higher attendance on average than a league game (Szymanski 2000: 3) but, while English league attendances have steadily risen from 1985, the FA Cup has not shared this recovery (ibid.: 4). Indeed, its popularity has fallen demonstrably: 'until the mid-1990s same division FA Cup matches always attracted at least 10 per cent more spectators over a season, while in the last three seasons the ratio has fallen below one' (ibid.: 5). Moreover, 'the relative decline of the FA Cup is not restricted to any particular division. The ratio of the FA Cup to League attendance has fallen in the Premier League, but it has also fallen in Football League Divisions One, Two and Three' (ibid.). This decline was demonstrated in 1999–2000 season by the woeful attendances for the competition especially in the rescheduled third round. The poor final between Chelsea and Aston Villa only exemplified the atrophy of this competition which the fans themselves recognised. While Chelsea fans were enthralled by the victory in the FA Cup in 1997, the triumph in 2000 was received very differently:

> We won the FA Cup in May and nobody is that bothered. I spent all summer trying to get someone to write a piece about what their day at the Cup Final was like. Now if I had done that in 1997 – I suppose it was slightly different because we hadn't won the Cup, we hadn't won anything, for twenty years so it was a lot more important but three years down the line people can barely raise a cheer about it. It rained on the Sunday on the Fulham Road [for the victory parade] and so hardly anyone turned up and suddenly you have a competition which everyone was very fond of and which

was held in great regard which is suddenly quite worthless ... It was very much like winning the League Cup. [James Edwards, personal interview, 10 August 2000]

One reason for the decline seems to be the concentration of power in the hands of the biggest clubs which is reducing uncertainty of outcome and therefore the attraction of the competition (Szymanski 2000: 6). For instance, there were only 25 cases of teams beating an opponent from two or more divisions higher than itself over the eleven years before 2000 compared with 42 cases between 1977 and 1989 (ibid.: 8). In 1974 the biggest earner in the Football League had an income 18 times greater than the smaller but by 1998 the multiple had reached 116, protecting the biggest clubs against defeats by smaller teams. The increasing inequality in the League may well be a factor in the decline of the FA Cup but other factors also seem highly relevant:

> I view the FA Cup and I think most people did view the FA Cup as the supreme competition because it was on television once a year. Outside the occasional England international – I think some of the home internationals used to be televised – it was the only match on telly. It was an all-day build up and your heroes got to be on national television. Most people didn't know who Ipswich's left-back was; after the Cup final, they would have done. That made it very important for football fans because everybody was looking at you. Now there is football on television everyday, there is so much more coverage in the press. It is not special anymore. [James Edwards, personal interview, 10 August 2000]

Although the decline in giant-killing may be relevant, the extensive coverage of other often superior games between the biggest clubs is likely to have undermined the special status of the FA Cup. Deregulated television has focused on the biggest clubs with the more skilful and well-known players and thereby reduced the attractiveness of FA Cup ties between lesser teams without star players. It is possible that the FA Cup may be redeemed in future seasons but it is unlikely that any action on behalf of the FA or the clubs could alter the organic decline in the FA Cup's importance to the fans themselves. Whatever the professions of faith on the part of those fans or the media who claim to speak for them, the final statement of a competition's popularity is registered in fan interest. In England, the decline in attendance denotes that this competition simply is not as important as it once was and it would take a quite dramatic social and cultural transformation for the long-term decline in attendance to be reversed.

This decline in the significance of domestic cup competitions is not limited to England. Infamously, in the same season, Barcelona withdrew from the equivalent King's Cup in farcical circumstances. Barcelona lost the first leg of the semi-final of this competition 3–0 to Atletico Madrid on 12 April 2000. At the return leg on 25 April, when the Barcelona team were due out on the Nou

Camp pitch, the captain Guardiola was sent to tell the referee that Barcelona could not field a team since nine of their players were away on international duty. The Atletico players returned to their dressing room having 'won' the tie without kicking a ball (King, J. 2000b: 271). Barcelona's coach, Van Gaal, did have a shortage of players, having signed only twenty professionals at the beginning of the season (ibid.) but by selecting reserve or youth team players, had he been minded to do so, he could have fielded a full, though obviously, weakened team. The club seemed to have been mounting a protest against the unreasonable burden of international football where federations demanded the availability of increasing numbers of the biggest clubs' players for more and more competitions. Although the demands of international football may have been the cause of this fiasco, the selection of the King's Cup for this protest was significant. It would have been inconceivable that they would have mounted such a protest for a league game or for the Champions League but the ignominious exit from the Cup demonstrated the low esteem in which that competition was held by the club.

Domestic leagues currently remain central to European football and they are likely to remain so for the foreseeable future but their continuing importance does not mean that their significance is unalterable. On the contrary, the development of the Champions League and, in particular, the inclusion of runners-up, third- and even fourth-placed teams has necessarily blunted these domestic competitions. Certainly, teams still want to win their domestic league but this achievement does not have the significance which it once did. The inclusion of non-champions in the Champions League has necessarily diminished the status of the leagues for the financial reward and prestige of entering the premier European competition is no longer exclusive to the league champions. This decline in the status of the domestic leagues was highlighted most obviously when Manchester United won the FA Premier League at the end of the 1999–2000 season by a record margin of 18 points, the title having been won some four games before the end of the season. Many United fans insisted that winning the league was the most important event and furiously rejected any suggestion that this easiest domestic triumph was an anticlimax:

> It is [an anticlimax] for some people because some people are dicks and they haven't got any sense of [tradition]. People who haven't maybe always supported United but who have just started coming in the last seven or eight years. They're knobheads. I started going in '87 and that's late on – when I was eight – and there are people who started going well before that and they will tell you: winning the league is the most important thing. It might seem like it's not when you've won it so easily, when you've won the league by 18 points but when you're not winning it, it is the only thing. [Stan, personal interview, 27 June 2000]

> If we're given a choice at the start of each season about which competition we would most like to win, it should always be the league. That's what we strive over for nine

months of the year. That's why we make long treks all over the country on any day of the week that Sky Sports tells us to. It's our bread and butter. Europe is the cake, and that's the way it should remain. Our first objective should always be to be crowned kings of our own backyard. Anything after that is a bonus. It was clear that's what the win at Southampton meant to the players and to 1400 diehards lucky enough to be there. But by the time of the Chelsea game two days later I sensed a feeling of smugness in certain quarters. It was probably generated by the day-tripping glory seekers wallowing in their reflected success, but those twats really don't deserve the football and the trophies we've had in the past decade. 'Only the league' might be disappointment to them, but as one who followed the lads home and away for every one of the 26 barren years between 1967 and 1993, I just can't get enough of the league. [*Red Issue* 2000a]

Masculine United fans asserted that only inauthentic United fans – day-trippers who are not proper men – regarded the 2000 league victory as something of an anti-climax. However, the very emphasis which fans like Stan or fanzines like *Red Issue* placed on this most recent victory demonstrated its very hollowness. In no other year had there been the slightest need for fans to emphasis how important winning the league was; domestic triumph was automatically the spur of the greatest celebration. It required no discussion. The emphasis of its continuing importance was a new phenomenon which denoted that even for those fans who insisted on its continuing centrality, the league had, in reality, lost some of its significance.[2]

Indeed, the decline of the league was recognised explicitly by some of the fans:

My impression is that most United fans want to win European Cup more than anything else. That was obviously the case before we won it but I know that there is another strand of opinion. I know that Andy [Walsh] is very defensive of the domestic game and feels that Europe shouldn't be overriding it. Certainly in terms of the European Superleague and things like that, I agree with that in the sense that unless we are getting something out of it, if it just for the sake of people making more money then I don't think they should be damaging the tradition of it which makes it what it is. The loss of the importance of the national league is very disappointing for a lot of people but they want to win in Europe because that is taking it to the next stage. [Duncan Drasdo, personal interview, 13 June 2000]

Duncan Drasdo was also explicit in the reasons for the renegotiation of the importance of competitions for United fans:

There is a devaluation of the competition in terms of letting the non-champions in for a start. I think that is more important as a devaluation of the national leagues in fact. It removes the prestige of actually winning the championship because you were the only ones who got in the European Cup before where the European Cup itself hasn't suffered that much because there are just a lot of good teams in it. It is actually more difficult to win now. [Duncan Drasdo, personal interview, 13 June 2000]

Drasdo's belief in the decline in the league's importance has been confirmed elsewhere: 'It just shows how far United have come in these last few years that we're now disappointed at only winning the league. In fact the defeat by Real, coming when it did was always going to take the gloss off our Championship win' (*United We Stand* 2000); 'Everybody knows that the Reds can lift the Premiership for the next five years in a canter like we have just proved. To me it's been an anti-climax this season' (*United We Stand*, Gus, 2000a).

These sentiments were affirmed more forcefully in the following season when the club once again won the domestic championship with ease but was knocked out in the quarter-finals of the Champions League. Clearly, the decline in the league's significance can be overstated and the attitudes of these United fans have to be considered in the light of the extraordinary ease of the team's victory in the league in 2000 and 2001, especially after the unique treble achievement of 1999. However, given the growing concentration of power among the biggest European clubs and the expansion of the Champions League, it seems likely that these clubs will qualify for that top competition regularly. Consequently, even without winning the league, their position in Europe is likely to remain unchallenged. The domestic league will of course remain extremely important to the biggest European clubs, but an organic shift which is rendering European football relatively more important than domestic league football, just as the FA Cup has diminished in value over the last twenty years, is currently observable. Of course, it is possible that this is simply a temporary trend but, given the context of deregulation and concentration, this does not seem likely. Over the next twenty years, a steady shift in balance between a developing European league and relatively declining domestic leagues is likely. It is just possible that there might come a point some time in the 2020s, given the decline of the league and the growing familiarity of the fans with other European teams and with the competition itself, that fan culture could find a genuine European Superleague meaningful. Such a league could only be possible given the development of relations between fan groups which would provide European football with a wider social context. At the moment we are living through a period of radical transition when the old order is fading rapidly but the new has not yet come fully into being. The entire social and economic basis of European football is changing but the new transnational regime has not yet become fully established.

Virtual Europe

The increased coverage of football on television has had a profound effect on the economic structure and cultural position of the sport. Given the importance of this new relationship between television and football, the perceptions and practices of the viewers are highly significant. This is particularly the case since the television viewers far outnumber the fans who actually attend the games; the Champions League averaged just under 5 million viewers in the major television markets in the 1999–2000 season. As Szymanski noted in his critique of the Restrictive Practices Court decision, there is a noticeable bias against this large television audience which is expressed through the press and, indeed, which has found itself into academic accounts (for example, Giulianotti and Williams 1994). Some of this bias comes from the attending fans themselves who resent the rescheduling of matches to inconvenient times, to maximise the television audience. Rightly, these attending fans recognise a divide of interests between themselves and the television viewer. Both Mark Longden and Monica Brady of IMUSA rejected the priority which the television viewers now seem to enjoy:

> The majority of people who go to football don't go because they see wonderful football. They go because it is their team playing and it bloody matters. And there are people who go and watch shit week in, week out because it is their team. They are the people who will always be there – when it is not popular anymore, when it is not trendy anymore. They are the people who are still going to want to go. But they are disregarding people like that. They are pandering to the TV audience: the passive market that will sit and watch it, 'This is great.' But there's no passion for the game. There's no love for the game ... If the kids only start to see football on television, you can support any team you want. If you don't have to travel to the bloody ground you can support any team you like. You could be a Real Madrid fan, if you wanted to be. It loses something in that situation. You will actually get to a situation where there is only support for a handful of clubs. [Monica Brady, IMUSA, personal interview, 13 June 2000]

Mark Longden and Monica Brady, like very many other attending fans, reject the process whereby television allows the development of global football fans where anyone can build a virtual relationship with any club, wherever they live and without ever attending that club's games. Given the transformation of football and the pressure which has been exerted on the 'traditional' fan, the growing recognition of the differing interests of television and attending fans is understandable. Moreover, as the attending fans have become a more self-conscious group, the categorisation of other groups as inauthentic is typical; it is a crucial way by which the group solidarity and legitimacy of the independent groups are sustained. Consequently, the attribution of inauthenticity to television fans by attending fans is socially coherent. The attending fans are also essential to the viability of football as a television sport. It is only insofar as they create an atmosphere at the ground, that televised football is a viable commodity. Silvio Berlusconi himself has recognised the indispensability of the attending fans predicting perhaps optimistically that in the future the attending fans will enter the stadia for free.

Nevertheless, despite the importance of the attending fans and the understandable denigration of television fans by the former, the idea that television fans are simply inauthentic – they are not real fans who do not 'love' the game – is mistaken. To accept this view is to take the understandable view of a prominent group of attending fans, which are threatened by the increasing importance of the virtual audience, as the reality itself. The television fans are certainly different kinds of spectators to the attending fans but their consumption of the game is in itself valid culturally. Watching games is a valid social practice through which these fans sustain certain social relations which are central to their identities. Whatever an observer might think of this form of social practice, it is one with determinate, and given the numbers who watch televised football, very significant social effects which cannot simply be ignored because this social practice clashes with the interests of other groups. In fact, many of those fans who would now be considered wholly authentic by Mark Longden and Monica Brady may have been attracted to United by the television coverage of the team in the past. Television fans are not inauthentic but they do consume the game differently from attending fans. Significantly, given the increasing control of the fans in the grounds in England, watching televised games in private homes or in pubs may become a less restrictive, more engaged and socially powerful event than attending itself. Ironically, those fans who used to attend the games from the 1960s onwards, seem to be demonstrating a growing preference for watching the games at home or in the pub, while those who watched the game in the comfort of their front-rooms, seem now to show more interest in attending games:

> Say I can pay for a pay-per-view thing so that I can have every Southampton game at the new stadium in my front room. And I say to four or five of my mates, 'What do you want to do on Saturday? Do you want to go down there [to the new ground] and pay £30 each or do you all want to come round my house, chip in four quid, get a load of beers in and watch the game live?' With a club like this, that is going to happen. Undoubtedly that is going to happen. Especially when you are looking at trying to recover 10,000 fans who have now lost the culture of going to matches. [Richard Chorley, SISA, personal interview, 22 June 2000]

Echoing Chorley's point, many United fans, appalled by the sanitised atmosphere at Old Trafford, no longer attend games but watch coverage of them and other matches in local pubs where the games are televised in various (not always entirely legal) ways (Bent et al. 2000).[3]

Given the authenticity of the television as a way of participating in football, the deregulation of European football and the increasingly live broadcast of European Cup games, in the form of the Champions League, is a very important social process. As Gruneau and Whitson (1993) demonstrated in their study of hockey night in Canada, televised sporting events are rituals by which imagined national communities are periodically re-created. Interestingly, anticipating processes which occurred in Europe from the 1990s, they presciently note that 'the sheer scope of the changes have made the equation between hockey and Canadianness increasingly problematic' (Gruneau and Whitson 1993: 268). As Durkheim demonstrated, the existence of coherent social groups relies upon periodic rituals in which they congregate. The Champions League constitutes a new ritual in Europe where a virtual audience gathers to watch the same event across the entire continent. In a myriad of parallel interaction rituals which occur in living rooms and in bars across Europe, fans renegotiate their relations with each other by reference to this new transnational context. Typically, fans align themselves with the opposing European team against the rival native teams. They do not want native English, German or Spanish teams to succeed against the clubs of other nations as a vindication of national superiority but to fail, since the success of a local rival is a threat. Concomitantly, the defeat of a fan's team by European opposition becomes a tool for ridicule in these interactions between viewers. Through face-to-face interactions during these viewing rituals, the transnational reality alters social relations at the most personal level, giving rise to increased local rivalry. Televised football, and especially the Champions League, illuminate the new realities of European football, in which the biggest city clubs are increasingly dominant. This league illustrates the decisive political economic transformations which have occurred in the New Europe. Deregulated television has created an important new ritual whereby the consumption of live football by fans in pubs, bars and their own homes has constituted an important way in which the New Europe can be created as an imagined community. These flickering images which transfix millions across Europe on winter's nights communicate the emergence of a transnational order.

The European Ritual

Whatever form European football takes in the future, this ritual is likely to constitute a key site for the expression of social solidarity and identity in Europe. As such, it is as rich and striking as the spectacles of ancient Rome which fascinate the modern reader and from which a deep understanding of that culture – and its profound differences from our own – is possible. It is difficult to gain an appropriate perspective on football since its very popularity dissuades academics from recognising the significance of this apparently trivial pastime. When viewed as a mere pastime, the significance of European football can be easily overlooked. Yet, when this social practice is viewed as a ritual and aligned with other unfamiliar rituals like the Roman spectacle, its importance becomes unignorable. In his famous discussion of status groups, Max Weber argued that status groups create themselves by selecting certain arbitrary criteria which distinguish members of the group from outsiders. The mere selection of such criteria of membership was not enough to form groups, however. Critically, 'intercourse which is not subservient to economic or any other purpose' (Weber 1968: 932) was essential. Groups require periods of exclusive interaction dedicated only to social purposes and in which there are no immediate extrinsic rewards to be had. These periods of exclusive social interaction are not supererogatory, groups already existing before they have engaged in periods of social intercourse. Rather, his social intercourse is the *sine qua non* of group formation. Throughout history, rituals have provided the arena in which this exclusive social intercourse has taken place and, consequently, rituals, including sporting ones, are essential elements in all social existence. Indeed, the ritual is, if anything, the prior social fact which precedes apparently more important aspects of social life such as economic production and human reproduction because the existence of certain social relations, enacted in the ritual, will determined the form which production and reproduction can take (Rappaport 2000).

European football does not provide food or shelter or basic economic goods but its apparent superfluity should not lead commentators to dismiss it as irrelevant to social life. The most important social relations and understandings are realised in the ritual and, in the New Europe, football is increasingly becoming the most prominent ritual in which emergent networks of social relations are affirmed. In European football, the social reality of the New Europe is brought to life in the powerful effervescence of the ecstatic crowd as it responds to the footballers illuminated in great silver domes of light around the Continent. Just as the arenas located in every major outpost of the Roman empire announced the reality of that political entity, so do the great amphitheatres of European football, whose lights illuminate the wintery skies above them, indicate the reality of the New Europe. In these new theatres, often located in the same cities which were at the heart of the Roman Empire, the European ritual is re-enacted to re-create and transform emergent social relations and solidarities. The Romans recognised the didactic values of their spectacles, where gladiatorial combat was intended to demonstrate an appropriate Roman stoicism towards death, the absolute authority of the emperor and the abjection of slaves (Hopkins 1983; Wilkinson 1975; Auguet 1994). Gladiatorial combats explicitly represented what it was to be a Roman, enacting the reality of that social order. It is vital that commentators on Europe begin to see that today's European ritual similarly illuminates the society in which we live. In the contemporary European ritual of football, the values and social relations of a transnational society in which the free market is dominant are enacted in the powerful and dramatic interplay of players and fans. The dying seconds of the 1999 European Cup Final, as Ole Gunnar Solskjaer was enveloped by his ecstatic team-mates while Sammy Kuffour pounded the Nou Camp turf, are enthralling moments of communal celebration and despair which transcend rational discussion. However, these moments – the very zenith of ritualistic effervescence – are inseparable outgrowths of the wider social reality which they inevitably reflect. Solskjaer's boot and Kuffour's fist reflect not some eternal human condition of triumph and ecstasy but rather the historically specific transformation of European society. These players playing for these particular clubs in this competition in front of these crowds are the products of an increasingly transnational social order. This era is dominated by the market but, against commentators like Pocock, this does not mean the end of politics or community. It involves the creation of new forms of solidarity and identification and new types of political activity. In this New Europe, football is likely to become an increasingly significant public ritual, providing this new social order with those necessary hours of creative effervescence. A strange landscape is appearing around us in which major European football clubs are become increasingly prominent features. Within their cavernous stadiums the reality of this new geography is illuminated with a brilliant silver light.

Notes

1 This tournament was plainly developed by FIFA in response to the growing power of UEFA as a result of the success of the Champions League.
2 It is interesting that in the *United We Stand* annual readers' survey for the 2000–01 season, 70 per cent of fans polled cited the European Cup as the trophy they most wanted to win (*United We Stand* 2001c. 29).
3 Bent et al. provide an interesting account of the way that, between 1992 and 1997, about 150 pubs in England adjusted their satellite settings illegally, allowing them to show live Premier League games being broadcast in Norway (Bent et al. 2000: 23–35). The matches were very popular and were very lucrative for the pubs involved.

Bibliography

Agnew, P. (2001), 'Roma on course', *World Soccer*, February, pp. 52–3.
Agnew, P. (2000), 'Racism and Refereeing put Soccer in the Shade', *World Soccer*, April, pp. 52–3.
Agnew, P. (1995), 'Forward Thinking', *World Soccer*, September, p. 15.
Aigner, G. (1999), 'A new attitude' *UEFAflash*, 104, December, p. 1.
Allan, J. (1989), *Bloody Casuals*, Scotland: Famedram.
Amin, A. and Thrift, N. (1994), *Globalization, Institutions and Regional Development in Europe*, Oxford: Oxford University Press.
Anderson, B. (1990), *Imagined Communities*, London: Verso.
Anderson, P. (1997), 'Under the sign of the interim' in Gowan, P. and Anderson, P. (eds), *The Question of Europe*, London: Verso.
Appadurai, A. (1996), *Modernity at Large: Cultural Dimensions of Globalization*, London: University of Minnesota Press.
Appadurai, A. (1994), 'Disjuncture and Difference in the Global Cultural Economy', in M. Featherstone (ed.), *Global Culture: Nationalism, Globalization and Modernity*, London: Sage.
Armstrong, G. (1998), *Knowing the Score: football hooliganism*, Oxford: Berg.
Armstrong, G. (1994), 'False Leeds: the construction of hooligan confrontations', in Giulianotti, R. and Williams, J. (eds) (1994), *Game without Frontiers*, Aldershot: Arena.
Armstrong, G. (1991), 'Football Hooliganism: theory and evidence', *Sociological Review*, 39(3), pp. 427–58.
Aschenbeck, A. (1998), *Fussball Fans im Abseits*, Kassel: Agon.
Auguet, R. (1994), *Cruelty and Civilisation*, London: Routledge.
Back, L., Crabbe, T. and Solomos, J. (2001), *The Changing Face of Football*, Oxford: Berg.
Back, L., Crabbe, T. and Solomos, J. (1996), *Alive and Still Kicking: An Overview Evaluation of Anti-Racist Campaigns in Football*, London: Commission for Racial Equality.
Baert, P. (1998), 'Foucault's history of the present as self-referential knowledge acquisition', *Philosophy and Social Criticism*, 24(6), pp. 111–26.
Baimbridge, M., Cameron, S. and Dawson, P. (1996), 'Satellite Television and the Demand for Football: a whole new ball game?', *Scottish Journal of Political Economy* 43(3), pp. 317–33.
Baldwin-Edward M. and Schain, M. (1994), 'The Politics of Immigration: Introduction', *West European Politics*, 17(2), pp. 2–33.

Bale, J. (1989), *Sports Geography*, London: E and F.N. Spon.
Bale, J. (1982), *Sport and Place*, London: C. Hunt and Co.
Balibar, E. (1991), 'Es gibt keinen Staat in Europa: Racism and Politics in Europe Today', *New Left Review*, 186, March/April, pp. 5–19.
Ball, P. (2002), *Morbo: the story of Spanish football*, London: When Saturday Comes.
Ball, P. (2000), 'Nod and a Wink', *When Saturday Comes*, 160, June, pp. 20–1.
Bance, A. (1992), 'The Idea of Europe: from Erasmus to ERASMUS', *Journal of European Studies*, 22, Part 1(85), pp. 1–19.
Banks, S. (1998), 'Cleaning up with Ajax', *World Soccer*, June, p. 8.
Banton, M. (1983), *Racial and Ethnic Competition*, Cambridge: Cambridge University Press.
Baringhorst, S. (1995), 'Symbolic highlights or Political Enlightenment? Strategies for fighting racism in Germany', in Hargreaves, A. and Leaman, J. (eds), *Racism, Ethnicity and Politics in Contemporary Europe*, Aldershot: Edward Elgar.
Baudrillard, J. (1990), *Fatal Strategies*, New York: Semiotext(e).
Beiersdorfer, D. (1993), *Fussball and Rassismus*, Gottingen: Verl. Die Werkstatt.
Bell, E. (1998), 'Nothing Super about this league for BSkyB – unless it's in the game', *Observer*, 9 August.
Bellamy, R. (1967), 'Draw enough for United', *The Times*, 16 November, p. 15.
Bent, I., McIlroy, R., Mousley, K. and Walsh, P. (2000), *Football Confidential*, London: BBC.
Betts, P. (1998a), 'Leading man chooses to play it cool in Italian drama', *Financial Times*, 4 December, p. 28.
Betts, P. (1998b), 'Moguls set for pitch battle', *Financial Times*, 16 December, p. 5.
Betts, P. and Gapper, J. (1999), 'News Corp in talks with Canal Plus', *Financial Times*, 11 February, p. 29.
Betts, P. and Gapper, J. (1998), 'Murdoch gains some ground in continental Europe', *Financial Times*, 24 November, p. 33.
Betts, P. and Studemann, F. (1998), 'Fininvest confirms Murdoch talks', *Financial Times*, 4 August, p. 24.
Bjorgo, T. (1997), '"The Invaders", "the Traitors", and "the Resistance Movement"', in Modood, T. and Werbner, P. (eds), *The Politics of Multiculturalism in the new Europe*, London: Zed Books.
Blainpain, R. and Inston, R. (1996), *The Bosman Case*, Leuven: Peeter, Sweet and Maxwell.
Blitz, J. (1999). 'Italy puts limits on Murdoch's TV football plans', *Financial Times*, 1 February, p. 19.
Bloch, M. (1997), *Ritual, History and Power*, London: Athlone.

Boon, G. (ed.) (2000a), *Annual Review of Football Finance: a review of the 1998/99 season*, Manchester: Deloitte and Touche.
Boon, G. (ed.) (2000b), *England's Premier Clubs*, Manchester: Deloitte and Touche.
Boon, G. (ed.) (1999), *Annual Review of Football Finance: a review of the 1997/98 season*, Manchester: Deloitte and Touche.
Boornscheier, V. and Ziltener, P. (1999), 'The Revitalisation of Western Europe and the politics of the "social dimension"', in Booje, T., Van Steenbergen, B. and Walby, S. (eds), *European Societies: Fusion or Fission?*, London: Routledge.
Bose, M. (1999), *Manchester Unlimited*, London: Orion Business Books.
Bose, M. (1998), 'Free market approach from Uefa', *Daily Telegraph*, 3 October.
Bourdieu, P. (1999), 'The State, Economics and Sport', in Dauncey, H. and Hare, G. (1999), *France and the 1998 World Cup*, London: Frank Cass.
Boyle, M., Findlay, A., Lebeivre, E. and Paddison, R. (1996), 'World Cities and the limits to global control', *International Journal of Urban and Regional Research*, 20(3), pp. 498–517.
Bowley, G. (1998a), 'Borussia sees float value of DM 350m', *Financial Times*, 16 February, p. 24.
Bowley, G. (1998b), 'Clubs push for stock market flotation', *Financial Times*, 24 June, p. 7.
Brewin, J. (2002), 'United in rivalry', 12 September, <www.soccernet.com>.
Brown, A. (2000), 'Sneaking in through the back door? Media company interests and the dual ownership of clubs', in Hamil, S., Michie, J., Oughton, C. and Warby, S., *Football in the Digital Age*, London: Mainstream.
Brown, A. (ed.) (1998), *Fanatics*, London: Routledge.
Brown, A. and Walsh, A. (1999), *Not for Sale*, Edinburgh: Mainstream.
Buford, B. (1992), *Among the Thugs*, London: Mandarin.
Bulmer, S. and Scott, A. (eds) (1995), *Economic and Political Integration in Europe*, Oxford: Blackwell.
Burns, J. (1999), *Barca: a people's passion*, London: Bloomsbury.
Butler, O. (1999), 'United's rule may not last long', *Soccer Investor*, 8 (October), p. 7.
Butler, O. and Nunns, H. (2001), 'Testing times', *World Soccer*, May, pp. 12–13.
Cable, V. (1995), 'The Diminished Nation-State: a study in the loss of economic power', *Daedalus* 124(2), pp. 23–53.
Calvocoressi, P. (1991), *Resilient Europe: 1870–2000*, London: Longman.
Cameron, C. (1995), *Football, Fussball, Voetbal*, London: BBC Books.
Campani, G. (1994), 'Immigration and Racism in Southern Europe: the Italian Case', *Ethnic and Racial Studies*, 16(3), pp. 517–26.
Castells, M. (1998), *The Information Age: Economy, Society and Culture. Vol. 1. The Rise of Network Society*, Oxford: Blackwell.

Castells, M. (1996), *The Informational City*, Oxford: Blackwell.
Castells, M. (1994), 'European Cities, the Informational Society and the Global Economy', *New Left Review*, 204, pp. 18–32.
Castles, S. (1993), 'Migration and Minorities in Europe. Perspectives for the 1990s: eleven hypotheses', in Wrench, J. and Solomos, J. (eds), *Racism and Migration in Western Europe*, Oxford: Berg.
Cave, M. (1997), 'Regulating Digital Television in a Convergent World', *Telecommunication Policy*, 21(7), pp. 575–96.
Chaudhary, V. (2001), 'Premier League fans pay more than ever', *Guardian*, 25 May, p. 7.
Chester, N. (1968), *Report of the Committee on Football*, London: HMSO.
Chilton, B., Day, M., Holt, P. and Williams, P. (1997), *If the Reds Should Play ... in Rome or Mandalay*, Sheffield: Jama.
Chippendale, P. and Franks, S. (1992), *Dished: the rise of fall of British satellite broadcasting*, London: Simon and Schuster.
Chryssochoou, D. (1996), 'Europe's Could-be Demos: Recasting the Debate', *West European Politics*, 19(4), pp. 787–801.
CIT (1999), 'The Media Map of Western Europe 1999', 25 November <www.elecoms-data.com/mwest.htm>.
Cochrane, A., Peck, J. and Tickell, A. (1996), 'Manchester Plays Games: Exploring the Local Politics of Globalisation', *Urban Studies*, 33(8), October, pp. 1319–36.
Cohen-Tanugi, J. and Rush, S. (2000), 'Transfer System', *Soccer Analyst*, 2(5), pp. 8–11.
Collins, Randall (1990), *Weberian Sociological Theory*, Cambridge: Cambridge University Press.
Collins, Randall (1979), *The Credential Society*, London: Academic Press.
Collins, Richard (1998), *From Satellite to Single Market*, London: Routledge.
Collins, Roy (1998b), 'High and mighty put the boot into romance', *Guardian*, 1 August, p. 3.
Commission of the European Communities (1999), *The Helsinki Report on Sport* (COM (1999) 644 Final), Luxembourg: Official Publications of the European Communities.
Commission of the European Communities (1992), *The European Community and Sport*, 2(1992), Luxembourg: Official Publications of the European Communities.
Commission of the European Communities (1990), *The European Community Policy in the Audiovisual Field*, Brussels: The Commission.
Conn, D. (1997), *The Football Business*, Edinburgh: Mainstream.
Corner, J. and Harvey, S. (1991), *Enterprise and Heritage*, London: Routledge.
Court of Arbitration for Sport (CAS), 98/200, AEK Athens and Slavia Prague vs UEFA, Lausanne: CAS.

Cox, K. (1995), 'Globalisation, Competition and the Politics of Local Economic Development', *Urban Studies*, 32(2), pp. 213–24.
Cresswell, P. and Evans, P. (1999), *European Football: a fans' handbook 1999–2000*, London: Rough Guide.
Creveld, M. Van. (1999), *The Rise and Decline of the State*, Cambridge: Cambridge University Press.
Crick, M. and Smith, D. (1989), *Manchester United: The Betrayal of a Legend*, London: Pan.
Curry, S. (1998), 'Uefa dig in for fight to finish', *Daily Telegraph*, 23 August.
Dauncey, H. and Hare, G. (1999), *France and the 1998 World Cup*, London: Frank Cass.
Dave (2000), 'Dear UWS', *United We Stand*, 91, April, p. 10.
Davis, H. and Levy, C. (1992), 'The regulation and deregulation of Television: a British/West European Comparison', *Economy and Society*, 21(4), pp. 453–82.
Davis, M. (1990), *City of Quartz*, London: Vintage.
Delanty, G. (1996), 'The Resonance of Mitteleuropa: a Habsburg Myth or Anti-Politics?', *Theory, Culture and Society*, 13(4), pp. 93–108.
Delanty, G. (1995), *Inventing Europe: Idea, Identity, Reality*, London: Macmillan.
Deloitte and Touche (2000), 'Rich list', *Four-Four-Two*, January, pp. 67–75.
Dempsey, P. and Reilly, K. (1998), *Big Money, Beautiful Game: saving soccer from itself*, London: Nicholas Brealey.
Derrida, J. (1992), *The Other Heading: reflections on Today's Europe*, Indianapolis: Indiana University Press.
Dicken, P. (1998), *Global Shift*, London: Paul Chapman.
Dobson, S. and Goddard, J. (2001), *The Economics of Football*, Cambridge: Cambridge University Press.
Downing, D. (2000), *Passovotchka*, London: Bloomsbury.
Drummond, P., Paterson, R. and Willis, J. (eds) (1993), *National Identity and Europe: The Television Revolution*, London: BFI.
Duclos, A. (1997), 'France', *World Soccer*, June, p. 34.
Dunford, M. and Kafkalas, G. (1992), *Cities and Regions in the New Europe*, London: Belhaven.
Dunning, E. (1999), *Sport Matters*, London: Routledge.
Dunning, E., Murphy, P. and Williams, J. (1988), *The Roots of Football Hooliganism*, London: Routledge and Kegan Paul.
Dunphy, E. (1991), *A Strange Kind of Glory*, London: Heinemann.
Durkheim, E. (1976), *The Elementary Forms of the Religious Life*, London: George Allen and Unwin.
Dyson, K. et al. (1990), *Broadcasting and the New Media Policies in Western Europe*, London: Routledge.

Eastham, J. (1999), 'The Organisation of French Football' in Dauncey, H. and Hare, G. (1999), *France and the 1998 World Cup*, London: Frank Cass.
Ecclestone, J. (1968), 'Manchester United make history', *The Times*, 30 May, p. 1.
The Economist (1998a), 'The cult of the true fan', 12 September, p. 884.
The Economist (1998b), 'Why Rupert Murdoch is polite', 11 April, p. 618.
The Economist (1997), *The Economist's Guide to the European Union*, London: Profile.
Edwards, G. and Spence, D. (eds) (1995), *The European Commission*, London: Catermill.
Ellwood, S. (1995), 'Spain is Different', in Hargreaves, A. and Leaman, J. (eds), *Racism, Ethnicity and Politics in Contemporary Europe*, Aldershot: Edward Elgar.
Everett, F. (1999), 'United in pride', *Manchester Evening News*, 27 May, p. 9.
Featherstone, M. (1997), *Undoing Culture*, London: Sage.
Evrigenis, D. (1985), *Committee of Inquiry into the rise of fascism and racism in Europe*, Luxembourg: Official Publications of the European Community.
Finn, G. and Guilianotti, R. (eds) (2000), *Football Culture*, London: Frank Cass.
Flower, J (ed.) (1997), *France Today*, London: Hodder and Stoughton.
Ford, G. (1991), *Committee of Inquiry on Racism and Xenophobia: Report on the findings of the inquiry*, Luxembourg: Official Publications of the European Community.
Forsyth, R. (1993), 'Argument for elite league undermined', *The Times*, 4 October, p. 27.
Foucault, M. (1977), *Discipline and Punish*, London: Allen Lane.
Fox, N. (1978), 'Substantial shadow joins Forest on the continental stage', *The Times*, 12 May, p. 20.
Fox, N. (1977a), 'Fair play given the boot at St Etienne', *The Times*, 16 September, p. 5.
Fox, N. (1977b), 'Liverpool at last reach Euro summit', *The Times*, 26 May, p. 12.
Fox, N. (1977c), 'United will offer evidence of Manchester Policemen', *The Times*, 21 September, p. 17.
Fox, N. (1974), 'When football was fun and the sweeper was someone who pushed a broom', *The Times*, 30 November, p. 6.
Frachon, C and Vargaftig, M. (1995), *European Television*, London: John Libbey.
Frame, D. (1968), 'Truce time – reds fans', *Manchester Evening News*, 29 May, p. 14.
Frampton, P., Michie, J. and Walsh, A. (2001), 'Fresh Players, New Tactics: Lessons from the Northampton Town Supporters' Trust', Research Paper

2000/01 for Supporters Direct, London: Football Governance Research Centre, Birkbeck.
Freeman, S. (2000), *Own Goal! How egotism and greed are destroying football*, London: Orion.
Fynn, A. and Guest, L. (1999), *For Love or Money*, London: Andre Deutsch.
Fynn, A. and Guest, L. (1994), *Out of Time*, London: Simon and Schuster.
Fynn, A. (1999), 'Super League to take Europe by storm', *The Sunday Times*, 6 December, p. 2.10.
Fysh, P. and Wolfreys, J. (1992), 'Le Pen, the National Front and the Extreme Right in France', *Parliamentary Affairs*, 45(3), pp. 309–40.
Gal, S. (1991), 'Bartok's Funeral: representations of Europe in Hungarian political rhetoric', *American Ethnologist*, 18(3), pp. 440–58.
Geertz, C. (1973), 'Deep Play: notes on the Balinese cockfight', in *The Interpretation of Cultures*, New York: Basic Books.
Giulianotti, R. (1999), *Football: a sociology of the global game*, Cambridge: Polity.
Giulianotti, R. and Williams, J (eds) (1994), *Game without Frontiers*, Aldershot: Arena.
Glanville, B. (1999), *Football Memories*, London: Virgin.
Glanville, B. (1991), *Champions of Europe*, London: Guinness.
Glanville, B. (1989), 'Italians chicken feed the Czechs', *World Soccer*, May, p. 27.
Glanville, B. (1977a), 'Football: all quiet on the UEFA front when facts on corruption are clear', *The Sunday Times*, 13 March, p. 31.
Glanville, B. (1977b), 'A suitable case for compensation', *The Sunday Times*, 22 May, p. 31.
Glanville, B. (1977c), 'A Trail of Deception', *The Sunday Times*, 30 October, p. 31.
Glanville, B. (1955), *Soccer Nemesis*, London: Secker and Warburg.
Glendinning, M (2000), 'French Football', *Soccer Analyst*, 2(1), pp. 3–7.
Goddard, V., Llobera, J. and Shore, C. (eds) (1994), *The Anthropology of Europe*, Oxford: Berg.
Gowan, P. and Anderson, P. (eds) (1997), *The Question of Europe*, London: Verso.
Greaves, J. (1999), 'Jimmy Greaves on Saturday', *The Sun*, 29 May, pp. 68–9.
Green, G. (1978), *There's only one United*, London: Hodder and Stoughton.
Green, G. (1977), 'Moves to make UEFA Cup into a European league', *The Times*, 10 November, p. 2.
Green, G. (1976), 'Move the make UEFA Cup into European league', *The Times*, 10 November, p. 2.
Green, G. (1974a), 'A night that goes into the black book of European competition', *The Times*, 11 April, p. 14.

Green, G. (1974b), 'Double Dutch makes sense in Spain's struggle for power', *The Times*, 18 September, p. 12.
Green, G. (1974c), 'Leeds on the threshold of a dream', *The Times*, 24 April, p. 8.
Green, G. (1974d), *Soccer in the Fifties*, London: Ian Allen.
Green, G. (1968a), 'Manchester United in the Final at Last', *The Times*, 16 May, p. 16.
Green, G. (1968b), 'Portuguese rush for tickets', *The Times*, 29 May, p. 15.
Green, G. (1968c), 'Seven Magic minutes that gave Manchester United the Cup', *The Times*, 30 May, p. 15.
Green, G. (1967a), 'New proposal for Super-League', *The Times*, 13 March, p. 6.
Green, G. (1967b), 'Thompson foils Naples by inspired display', *The Times*, 9 February, p. 5.
Green, G. (1967c), 'United can look ahead to rising hopes', *The Times*, 30 November, p. 13.
Green, G. (1957), 'Manchester United face two goal deficit', *The Times*, 12 April, p. 14.
Gruneau, R. and Whitson, D. (1993), *Hockey Night in Canada*, Toronto: Garamond.
Guest, L. and Law, P. (1997a), 'The Revolution will be Televised', *World Soccer*, January, pp. 14–17.
Guest, L. and Law, P. (1997b), 'The Television Revolution: Part 2', *World Soccer*, February, pp. 24–5.
Haas, E. (1964), *Beyond the Nation-State*, California: Stanford University Press.
Habermas, J. (1993), 'The Second Life Fiction of the Federal Republic: we have become "Normal" Again', *New Left Review*, 197, January/February, pp. 58–66.
Hamil, S., Michie, J., Oughton, C. and Warby, S. (2000), *Football in the Digital Age*, London: Mainstream.
Hamil, S., Michie, J. and Oughton, C. (1999), *The Business of Football*, London: Macmillan.
Hammer, Max (n.d.), *Blood and Honour: The Way Forward* <http://www.bloodandhonour.com/index.html>.
Harding, A. (1997), 'Urban Regimes in a Europe of Cities', *European Urban and Regional Studies*, 5(4), October, pp. 291–311.
Hare, G. (1999), 'Towards the demassification of French Television in the 21st Century', *Modern and Contemporary France*, 7(3), pp. 307–17.
Hare, G. (1997), 'The Broadcasting Media', in Flower, J (ed.), *France Today*, London: Hodder and Stoughton.
Harveson P. (1996), 'It's a new ball game as takeover talk hits fever pitch', *Financial Times*, 16 October.

Hegel, G. (1977), *The Phenomenology of Spirit*, trans A. Miller, Oxford: Oxford University Press.
Hegel, G. (1967), *The Philosophy of Right*, trans. T. Knox, Oxford: Oxford University Press.
Held, D. (1991), 'Democracy, the Nation-State and the Global System', *Economy and Society*, 20(2), pp. 138–72.
Henderson, J. and Castells, M. (eds) (1987), *Global Restructuring and Territorial Development*, London: Sage.
Herman, E. and McChesney, R. (1997), *The Global Media*, London: Cassell.
Hince, P. (1999), 'I believe in miracles', *Manchester Evening News* (sports), 27 May, pp. 8–9.
Hobsbawm, E. and Ranger, T. (eds) (1983), *The Invention of Tradition*, London: Macmillan.
Holt, O. (1997), 'Juventus' dynasty turns to dust', *The Times*, 30 May, p. 40.
Hopkins, K. (1983), *Death and Renewal*, Cambridge: Cambridge University Press.
Horridge, D. (1965), 'Liverpool crash – blame ref', *The Mirror*, 13 May, p. 31.
Hughes, R. (1996a), 'Money means more than glory to Europe's finest', *The Times*, 15 October, p. 48.
Hughes, R. (1996b), 'Slick men of Europe devaluing game's honoured traditions', *The Times*, 10 February, p. 46.
Hughes, R. (1993), 'Uefa establishes European Cup cartel', *The Times*, 3 December, p. 40.
Hume, M. (1999), 'Football has become not so much the new rock 'n' roll as a cross between the new royalty and the new religion', *The Times*, 27 May, p. 24.
Humphreys, P. (1990), *Media and Media Policy in West Germany*, Oxford: Berg.
Hutchinson, J. and Smith, A. (1994), *Nationalism*, Oxford: Oxford University Press.
Ingham, R. (ed.) (1978), *Football Hooliganism: the wider context*, London: Interaction.
Inglis, S. (1991), *The Football Grounds of Great Britain*, London: Collins Willow.
James, C.L.R. (1963), *Beyond a Boundary*, London: Hutchinson.
James, T. and Sturgess, B. (1997), 'What price European football?', *Soccer Analyst*, 10, pp. 2–14.
Jameson, F. (1991), *Postmodernism or the Cultural Logic of Late Capitalism*, London: Verso.
Jenkins, B. and Sofos, S. (eds) (1996), *Nation and Identity in Contemporary Europe*, London: Routledge.
Jensen-Butler, C., Shachar, A. and van Weesep, J. (eds) (1997), *European Cities in Competition*, Aldershot: Avebury.

Jones, K. (1968), 'From the brink of disaster ... Matt's night of glory', *The Mirror*, 30 May, pp. 26–7.
Keating, M. (1998), *The New Regionalism in Western Europe*, Cheltenham: Edward Elgar.
Keating, M. (1988), *State and Regional Nationalism*, London: Harverster Wheatsheaf.
Keating, M. and Jones, B. (eds) (1985), *Regions in the European Community*, Oxford: Clarendon.
Keating, M. and Loughlin, J. (eds) (1997), *The Political Economy of Regionalism*, London: Frank Cass.
Kelly, J and Radnedge, K. (1996), 'Ball of Confusion', *World Soccer*, April, pp. 18–19.
King, A. (2000), 'Football and Post-National Identity in the New Europe', *British Journal of Sociology*, 51(3) pp. 419–42.
King, A. (1999a), 'Baudrillard's Nihilism and the End of Theory', *Telos*, 112 (Summer), pp. 89–106.
King, A. (1999b), 'Football Hooliganism and the Practical Paradigm', *Sociology of Sport Journal*, 16(3), pp. 269–73.
King, A. (1998a), 'A Critique of Baudrillard's Hyperreality: towards a sociology of postmodernism', *Philosophy and Social Criticism*, 24(4), pp. 47–66.
King, A. (1998b), 'Thatcherism and the Emergence of Sky Television', *Media, Culture and Society*, 20(2), pp. 277–93.
King, A. (1998c), *The End of the Terraces: the transformation of English football in the 1990s*, London: Leicester University Press.
King, A. (1997a), 'The Lads: masculinity and the new consumption of football', *Sociology*, 31(2), pp. 329–46.
King, A (1997b), 'The Postmodernity of Football Hooliganism', *British Journal of Sociology*, 48(4), 1997, pp. 576–93.
King, A. (1995), 'Outline of Practical Theory of Football Violence', *Sociology*, 29(4), pp. 635–41.
King, J. (2000a), 'Camp Nou Nightmare', *World Soccer*, December, pp. 70–1.
King, J. (2000b), *FC Barcelona: Tales from the Nou Camp*, London: Macmillan.
Kipker, I. (2001), 'Champions League vs. Superleague', *Soccer Analyst*, 2(6), pp. 11–16.
Kipker, I. (2000a), 'Bosman Ruling: How German Football Reacted to the New System', *Soccer Analyst*, 2(4), pp. 3–6.
Kipker, I. (2000b), 'The Bundesliga', *Soccer Investor*, 8, pp. 6–10.
Klein, M. and Welfens, P. (eds) (1992), *Multinationals in the New Europe and Global Trade*, London: Springer-Verlag.
KPMG (1998), *European Super League: results of a survey conducted by MORI on behalf of the KPMG European Football Unit*, Huddersfield: KPMG.

Kuhn, R. (1995), *The Media in France*, London: Routledge.
Kuypers, T. (1997), 'Football on the Box', *New Economy*, 4(4), pp. 207–11.
Lash, S. and Urry, J. (1993), *Economies of Signs and Space*, London: Sage.
Ledbrooke, A. (1957), 'Blanchflower kicked, Berry tripped, Whelan winded in Cup', *The Mirror*, 12 April, p. 21.
Lindberg, L. and Scheingold, S. (1970), *Europe's Would-be Polity*, New Jersey: Prentice Hall.
Lomax, B. (1999), 'Supporter Representation on the board: the case of Northampton Town FC', in Hamil, S., Michie, J. and Oughton, C. (eds) (1999), *The Business of Football*, London: Mainstream.
Lovejoy, J. (1998a), 'Eurotrash meets fantasy football', *The Sunday Times*, 9 August, p. 2.12.
Lovejoy, J. (1998b), 'Gunning for Europe', *The Sunday Times*, 13 September, p. 2.7.
Lovejoy, J. (1995), 'Rijkaard's grace amid the greedy', *The Sunday Times*, 28 May, p. 2.14.
Maguire, J. (1999), *Global Sport*, Cambridge: Polity.
Macdonald, R. (1968), *Manchester United in Europe*, London: Pelham.
Macwilliam, R. (2000), *The European Cup*, London: Aurum Press.
Manchester Evening News (1958), 'United Cup XI: 28 die', 6 February, p. 1.
Manchester Evening News (1957), 'The Drama of Madrid', 12 April, p. 19.
Mann, M. (1993), 'Nation-States in Europe and Other Developing Continents: diversifying, developing, not dying', *Daedalus* 122(3), pp. 115–40.
Marchesi, A. (ed.) (1998), *Italian Serie A: Deloitte and Touche Financial Review* Manchester: Deloitte and Touche.
Marsh, P., Rosser, E. and Harré, R. (1978), *The Rules of Disorder*, London: Routledge.
McCarra, K. (1999), 'Hitzfeld magnanimous in defeat', *The Times*, 29 May, p. 31.
McGhee, F. (1957), 'Our Champions go down fighting', *The Mirror*, 26 April, p. 17.
McKeever, L. (1999), 'Reporting the world cup: old and new media', in Dauncey, H. and Hare, G. (1999), *France and the 1998 World Cup*, London: Frank Cass
Meek, D. (1988), *Red Devils in Europe*, London: Cockerel Books.
Meek, D. (1968a), 'Hearts trump United', *Manchester Evening News*, 29 May, p. 14.
Meek, D. (1968b), 'Tonight their finest hour', *Manchester Evening News*, 29 May, p. 1.
Meek, D. (1967), 'Triumph of temperament', *Manchester Evening News*, 16 November, p. 30.
Mellor, G. (2000), 'The Genesis of Manchester United as a National and International "Super-Club", 1958–68' *Soccer and Society*, 1(2), pp. 151–66.

Melotti, U. (1997), 'International Migration in Europe', in Modood, T. and Werbner, P. (eds), *The Politics of Multiculturalism in the New Europe*, London: Zed Books.
Melucci, A. (1989), *Nomads of the Present*, London: Hutchinson.
Melucci, A. (1988), 'Social Movements and the Democratization of Everyday Life', in Keane, J. (ed.), *Civil Society and the State*, London: Verso.
Merkel, U. and Tokarsi, W. (eds) (1996), *Racism and Xenophobia in European Football*, Aachen: Meyer and Meyer.
Michie, J. and Ramalingam, S. (1999) 'Whose game is it anyway? Stakeholders, Mutuals and Trusts', in Hamil, S., Michie, J. and Oughton, C. (eds) (1999), *Business of Football*, London: Mainstream.
Michie, J. and Walsh, A. (1999) 'What future for football?', in Hamil, S., Michie, J. and Oughton, C. (eds) (1999), *The Business of Football*, London: Mainstream.
Middlemas, K. (1995), *Orchestrating Europe*, London: Fontana.
Miles, R. (1993), 'The Articulation of Racism and Nationalism: Reflections on European History', in Wrench, J. and Solomos, J. (eds), *Racism and Migration in Western Europe*, Oxford: Berg.
Mignon, P. (2000), 'French Football after the 1998 World Cup: the state and modernity of football', in Finn, G. and Giulianotti, R. (eds), *Football Culture*, London: Frank Cass.
Miller, D. (1991), 'Milan choking on champagne', *The Times*, 8 March, p. 39.
Milward, A. (1992), *The European Rescue of the Nation State*, London: Routledge.
Mingione, E. (1993), 'Italy: the resurgence of regionalism', *International Affairs*, 69(2), pp. 305–18.
The Mirror (1999), 'The United Kingdom: the nation is gripped by red fever', 26 May, p. 7.
MMC (Monopolies and Mergers Commission) (1999), *British Sky Broadcasting and Manchester United PLC*, London: HMSO.
Moore, G. (1998), 'Nou Camp thriller shows Europe's premier competition is moving in right direction', *The Independent*, 27 November, p. 30.
Moore, G. (1996), 'UEFA acts to frustrate breakaway', *The Independent*, 8 February, p. 27.
Morley, D. and Robins, K. (1990), 'No Place like Heimat: images of Home(land) in European Culture', *New Formations*, 12 (Winter), pp. 1–23.
Morrow, S. (1999), *The New Business of Football*, London: Macmillan.
Morrow, S. (1997), 'The City's Match of the Day', *New Economy*, 4(4), pp. 202–206.
Muller, W. and Wright, V. (1994) 'Reshaping the State in Western Europe', *West European Politics*, 17(3), pp. 1–11.
Motson, J. and Rowlinson, J. (1980), *The European Cup*, London: Queen Anne Press.

Murdoch, R. (1989), 'Television Choice – and Quality', *The Times*, 26 August, p. 8.
Murphy, P., Williams, J. and Dunning, E. (1990), *Football on Trial*, London: Routledge.
Nairn, T. (1981) *The Break-up of Britain*, London: New Left Books.
Nash, R. (2001), 'English Football Fan Groups in the 1990s: class, representation and fan power', *Soccer and Society*, 2(1), pp. 39–58.
Nelson, B. and Stubb, A. (eds) (1994), *The European Union*, London: Lynne Rienner.
Newman, C. (1999), 'Vivendi deal helps Murdoch broaden his European vision', *Financial Times*, 18 June.
Networking Against Racism in Europe (1999), *Report of the Vienna Seminar* Vienna: Fairplay.
Nottage, J. (1986), 'Milan into battle by helicopter', *World Soccer*, October, pp. 30–31.
Ohmae, K. (1993), 'The Rise of the Region-State', *Foreign Affairs*, 72(2), pp. 78–87.
Ostergaard. B. (ed.) (1993), *The Media in Western Europe*, London: Sage.
Parkinson, M. and Harding, A. (1995), 'European Cities toward 2000: entrepreneurialism, competition and social exclusion', in Rhodes, M. (ed.), *The Regions and the New Europe*, Manchester: Manchester University Press.
Paxman, J. (1999) *The English*, Harmondsworth: Penguin.
Pearson, J. (1968), 'Portuguese Rush for tickets', *The Times*, 29 May, p. 15.
Peck, J. (1995), 'Moving and Shaking: Business Elites, State Localism and Urban Privatism', *Progress in Human Geography*, 19(1), March, pp. 16–46.
Peck, J. and Tickell, A. (1995), 'Business Goes Local: dissecting the business agenda in Manchester', *International Journal of Urban and Regional Research*, 19(1), March, pp. 55–78.
Pietersee, J. (1991), 'Fictions of Europe', *Race and Class*, 32(3), pp. 3–10.
Pocock, J.G.A. (1991), 'Deconstructing Europe', *London Review of Books*, 13(24), December, pp. 6–10.
Podaliri, C. and Balestri, C. (1998), 'Racism and Football Culture in Italy', in Brown, A. (ed.), *Fanatics*, London: Routledge.
Potter, B. (1999), 'Man United chief bemoans "low" TV rights', *Daily Telegraph*, 11 February.
Power, P. (2000), 'Kick racism out of football', in Hamil, S., Michie, J., Oughton, C. and Warby, S. (eds) (2000), *Football in the Digital Age*, London: Mainstream.
Radnedge, K. (1999a), 'Down the drain or up the table?' *World Soccer*, Summer, p. 4.
Radnedge, K. (1999b), 'Germany', *World Soccer*, January, p. 27.
Radnedge, K. (1998a), 'D-Day in Jerusalem', *World Soccer*, December.

Radnedge, K. (1998b), 'Superleague is no Idle Threat', *World Soccer*, September, p. 4.
Radnedge, K. (1997a), 'Ajax wheels are coming off', *World Soccer*, June, p. 4.
Radnedge, K. (1997b), 'Foreign Legions – Bosman one year on', *World Soccer*, February, pp. 22–3.
Radnedge, K. (1997c), *The Ultimate Encyclopedia of European Soccer*, London: Hodder and Stoughton.
Radnedge, K. (1995a), 'The Good, the Bad and the Utterly Ridiculous', *World Soccer*, November, pp. 8–9.
Radnedge, K. (1995b), 'The Vision Thing', *World Soccer*, March, pp. 33–5.
Radnedge, K. (1986), 'Boniperti Calls for Euro-Seeding System', *World Soccer*, November, pp. 4–5.
Radnedge, K. (1985a), 'World Soccer Diary', *World Soccer*, September, pp. 26–7.
Radnedge, K. (1985b), 'World Soccer Diary', *World Soccer*, December, pp. 26–7.
Rappaport, R. (2000), *Ritual and Religion in the Making of Humanity*, Cambridge: Cambridge University Press.
Reade, B. (1999), 'Why I back Bayern', *The Mirror*, 26 May, p. 6.
Redhead, S. (1991a), 'The Era of the end, or the end of an era: football and youth subculture in Britain', in Williams, J. and Wagg, S. (eds), *British Football and Social Change*, Leicester: Leicester University Press.
Redhead, S. (1991b), *Football with Attitude*, Manchester: Wordsmith.
Redhead, S. (1986), *Sing When You're Winning*, London: Pluto.
Red Issue (2001), 'Toy Towns', 43, March, p. 9.
Red Issue (2000a), 'Baggy's Shorts' 34, May, p. 12.
Red Issue (2000b), 'Flicker Haircuts and Cagools: Bohemian Away, 1981', 30, February, pp. 30–31.
Red Issue (2000c), 'Lacoste Comes to Manchester: more politically incorrect tales from the eighties. Nuremberg/Vienna 1980', 31, March, pp. 28–31.
Red Issue (2000d), 'Welcome to our World', 40, Christmas, p. 8.
Red Issue (1997), 'Editorial', 9(10), April, p. 1.
Restrictive Practices Court (1999), 'The Office of Fair Trading against the Premier League', London: HMSO.
Rhodes, M. (ed.) (1995), *The Regions and the New Europe*, Manchester: Manchester University Press
Rippon, A. (1980), *The European Cup*, London: Mirror Books.
Roberts, G. (1992), 'Right-Wing radicalism in the new Germany', *Parliamentary Affairs*, 45(3), pp. 324–50.
Robertson, R. (1992), *Globalization*, London: Sage.
Robillard. S. (1995), *Television in Europe: Regulatory Bodies*, London: John Libbey.

Robson, G. (2000), *No One Likes Us, We don't Care: the myth and reality of Millwall fandom*, Oxford: Berg.
Rosentraub, M. (1999), *Major League Losers*, New York: Basic Books.
Rotmil, A. (1995), 'Germany', *World Soccer*, January.
Rotmil, A. (1986a), 'Long Summer Break Costs Money', *World Soccer*, October, p. 28.
Rotmil, A. (1986b), 'Star Exodus Continues', *World Soccer*, September, p. 28.
Rotmil, A. (1985), 'Bundesliga Debts', *World Soccer*, September, pp. 28–9.
Russell, D. (1997), *Football and the English: a social history of association football in England, 1863–1995*, Preston: Carnegie Publishing.
Sassen, S. (1991), *The Global City*, Chichester: Princeton University Press.
Schafer, T. and Owen, D. (2001), 'A weight off Real shoulders', *Financial Times*, 25 May.
Schaffrath von, Michael (1999), 'Free-TV, Pay-TV oder Pay-per-View?', in Schaffrath von, Michael (ed.), *Die Zukunft der Bundesliga*, Gottingen: Verl. Die Werkstatt.
Schlesinger, P. (1994), 'Europeanness: a new cultural battlefield?', in Hutchinson, J. and Smith, A. (eds), *Nationalism*, Oxford: Oxford University Press.
Scruton, R. (2000), *England: An Elegy*, London: Pimlico.
Schmidt, V. (1995), 'The New World Order, Incorporated: the rise of business and the decline of the nation-state', *Daedalus*, 124(2), pp. 75–106.
Scholar, I. (1992), *Behind Closed Doors*, London: Andre Deutsch.
Screen Digest (1998), 'Europe's Digital TV Platforms', December, pp. 273–80.
Seve and Claudio (1999), *Il Gruppo*, Turin: Tecno Grafica.
Siedentop, L. (2000), *Democracy in Europe*, Penguin: Allen Lane.
Sharpe, L. (1993), *The Rise of Meso Government in Europe*, London: Sage.
Shaw, K. (1993), 'The development of a new urban corporatism', *Regional Studies* 27(3), pp. 251–8.
Shelley, M. and Winck, M. (1993), *Aspects of European Cultural Diversity*, London: Routledge.
Sheridan, M. (1995), 'Political Theatre', *The Times Literary Supplement*, 4788, 6 January, pp. 27–8.
Shore, C. and Black, A. (1994) 'Citizen's Europe and the construction of European identity', in Goddard, V., Llobera, J. and Shore, C. (eds), *The Anthropology of Europe*, Oxford: Berg.
Smith, A. (1992), 'National Identities and "Europe": National Identity and the idea of European Union', *International Affairs*, 68(1), pp. 55–76.
Smith, T. (1999), 'Why I back Man U', *The Mirror*, 26 May, p. 6.
Soccer Analyst (2000a), 'Dupont Interview', 2(1), pp. 10–11.
Soccer Analyst (2000b), 'Galliani Interview' 2(3), pp. 13–15.
Soccer Analyst (2000c), 'Meier Interview', 2(2), pp. 15–16.
Soccer Analyst (2000d), 'Transfer Reform: For the Good of the Game?', 2(4), pp. 1–2.

Soccer Analyst (2000e), 'The Transfer System', 2(5), pp. 8–11.
Soccer Investor (2000a), 'European News', 9, p. 10.
Soccer Investor (2000b), 'International News' 8, p. 18.
Soccer Investor (2000c), 'Sponsorship News', 8, p. 20.
Soccer Investor (2000d), 'Telefonica Superleague Plan', 10, p. 15.
Soccer Investor (2000e) 'TV Deals', 10, p. 19.
Soccer Investor (2000f), 'TV Rights Deals', 8, p. 19.
The Square Ball (1992), 'The Temptation of Cantona', p. 5.
Stern (1999), 'Kassen-Kampf', 8, 18 February, pp. 66–7.
Storper, M. (1995), 'The Resurgence of Regional Economies, Ten Years Later', *European Urban and Regional Studies*, 2(3), pp. 191–221.
Stott, R. and Reicher, S. (1998), 'How Conflict Escalates: the inter-group dynamics of collective crowd violence', *Sociology*, 32(2), pp. 353–77.
Strange, S. (1995), 'The Defective State', *Daedalus*, 124(2), pp. 55–74.
Studemann, F. (1998a), 'Kirch licks his wounds after Brussels blocks pay-TV deal', *Financial Times*, 29 May.
Studemann, F. (1998b), 'Murdoch set to lift German TV interests', *Financial Times*, 15 June.
Sturgess, B. and Mounsey, J. (2000), 'Fan Investors: Part One: A Neglected Opportunity?', *Soccer Analyst*, 2(5), pp. 3–7.
Sturgess, B., Mounsey, J. and Hamilton, B. (2001), 'Fan Investors: Part II. Part Two: A Share for all Seasons', *Soccer Analyst*, 2(6), pp. 3–7.
Sugden, J. and Tomlinson, A. (1998), *FIFA and the Contest for World Football*, Cambridge: Polity.
Supporters' Direct (2001), 'Owls trust takes off', 3, June, p. 1.
Swann, D. (1995), *The Economics of the Common Market*, Harmondsworth: Penguin.
Sznajder, M. (1995), 'Italy's Right-Wing Government: Legitimacy and Criticism', *International Affairs*, 71(1), pp. 83–102.
Szymanski, S. (2000a), 'The Decline of the FA Cup', *Soccer Analyst*, 2(2), pp. 3–8.
Szymanski, S. (2000b), 'Hearts, Minds and the Restrictive Practices Court Case', in Hamil, S. et al. (eds) *Football in the Digital Age*, London: Mainstream.
Szymanski, S and Kuypers, T. (1999), *Winners and Losers*, London: Viking.
Tassin, E. (1992), 'Europe: A Political Community?', in Mouffe, C. (ed.), *Dimensions of Radical Democracy*, London: Verso.
Taylor, I. (1971), 'Soccer and Soccer Consciousness', in Cohen, S. (ed.), *Images of Deviance*, Harmondsworth: Penguin.
Taylor, Lord Justice P. (1990), *The Hillsborough Stadium Disaster 15th April 1989*, London: HMSO.
TEAM (1999), *UEFA Champions League: Season Review 1998/9*, Lucerne: TEAM.

TEAM (2000), *UEFA Champions League: Season Review 2000/1*, Lucerne: TEAM.
Team Manchester (2000), 'So Proud', *Red Issue*, 33, Easter, p. 15.
The Times (1999a), 'Ten reasons to support Bayern tomorrow', 25 May, p. 3.
The Times (1999b), 'Ten reasons to support United tomorrow', 25 May, p. 2.
The Times (1965a), 'Mersey sound in Milan to help Liverpool', 12 May, p. 3.
The Times (1965b), 'Wembley final a triumph for football', 20 May, p. 4.
The Times (1963a), 'Benfica's heaviest defeat for three years', 15 November, p. 5.
The Times (1963b), 'Benfica lose European Cup', 23 May, p. 4.
The Times (1963c), 'Physical strength is not enough', 19 September, p. 3.
The Times (1962a), 'Brave Bangor yield at last to Naples', 11 October, p. 4.
The Times (1962b), 'Faint hope now for Ipswich', 15 November, p. 4.
The Times (1962c), 'Ipswich foiled by policy of containment', 29 November, p. 4.
The Times (1962d), 'Stunned silence at Ibrox', 12 December, p. 4.
The Times (1962e), 'Tottenham fight to last but fail', 6 April, p. 4.
The Times (1962f), 'Two Mistakes and Two Goals Down', 22 March, p. 3.
The Times (1961a), 'Burnley two goals up but Hamburg still in the hunt', 19 January, p. 3.
The Times (1961b), 'Spurs fight back from desperate position', 14 September, p. 4.
The Times (1956), 'Anderlecht Swamped', 27 September, p. 4.
Touraine, A. (1994), 'European Countries in a Post-National Era', in Rootes, C. and Davis, H. (eds), *Social Change and Political Transformation*, London: University College London Press.
Touraine, A. (1988), *The Return of the Actor*, Minneapolis: University of Minnesota Press.
Touraine, A. (1981), *The Voice and the Eye*, Cambridge: Cambridge University Press.
Touraine, A. (1971), *The Post-Industrial Society*, New York: Random House.
Turner, G. (1998), 'Spain', *World Soccer*, December, p. 32.
Turner, V. (1969), *The Ritual Process*, Harmondsworth: Penguin.
UEFA (1998), *UEFA Champions League: A Solidarity System for European Football*, Nyon: UEFA.
UEFAflash (2001), 'One billion swiss francs for European football', 123, July, p. 3.
UEFAflash (2000), 'A global vision', 113, September, p. 1.
United We Stand (2001a), 'Annual Readers Survey (no. 11)', 104, September, pp. 28–9.
United We Stand (2001b), 'Ask: Eric Harrison', 102, May, pp. 18–19.
United We Stand (2001c), 'Manchester c'est merde', 102, May, p. 30.
United We Stand (2000a), 'Gus', 90 March, p. 7.

United We Stand (2000b), 'Mad Cyril', 93, Summer, p. 6.
United We Stand (2000c), 'Starting something you just can't finish', 93, Summer, p. 16.
United We Stand (1999a), 'A Tale of One City', 8, May, p. 23
United We Stand (1999b), 'A Tale of Two Cities: Manchester versus Birmingham', 79, March, pp. 22–3.
United We Stand (1999c), 'A Tale of Two Cities: Manchester versus Leeds', 80, April, pp. 16–17
United We Stand (1999d), 'Redheaded: We people who are darker than blue', 81, April, pp. 22–3.
United We Stand (1998a), 'Men Behaving Badly', 71, May, pp. 18.
United We Stand (1998b), 'UWS Letters', 68, February, pp. 11.
United We Stand (1998c), ' UWS Letters: England for me means nothing', 67, January, p. 8.
United We Stand (1997), 'Redheaded: we people who are darker than blue', 66, December, p. 29.
United We Stand (1996), 'Irwellian Thoughts', 58, December, p. 6.
United We Stand (1995), 'Abbey Hey', 49, October, pp. 26–7.
Urwin, D. (1991), *Western Europe since 1945*, London: Longman.
Vasta, E. (1993), 'Rights and racism in a new country of immigration: the Italian case', in Wrench, J. and Solomos, J. (eds) (1993), *Racism and Migration in Western Europe*, Oxford: Berg.
Venturi, R., Scott Brown, D. and Izenour, S. (1977), *Learning from Vegas*, London: MIT Press.
Wallace, W. (1997), 'Rescue or Retreat? The Nation State in Western Europe, 1945–93', in Gowan, P. and Anderson, P. (eds), *The Question of Europe*, London: Verso.
Wallace, W. (1990), *The Transformation of Western Europe*, London: Pinter.
Walker, M. (1998), 'Shearer "slates" money driven superleague', *Guardian*, 1 September, p. 28.
Ward, C. (1989), *Steaming In*, London: Sportspages.
Weber, M. (1968), *Economy and Society*, Berkeley: University of California Press.
Weiler, J., Haltern, U. and Mayer, F. (1995), 'European Democracy and its Critique', *West European Politics* 18(3), pp. 4–39.
Weiler, J. (1997), 'Does Europe need a constitution?', in Gowan P. and Anderson P. (eds), *The Question of Europe*, London: Verso.
Weymouth, T. and Lamizet, B. (1999), *Markets and Myths*, New York: Addison Wesley and Longman.
White, C. (1992), 'Leeds may share £15 million prize', *The Times*, 3 September, p. 25.
Wilkinson, L. (1975), *The Roman Experience*, London: Paul Elek.
Williams, A. (1992), *The European Community*, Oxford: Blackwell.

Williams, J., Dunning, E. and Murphy, P. (1990), *Hooliganism Abroad*, London: Routledge.
Williams, R. (1990), *Television: Technology and Cultural Form*, London: Routledge
Wilpert, C. (1993), 'Ideological and Institutional Foundations of Racism in the Federal Republic of Germany', in Wrench, J. and Solomos, J. (eds), *Racism and Migration in Western Europe*, Oxford: Berg.
Wilson, T. and Smith, M. (1993), *Cultural Change and the New Europe*, Oxford: Westview.
Winner, D. (2000), *Brilliant Orange*, London: Bloomsbury.
Winton, O. (2001), 'From the Banks of the River Irwell', *United We Stand*, 104, p. 26.
Woever, O. (1995), 'Identity, Integration and Security: studying the sovereignty puzzle', *Journal of International Affairs*, 48(2), pp. 389–431.
World Soccer (2001), 'What they say', May, p. 13.
World Soccer (1996), 'Brian Glanville's last word', April, p. 65.
World Soccer (1985), 'Italy to "beat" ban', April, p. 30.
Wrench, J. and Solomos, J. (eds) (1993), *Racism and Migration in Western Europe*, Oxford: Berg.

Index

1860 Munich 219
  vs West Ham 46
AC Milan
  Champions League 142
  debts 64–5
  domination 65
  and the European Cup 38
  vs Liverpool 46
Adams, Mike 203, 211
Adams, Victoria 197, 198
Aigner, Gerhard 90
Ajax 49, 82, 85, 139, 140
  Champions League 143
Allodi, Italo 54
Amorfini, Jean-Jacques 94
Anderlecht 6
Anelka, Nicholas 78, 83–4
anti-racism
  Austria 238–9
  England 237–8
  and football 237–41
  Germany 238
  Italy 238
  and realities of football 241–3
  UEFA 241
  see also racism
architecture, postmodern 131
Arkan, influence 236
Arsenal, sponsorship 128
Aston Villa, and NTL 113
Atlantic League 85, 86
Atletico Bilboa 92
Atletico Madrid
  vs Barcelona 252–3
  vs Celtic 51

Austria
  anti-racism 238–9
  Freedom Party 228

BAFF (Association of Active Fans), Germany 183–4
Baggio, Roberto 128
Balestri, Carlo 238, 242
Ball, Phil, *Morbo: the story of Spanish football* 169
Bangerter, Hans 49–50
Banton, Michael, on race 223–4
Barcelona
  and Catalan identity 88, 219
  and the Champions League 143
  fans 185–6
  L'Elefant Blau 185–6, 187, 242
  localism 88
  merchandising 127
  vs Atletico Madrid 252–3
  vs Newcastle United 159–60
Baudrillard, Jean, on television 131
Bayern Munich
  antipathy to 192–3
  club badge 172
  fans 185
  localism 219
  vs Besiktas 233–4
  vs Manchester United 3, 9–12, 219
  vs Schalke 04 193
Beckenbauer, Franz 121, 124, 161, 246
Beckham, David 3, 87
  abuse by fans 197–8, 199, 205
  George Best, compared 196–7
Benfica
  European Cup 38

vs Manchester United 3
vs Rapid Vienna 55
Benz, Marcel 155
Berlusconi, Silvio 65, 80, 100, 112, 140, 246, 257
Bernabeu, Santiago 37, 42
Besiktas, vs Bayern Munich 233–4
Best, George 15, 61, 87
  David Beckham, compared 196–7
Bettega, Roberto 105–6, 122, 130, 151
Blackburn Rovers 139–40
Blanchflower, Jackie 49
Blomquist, Jesper 3
Bolton 216, 217
Boninsegna, Roberto 50
Boniperti, Giampiero 52, 138
Borussia Dortmund
  vs Internazionale 50
  vs Manchester United 7
Bosman, Jean-Marc 71–2, 75
Bosman ruling 71–7
  impact 77–95
Bosvelt, Paul 245
Brady, Liam 116
Brady, Monica 256, 257
branding
  football clubs 125–6
  Manchester United 171–2
Brennan, Shay 5
Bretton Woods monetary system, collapse 23–4
Brierley, Roger 175
Britain
  concept of 248
  domestic league, broadcasting 103
  National Front 226, 234
  satellite broadcasting 98
  see also England
broadcasting
  competition, and the European Commission 101
  deregulation 97–9
  domestic football 103–9

beneficiaries 110–12
Britain 103
collectivist deals 108–9
France 103
Germany 103–4
Italy 104–6
Spain 106–7
see also public service broadcasting; satellite broadcasting; television
Brondy FC, Champions League 143
Brown, Adam 114
Brown, Andy 175
BSkyB 98, 100
  and the English Premier League 102, 109, 113
  Manchester United bid 112–13, 175
'Busby Babes' 4
Busby, Matt 41, 42, 43, 61, 87, 138
  statue 132–3

Cantona, Eric 76, 126, 194–5
CAP (Common Agricultural Policy) 21, 22
capitalism, and television 132
Caraben, Armand 185, 186, 187, 242
Catalan identity, and Barcelona Football Club 88, 219
Celtic, vs Atletico Madrid 51
Champions League
  AC Milan 142
  Ajax 143
  and Barcelona 143
  Brondy FC 143
  criticism 157–8
  and Euro 2000 246
  finance
    benefits 142–3
    distribution 147, 149–51
  G14 proposals 250
  origins 142–3
  reforms 148–9, 163–5, 250
  and romance 160–1
  and television 142–3, 256

and UEFA 143–4
  see also European Superleague
Charles, John 49
Charlton, Bobby 44, 51, 87
Chelsea 251–2
Chorley, Richard 173–5, 188, 191–2, 220, 257
Churchill, Winston 19
cities, and globalisation 28–9
Clough, Brian 52, 54
Club Nummer 12 185, 186
Cole, Andy 3, 234
collectivist deals, football broadcasting 108–9
Collins, Roy 156–7
commodities, 'sign-value' 125
'continental', meaning 5
corporations, and the region-state 27–8
corruption, European Cup 51–4
Council of Europe 20, 26
Council of Ministers 20
Cragnotti, Sergio 241–2
Crick, Michael 175
Crozier, Adam 90, 114, 155
Cruyff, Johann 49, 69, 88, 186
currency, single European 25, 26
customers, fans as 170–1

Dein, David 84, 153, 164–5
Derby County, vs Juventus 52
deregulation
  broadcasting 97–9
  and hooliganism 196
  television 103–9, 115–17
  transfer market 80–5
Di Stefano, Alfredo 42–3, 49
digital television *see* television, digital
Docherty, Tommy 61
Drasdo, Duncan 171, 183, 187, 254–5
Drewry, Arthur 44
Dreyfus, Robert Louis 123
Dunkerque 71

Dunne, Tony 5
Durkheim, Emile 258
  The Elementary Forms of the Religious Life 12–14
Dykes, Stuart 183–4

Edwards, Duncan 44, 87
Edwards, James 162, 198, 252
Edwards, Martin 59, 119, 135, 181
EEC (European Economic Community) 20
  see also EU
Ekersley, Ray 218
Ellis, Doug 119
England
  anti-racism 237–8
  nationalism 248
English Professional Football Association 91
Eriksson, Sven Goran 246
EU (European Union)
  Fordism 23–4
  integration 25, 32–3
  origins 19–23
  post-Fordism 25
  and sport 70–1
  supranationalism 30–2
  US, comparison ix
EURATOM 20
Euro 2000, and the Champions League 246
Europe
  meaning ix
  neo-Nazism 229
  racism 225–31
'European', meaning 5
European Coal and Steel Community 20, 22
European Commission, and broadcasting competition 101
European Cup
  Benfica 38
  corruption 51–4

economics 41–7
and European integration 40
and the Football League 44–5
foul play 49–50
hooliganism 54–9
Internazionale 38
Liverpool 59
origins 37–8
playing standards, decline 59–64
Real Madrid 37–8
reforms 141–2
seeding system 139–40
structure 45
and television 62–3
European Cup Final (1968) 3–9
European Cup Final (1999) 3, 9–12, 102, 247, 260
European Superleague 85, 112
and national sovereignty 137
proposals 137–41, 248–55
see also Champions League
Eusebio 7
Everton, vs Internazionale 46

FA Cup, decline in prestige 251–2, 255
Fagan, Joe 61
Falklands War, and hooliganism 56
fan culture
and fashion 200–1
and ISAs 179–80
and masculinity 175–6, 200–1
and social class 176–80
fans
abuse of David Beckham 197–8, 199, 205
Bayern Munich 185
and collective memory 161–3
as customers 170–1
football clubs 134–5
Germany 183–5
Leeds United 194–5
Liverpool, nationalism 214–15
Manchester United 171–2

England, rejection of 209–15
European travel 202–5
magazines 205
Mancunian identity 205–9
songs 205
racism 224–5
rivalry 196–9, 205–9, 219
and romance of football 161–2
Southampton 220
Spain 169–70
television 257
see also BAFF; fan culture; IMUSA; INUSA; ISAs; SISA
FARE (Fans Against Racism in Europe) 238–40
Farina, Giuseppe 65
Farmer, Jeff 160, 163, 250
fashion, and fan culture 200–1
Ferdinand, Rio 195
Ferran, Jacques 38
Feyenoord 85
FIFA 39, 143
FIFPro 75, 91
Figo, Luis 120, 196
flotation
football clubs 121–5
Manchester United 121
football
academic research 181
and anti-racism 237–41
domestic league broadcasting 103–9
and nationalism 247–8
new geography of 85–90
and New Labour 181
other sports, comparison 102
and racism 231–2
ritual of 12–16, 258–60
and romance 159–63
sociology of 16
and television 83, 101–9, 256–8
value
Britain 109
France 109–10

Germany 110
Italy 110
Spain 110
football clubs
  branding 125–6
  competitive balance 115–17
  dominance 247–8
  fans 134–5
  flotation 121–5
  France, business structure 123
  Germany, business structure 124
  grounds 129–33
  media, vertical integration 112–14
  and nation 8–9
  Spain, business structure 124–5
  sponsorship 127–9
    Germany 128
  vertical integration 89
Football Governance Research Centre, Birkbeck College 181
Football League, and the European Cup 44–5
Football Supporters' Association 182
football teams, transnational composition 9
Fordism
  EU 23–4
  see also post-Fordism
Foster, Norman 131
Foucault, Michel, *Discipline and Punish* 4
foul play, European Cup 49–50
Fox, Norman 50
France
  domestic league football, broadcasting 103
  Euro 2000 victory 246
  football, value 109–10
  football clubs, business structure 123
  National Front 226
  satellite broadcasting 99
Franchi, Artemio 70
Freedman, Edward 125, 126

Freedom Party, Austria 228
Fynn, Alex 140–1

G14 group
  Champions League proposals 250
  importance 153–4
  membership 152–3
  and Rodolfo Hecht 153
  and UEFA 154–5, 164
Galliani, Adriano 122
Gandini, Umberto 86, 89, 92–3, 105, 122, 128, 141, 151, 152–3, 159, 164, 249
Germany
  anti-racism 238
  BAFF 183–4
  domestic league football, broadcasting 103–4
  fans 183–5
  football, value 110
  football clubs
    business structure 124
    merchandising 126–7
  racial violence 227
  Republican Party 226
  right wing parties 226–7
  satellite broadcasting 99
Giggs, Ryan 3, 87
gladiatorial shows 14–15, 259
Glanville, Brian 39, 52–3, 59
glass, use in football grounds 131–2
globalisation
  and cities 28–9
  and localism 200
  and the nation-state 26–7, 210–11
  and racism 229–31
Godall, Alfons 185, 186, 187
Gori, Cecchi 112
Gornik Zabrze FC 5
Granada company, and Liverpool 113
Grasshoppers Zurich 93–4

Green, Geoffrey 4–5, 6, 7, 8, 10, 44, 51–2, 102, 138
  Soccer in the Fifties 50
grounds
  atmosphere 173
  exploitation 129–30
    Manchester United 130–3
  football clubs 129–33
  use of glass 131–2

Haider, Joerg 228
Hall, John, Sir 119
Haller, Helmut 52
Hammer, Max 229–30
Hanot, Gabriel 42, 50, 137
Hardaker, Alan 39–40
Hargreaves, Owen 91
Hecht, Rodolfo Lucari 116–17, 158, 159
  European Superleague proposals 144–51, 249–50
  and G14 group 153
Heysel stadium disaster (1985) 57, 58–9, 64, 215
Hiddink, Guus 246
Hillsborough disaster (1989) 182
Hoeness, Uli 62, 193
Holland, vs Italy 245
Honved, vs Wolverhampton Wanderers 42
hooliganism
  and deregulation 196
  European Cup 54–9
  and the Falklands War 56
  and ISAs 174
  and Manchester United fans 55–6, 211–14
  and masculinity 56, 169–70
  and moral panic 54–5
  and nationalism 56–7
Hughes, Robert 156
Hytner, Richard 175

identity, and post-Fordism 199

IMUSA (Independent Manchester United Supporter's Association) 174, 175, 186, 187, 201, 256
Internazionale
  and the European Cup 38
  vs Borussia Dortmund 50
  vs Everton 46
INUSA (Independent Newcastle United Supporter's Association) 174
  and Schalke 04 187–8
Irriducibili group 235–6, 241, 242
ISAs (Independent Supporters' Associations)
  European 183–6
  and fan culture 179–80
  formation 173
  future 182–3
  and hooliganism 174
  membership 174–5
  purpose 173–4
  and share ownership 181
  strategies 180–3
  transnational relations 186–9
  see also IMUSA; INUSA; SISA
Italy
  anti-racism 238
  domestic league football, broadcasting 104–6
  foreign players 69–70
  racial violence 228
  racism 230, 235–6
  satellite broadcasting 99
  vs Holland 245

James, C.L.R. 16
Jameson, Frederick 131
Johansson, Lennart 156
Juventus 49
  antipathy to 194
  vs Derby County 52
  vs Liverpool 58
  vs Real Madrid 138

Kavanagh, Brian 186
Keane, Roy 77–8, 126, 134
Kelly, Bob 44
Kenyon, Peter 78, 79–80, 86, 104, 107, 126, 148
Kidd, Brian 61, 87
King's Cup, Spain 252–3
Kuffour, Sammy 3, 16, 260
Kurt, Richard 204, 216

La Porta, Joan 185, 186
Laudrup, Michael 196
Law, Denis 87
Le Pen, Jean-Marie 226
Leeds United, fans 194–5
Leigh, Jon 186
L'Elefant Blau, Barcelona 185–6, 187, 242
Lenz, Advocate General
  ruling
    foreign players 75–7
    transfer fees 73–5
Liverpool 5
  and the European Cup 59
  fans, nationalism 214–15
  and Granada company 113
  vs AC Milan 46
  vs Juventus 58
Lo Forte, Domenico 194, 232, 233
Lobo, Francisco 52
localism
  Barcelona 88
  Bayern Munich 219
  and globalisation 200
  Manchester United 87–8, 201, 209–19
  racism 235–7
  Southampton 220
Lombardo, Massimo 93–4
Longden, Mark 186–7, 256, 257
Luxembourg Compromise 20–1, 22, 23

Maastricht Treaty 77
McQueen, Gordon 195

Malmo, vs Nottingham Forest 60
Manchester
  diversity 216–19
  and Manchester United 217–18
Manchester United
  1968/1999 teams, comparison 87
  antipathy to 191–2
  BSkyB bid 112–13
  club badge 171–2
  fans 171–2
    England, rejection of 209–15
    European travel 202–5
    hooliganism 55–6, 211–14
    magazines 205
    Mancunian identity 205–9
    songs 205
  flotation 121
  localism 87–8, 201, 209–19
  and Manchester 217–18
  merchandising 125
  national status 11
  and Nike 129
  Premier League champions 253–4
  sponsorship 128–9
  stadium, symbolism 130–3
  and Vodafone 128–9
  vs Bayern Munich 3, 9–12, 219
  vs Benfica 3, 9–12
  vs Borussia Dortmund 7
  vs Real Madrid 6–7, 49
  vs St. Etienne 57–8
  World Champion Clubs' Cup 251
Maradona, Diego 69–70, 76
Marshall Plan 19
masculinity
  and fan culture 175–6, 200–1
  and hooliganism 56, 169–70
maximum wage, abolition 69, 77, 195
media, football clubs, vertical integration 112–14
Media Partners
  European league proposals 144–51, 156, 249

criticism 156–8
Meek, David 5, 6, 7, 41–2
Meier, Michael 109
Mellor, Gavin 178
memory, collective, and fans 161–3
Mendoza, Ramon 141
merchandising
   Barcelona Football Club 127
   football clubs, Germany 126–7
   Manchester United 125–6
   Real Madrid 127
Michie, Jonathan, Prof 175, 181, 182
Mihajlovic, Sinisa 236
Miles, Kevin 174, 187
Miles, Robert 224
Miller, David 156
Milward, Andrew 21–3, 26
Mitten, Andy 203, 217, 218
models, nation 226
moral panic, and hooliganism 54–5
Moratti, Angelo 53–4
Munich aircrash (1958) 46
Murdoch, Rupert 97–8, 100
Murray, David 141

Nash, Rex 177
nation
   and football clubs 8–9
   models 226
nation-state
   and globalisation 26–7, 210–11
   and post-Fordism 26–7
   role 27
   and the Treaty of Rome (1957) 22–3
National Front
   Britain 226, 234
   France 226
nationalism
   England 248
   and football 247–8
   and hooliganism 56–7
neo-Nazism, Europe 229
Neville, Gary 87

Neville, Phil 87
New Labour, and football 181
Newcastle United
   and NTL 113
   vs Barcelona 159–60
Nike, and Manchester United 129
Nottingham Forest, vs Malmo 60
NTL
   and Aston Villa 113
   and Newcastle United 113
Nunez, Josep 242

OFT (Office of Fair Trading), and
   English Premier League 108, 113
Ogilvie, Campbell 141
Ohmae, Kenichi 27–8
Olympic Marseilles 123
Onieva, Juan 92, 93, 107, 120, 151, 249

Paisley, Bob 61
Papin, Jean Pierre 80
Paris Saint-Germain 83, 123
Parry, Rick 71, 72, 78, 86, 92, 104, 154, 246–7
Perez, Florentino 120–1, 127
Perugia case 93–5
players, foreign
   Italy 69–70
   Real Madrid 40
   restrictions on 8–9, 61–2, 64
      lifting of 70–1, 75–7
   Spain 69, 92
playing standards, decline, European Cup 59–64
Pocock, John 33, 260
post-Fordism
   EU 25
   and identity 199
   and the nation state 26
   see also Fordism
Power, Piara 238
Premier League (English) 83

and BSkyB broadcasting 102, 109, 113
decline 253–5
Manchester United 253–4
and the OFT 108, 113
Progetto Ultra 238, 239
Project 1992 25, 76–7
PSV Eindhoven 83, 85
public service broadcasting
Europe 97
see also television

Quintin, Odile 239–40
Quixall, Albert 43

race, Michael Banton on 223–4
racial chants 232–4
racial violence
Germany 227
Italy 228
Spain 227
racism
among fans 224–5
Europe 225–31
and football 231–2
and globalisation 229–31
Italy 230, 235–6
localism 235–7
organic 232–4
political groups 235
Spain 236–7
see also anti-racism
Rapid Vienna
vs Benfica 55
vs Real Madrid 44
Reade, Brian 10
Real Madrid 4
and the European Cup 37–8
finances 120
foreign players 40
merchandising 127
vs Juventus 138
vs Manchester United 6–7, 49

vs Rapid Vienna 44
region-state, and corporations 27–8
Republican Party, Germany 226
ritual
football as 12–16, 258–60
function 32
Robson, Garry 175–6
romance of football
and the Champions League 160–1
and fans 161–2
and football 159–63
Ronaldo 128
Rummenige, Karl Heinz 116

St. Etienne, vs Manchester United 57–8
Sanz, Lorenzo 84, 95, 147
satellite broadcasting
Britain 98
emergence 97–8
France 99
Germany 99
Italy 99
see also BSkyB
Schalke 04
and INUSA 187–8
vs Bayern Munich 193
Schmeichel, Peter 3
Scholar, Irving 140
Scholes, Paul 87
Schumann, Robert 19–20, 22
season tickets, cost 129, 171
Serie A League 83
Shankly, Bill 60, 61
share ownership, and ISAs 181
Shareholders United Against Murdoch 175, 181
Shearer, Alan 157
Sherringham, Teddy 3
'sign-value', commodities 125
Single European Act (1992) 25

SISA (Southampton Independent Supporter's Association) 174, 188–9, 257
Smith, Tommy 9, 10
Sobriques, Jaume 93
social class, and fan culture 176–80
Solskjaer, Ole Gunnar 3, 260
Solti, Dezco 52
Sorensen, Bent 240
Southampton
  fans 220
  localism 220
Spain
  domestic league football, broadcasting 106–7
  fans 169–70
  football, value 110
  football clubs, business structure 124–5
  foreign players 69, 92
  King's Cup 252–3
  racial violence 227
  racism 236–7
Spice Girls 197
sponsorship
  Arsenal 128
  football clubs 127–9
    Germany 128
    Manchester United 128–9
sport
  and the EU 70–1
  ritual of 14
  and television 101–2, 258
Sprengers, Mathieu 240
stadiums *see* grounds
Stam, Jaap 126
Standard Liege 71, 72
status, Max Weber on 224, 259
Stein, Jock 44
Strasbourg 123
Sugar, Alan 119
Sunderland 6
supporters *see* fans; ISAs

supranationalism, EU 30–2

Taylor, Gordon 91–2, 93, 94
Taylor, Ian 195–6
Taylor Report (1990) 129
Taylor, Rogan 182
TEAM (Television Event and Media Marketing) 141–2, 249
Telefonica, European Superleague proposals 249
television
  and capitalism 132
  and the Champions League 142–3, 256
  deregulation 103–9, 115–17
  digital 100–2
  and the European Cup 62–3
  fans 257
  and football 83, 101–9, 256–8
  Jean Baudrillard on 131
  and sport 101–2, 258
  see also satellite television
Thompson, Phil 87
Tocqueville, Alexis de ix
transfer fees 73–5, 94
transfer market 72
transnationalisation 80–5
Treaty of Rome (1957) 20
  and the nation state 22–3
Tyldesley, Clive 10

UEFA (Union of European Football Associations) 8, 38, 39, 90
  anti-racism 241
  Champions League 143–4
  European Cup reforms 141–2
  and G14 group 154–5, 164

value, football
  Britain 109
  France 109–10
  Spain 110
Van Gaal, Louis 88, 253

Viera, Patrick 236
Vieri, Christian 78
violence *see* hooliganism
Vodafone, and Manchester United 128–9
Vogts, Berti 246

wage increases 77–80
Walker, Jack 119
Walsh, Andy 174, 175, 186
Weber, Max, on status 224, 259
Wenger, Arsene 83

West Ham, vs 1860 Munich 46
White, Jim 175
Winton, Oli 186
Wolverhampton Wanderers, vs Honved 42
World Champion Clubs' Cup, Manchester United 251
World Cup Final (1966) 10
Worth, Richard 72, 144, 160

Yorke, Dwight 3, 234